Playing in the Shadows

MICHIGAN MONOGRAPH SERIES IN JAPANESE STUDIES

NUMBER 88

CENTER FOR JAPANESE STUDIES
UNIVERSITY OF MICHIGAN

Playing in the Shadows

Fictions of Race and Blackness in Postwar Japanese Literature

Will Bridges

University of Michigan Press
Ann Arbor

Published in the United States of America by the
University of Michigan Press
Printed and bound by CPI Group (UK) Ltd, Croydon, CR0 4YY

A CIP catalog record for this book is available from the British Library.

Library of Congress Cataloging-in-Publication data has been applied for.

First published February 2020

ISBN: 978-0-472-07442-6 (Hardcover : alk paper)
ISBN: 978-0-472-05442-8 (Paper : alk paper)
ISBN: 978-0-472-12652-1 (ebook)

To the folks with an empty seat next to them on a full train

Acknowledgments

If it takes a village to raise a child, what does it take to raise a monograph from its conception to its completion? Knowing myself the way I do, I know that this book would have played in the shadows for much longer than it did if not for generous contributions—some tangible, like a good book or a warm meal, some intangible, like a good idea or a warm word of encouragement—of a network of colleagues that spans, by my count, three continents. Here are a few words of acknowledgment in thanks for the part their contributions have played in helping this project come to life.

It would not be too hyperbolic to say that Atsuko Ueda taught me how to read and write. I am thankful for many things about Atsuko, but I am most thankful for her brilliance, her rigor, and her generosity.

Valerie Smith guided me during the uneven toddles of my first foray into African American literature. Black literature seems to come to life when Valerie reads it; I can only hope that she transferred some of her magic to me during our time together.

If I spelled out the contributions I received from my graduate school cohort by name and number, these acknowledgments would become another chapter. So I'll provide an open and standing invitation to give each of you your acknowledgment in person: on finding this sentence, you are officially entitled to one cup of coffee on me.

I once heard or read somewhere that we spend the first half of our lives running toward our influences and the second half running away from them. As a middle-aged person, I don't know where I'm going. But I know that the thought of John Russell should be celebrated. That is, in short, what I hope the pages of this book do.

I admired Nina Cornyetz from afar—her scholarship shaped and reshaped many of my thoughts on our shared scholarly interests—long before I was able to call her a friend and a mentor.

Doug Slaymaker has an uncanny way of providing the right idea at the right time.

Anne McKnight's and Eve Zimmerman's work on Nakagami Kenji gave me a sense of what was possible.

Nahum Chandler's foresight gave me a glimpse of the future.

Anonymous readers made murky arguments legible and dull ideas sharper.

The last words of this book are written with the generous support I have received from the Fulbright and Japan Foundations in mind.

I have had the good fortune of having three sets of supportive colleagues over the course of writing this book. My thanks to Karil Kucera, Hiroe Akimoto, Rika Ito, Kathy Tegtmeyer Pak, Barbara Reed, Ka Wong, Bob Entenmann, Michael Fuller, Kyung Hyun Kim, Susan Klein, Mimi Long, Bert Scruggs, Serk-Bae Suh, Hu Ying, Chungmoo Choi, Martin Huang, Jim Fujii, Joanne Bernardi, Robert Doran, John Givens, and David Holloway for the contributions they made to this project.

I found intellectual homes away from my intellectual home in Japan. Takahashi Toshio taught me what the word *sensei* means. The Department of English at Tsuda University, the Graduate School of Language and Society at Hitotsubashi University, Miyamoto Keiko and the Department of Literature at Seinan Gakuin University, and the Japanese Association for Black Studies made this book possible.

My family supported me during times of doubt (I'll never forget how my brother put and pulled it all into perspective for me: "But they pay you to read books, right?"), so I thank Lillie, Kwame, Nakeisha, Daiki, Haruki, and Akira. Keiko has made a herculean amount of sacrifices over the years—often with a smile. For every word written here, there is a corresponding moment when Keiko was taking care of something I had forgotten to do, so I dedicate the words written here to her.

And here, as I acknowledge the support I've received from my family over the years, it seems fitting to express my thanks to Professor Richard Okada. Shortly after I received the contract for this book, Richard came to me in a dream. He proceeded to poke and prod, to tease out every shortcoming and unquestioned assumption that remained in the manuscript. This—an angry spirit sent in love and the hope of better thinking—sounds about right to me; it sounds like the Richard I know. I would have preferred to have had this conversation with him in person, but with Richard you take what you can get. My time with Richard was too short, but I received too much from him during that time. I know this comes a little too late, but, given his thoughts on belatedness, I'll say it anyway: thank-you.

Contents

Digital materials related to this title can be found on the Fulcrum platform
via the following citable URL: https://doi.org/10.3998/mpub.11301772

Introduction

Playing in the Shadows, Fictions of Race, and Blackness in Postwar Japanese Literature

> For your average Japanese person, the only thing they know about black folks is what they've read in storybooks.
>
> —Honda Katsu'ichi, *Amerika gasshūkoku*
> (The United States of America)

Playing in the Shadows

"The secret of the birth of the modern novel (*kindai shōsetsu*)" in Japan, literary critic Tanaka Minoru proposes, can be discovered by determining how the country "came to terms with the impact of the arrival of the . . . black ships."[1] In 1853, Commodore Perry's black ships brought a combination of epistolary and gunboat diplomacy to the shores of Japan. Almost as if to ensure that the message of the warships wasn't overly adulterated by the cordiality of President Millard Fillmore's letter to the Tokugawa shogunate, Perry—who was known to choreograph and rehearse his audiences with foreign officials—presented the Japanese with a cipher for interpreting these competing modes of diplomacy: black bodies. From the very moment Perry set foot on Japanese soil, he put African American soldiers and servants on display in a bid to impress and intimidate the Japanese.[2] When Perry delivered President Fillmore's letter, for example, he was, as Perry himself wrote in his account of the expedition, flanked by two "negro[es], armed to the teeth . . . blacks, selected for the occasion . . . [and] two of the best-looking fellows of their color that the squadron could furnish."[3] By attempting to instill fear in his Japanese audience by "furnishing negroes" for the occasion,

Perry intimated what would await Japan if it were to show resistance in the face of American might.

If Perry's first audience simply intimated, his follow-up performance was a bit more explicit. On his 1854 return, Perry brought with him "Plantation 'Niggas' of the South." Some four days before the signing of the Treaty of Kanagawa, Perry invited Japanese commissioners aboard the USSF *Powhatan* for dinner and entertainment. Among the festivities was a performance by the "Japanese Olio Minstrels," musically inclined members of Perry's crew who put on an "Ethiopian entertainment" in blackface.[4] This minstrel show proved to be a powerful facilitator of US-Japanese solidarity. On seeing the show, "Matsusaki [a secretary to the chief Japanese envoy] flung his arms around the commodore's neck and remarked . . . 'Nippon and America, all the same heart!'"[5]

In finding "the same heart" with America on viewing a minstrel show, the events of the opening of Japan make Toni Morrison's (1931–2019) thoughts in *Playing in the Dark: Whiteness and the Literary Imagination*, which was translated into Japanese in 1994 as *Shirosa to sōzōryoku* (Whiteness and the Power of the Imagination), revelatory in thinking through how modern Japanese literature has come to terms with the impact of the arrival of those black ships. Morrison writes that blackness, even when silhouetted, "informs in compelling and inescapable ways the texture of American literature. It is a dark and abiding presence, there for the literary imagination as both a visible and an invisible mediating force."[6] "As metaphor for transacting the whole process of Americanization," Morrison continues, blackness "may be something the United States cannot do without."[7] If, as Tanaka Minoru suggests, the American opening of Japan had an indelible impact on the development of modern Japanese literature, this book asks how our readings of postwar Japanese literature might be enriched by the reminder that "American" also always includes "African American." It asks if, in the process of "Japanization," blackness might be something postwar Japanese literature cannot do without.

This book explores the body of literature engendered by post–World War II Japanese authors' robust cultural exchanges with African Americans and African Americana. Previous studies of blackness in postwar Japanese literature have been concerned primarily with the representation of black characters: blackness is "in" a work of Japanese literature insofar as the text represents some blackness that is already out there in the world.[8] According to this scholarly vision, the blackness of a work of Japanese literature is, primarily, blackness that can be seen with the naked eye. Rather than focusing on representations of African Americans in Japanese literature, this book supposes that the black characters who rise to the textual surface are just the tip of the signifying iceberg. Beneath those representations (or, in some texts, even in the absence of representations of black characters) there runs a rich history of Afro-Japanese literary and cultural exchange, a history characterized by cross-cultural pollination and creative experimentation that spans the Pacific. This book proposes what I call reconstructive readings of how blackness, in the fullest sense of the term, has been written into postwar Japanese literature. I argue that the blackness in Japanese fictions of race provides visions of the way in which postwar Japanese authors reimagine the ascription of race to bodies—be they bodies of literature, the body politic, or the human body itself.

The notion of "blackness" has constitutive power in the postwar Japanese racial and literary imagination. With this in mind, this book proposes that a fuller accounting of postwar Japanese literature requires rereading how blackness has been written into this body of literature. This means, in turn, rereading postwar Japanese literature comparatively alongside African American literature, history, and literary criticism. In short, this book is an attempt to read postwar Japanese fiction as a kind of black literature.

I am interested primarily in the history of blackness in postwar Japanese literature as a history of racial thinking in postwar Japan. I also explore the hermeneutics of blackness best equipped for reading such a history. In the introduction to *Traveling Texts and the Work of Afro-Japanese Cultural Production*, I refer to this hermeneutic as reading texts in motion, but I refer to it here as "reconstructive reading." The readings proposed in this book are reconstructive insofar as they focus less on critiquing representational faux pas than on reconstructing the (stylistic, subjective, intellectual, historical, cultural, intertextual, and other) roots and outgrowths of the writing of blackness in postwar Japanese fiction. A guiding premise of this book is that the literary history under discussion here becomes legible only after it has been reconstructed. The remainder of this introduction addresses this premise.

Fictions of Race

I use the phrase "fictions of race" to highlight three of the foundational hypotheses of this study. First, I mean that race itself may be a kind of fiction. Right on the cusp of the twenty-first century, Bill Clinton—a figure deemed by no less than Toni Morrison to be a kind of fictional surrogate for "our first black President"—commemorated the completion of the human genome project with this: "One of the great truths to emerge from this triumphant expedition inside the human genome is that in genetic terms, all human beings, regardless of race, are more than 99.9 percent the same."[9] The human genome itself seems to retell the tale that scholars of the humanities and interpretive social sciences (not to mention both African American and Japanese authors) have long reported. As the American Anthropological Association (AAA) wrote in its Smithsonian exhibit on race, "The essentialist view [of race] is not a valid biological concept, nor does it fit the data."[10] Even those who still adhere to the biological reality of what the AAA calls the "population concept" of race must concede, in the words of evolutionary biologist David Barash, that the biological definition of race itself is "socially constructed," and the biological definition of race is based on whatever "trait(s) emerge as useful, consistent and convenient."[11]

To advocate that more attention be paid to the nonessentialist realities of race is to extend an invitation to listen to stories of what has been "useful, consistent and convenient" with regard to race, to explore how the "traits" that determine that trio of adjectives often undercut the truth of human variation and singularity, and to imagine different, and perhaps better, ways of organizing human community.

In *The Self Comes to Mind*, Antonio Damasio writes that the self is a narrative spun by a "novel-writing machine," the human mind. "In brains endowed with abundant memory, language, and reasoning, narratives with . . . simple origin and contour are enriched and allowed to display even more knowledge, thus producing a well-defined protagonist, an autobiographical self."[12] If the racial self, too, is more like a narrative than like a fixed essence, then there is a second implication of the expression "fictions of race," for the materials and techniques of literary studies have much to contribute to a conversation on blackness in Japanese cultural discourse. It is for this reason that this book focuses primarily on prose fiction. Furthermore, if race is a narrative, then its genre is creative nonfiction—race is a social fiction that tells its story through the language of verifiable fact, quite literally creating nonfictional essences where there were originally none. It is for this reason that, whenever possible, I try to capture the interplay between a given author's nonfictional musings on race and blackness and his or her translations of these musings into works of fiction. It is somewhere between these nonfictional musings and their fictional translations that the truths of fictions of race reside.

A third implication of "fiction of race" stems from a question inherent to its second meaning: how should we read texts that hover in the space between the fictional and the nonfictional? One argument I have in mind when I call this a study of fictions of race is the program set by Martha Nussbaum in "Fictions of the Soul." She writes, "No stylistic choice can be presumed to be neutral—not even the choice to write in a flat or neutral style. My aim . . . is to begin working on the complicated connections between a view of what a human soul is and a view about how to address that sort of soul in writing."[13] Following Nussbaum, this study assumes that fictions of race are best served by readings that pay sustained, deliberative attention to the "complicated connections" between a view of what a black human soul is and a view about how to address that sort of soul in writing. I am particularly interested in considering the implications of Nussbaum's claim that no choice can be presumed to be neutral for the reading of fictions of race. In other words, how does the impossibility of stylistic neutrality inform the interpretation of fictions of race?

Some of the previous studies of blackness in Japanese culture, particularly scholarship composed beyond the field of literary studies, have what Paul Ricoeur might call a first faith in the ability of readings to produce definitive interpretations of *the* Japanese representation of blackness.[14] Over the course of three decades of study, John Russell, for example, has set the standard for investigations of blackness in contemporary Japanese culture. Russell's groundbreaking "Race and Reflexivity: The Black Other in Contemporary Japanese Mass Culture" is predicated on faith in transparent representations. Russell contends that even a "brief survey of literary and visual representations of blacks in contemporary Japan *reveals* [my emphasis] the persistence of racial stereotypes which ascribe to blacks the following characteristics: (1) infantilism, (2) primitivism, (3) hypersexuality, (4) bestiality, (5) natural athletic prowess or physical stamina, (6) mental inferiority, (7) psychological weakness, and (8) emotional volatility."[15] The assumption here is that a survey of representations might reveal that which is deemed representative. In this case, representative reading reveals eight stereotypes of "the view of the blacks that permeates virtually all aspects of Japanese discourse on the black Other."[16]

Before I go any further, I should reiterate that the questions of representation are profoundly significant.[17] Given the ubiquity of moments of misrepresentation in the modern history of Afro-Japanese cultural exchange, it might even be argued that the Afro-Japanese critic has a kind of ethical obligation to pose representational questions. Moreover, in light of Gayatri Spivak's reminder of the two meanings of *representation*—"representation as 'speaking for,' as in politics, and representations as 're-presentation,' as in art or philosophy"—there is clearly something commendable in the corrective impulse behind representational readings.[18] Representative readings run the risk of emphasizing strategic essentialism and hermeneutic stability at the cost of reduction of the contradictory complexities of fictions of race. But the potential reward of representational gambles is interpretations of blackness that are more democratic, more imaginatively capacious, and more just in their attempt to bridge the divide between the plentitude of blackness and the paucities of its representations. The project I propose here simply would not be possible without the foundation set by work such as Russell's. In the words of Rachael Hutchinson and Mark Williams, such representative research cultivates a key "question to be asked: how did representing the Other lead Japanese authors to new definitions of what it meant for them to be 'Japanese'? . . . The moment of recognition that occurs in the space of the representational process is often uncomfortable, but always crucial."[19]

In this study, however, I aim to repay my debt to previous research by cultivating a set of questions related to but different from the primary inquiries of representation-focused studies of blackness. There are, to be sure, places throughout this study where I address questions of representation. Questioning representations, however, is my secondary focus. My primary focus is on the questions that arise before, after, and even beyond the concerns of representation.[20] My primary focus, in other words, is not on how postwar Japanese writings of blackness can be reproductive but on how this writing can be generative. By building on previous research with an approach that thinks both about and beyond representation, my goal is to supplement readings of the blackness in postwar Japanese literature with what W. E. B. DuBois might call a kind of second sight. Blackness in postwar Japanese literature becomes visible in all its plentitude when we think not only about how blackness is represented in a text but also about how texts efface blackness, as well as about how authors write blackness in ways that are not "represented" in the text at all (e.g., when Japanese authors are inspired by black authors to write works that do not feature black characters).

In other words, I am asking that we step back and reassess one of the foundational assumptions of the study of blackness in Japanese literature and culture: that the operative framework for such studies is the "representation" of the "black Other." To start with the term *Other*, it is clear that there is a theoretical *difference* between blackness and, for lack of a better term, Japaneseness. But one guiding premise of this book is that racial difference is not necessarily equivalent to Otherness. When Nakagami Kenji refers to himself as a black man from Japan, or, for that matter, when Muhammad Ali refers to himself as an Asiatic black man, I do not think that *Otherness* is the operative term for the way these thinkers are imagining Afro-Japanese racial difference. Sometimes racial difference will be othering and sometimes it won't, and sometimes it will think that it is not othering even though it is. The chapters that follow are interested in untangling this messy difference, which cannot be untangled if we begin with the assumption that writing blackness means always representing the black Other.

It is for this reason that this book follows (a slightly more constructivist rendition of) what Michael O. Hardimon has called a deflationary realist approach to race. Hardimon sees race as a "series of four distinct but interrelated concepts": racialist (or racist) race, minimalist race, populationist race, and "socialrace."[21] Much of the confusion in contemporary conversations about race, according to Hardimon, comes from conflationary conceptual leaps between the racist, othering concept of race and its minimalist and social conceptual counterparts. This study hopes, along with Hardimon, that it is possible to recognize, respect, be real about, and deflate (minimalist) racial difference without othering it.

As for representation, Hutchinson and Williams contend that one of "the most intractable problems with the binary structure [of the representing Self and the represented Other] is, as Jacques Derrida maintains, the fact that two totalistic entities cannot actually exist."[22] Representational readings of blackness run the risk of forgetting that Derrida's insight holds not just for identities but for language itself. The language that represents the Other is rarely self-identical and is often messy and contradictory. Even in the savviest of representational readings, however, there inevitably comes a moment when the analysis focuses on extrapolating the "representativeness" of the passage under discussion. At that moment, it becomes much more probable that our reading might take a reductivist approach to the layers of text, intertext, and context that are not representative of the argument being made or represented in the text itself. It is, in other words, at this moment that representation-driven studies of reading blackness in Japanese cultural productions run the risk of cross-applying some of our missteps from reading race in general to the reading of racialized texts. The critic might speak for the text rather than letting it speak for itself and judge the text according to what we have said on its behalf rather than on what it has actually said. In the micromoments of racial judgment, readers are quick to essentialize and rarely have time to regard the text with what Giorgio Agamben calls the purity of the example, to regard it as a singular instantiation that *we* must work to connect to larger discourses, to ask it where it came from, how it got here, and where it is going.[23] The danger of representative studies is the same danger inherent in our reading of race in general: we don't go to the trouble of allowing the text to travel.

There is a degree to which representative focus is an unavoidable component of any act of interpretation. The Derridean observation noted by Hutchinson and Williams, however, is helpful during such acts of interpretation because it serves as a reminder that "the instant of decision is madness (*la folie*)."[24] In the context of this study, this suggests that representative readings run the risk of a kind of "folly," selecting one component of the text and deeming it more representative than some other putatively peripheral component, a process of representational selection that often says more about the reader than it does about the read. Derrida's reminder is informative because of an admittedly simplified synopsis of the central concern of his philosophical project: what are we to do with systemic failure? Whether the system in question is language, logic, literature, multiethnic democracy, or representative interpretation, a common response to systemic failure is to proceed as if the moment of failure never occurred. Derrida asks how we are to proceed if we respect and acknowledge that such failure is a constitutive element of man-made systems. Such an approach holds the potential to provide rich, rigorous readings of fictions of race, which are inherently riddled with contradictions and moments of failure.[25]

It is important to note that, even if the moment of interpretative decision making is one of "madness" (that is to say, marked by an indeterminacy that suggests the impossibility of finding *the* representative interpretation of fictions of race), the upshot of this condition is not the end of reading fictions of race. Rather, it can be the beginning of their readings. At this juncture, Tanaka Minoru—who proposed that "the secret of the birth of the modern novel (*kindai shōsetsu*)" in Japan can be discovered by determining how Japan "came to terms with the impact of the arrival of the . . . black ships"—is insightful.[26] The black ships brought with them, Tanaka continues, visions of the other side (*mukō*) and of an Other with "irreducible plurality" (*kangen fukanō na fukusūsei*).[27] The irreducible plurality of this Other is not unlike the irreducible plurality of literary texts; this is why literature, Tanaka suggests, and the modern novel in particular become a premier venue where Japan "comes to terms" with the irreducible plurality of the Other.[28] This irreducible plurality, which Tanaka also refers to as "anarchy" and "the absurdity of reading" (*yomi no hairi*), however, does not spell the deconstruction of literature.[29] Rather, it spells the reconstruction of the self and reading in the truest sense of the term. For Tanaka, reading literature entails the "deconstruction" (*tōkai*) and subsequent "reconstruction of the [reading] subject" (*shutai no saikōchiku*), which occurs when texts are accepted as an irreducibly plural Other that is fundamentally different from the reading Self.[30]

Following Tanaka, this book steps away from critiques of representations and moves toward reconstructive examinations of Japan's postwar fictions of race. To reiterate, by "reconstructive," I mean readings that focus less on critiquing representational faux pas and more on reconstructing the (intellectual, subjective, historical, cultural, intertextual, and other) roots and outgrowths of the stylistics of writing blackness in postwar Japanese fiction. Tanaka's approach has something in common with Marielle Macé's notion of the stylistics of existence. Macé contends that there are "phenomena belonging to reader experience that produce durable effects in the grammar of existence," which organizes the expressive possibilities by which readers might articulate their being in the world. As readers read, Macé continues, literary forms "seize . . . hold of them [with] a power that tugs the threads and possibilities of being within [them]."[31] This book asks how engagements with literary blackness (and also black music, thought, history, people, and so on) produce durable effects in the grammar of Japan's postwar fictions of race. How does the idea of blackness seize hold of Japanese authors as they attempt to rewrite and reconstruct racial being according to a new postwar grammar? What are the stylistics of racial existence in postwar Japan, and in what way is blackness the cynosure of this question for postwar Japanese authors?

John Russell has done remarkable work on antiblack *racism* in Japanese culture. I would like to discuss blackness and *race* in its postwar literature even if questions of racism always linger on the horizon. I am less interested in questions of racism, its attempts to unmake and undo the subject, and the representation of blackness in postwar Japanese fiction and more interested in how blackness becomes a constitutive component of the rewriting of fictions of race in postwar Japan even in spite of those attempts. I argue, in short, that the blackness of postwar Japanese literature should not be read primarily in search of representations and, more often than not, misrepresentations of blackness but in search of the existential possibilities literature opens for its readers. We should read it, as I argue in chapter 2 of this book, primarily in search of the ways of thinking, seeing, being, hearing, feeling, and moving in the world made possible by reading fictions of race.

In other words, with "reconstructive reading," I want to split the difference between respecting *différance* and refusing to defer dreams irrevocably. Reconstructive reading is the culmination of the combination of post-Derridean thought (by which I mean simply how we can think about things after reading Derrida) and the spirit of reconstruction, that desire to rebuild racial, cultural, and spiritual infrastructures after an uncivil war. This approach to reading Japan's postwar fictions of race should highlight two things: first, the possibility that Derrida and Tanaka's notion of respect for the irreducible plurality of the text might be the prerequisite for becoming better readers of the fiction of race; and, second, that the answer to misrepresentations of blackness might come not from more representative readings but from questioning the hermeneutic tools used to read and imagine blackness. An exclusive focus on representations, no matter how well done, always runs the risk of reifying binary oppositions and reducing matters in terms of black and white. Thus, rather than anticipating encounters—however transformative these encounters may be—between a fully formed Japanese Self and representations of its black Other, I am asking that we consider how multivalent writings of blackness generate and constitute multivalent imaginings of fictions of race (the fiction of a homogeneous Japanese body politic, for example, or the fiction of postwar Afro-Japanese solidarity or the fiction of postwar Japanese authors as participants in a Global South) in postwar Japanese literature.

A paradigmatic example—and the example from which this book draws its title—of the risks associated with representative readings of blackness and the need for reconstructive reading can be seen in a key passage of Tanizaki Jun'ichirō's (1886–1965) 1933 *In'ei raisan* (In Praise of Shadows). *In Praise of Shadows* is Tanizaki's *zuihitsu*-style treatise on what he deems to be a key difference between Japanese and western aesthetics. *Zuihitsu* is a genre of essayistic writing in which writers follow the flow of their thoughts wherever they may take them. The genre is characterized by aphoristic, fragmentary pieces rather than structured writing.[32] Tanizaki's *In Praise of Shadows* proposes that, whereas modern western beauty glows under ostentatious illumination, traditional Japanese beauty has thrived in the darkness of shadows. He writes:

> For the Japanese complexion, no matter how white, is tinged by a slight cloudiness. . . . But the skin of the Westerners, even those of a darker complexion, had a limpid glow. Nowhere were they tainted by this gray shadow. . . .
>
> We can appreciate, then, the psychology that in the past caused the white races to reject the colored races. A sensitive white person could not but be upset by the shadow that even one or two colored persons cast over a social gathering. . . . Those with the slightest taint of Negro blood, be it but a half, a quarter, a sixteenth, or a thirty-second, had to be ferreted out and made to suffer. . . . And so we see how profound is the relationship between shadows and the yellow races.[33]

This passage, with its undertones of racial self-loathing and apologist sympathy for western colorism, might, either explicitly or implicitly, send a representational reading down a path that Kobena Mercer has referred to as "reflectionist." Mercer defines a reflectionist approach as one that "holds that the fight for Black representation and recognition—against White racist stereotypes—must reflect or mirror the real Black community, not simply the negative and depressing representations of it."[34] A reflectionist reading, however, although undeniably well intentioned, would run the double risk of short-circuiting analysis beyond the representative aspects of this passage, as well as shortchanging the complexity of Tanizaki's text. In the Japanese original, for example, Tanizaki describes the relationship between shadows and the yellow races as *fushigi*. Harper and Seidensticker translate this as "profound." *Fushigi*, however, is a loaded, evocative term. It can be translated as "wonderful," "miraculous," "mysterious," "marvelous," "curious," and, finally, "strange." If the relationship between shadows and the yellow races is wonderful, it is also, by virtue of this single word, marvelous and curious, and strange. Alongside this putative racial self-loathing, then, there is also Tanizaki's titular celebration of shadows: "I would call back at least for literature this world of shadows we are losing. In the mansion of literature I would have the eaves deep and the walls dark, I would push back into the shadows things that come forward too clearly."[35]

The contradiction engendered in this single word encapsulates the complexities of writing about race. There is a *fushigi*ness to the written word, and there is always the possibility of mobilizing literary language in multifaceted, metaphoric, and malleable ways. It is not impossible for representative readings to account for such malleability—the best ones certainly do. The messiness of Tanizaki's literary mansions, however, clearly challenges the representational cleanliness of Morrison's *Playing in the Dark*. For Morrison, the language of racial ideology, particularly in its literary manifestation, functions powerfully precisely because it is transparent, coating the meaning of texts with an invisible film that we would be able to see through if only we would take the time to do so. "It is as if," Morrison writes, "I had been looking at a fishbowl . . . and suddenly I saw the bowl, the structure that transparently (and invisibly) permits the ordered life it contains to exist in the larger words."[36] When she "began to rely on [her] understanding of what the linguistic struggle requires of writers," she says, "what became *transparent* were the *self-evident* ways that Americans choose to talk about themselves *through* a[n] . . . always choked representation of an Africanist presence.[37]

It seems, however, that the language of race—literary or otherwise, Japanese, American, or somewhere in between—is shadowed, with race as something that is always just beyond our ability to represent with transparent, illuminating finality. The writing of fictions of race is arguably less like Morrison's fishbowl and more like Tanizaki's *zuihitsu*. Reconstructive reading is an attempt to think about the *zuihitsu* of race and blackness in postwar Japanese literature on its own terms. It is easy to judge the representation of "Negro blood" in Tanizaki's treatise, but this easy critique might occlude literary questions and investigations of greater import. How, for example, does the language of blood quantums end up in a 1933 essay from Japan? On what transpacific current did this racial discourse flow, how did it circulate throughout Japan, how did this circulation transform Japanese discourses of race, and how were these currents recirculated to the other side of the Pacific?

Blackness in Postwar Japanese Fiction

Reading fictions of race according to the terms outlined above—that is, reading fictions of race with three commitments, an intellectual commitment to the notion of race as a construct, an attentive commitment to the interplay between fictional and nonfictional narratives of race, and a reconstructive commitment to exploring what (stylistic) form suggests about the (conceptual) formation of race—calls for a redefinition of the term *blackness*. It also calls for a redefinition of what we mean when we say that there is "blackness in postwar Japanese literature." To reiterate, studies of blackness in postwar Japanese literature have been concerned primarily with the representation of black characters. Under the representational paradigm, there is blackness already out there in the "real world," and this blackness is in a work of Japanese literature when the literary world represents real-world blackness. In his study of Japanese literary representations of Afro-Jamaican blackness, for example, Marvin Sterling defines blackness as the intersection of "biological" and "imagined fixity" of the identity of people of sub-Saharan African descent and the fluid "range of ideological agendas facilitated" by this imagined fixity.[38] One of Sterling's insights is that blackness is both a description of a real-world, "biological" community/communality and a marshalling of sociopolitical energy in response to that description. Sterling's definition of blackness is composed with an eye turned toward how the reality of blackness is fictionalized in Japanese literary representations.

In order to enrich the conversation on representation, I would like to add something to Sterling's definition: that the terms delimited by any definition of blackness must reach beyond a discussion of a particular identity—in Sterling's case, people of sub-Saharan African descent—and toward a definition of the conditions of the possibility of identity itself. In other words, an attempt to define blackness is also an attempt to define ontology, an attempt to think through being (or, perhaps, nonbeing) in the social world. According to the logic of race-based systems of social oppression such as Jim Crow and apartheid, blackness does more than simply denote a racial category—it determines what kind of human being a person is. Or, more accurately, it determines whether or not a person is fully a human being. An insidious reminder of the link between the question of blackness and the question of humanity is the Three-Fifths Compromise of 1787, which recognized only a fraction of the humanity of slaves. Any cultural conversation on blackness carries this historical baggage, even, or maybe especially, when the conversation crosses the Pacific. To talk about blackness is to talk about what kind of human being a person is, or, in more pernicious variants of this conversation, it is to talk about whether or not a person is a human being at all. This is why Jared Sexton proposes that "the province of the field of investigation called black studies" is the "sustained response" to the following constellation of inquiries.

> What is the nature of a form of being that presents a problem for the thought of being itself? More precisely, what is the nature of a human being whose human being is put into question radically and by definition, a human being whose being human raises the question of being human at all? Or, rather, whose being is the generative force, historic occasion and essential byproduct of the question of human being in general? . . . What can be said about such a being and how, if at stake in the question is the very possibility of human being and perhaps even possibility as such?[39]

Sexton's delineation of the province of African American studies has profound purchase on the contributions that might be made by Afro-Japanese studies, particularly in the postwar context. This book is an attempt to travel to Japan with Nahum Chandler and ask what it means to consider the problem of the Negro as a problem for Japanese thought and, perhaps more important, to ask why postwar Japanese authors themselves see the "Negro problem" as a problem for Japanese thought. It is more than mere coincidence that organizations such as the Kokujin kenkyū no kai (Japanese Association for Negro Studies, founded in 1954) and literary endeavors such as the *Kokujin bungaku zenshū* (The Complete Works of Black Literature), a twelve-volume collection of Japanese translations of the likes of Richard Wright, James Baldwin, Jean Toomer, and Langston Hughes published between the years 1961 and 1963, emerged in the postwar period—after Nagasaki, after Hiroshima, and after the American Occupation of Japan.

When authors, Japanese or otherwise, turn to questions of blackness, they are, more often than not, playing with and reimagining how we think about racialized human beings, testing the epistemological limits of the relationship between race and being. Fred Moten asks, "What if blackness is the name that has been given to the social field and social life of an illicit alternative capacity to desire?"[40] When E. Taylor Atkins, riffing on Amiri Baraka, writes "If blues-based music is . . . an *outlook* or 'mode of being' . . . I present the experiences of Japan's jazz artists and aficionados with the intention of asking the reader to consider the possibility that Japanese too might be 'blues people,'" he has effectively recapitulated the suggestion I would like to make here: that there is a palpable "illicit alternative capacity [and] desire" for new ways of imagining racial being present in the writing of blackness in postwar Japanese literature.[41] (There are also, to be sure, instances in which there is a desperate desire to recodify the racial paradigms of yesteryear, but this, too, is in a sense a kind of reimagining.) To reduce this desire solely to the representations of blackness that rise to the surface of texts is to render invisible the stakes and techniques of postwar Afro-Japanese cultural exchange.

In short, the relationship between blackness and postwar Japanese literature is—to revisit the translation of *fushigi* in Tanizaki's *In Praise of Shadows*—much more "profound" than representative readings, in and of themselves, can portend. If blackness can be seen as, in addition to Sterling's imagined fixity, a mode of being in the world, as well as a way of signifying that mode to the world, to say that there is blackness *in* postwar Japanese literature should mean much more than the representations of black characters that appear on the surface of Japanese texts, which, all too often, only run skin deep. The blackness in Japanese literature is everything—Afro-Japanese intertextuality, Japanese experimentation with black literary techniques and tropes, Japanese translations and receptions of black stories, Japanese literati's encounters with black thought, culture, history, people, and politics and the way that such encounters inevitably colored their thematic concerns, and so on—and all the engagements by which postwar, "post-Occupation" Japanese authors struggle to rearticulate racial being and reconstruct their fiction of race in the postwar period.

John Dower writes that the Pacific War was "also a race war," which "ultimately . . . brought about a revolution in racial consciousness throughout the world that continues to the present day."[42] That is to say, in the Pacific War race played a central role both in the imagining of "the enemy" and in justifying the violent means required to defeat it. If we accept the postwar era as a valid periodization for the study of Japanese literature, then this implies that there are insights to be gained from a body of literature written in the wake of a race war. To read the blackness—here in the expanded sense of the term—in postwar Japanese literature is to consider how Japanese authors wrote themselves into Dower's "revolution in racial consciousness."[43]

The writing of blackness and fictions of race in modern Japan, as the previous excerpt from Tanizaki suggests, preceded the postwar period. It was not long after the arrival of those black ships that Japanese authors began to translate cross-cultural encounters with black people into fictions of race. There are references to "countries of sun-kissed darkies (*kuronbō*)" and "darkies from the African states hired on the cheap" as early as Kanagaki Robun's (1829–94) *Aguranabe* (The Beefeater, 1871) and *Seiyō dōchū hiza-kurige* (Shank's Mare Round the West, 1870–76).[44] These early Meiji references were revisited and updated in the late Meiji era by figures such as Natsume Soseki (1867–1916), who wrote in *Sanshirō* (1908), "If it's an African hero you need, you've got Ogawa here, the Kyushu black man," and Nagai Kafū (1879–1959), who described Washington, DC, in *Amerika monogatari* (American Stories, 1908) as enveloped by a "mass of hideous negroes."[45]

In *From White to Yellow: The Japanese in European Racial Thought, 1300–1735*, Rotem Kowner notes that, when seen in "racial terms," the opening of Japan by America in 1854 "was the final step in the gradual repositioning, if not decline, of the Japanese 'race.'"[46] Several of the fictions of race of the Meiji period mobilize blackness in order to think through the relationship between "civilization" (*bunmei*) and the discourse of a racialized Great Chain of Being. Think, for example, of Fukuzawa Yukichi's (1835–1901) comparison of advanced civilizations such as America's, "semi-developed" countries such as Japan, and "primitive lands" such as Africa in his *An Outline of a Theory of Civilization* or of Rachael Hutchinson's research on Kafū's writing of "flexible positioning," Kafū's attempt to see racial and civilizational status markers "as something that can shift depending on one's positions vis-à-vis other people and other places."[47]

During the interwar period, Japanese writings of blackness would find their way into literary projects that stemmed from Meiji era conversations on civilization. One example is Abe Tomoji's (1903–73) "Shinema no kokujin" (A Negro in Cinema, 1930), which borrows the figure of Stephin Fetchit (1902–85) for a Japanese rendition of modernist literature's fascination with black primitivism. The interwar period also saw, however, new imaginings of the place and purpose of blackness in Japanese letters. The Indonesian "black brothers" of Ema Shū's (1889–1975) 1928 "Kokujin no kyōdai" (Black Brothers), for example, is a precedent-setting example of the power of imagining global blackness and transoceanic "black" solidarity in proletarian prose. A second example of new imaginings is Lieutenant General Satō Kōjirō's (1862–1923) *Nichi-bei sensō yume monogatari* (A Fantasy of the US-Japanese War, 1921), which prognosticated the Pacific War some eighteen years before its actual onset. Satō, who participated in both the Sino- and Russo-Japanese wars, produced a fantastic, propagandistic vision of the US-Japanese war, in which the Japanese defeat the US Pacific fleet in a surprise attack, occupy Hawaii, and, with ten million "Negro" reinforcements led by Marcus Garvey, invade mainland United States.

I make note of these Meiji and Taisho era texts to suggest that there are enough prewar fictions of race and blackness in Japan to quite literally fill a book of scholarship. In light of this prehistory, I focus on the period from the postwar to the present with several things in mind. The Allied Occupation brought an influx of African American soldiers, families, and culture to Japan. This influx came right into the homes of Japanese writers, as television, radio, newspaper, film, and books brought black politics, culture, and literature to Japan with a tangibility unseen in the preceding periods. Moreover, the conditions under which black people and culture came to Japan—that is, as second-class enforcers of the occupation of a defeated Japan—served as a galvanizing prompt for prolific writings of fictions of race. In addition to this influx, this period also saw an unprecedented uptick in translations of black literature and ideas into Japanese, with Japanese fictions of race now informed by black voices, as well as Japanese authors' observations during their travels abroad and readings of fictions of race by nonblack authors.

I begin with this moment of postwar exchange and trace a history into contemporary times, rather than focusing solely on Occupation period writings, in order to address the shifting signification of blackness in postwar Japanese literary history. Even if two authors—take, for example, Ishikawa Jun (1899–1987) and Yamada Eimi (1959–)—both use the term *kokujin* (black person), the significance of this word in Ishikawa's 1946 works is fundamentally different from its significance in Yamada Eimi's writings in 2016. Finally, I hope that the periodological shortcomings of this study may prompt future scholars to write fuller accounts of this rich, understudied chapter of comparative literature.

The postwar period includes some of the richest chapters in the story of Afro-Japanese cultural exchange. The culmination of the Pacific War and the onset of the Allied Occupation of Japan made for heady times in the encounters between African Americans and Japanese people. The "Double V" campaign, which promised that African American contributions to the war abroad would translate into "victories" in the battle against racial inequality on the domestic front, ended in only a partial victory, for African Americans' contributions to the war effort did not translate into immediate civil rights or economic opportunity. Postwar African Americans enlisted in droves in search of a better life on the other side of the Pacific. The Allied Occupation was less than a week old when the Twenty-Fourth Infantry Regiment, one of the army's largest and oldest African American commands, was assigned to garrison duty in Japan. Throughout the Occupation, the number of black servicemen stationed in Japan "generally fluctuate[d] between ten and fifteen thousand," a number that was bolstered by black military families in Japan.[48] Add to this the vertiginous inversion of power dynamics that came with the Occupation, as Japan, revered as the big brother of the colored races since its defeat of Russia, was now occupied by a white nation.

This shift in the power dynamic significantly altered the tenor of black-Japanese racial solidarity. Up to this point, Afro-Japanese affinities had been buoyed primarily by black quixotism and Japanese propagandism and opportunism. The Occupation, however, saw both the genuine empathy and the messy disillusionment that comes with the lived experience of cross-cultural exchange. For the Japanese, African Americans were both powerful occupiers and (fellow) second-class citizens "beneath" white soldiers in the racial world order, and African Americans couldn't help but notice the irony of enforcing a color line—the "SCAP Personnel Only" signs, the elections monitored by black soldiers—that they themselves hadn't fully crossed.[49] Add to this the fact that African Americans served as the stewards of the Occupation, filling positions (such as guarding cargo as service battalion worker) that often put them in close contact with the Japanese. This rich contact extended beyond the drudgery of duty and into the soldiers' rest and relaxation: "Black GIs experienced discrimination both on base and off. But in the off-base establishments where they felt at home, a vital Creolised counter-culture grew up. Many of Japan's leading postwar jazz artists and popular entertainers got their start in this marginalised *demi-monde* of drugs, booze and black-marketeering where the creative juices could flow freely, undisturbed by convention and the prying eyes of whites."[50]

In sum, the postwar period gave birth to a vast body of cultural artifacts that Mary Louise Pratt calls arts of the contact zone. "Autoethnography, transculturation, critique, collaboration, bilingualism, mediation, parody, denunciation, imaginary dialogue, vernacular expression—these are some of the literate arts of the contact zone. Miscomprehension, incomprehension, dead letters, unread masterpieces, absolute heterogeneity of meaning—these are some of the perils of writing in the contact zone."[51] One objective of this study is to see how the "arts and perils" of the Afro-Japanese contact zone—transculturation, parody, imaginary dialogue, miscomprehension, incomprehension, and so on—play out on the pages of postwar Japanese literature.

It is in the muck of the postwar contact zone that the texts addressed in the first chapter of this book were produced. John Russell suggests that "contemporary Japanese discourse reduces the Black Other to a mute object of the lingering gaze" and "privilege[s] discourse *about* blacks while effectively precluding any dialogue" between black and Japanese characters, thereby "silenc[ing] the Black Other."[52] In part as an acknowledgment of my debt to Russell and in part as an attempt to open up a new way of thinking about Afro-Japanese cultural exchange, chapter 1, "Unspeakable Things Unspoken: Moments of Silence, Racial Preoccupation, and the Hauntology of Blackness in the Fiction of Occupied Japan," advances two arguments: first, that an overemphasis on representative readings of blackness might run the risk of exacerbating the very silencing of blackness that these readings critique in that literature; and, second, that "haunting" (rather than "silent") is an apt metaphor for the presence of blackness in the fiction written under the watchful eye of Occupation censors. I advance these arguments by reading the haunting significance of racial specters and silence in the short fiction of Ishikawa Jun (1899–1987), Kojima Nobuo (1915–2006), and Matsumoto Seichō (1909–92) alongside Derrida's notion of hauntology.

The contact zones of the Occupation gave rise to much more than representations of black characters. They engendered new ways of thinking about racial being; this is the "revolution in racial consciousness" of which Dower writes in *War without Mercy*.[53] The second and third chapters address these new ways of thinking. From the late 1950s through the 1960s, Ōe Kenzaburō (1935–) was a key figure in this revolutionary pivot in racial thinking. In 1959 Ōe wrote, "When it comes to the American Negro problem, the Japanese stand on the side of the Negro. I imagine that there isn't a single Japanese person who prefers the whites who do the beating over the Negroes who receive them."[54] Here Ōe is imagining himself as an ally and fellow "colored person," and he would rather stand with his brethren than inflict bodily harm on them. Ōe's words of Afro-Asian camaraderie voice the aspiration of Afro-Japanese exchange during the tumultuous times of the 1960s. If Afro-Japanese exchange was characterized by vicarious wish fulfillment and proxy politics in the first half of the twentieth century, 1960s writings aspire (even if there are moments in which this aspiration is not met) to a kind of affinity politics—with *affinity* here resonating both as the force that bonds people together and kinship based on something other than consanguinity. The contemporaneity of the civil rights, ANPO, and Zengakuren movements sparked an era of rich, authentic, transpacific synergy that might be called the golden age of Afro-Japanese exchange.[55]

The view of this synergy from Japan would include the hosting of the Asian-African Writers Conference in 1961, the rise of the Japanese Association for Negro Studies and the intellectual coming of age of Furukawa Hiromi—a seminal figure in the association and coauthor of the epochal *Nihonjin to Afurika-kei Amerikajin: Nichi-Bei kankeishi ni okeru sono shosō* (The Japanese and African Americans: Facets of Afro-Japanese Interaction in the History of Japanese-American Relations), travels through black America documented by artists and intellectuals ranging from Fulbright recipient Yoshida Ruiko to translator of *Roots* Yasuoka Shōtarō, and the swinging jazz riffs of Akiyoshi Toshiko. The view from the other side of the Pacific would include the some four thousand haiku penned by Richard Wright, the rise and fall of Amiri Baraka's *Yūgen*, Yuri Kochiyama on the cover of *Life* magazine cradling the dying body of her colleague and friend Malcolm X, and the heavyweight champion of the world—Muhammad Ali—declaring, "I am not a Negro . . . I am an Asiatic black man."[56] The era was characterized by black language coming from Japanese mouths and Japanese forms in black ink.

It was against this backdrop that Ōe posited an existential analogy between postwar, post-Occupation Japanese people and civil rights era African Americans. Chapter 2, "In the Beginning: Ōe Kenzaburō and the Creative Nonfiction of Blackness," takes up Ōe's Afro-Japanese analogy. It was "around the time when the Afro-Asian Writers' Conference was held [1961] that I [Ōe] began to carry black literature (*kokujin bungaku*) and works concerning Africa with me and nothing else and read them like a man who had been washed onto a deserted island."[57] Indeed, throughout the 1960s, Ōe participated in conferences held by the Afro-Asian Writers Association and the Japanese Association for Negro Studies, read black literature extensively, and met with Ralph Ellison at Harvard. I argue that these encounters held transformative power for Ōe; after rich engagement with African and African American literature, he translated his interest in Sartrean existentialism into a series of nonfiction writings that posit a new vision of the Japanese as "colored." These essays are, quite literally, creative nonfiction, as Ōe creates an existential analogy between postwar, post-Occupation Japanese and Civil Rights era African Americans.

I also argue, however, that Ōe's analogy—like any analogy—contains an element of falsity. Chapter 2 also addresses the inevitable fallacy of Ōe's black-Japanese analogical thinking: to focus solely on affinity, on how Japanese people are "like" their African American counterparts and vice-versa, is to do violence to the singularity of their struggles. Here I would like to briefly consider the violence of analogy by way of Afro-Japanese relations in Okinawa. I turn to Okinawa in order to highlight the fact that the chapters of this book do not adequately address the profound parallax vision that occurs when blackness is viewed vis-à-vis Okinawa, itself a "limit," to borrow Wendy Matsumara's recent articulation, of Japan's thinking of itself.[58]

Given Japan's amicable atmosphere for African Americans relative to other Asian stations, the US military, as previously mentioned, sent waves of black soldiers to its bases there. Many of these soldiers were shipped in turn to Okinawa; the aforementioned Twenty-Fourth, for example, was stationed in Okinawa until its 1947 transfer to Camp Gifu. The history and legacy of the America's administration of Okinawa (1945–72) holds within it a history of Afro-Japanese cultural exchange. To be sure, some of this contact takes the shape of the golden age exchange outlined above. Take, for example, Arakawa Akira's "The Colored Race," a series of poems published in *Ryūdai bungaku*, a student literary magazine housed at the University of the Ryukyus. The series includes "A Poem for the Black Troops," which begins, "Your skin, like ours, is not white. / A rugged dark brown, it is / The color of iron. / Covering ineradicable welts / from the whip, / Your brown skin is / Strong, like stone."[59]

There is also, however, a history of racial tension and strife in Okinawa, both of which have been exacerbated by extraterritoriality and crimes perpetrated by US servicemen. In the words of Inamine Susumu, mayor of Nago, Okinawa, "Since we survived the end of the war, the San Francisco Treaty, [and] the 'return' to Japan, we . . . have to live with 74% of US military bases on Okinawa. . . . We will have to live not only with the bases, but with the accidents and the crimes that they cause, so that after we die we will leave our children and grandchildren a legacy of misery."[60] It is true that Okinawans have suffered at the hands of servicemen of all colors; the accusations of rape of Okinawan girls by US soldiers is yet another scar on the history of US-Okinawan relations. It is also true, however, that the myth of black criminality has planted firm roots in Okinawan soil. Perhaps future scholarship will have more to say about what Mitzi Uehara Carter calls these "nappy routes," which are often "inscribed in local literature, poetry, or art."[61]

A painfully fitting literary reminder of this dynamic can be found in Chinen Seishin's (1941–2013) *Jinruikan* (The Human Pavilion, 1976), a satirical dramatization of the displaying of Okinawans at the 1903 Fifth World Trade and Industrial Exhibition held in Osaka. In the room next to the Okinawan exhibit, the trainer/guide tells the audience, "We have a display of the Negro race. (*He says threateningly*). They're black, their entire bodies, really and truly black. It'll send shivers tingling down your spines. Let me warn guests with weak hearts or high blood pressure not to enter here."[62] This scene quite literally exhibits both the analogy between Okinawans and "Negroes" as oppressed peoples and the myths of blackness that circulate throughout Japan, including Okinawa. The juxtaposition of blackness and Okinawa here serves as a reminder that black-Okinawan encounters do not automatically engender the "cross-racial fraternity" of Arakawa's "colored races"; in addition to the possibility of affinity, there is also a history of dehumanizing violence between Okinawa and the black people who have occupied its soil.

A second reminder of the violence of Ōe's analogy can be found in the work of Nakagami Kenji (1946–92). Nakagami took the project initiated by Ōe and turned it on its head. For Nakagami there is indeed something analogous about the existential conditions of African Americans and Japanese people. This analogy, for him, is all the more true for the *burakumin*, Japan's largest social minority. If Ōe created an analogy between African Americans and Japanese people in the 1960s, Nakagami plays with that analogy like a jazz riff, questioning what it means for someone, or some body—literary or somatic—to be African American, Japanese, or any other identity. Chapter 3, "Of Passing Significance: Pronominal Politics, Nakagami Kenji, and the Fiction of *Burakuness*," addresses the work of Nakagami Kenji, the first author born in the postwar period to receive the Akutagawa Prize. Nakagami was also the first postwar author to self-identify as a member of the *burakumin*. This chapter considers Nakagami's borrowing of the rhetoric and tropes of 1960s black artistic movements (e.g., he once declared that *buraku* is beautiful) in light of pertinent works of black literary theory. I am particularly interested in Nakagami's self-proclaimed affinity with passing, Henry Louis Gates's notion of signifying, and jazz improvisation. In concert, these three tactics inspire what I call the passing significance of Nakagami's writing of improvised identities.

The second and third chapters consider the precedents of Afro-Japanese identity and affinity politics set by two canonical authors in the 1960s, a golden age of exchange across the Black Pacific. The final two chapters turn to the contemporary experiments that build on and move beyond those precedents. Ōe and Nakagami produced precedents—Afro-Japanese analogy from Ōe and black-Japanese improvisational affinity, as the wellspring of new ways of imagining racial being, from Nakagami—that would form a foundation for the racial thinking of the literature of the long 1970s. Andrew Gordon suggests that the period from the late 1960s through the early 1980s, which I call the "long 1970s," was characterized by Japan's "greater openness to the world" due to the fact that "the United States and Japan were more interdependent than ever."[63] And yet this interdependence existed alongside the belief that "the American government did not fully trust the Japanese state or regard it as an equal partner."[64] If a "new race" (*shinjin-rui*, a pun first recorded by the *Asahi shimbun* to describe the transformed Japanese people who came of age during the long 1970s) of Japanese people was born of interdependence with and unequal status in the eyes of the American government, it should come as no surprise that the literature of this era thought of itself in terms of blackness.

The literature of the long 1970s experiments with race and blackness in a way that amalgamates the black-Japanese analogy of Ōe with the blurring of the borders of racial being seen in the experiments of Nakagami (whose writings on blackness coincide largely with the long 1970s). In chapter 4, "Genre Trouble: Breaking the Law of Genre and Literary Blackness in the Long 1970s," I consider texts of the long 1970s ranging from the photorealistic journalism of Yoshida Ruiko (1938–) to the science fictional work of Abe Kobo (1924–93). Prompted by phenomena such as the spectacular Japanese media coverage of the events in black America throughout the 1960s (e.g., the Harlem Riots) and Japanese authors' travels throughout black America, the long 1970s saw a proliferation of black characters, settings, motifs, and stylistics in Japanese literature. From the reportage of Honda Katsu'ichi (1932–) to the murder mysteries of Morimura Seiichi (1933–), this explosion reverberated across the genres. The chapter poses two intertwined questions: how do various genres, each with their own generic conventions, think through blackness; and which shared aspects of these texts cut across genre borders, thereby becoming "generic" to the era's writings of blackness?

Following the long 1970s, the mid-1980s saw "booms" on both sides of the Pacific. In Japan journalists coined the term *black boom* (*kokujin būmu*) to describe the Japanese fascination with all things African American. In black America, a fascination with Asian culture that had a decidedly Chinese inflection—this is the age of Bruce Leroy and Wu Tang—grew to include black-Japanese "*collabos*," or, collaborations. At the heart of these twin booms was the global rise of hip hop, a cultural phenomenon that, as Ian Condry (channeling Cornel West) argues in his *Hip-Hop Japan: Rap and the Paths of Cultural Globalization*, had the potential to establish "a new cultural politics of affiliation."[65]

Afro-Japanese cultural production in the age of hip hop is both prodigious and problematic. Building on the foundation laid during the golden age, its prodigy resides in the incredible velocity at which Afro-Japanese exchange takes place—a speed that only increases with the ever-increasing sophistication of digital technologies and the mastery that black and Japanese artists wield over their localized versions of global culture (Lenard Moore is

a case in point)—and the power such nonessentialist, transnational borrowings have in helping us navigate political and cultural spaces.[66] Or perhaps
purchases should be substituted for *borrowings*. Decidedly estranged from the
foundation established in the long 1970s, the difficulty of exchange during
this period stems from its tendency toward commodification, fetishization,
and (racial) reification—transaction in lieu of interaction. This tendency,
moreover, is often coupled with a borrowing akin to that of Azuma Hiroki's database animals.[67] Whereas the artists and intellectuals of the 1960s
and 1970s rooted racial affinity in what they saw as a common critique
of a suffocating master narrative, much hip hop era exchange is obsessed
with borrowing only styles and surfaces, many of which are divorced from
any narrative whatsoever. This explains, in part, the odd coexistences of the
Afro-Japanese cultural production of this period; for every innocuous "superflat" collaboration between black rappers and Murakami Takashi, there
are heard an equal number of disparaging remarks about African Americans
from politicians such as Nakasone Yasuhiro, Watanabe Michio, and Kajiyama Seiroku.[68]

In chapter 5, "Japanese Literature in the Age of Hip Hop: A Mic Check,"
I think through these odd coexistences by way of the lyrics and music criticism of rapper/novelist Itō Seikō (1961–), a novel by writer/turntablist
Mobu Norio (1970–), and the literature of the self-styled Japanese dean of
black culture, Yamada Eimi (1959–). This chapter addresses a new mode
of Japanese writing that followed the experimentation of the long 1970s:
hip-hop-informed Japanese literature. It explores the writing of blackness
in Japanese literature in an age in which the hip-hop-inspired signs and
techniques of the "postracial" exist side by side with the legacies and realities
of the racial.

In *Becoming Yellow: A Short History of Racial Thinking*, Michael Keevar
asks us to think of "color terms" as inventions with "complex and often
surprising histor[ies]."[69] The five chapters presented here adumbrate the inventions of blackness in Japanese cultural and literary discourse from the
end of the Pacific War to the rise of hip hop in Japan—a complex and often
surprising history of postwar Japan's racial thinking. It seems to me that
an exclusive focus on representations of blackness might obfuscate visions
of the power these inventions had for postwar Japanese storytellers as they
reconstructed what it meant to be "Japanese" in the ruins of a lost race war.

The guiding premise of this book is the assumption that a history of
blackness in postwar Japanese literature is also a history of racial thinking in
postwar Japan and that this transpacific view of blackness is, in turn, also a
step toward understanding a global history of blackness in its plentitude. I

say more about this conjecture in the "Conclusion." But for the time being I will note simply that a historical view of the contours of blackness in post-war Japanese literature charts a course that begins with the racial amnesia and discombobulation of the postwar period, works toward the affinities of Afro-Japanese thought in the face of American power exhibited in the 1960s–80s, and concludes with contemporary gestures toward deconstructive, postracial, and/or hypercommodified exchanges with blackness. This course traces the very contours of the thinking of race in postwar Japan.

For the purposes of this study, by "racial thinking" I mean a hermeneutics of race or, more pointedly, a hermeneutic circle of race. The hermeneutic circle is one of the fundamental building blocks of the study of interpretation. On the one hand, the part cannot be understood without some preliminary conceptualization of the whole and, on the other hand, the whole cannot be understood without some sense of how its parts lead to its emergence. The hermeneutic circle provides a visualization of the interpretative process, a kind of feedback loop in which the interpreter begins with a preconceived notion of the whole, which provides an interpretative framework for the creation of discernible parts, and the discernment of parts, in turn, reconfigures the image of the framing whole. By racial thinking, I mean that the presence of race on the level of the part or the whole inevitably colors the feedback between the part (the character, the metaphor, the sentence, the solitary postwar Japanese reader reading in his or her bedroom, postwar Japanese literature, or what have you) and the whole (the story, the concept being metaphorized, the novel, any and all readers on any part of the globe, post-world-war literature, or what have you), and that race inevitably mediates the interpretation of the relationship between the part and the whole. When a single black drug user becomes a part of the population criminalized during a crack epidemic or when a single white opioid addict becomes a bellwether of a public health crisis and the failures of globalization, racial thinking as it is defined here is in play. The tools, techniques, and procedures of representative readings, which often assume that the black Other is wholly apart from and moves in different circles than the Japanese Self, might make this history of racial thinking in postwar Japanese literature less, rather than more, visible.

In proposing reconstructive readings in lieu of representative ones, I aim to develop at least four heuristics for the analysis of postwar Japan's literary racial thinking: translation, intertextuality, experimentation, and shared history. With the first heuristic, translation, I am thinking in two directions. The first of these is the mediating power actual translations of black literature and culture have for Japanese writings of fictions of race. How do translations of authors such as Richard Wright (1908–60), Ralph Ellison (1914–94), and James Baldwin (1924–87) (chapters 2 and 3) or of hip hop English (chapter 5) give rise to new ways of thinking and talking about race in Japanese fiction? The second suggestion I have in mind considers translation in the broader sense of the term. The *Oxford English Dictionary* defines *translation* as "the removal or conveyance from one person, place, or condition to another; . . . changing or adapting to another use; renovation."[70] The "renovations" of blackness that occur in Japanese literature—Abe Kōbō's translation of the Harlem Riots of 1964, for example, in his *The Face of Another* (chapter 4)—are revelatory in their ability to make visible the assumptions, stakes, and implications of Japan's fictions of race.

In this regard, it can be more productive to think of Japanese "translations" of blackness in the broader sense of the term—their removals, conveyances, changes, adaptations, and so on—rather than Japanese representations of blackness. If the task of the translator is indeed to "serve the purpose of expressing the innermost relationship of languages to one another,"[71] viewing Afro-Japanese literary relations through the lens of translation might fundamentally transform the task of the Afro-Japanese literary critic. How does the mediation of translation serve the purpose of expressing the innermost relationships of human races with one another? Or what new ways of thinking about and articulating race are born when the relationship between the self and the "racial Other" is seen as a kind of translation? Throughout this book, I often refer to "writings" and "constructions of blackness" rather than "representations of the black Other." I do this not to be circumlocutious but to remind readers of translation as a heuristic; maybe we are dealing with a "representation of the black Other," but our analysis will be enriched if we consider the processes of translation that enable and enliven a given representation.

Such translations often facilitate intertextuality. Here, too, it might be helpful to think both literally and metaphorically. There is, thanks in large part to linguistic translations, a rich network of Afro-Japanese intertextuality in Japan's postwar fiction. But a broader sense of the term *intertextuality* opens new avenues for considering this body of literature. In *Writing between the Lines: Race and Intertextuality*, Aldon Nielsen asks what it might mean to think of intertextuality as not simply a relationship between bodies of literature but also a relationship between human bodies and the body politic. For Nielsen "the transposition of sign systems lead[s] . . . to a new positionality"—"identity formation[s] in transit"—which gives rise to articulations of race that are "not wholly given . . . at birth, but neither . . . [are a] wholly owned psychic subsidiar[y] of the hegemonic system of racial identification."[72] The border-crossing intertextuality of Japanese play in the shadows engenders such new positionalities and in so doing provides new models for transracial connectivity. Moreover, the transpacific circulation of texts creates heretofore underexplored networks of world literature. This is what Karen Thornber has referred to as transculturation by way of dynamic intertextuality.

I am interested in a possible difference between allusion and intertextuality. With allusion, a self-determined, self-contained work of literature refers to another text under the assumption that familiarity with the allusion brings to light some aspect of the alluding work. Intertextuality, on the other hand, supposes that the texts are, as the term's etymology suggests, woven together, that "any text is the absorption and transformation of another."[73] Intertextuality provides a model of thinking through racial difference that might be closer to the actual process of imagining racial identities; it is not that one race "alludes" to another but that the act of imagining racial difference becomes a constitutive aspect of conceptualizing one's own racial identity. It is with this in mind that this book, whenever possible, teases out intertextual links between works of Japanese literature and African American writings.

Literary play with race often occurs in shadowy, unexplored territories. So it follows that the style of such play tends to be experimental, the third heuristic suggested here. Experimentation with literary technique pushes at the very borders of discursive possibility, providing new languages for the discussion of race. This book sees Japanese fictions of race as themselves theoretical imaginings of racial possibilities. Theoretical experimentation often takes the shape of stylistic innovation, and one guiding heuristic of this study is to put this experimentation into dialogue with theories of race and literature.

By "shared history," the fourth heuristic, I have in mind the implications of Hans Robert Jauss for the reading and writing of blackness in postwar Japanese literature. Moving toward his horizon of expectation, Jauss writes, "A literary work, even if it seems new, does not appear as something absolutely new in an informational vacuum, but predisposes its readers to a very definite type of reception by textual strategies . . . familiar characteristics or implicit allusions. It awakens *memories of the familiar*, stirs particular emptions in the reader and with its 'beginning' arouses expectations for the 'middle and end.'"[74] My emphasis here is on memories of the familiar. What does it mean for Japanese authors to include references to historical events with the expectation that both Japanese and African American readers will sense something familial (this is, after all, what the "familiar" gestures toward) and the expectation that a single story might speak to a shared Afro-Japanese beginning, middle, and end?

This final heuristic is informed by what Nahum Chandler has recently called "another archive."[75] In reading postwar Japanese fiction, it is easy to develop tunnel vision in the archives of Japan. This fiction, however, is best read alongside archives well beyond the boundaries of Japan; it is almost impossible to read postwar Japanese fiction without referencing postwar Japan's shared history with the United States. By "shared history," I have in mind the readings enabled when the historical context of postwar Japanese literature is expanded to include events in African American history.

This list of heuristics is far from exhaustive. It should, however, provide prompts for reading blackness in postwar Japanese literature beyond its representations of blackness. There is a way in which, when viewed reconstructively, the texts addressed in this book become representative, for they represent responses to how race was articulated in Japan's postwar past, as well as a means of reimagining how race might be rearticulated in the future.

CHAPTER I

Unspeakable Things Unspoken

Moments of Silence, Racial Preoccupation, and the Hauntology of Blackness in the Literature of Occupied Japan

'The niggers ran off into those mountains. Be careful, and get home safely.' . . . When he got home, he found Yoshiko frozen in place, still stretched out under the mosquito net. She didn't moan, she didn't move. . . . Something about her reminded him of a ghost.

—Matsumoto Seichō, "Kuroji no e"

Something Out of Nothing: Toward a Hauntology of Blackness in Postwar Japanese Literature

My grandmother—whose first job was picking cotton in the very fields where our ancestors once labored in that most peculiar of institutions—had an expression she would repeat in times of trouble: "We'll make something out of nothing." For her the meaning of black life was never far removed from memories of the cotton field. She understood black life as one of limited social, political, and economic resources, so much so that one might say it is a life of nothing. But "nothingness" here is not to be confused with purposelessness, and limited social, political, and economic means is not to be confused with meaninglessness. Nothing can be productive, big bangs of meaning, hence "something out of nothing."

It is with my grandmother in mind that I enter the conversation initiated by John Russell. Over the course of three decades of study, John Russell has set the groundwork for investigations of how the "physical and cultural *presence* of blacks in Japan . . . has been and continues to be constructed in mass culture and what that suggests about the construction of blackness, both locally and globally."[1] Russell's investigations engage, more often than not, in "examination[s] of the performative and ludic aspects of its [blackness in Japanese cultural discourse] representation."[2] Russell finds the representation of this presence to be lacking something: authentic black voices. He writes, "Contemporary Japanese discourse reduces the Black Other to a mute object of the lingering gaze, desire and dread. These narratives privilege discourse about blacks while effectively precluding any dialogue."[3] This conjecture has been reiterated by scholars such as Michael Molasky ("Blacks themselves have been given practically no voice in shaping this racial discourse, other than by providing soundbites or stereotypical, disembodied images") and Theodore Goossen ("The 'actual,' in other words the authors who actually live there [read black authors], aren't given an opportunity to speak for themselves; the recipient is narrated in the words of the self," which is "a kind of literary imperialism [*bungakuteki teikokushugi*]").[4]

In the remaining chapters of this book, I argue against these conjectures using the weight of the archive. The blackness of the body of literature composed by postwar Japanese authors simply does not bear out the claim of mutism. In this chapter, however, rather than sidestepping the concerns outlined above with counterexamples, I want to speak to Russell's critique on his terms. There is a sense in which Russell is absolutely correct, particularly as his assessment pertains to the Occupation period. Given that "Japanese literary and visual representations of blacks rely heavily on imaginary Western conventions," there is a way in which blackness in Japanese literary discourse becomes a kind of nothingness, just as it is in its American counterpart; thus blackness becomes the absence on which "something" (read: Japaneseness or whiteness) is defined.[5] How could one witness, for example, SCAP's segregationist policies and not see something on one side and nothing on the other?[6]

If this is the case, the question becomes: What can be made of social death, or what can be made out of nothing? It is here, I think, that Russell and I disagree. Russell contends that there is "a negative view of the blacks that permeates virtually all aspects of Japanese discourse on the black Other."[7] It seems to me that such a judgment call is best made on a case-by-case basis, but, for the sake of dialogue, I wonder if such moments of negativity can be read positively—as generative, productive, and meaningful? And it helps that Fred Moten agrees with my grandmother. "If the slave is," Moten writes, "in the end and in essence, nothing, what remains is the necessity of an investigation of that nothingness. What is the nothingness, which is to say the blackness, of the slave?"[8] Moten's investigation promises an opportunity to rethink the "relationship between fantasy and nothingness: what is mistaken for silence is, all of a sudden, transsubstantial."[9]

I think that Russell is right to suggest that "Japanese images of blackness" (to borrow Russell's articulation) are often "insubstantial as a simulacrum" (to borrow Derrida's articulation) of that blackness.[10] But this chapter proposes that the insubstantial and the spectral—particularly in the ruins of postwar Japan—might be charged with potential, that something can and should be made out of nothing. The fact that incomplete representations of black bodies appear and reappear in works of postwar Japanese literature is not necessarily a defect; it can be read as a feature of the literature's discourse on race in the aftermath of a lost race war.

In works such as *Specters of Marx* and "Spectrographies," Derrida outlines the differing scholarly objectives of ontology and hauntology. Ontology is the study of flesh and blood. It is interested in the difference between the real, what is "actually there," and the unreal. *Hauntology*, a homophone of *ontology* in the French original, is an attempt to think beyond the purity of the binary difference between presence and absence, or between authentic and inauthentic representations, in order to provide more thorough responses to texts on their own terms. There is something apposite in a hauntological approach when the theme in question is representations of blackness in postwar Japanese literature, which often appear as ghostly projections of the "real thing." More important than this, however, is the place of hauntology as a kind of conceptual metaphor for literary studies. The incompleteness of a haunting specter can be seen as both "a productive opening of meaning" and a conceptual metaphor for "the processes of literature and textuality in general."[11] In a word, the difference between ontology and hauntology is whether or not we believe in ghosts. Are ephemeral moments that don't accurately represent mundane reality something to be dismissed or something that might fundamentally redefine our reading of reality itself?

A "post-European" culture such as Japan's, Rey Chow suggests, "already contains, in its many forms of self-writing, imprints of a fraught and prevalent relation of comparison/judgment in which Europe haunts it as the referent of supremacy."[12] I would add to Chow's insight only that, even before it was occupied, Japan was just as haunted by the United States—preoccupied with a concern about its place in the face of America as the supreme referent. And this is where the specters of blackness arise. This preoccupation quite often took on a racial valence in the postwar period, as "to a conspicuous degree, the racial and racist ways of thinking which had contributed so much to the ferociousness of the war were sublimated and transformed after August 1945 . . . capable of being revived by both sides in times of crisis and tension."[13] Blackness haunts postwar Japanese literary discourse as authors attempt to reimagine racial being under the shadow of this new world order.

In his call for a "poetics of silence," David Danow writes, "In critical analyses scholarly interest has focused almost entirely . . . on the presence of the Word, rather than on its frequently telling absence. . . . *But what if the extraverbal mode, if only temporarily or periodically, emerges as the primary means of communication?* What might we learn if our focus remains concentrated on the moments of dialogue of *communicative* silence?"[14] This chapter, the only one in which the representation of blackness is my central concern, serves as a kind of simile for the chapters to come. There is a rich dialogue between postwar Japanese authors and black culture and literature that takes place directly beneath the textual surfaces on which Japanese authors represent blackness, and this dialogue is ongoing even when blackness is spectral and silent. My concern here is the ways in which representative analyses—readings that are interested in what blackness "is" and how it is represented in Japanese cultural productions—potentially short-circuit the reading process, ignoring elements of a text that are not representative of the interpretation being argued. This chapter considers the dialogues that occur in silence between black and Japanese characters in racially preoccupied postwar fiction, namely, the fiction of Matsumoto Seichō, Ishikawa Jun, and Kojima Nobuo.

"Exhuming a Buried Past": The Kokura Riots and the Painting on Black Canvas

The Allied Occupation was less than a week old when the Twenty-Fourth Infantry Regiment—the regiment of buffalo soldier lore—was assigned garrison duty in Okinawa. The Twenty-Fourth would remain in Okinawa until 1947, when it was transferred to Camp Gifu. Its time in Gifu would prove to be short-lived, however, and in June 1950, when the Korean People's Army (KPA), the North Korean military force, crossed the thirty-eighth parallel, the regiment was reassigned to Camp Jōno in Kokura, Japan (present-day Kitakyushu). Even though the Twenty-Fourth was underequipped and had little combat experience, it was to serve on the front lines throughout the Korean War, a fact that many soldiers of the predominately African American unit anticipated. Camp Jōno served as the way station for the regiment until its deployment in the Korean War. Camp Jōno, however, did not have sufficient facilities to house the soldiers. Nor were there adequate vessels to ship them to Korea; they were to be transported "in a hastily assembled flotilla of fishing boats, fertilizer haulers, coal carriers and tankers."[15]

"It was against the background of this chaos," Tessa Morris-Suzuki writes, "as the miseries of their situation and the prospect of impending death confronted the soldiers, that [a] mass breakout and riot occurred."[16] July 11, 1950, marks the beginning of the Kokura Riots, in which some two hundred soldiers from the Twenty-Fourth absconded from Camp Jōno, escaping from the base, most likely, through drainage passageways.[17] On the other side of the camp fence, the soldiers divided themselves into miniature battalions of anywhere from two to five soldiers. Over the next few days, the soldiers rioted and perpetrated a variety of crimes. According to sources ranging from the US National Archives to the Fukuoka Prefectural Police, the crimes most commonly reported were assault, theft, unlawful entry, and attempted sexual assault.[18] There is a critical discrepancy in the reports; whereas a cursory investigation of the riots conducted by US military authorities determined that there had been no deaths or injuries, Japanese police alleged one murder and two sexual assaults (as well as the possibility of unreported sexual assaults).[19]

The people and authorities of Kokura had little recourse over the several days of the Kokura Riots. One imperfect barricade between the people of Kokura and the riotous soldiers, however, was the *Asahi shimbun*, which has a main office in Kokura. As news of the riots reached *Asahi*, the newspaper assisted the military police by patrolling the areas where crimes had been reported and cautioning residents to stay indoors and secure their premises. The voice of *Asahi*, however, was muffled by SCAP, which heavily censored both the announcement and the subsequent reporting on the incident. It was not until 15 July, some five days after the riots, that the Kitakyushu edition of the *Asahi shimbun* would run a report by the military police on the absconded soldiers. This report included a message from Captain John O. Roberts to the people of Kitakyushu. Captain Roberts announced that there were "several black and white soldiers who hadn't reported back to their proper attachments" and any derelict soldiers should be reported to the proper authorities.[20] (Note here the reference to white soldiers. The fiction of race produced after the Kokura Riots has a kind of amnesia, a habit of highlighting the conduct of violent black soldiers and forgetting the violence of white ones.) This report was followed by a second Kitakyushu *Asahi* report on 18 July, "With Regrets from the US Armed Forces," a euphemistic apologia for the Kokura Riots.

It is easy to imagine Matsumoto Seichō, an author who would go on to become the godfather of Japanese mystery fiction, puzzling over the censored *Asahi* reports. At the time of the Kokura Riots, Matsumoto worked in the advertising department of a branch office of the *Asahi shimbun* in Kitakyushu. As his department prepared advertisements of smiling American faces promoting cosmetic goods—several such ads line the very pages that euphemized the riots—Matsumoto's colleagues were being censored and editing nonadmissions of guilt. On his transfer to the Tokyo office of the *Asahi shimbun*, Matsumoto was shocked to discover that many of his colleagues in Tokyo had never heard of the Kokura Riots. It is for this reason that Matsumoto penned "Kuroji no e" (Painting on Black Canvas, 1958), a short story/literary exposé of the riots. Or, in Matsumoto's words, "Painting on Black Canvas" "exhumes a buried past."[21]

"Painting on Black Canvas" unburies this history in two parts. The first half of the story tells of the brutal rape of Yoshiko at the hands of six black soldiers from the Twenty-Fourth. The story is told primarily from the perspective of Tomekichi, Yoshiko's husband. The second half of the story has Tomekichi working at the American Graves Registration Service (AGRS), a processing center for American soldiers killed in the Korean War that was—both in the story and in actual postwar Japan—located in Kokura. Tomekichi's work with AGRS facilitates his search for the ringleader of the men who raped his wife, from whom he is now estranged. This body is easily identified: it is the ghastly museum for the eponymous "painting on black canvas"—a large tattoo of a bald eagle on the black soldier's chest. Tomekichi does indeed find the painting, and the story concludes with him cutting into the corpse with a scalpel.

In "A Darker Shade of Difference," Molasky notes that "Painting on Black Canvas" vacillates between two voices: a journalistic voice that "locates the story's events within a specific temporal and political context, lending it an air of objectivity and hinting at the 'truth' of the account"; and a fictional voice that "examines the impulses and instincts that propel the soldiers to their criminal act."[22] This second, fictional voice, Molasky continues, is "informed by a philosophy of racial determinism" and "is reserved for those facets of the narrative for which there is no objective documentation."[23] Through these two voices, "Painting on Black Canvas" attempts to navigate the messy intersection of the undervaluation of black life, on the one hand, and the heretofore euphemized postwar violence perpetrated on Japanese bodies in Kokura on the other. Molasky suggests that Matsumoto errs on the side of the Japanese, with the journalistic voice "lending veracity to the egregiously racist reconstructions of the motives behind the rape" narrated in the fictional voice.[24] And yet, even as he errs on the side of exhuming Japanese history, Matsumoto cannot fully abandon the project of exhuming the value of black life. This amounts, according to Molasky, to representations of black soldiers through "a relentless series of racial stereotypes partially offset by a grudging sympathy."[25]

The addition I want to make to Molasky here is the difference between ontology and hauntology. Molasky, for example, makes quick work of the "fleeting moment" in "Painting on Black Canvas" in which there is a "hint at a parallel between the soldiers and Tomekichi."[26] Such ephemeralities, however, are the central focus of a hauntological reading, and so addressing these peripheral moments of parallelism are the crux of the reading of Matsumoto's "Painting on Black Canvas" proposed here. In other words, I am less surprised by Matsumoto's "egregiously racist" representations of black motives and more intrigued by the text's momentary lapses, its inability to commit fully to such egregious, racist logic. This inability speaks to the haunting power of blackness. As Morris-Suzuki writes in "Lavish Are the Dead," "In their first six weeks in Korea the 24th Infantry Division suffered 883 battle casualties. Many of those who had passed through Camp Jōno on their way to Korea returned to the camp in the ghost ships, to be laid out on its bleak antiseptic tables where even in death—even in the effort to return their bodies to their families—their mortal remains were viewed through the prism of the race that had overshadowed their lives."[27] Tomekichi and his "Painting on Black Canvas" are haunted by that shadow; in a nonfictional essay, Matsumoto himself writes, "The black soldiers were well aware that they were being pushed into a graveyard [on the front lines of Korea], and so they abandoned themselves to their despair."[28] In "Painting on Black Canvas," "egregiously racist" representations of blackness are paired with hesitantly empathetic explorations of this abandonment and despair. With this in mind, the text's "fleeting moments" of black-Japanese parallelism suggest the haunting similarities between the black soldiers and the victims of the Kokura Riots, all of whom are caught in the violent Korean conflict.

Part 1 of "Painting on Black Canvas" begins with a series of news wires that contextualize the escalating conflict on the Korean peninsula. These tell primarily of American setbacks in Korea, and they conclude with a brief note on President Truman's decision to increase the number of American troops in Korea by six hundred thousand. Although these news wires were inspired by historical events, they are fictionalized renditions of news articles of the time (particularly articles in the 5 and 12 July issues of *Nippon Times*). In other words, from the first word of "Painting on Black Canvas," Matsumoto underscores the need for a prosthesis in the telling of this story. Simulated news speaks to the phantom pains of history, and "Painting on Black Canvas" provides a literary prosthesis for a history effaced and suppressed from its very origins. Or, as Toeda Hirokazu writes, for Matsumoto—who grew up in the age when newspapers rose to prominence in Japan, cultivated a fascination with newspapers in his early years, and didn't have an opportunity to pursue a secondary education—the newspaper served as a "substitute for school, a precious opportunity for autodidactic education."[29]

With its historical stage set, "Painting on Black Canvas" shifts from its journalistic voice—which is also its fictional voice—to storytelling proper (which here doubles as a kind of journalistic historiography). From the first line of the story proper, the reader is transported to the Kokura Gion festival: "In the few days leading up to the festival, drumming reverberated limitlessly throughout every part of the city."[30] This drumming serves as the bass line for the story's stereotypical representations of the black soldiers. In addition to describing them as thick-lipped monkeys with bulging eyes, Matsumoto has the soldiers respond to the drums as semiautonomous, primitive savages. "The black soldiers, their chests throbbing with angst, must have perked up at the sound of the percussion. Ba-boom, ba-boom-boom, ba-boom, ba-boom-boom—there was something of a melodic charm buried within the incantation of this simple rhythm. . . . Its sound was reminiscent of the drumming that rumbles from deep within the jungle from the drums of savages as they perform their rituals."[31]

An ontological interpretation would have the reader stop here. Insofar as the black soldiers of the Twenty-Fourth respond to the "melodic charm" of primitive drumming with riotous savagery (whereas their white and Japanese counterparts recognize the drumming as the remnant, ritualized reverberations of the primitive world), we have heard all we need to hear about Matsumoto's surround-sound stereotyping of blackness. But what might a hauntological reading add to this writing of blackness? Matsumoto's story makes no mention of the historical roots of the Kokura Gion festival, and, because this history is not present or represented on the story's textual surface, neither will any ontological reading. The construction of Kokura Castle was followed by the building of the Kokura Gion shrine and the 1618 inauguration of the Kokura Gion festival. As Junko Hayakawa writes, "In 869, the festival was first conducted at Gion, a district located in Kyoto, to protect against an epidemic that was sweeping the city. The festival . . . aimed at pacifying malevolent spirits believed to be the cause of the epidemic. The Kokura Gion festival, a more musically-inspired version of its Kyoto counterpart, incorporates ritualized *Shinto* drumming in its attempt to appease malevolent spirits."[32]

This haunting history gestures toward a second reading of Matsumoto's Twenty-Fourth. Although the soldiers' riotous response to the festival drumming does suggest "savagery," it also speaks to the refusal of malevolent black spirits to be pacified in the face of death. The double possibilities of Matsumoto's drumming—the reverberating tension between hearing the Kokura

Riots as both "proof" of primitive black savagery and a haunting resistance to the undervaluation of black life—resound throughout the first half of the text. This is why, alongside passages that refer to the members of the regiment as thick-lipped simians, "Painting on Black Canvas" includes passages such as this:

> The black soldiers had been shipped down from Gifu, and in a few days' time they would be shipped again to their final destination: a meeting with the Korean People's Army on the battlefields of Korea. We can only imagine that they had a sense of their dark destiny (*kurai unmei*), and shuddered in hopelessness. . . .
>
> The black soldiers walked to the light [of the residences of Kokura]. They knew absolutely nothing about the lay of the land. And that was exactly how much they knew about what tomorrow planned to do with their lives. But, even if they hadn't been briefed, they were highly attuned to the fortunes of war on the other side of the sea, and they knew that every inch the US Army gave up brought them one step closer to death. They would be thrown into that sliver of space between their retreating comrades and their pursuant enemies. Undoubtedly, they had some vision of what was to come for them—army crawls on severed limbs on a battlefield of seared trees and tank carcasses. But they were several days and many more miles removed from the reality of it all. They wanted—for just an hour, or even a minute—to erase those encroaching visions. It was less of a "want" and more along the lines of a prayer.
>
> In the beginning, the drums of savages that echoed out of the depths of African jungles held a kind of ritualized prayer. When their ancestors were brought to the American colonies as laborers, they were taught by white people about the grace of God. This inspired them, and they found hope within the shackles of slavery and created Negro spirituals. And even in these spirituals can be heard a rhythm that is distinct from the rhythm of God: this is the primitive rhythm of Africa, a rhythm of incantatory prayer that flows deep within these spirituals.
>
> The drums [of the Kokura Gion festival] reverberated endlessly in the distance. It was a dull, spellbinding sound. Maybe the black soldiers said a prayer for their hopeless lives.[33]

In the moment when the drumbeat of the Kokura Gion festival overlaps with the "rhythm of incantatory prayer that flows deep within [Negro] spirituals," Matsumoto forges a structural similarity between the predicament of the soldiers of the Twenty-Fourth and the people of Kokura. Just as the regiment will be "thrown into that" violent "sliver of space" between white American might and Korean resistance, the people of Kokura are thrown into that violent space between white American might and black resistance. Moreover, by positing slavery and American colonization as America's original sins of race-based violence, Matsumoto implies a second parallel between the Twenty-Fourth and the people of occupied Kokura.

There is one sense, then, in which the people of Kokura are victims of racial violence at the culpable hands of the Twenty-Fourth. Matsumoto responds to this by drumming home stereotypical clichés of black savagery. There is another sense, however—a "second rhythm that is distinct from the rhythm of God"—in which the black condition speaks to the Japanese condition. In this second rhythm, the Kokura Riots become symptomatic of racial violence set in motion by the American state and perpetrated on black and Japanese bodies alike. Matsumoto responds to this with haunting and possessions, as Tomekichi and Yoshiko take on the apparitional features of their black perpetrators.

These two sensibilities collide with the rape of Yoshiko, a gruesome act of racial violence. Following that first sense, Yoshiko's rapists are depicted as the clichéd myth of the black rapist come to life—pure black, animalistic, primitive savagery incarnate. With the exception of their white eyes and "thick pink lips," every part of their face is "jet black." One speaks "gutturally, like a growling dog," they all smell like "rancid animals," and they are "six gargantuan, black massifs" with "cylindrical torsos like monkeys" who strip naked in Tomekichi and Yoshiko's home and laugh and "keep time with their feet and prance around" and "bounce their shoulders rhythmically" as they wait for their "turn" to sexually assault Yoshiko.[34] The composite of the soldiers as primitive (hence the ritualistic dancing), animalistic, and morally bankrupt marks the abjection of racial difference, a stark divide between the inhuman/inhumane black soldiers and their innocent Japanese victims.

And yet, following that second sense, this abject racial difference is juxtaposed with a kind of intersubjective overlap among Tomekichi, Yoshiko, and the black soldiers. The first hint of this occurs as Tomekichi and the soldiers argue in a Japanese-English pidgin. Tomekichi notes that "he could see clearly, even in this black . . . round face, an expression of animosity—it was as if he were dealing with a fellow Japanese person."[35] Moreover, Matsumoto employs the same verb, *yokotawaru* (to lie down, to stretch out), to describe both Yoshiko during her assault and the black soldiers' nightmarish daydreams of themselves under assault on the battlefields of Korea. The shared humanity of the black soldiers and Tomekichi is thrown into haunting relief as Tomekichi tries to console Yoshiko after the assault by cleaning her bloody body. Tomekichi "pushed aside the robe that covered his wife's body. She tried to fend him off with her legs. He used his own legs to restrain her."[36] In his attempt to console his wife, Tomekichi reenacts symbolically the very violence enacted by the black soldiers. I do not think that the issue here is, to borrow Molasky's articulation, one of "grudging sympathy." Rather, it is a question of racial possession: Tomekichi embodies the very features of the black specters that haunt him.

The tension between stereotypical primitive blackness and American discrimination against "colored races"—black and Japanese alike—as competing impetuses for the Kokura Riots is, quite literally, embodied. One example is that one of Yoshiko's rapists is "clearly of mixed blood."[37] The soldier with "white blood" is the only one described as having beautiful features. He is also the only culprit to show any remorse. When he "took a glance at Tomekichi, there was, for just a brief moment, a flash of frailty in his eyes."[38] By humanizing, however fleetingly, the biracial soldier, Matsumoto simultaneously magnifies the savagery of the "pureblood" black soldiers even as he marks the only rapist of white descent as the embodiment of buried guilt and responsibility. A second example is the eponymous "painting on black canvas." Preceding the rape of Yoshiko—that is, in the very moment that the logic of racial determinism and the myth of the black rapist should carry unquestionable explanatory power—one of the black soldiers removes his shirt to reveal a tattoo of an "eagle with its wings spread," a symbol of American democracy and freedom in flight.[39] Here, too, is an embodiment of that tension. The naked black body suggests savage primitivism—wild, uncontrollable, riotous movement and freedom. And yet this body is branded with a freedom it cannot fully possess, the Kokura Riots an attempted flight from the very eagle that is seared into black American skin no matter where it goes. Any possibility of black agency is usurped by the painting, for which it is nothing more than a "black canvas."

For our purposes, it is crucial to note that the tension between these two explanations of the events of the Kokura Riots is not only embodied but also disembodied. This disembodiment is palpable in the immediate aftermath of the rape scene. Yoshiko is described as "reminiscent of a ghost," "like the dead," and "like a vengeful ghost" as her dialogue degrades into eerie incantations of "kill me, kill me."[40] This is simply *shinu*, which evokes both the present and the future in Japanese and further blurs the line between life and death and present and phantasmal projection. Hence Yoshiko's "Death. I'll die as soon as I can, tomorrow even."[41] Yoshiko has become, much like her assailants, caught in purgatory between life today and death tomorrow.

This uncanny sensation of haunting disembodiment is given voice by the narrator, who tells this story as a kind of ghost tale. Floating in and out of time and space, the narrator provides lines such as (directly preceding Yoshiko's rape) "they weren't afraid yet."[42] This implies, of course, that they *will be* afraid at some point in time, and that the narrator—a disembodied presence who views these events from a time and space beyond the story's diegetic realm—knows this before the characters within the story do. Such ghoulish narration speaks to "Painting on Black Canvas" as a kind of historical ghost story that resurrects the buried history of the Kokura Riots. Or, as the narrator concludes in part 1, "It is hard for anyone to know what exactly happened on that night of 11 July 1950, when the black soldiers of Camp Kokura absconded and committed their acts of violence. The records have been almost entirely expunged. But we know this for sure: they were the black soldiers of the Twenty-Fourth Infantry Regiment of the Twenty-Fifth Infantry Division."[43]

This haunting bleeds over into part 2 of "Painting on Black Canvas," as the two competing rationales for racial violence haunt Tomekichi's search for catharsis. Part 2 finds Tomekichi, now estranged from Yoshiko, working for the "Army Grave Registration Service," a fictional counterpart of the AGRS) group located in Kokura. As Morris-Suzuki writes, the AGRS assembled teams of Japanese anthropologists and laborers and American experts to "register" the corpses of American soldiers killed in the Korean War. "On busy days . . . [the teams] examined as many as sixty to eighty corpses a day, most of them severely decomposed because they had been temporarily buried where they fell when US troops retreated before the onslaught from the north, and then unearthed and sent to Japan when the tides of war turned."[44]

In shifting the setting of from Tomekichi's home to the AGRS, part 2 of "Painting on Black Canvas" forces historical exhumation, which drives the text's narrative techniques, to collide with representations of actual exhumed black bodies. This collision is Matsumoto's attempt at an evenhanded counterbalance to the savage representations of the Twenty-Fourth featured in part 1; the AGRS setting of part 2 allows for the "registering" of the meaning and value of black life and death. After a second series of contextualizing newswires, part 2 begins with descriptions of the AGRS and the labor that occurs there. The AGRS is "not a place where [the dead] are dissected, but where they are put together."[45] The fallen soldiers of the Korean War, Matsumoto writes, "have rights" because *the dead are not 'nothing'*—their existence is still assertive."[46] It is the members of the AGRS group, Tomekichi included, who meet the demands of the dead, and in so doing ensure that the "rights" the dead were denied in life are met in death. "In short, the autopsy room is a place where the dead are resurrected."[47]

If part 1 fixates on the riotous, primitive savagery of the half-dead black soldiers of the Twenty-Fourth, part 2 effectively inverts this strategy. Now deathly still, the soldiers are granted rational motivations befitting human beings, a psychological life that goes beyond "percussion hypnosis." Dr. Kōsaka, a dentist with the AGRS who befriends Tomekichi and serves as his psychological foil, acts as speaker for the dead. The doctor tries to convince Tomekichi that both black and Japanese people are, as fellow members of the "colored races," targets of American discrimination, the only difference being whether one is targeted in the workplace or on the battlefield. The doctor receives unequal pay for equal work, and black corpses outnumber white ones in the AGRS even though both were fighting in the same American war.[48] The doctor forces Tomekichi to consider how knowledge of impending death might influence the way the black soldiers lived. And it is through the doctor's prodding that the text captures—ontologically speaking—what black life is to Tomekichi. Tomekichi replies, "The niggers are pitiable. The niggers are pitiable, but . . ."[49] Even as it holds onto the racist logic that characterizes part 1 (hence "the niggers"), part 2 exhumes the endless reverberations of racial discrimination as a kind of violence, the rationale buried just beneath the surface of part 1, as an explanation potent enough to have Tomekichi "pity" the soldiers who raped Yoshiko.

But what I want to do here is dig beneath the surface of the text and expose the unspoken specters of racial injustice as they possess Tomekichi himself. That is to say, I am less interested in what Tomekichi says than in what he doesn't say. I am more interested in the ellipses themselves than in the phrase that precedes them: "The niggers are pitiable, but . . ." what? The first answer that comes to mind, of course, is: "but . . . even this does not justify the Kokura Riots." And that may be. But the ellipses that pervade part 2 point to something more. Molasky notes that there is an "ironical twist in 'Painting on Black Canvas': the rapists are brought to justice only through America's system of racial injustice."[50] Reading the ellipses of part 2 can add this to Molasky's insight, for in order to exact revenge Tomekichi must first be possessed by the very features that characterize the black ghosts he wishes to exorcise: social stigmatization rooted in the body itself and violent outbursts in protest of his living conditions.

The first hint of this emerges during the opening moments of part 2 as Tomekichi becomes associated with the smell of death. In an opening passage of part 2, the narrator notes the "egregiously high wages" paid to

AGRS workers. Their labor "aroused disgusting visions of gripping crumbling corpses and decomposing chunks of flesh; the severity of the work was, more or less, paid for by the high compensation."[51] This (over)compensation, moreover, must also overcome the social stigma associated with working with dead bodies. The stench of death serves as a metonym for such stigma: "Some people say that you can tell immediately who works with the dead, because a strange smell radiates from their bodies. So, for example, if one of those people gets on a train, you can tell, just by the smell, that he deals with the dead."[52] In order to search for the corpses of the Twenty-Fourth, Tomekichi must become one of "those people"; he has to get his hands dirty. In so doing he, too, is marked by the stench of death and its accordant stigma. Tomekichi's first encounter with the doctor is a case in point. The doctor is able to deduce Tomekichi's line of work not because he recognizes his face but because "the smell of dead bodies is stuck on you."[53]

With this in mind, we can reread Tomekichi's comments about "the niggers" for its hauntological significance. Tomekichi claims that the "niggers are pitiable, but . . ." or, in a more colloquial translation, that he "feels sorry for the niggers, but . . ." Following the ellipses, the passage continues, "Mumbling this, Tomekichi turned his back on the dentist. The dentist again smelled the stench of death coming off Tomekichi's shoulders."[54] The exchange ends here, and the narrative breaks and shifts to an update on the Korean War. A surface reading of this passage might note the ambivalent mix of sympathy and racism present in Tomekichi's dialogue, the term *nigger* vocalizing the antiblack racism engendered by the pain of the Kokura Riots even given Tomekichi's recognition of the soldiers' tragic dilemma.

It seems to me, however, that beneath the textual surface this passage is haunted. Why is it that the most ostensibly racist passage in the text is punctuated with the lingering smell of death, which serves as both a metonym for social stigma and a reminder of the members of the Twenty-Fourth, who lived between life and death? In light of *Buraku mondai kenkyūjo* reports that many of the *burakumin*, Japan's largest social minority, were "displaced by [the US military] . . . for new military facilities . . . [and] migrated to northern Kyushu," I do not think it is too speculative to answer this question by suggesting that Tomekichi's search for the corpses of the Twenty-Fourth makes visible—or perhaps, "olfactible"—the similarities in the conditions that define Tomekichi's life as a Japanese man in occupied Japan and the soldiers of the Twenty-Fourth, who have to fight both Jim Crow and the KPA.[55] "Painting on Black Canvas" does not explicitly note whether Tomekichi identifies as *burakumin*. The story does mention "rumors" of the reticence of "regular workers" to take jobs with the AGRS, but it also mentions workers overcoming this reticence because of the relatively high wages.[56] Although the story—in a move reminiscent of what Anne McKnight has called writing *burakumin* identity under erasure—leaves the question of Tomekichi's "true" identity unanswered, it plays on the literary and cultural trope of the supposed impurity of *burakumin* having a discernible smell, which marks the physiological difference between the *burakumin* minority and "average" Japanese people. The simile of smelling like death marks Tomekichi as akin to a social minority, which in turn makes his status crudely analogous to that of the members of the Twenty-Fourth, who are racial minorities. In other words, Tomekichi's quest for vengeance marks him with the smell of a haunting, inescapable blackness or, perhaps, *burakuness* (a concept I revisit in chapter 3 by way of Nakagami Kenji). With this, the tension between black stereotyping and a shared Afro-Japanese experience of discrimination that runs beneath part 1 of "Painting on Black Canvas" is resurrected in part 2.

If this return is prefigured by the stigmatizing smell of death, it culminates in the return of the dead black bodies from Korea. The story concludes with Tomekichi in an autopsy room of the AGRS. Having found the soldier with the painting, he takes a knife and adds several "strokes" to the canvas: "The torso of the bloated, armless corpse rolled about in front of Tomekichi. The black skin canvas now had red strokes drawn into it. The eagle with its wings spread had been cut into thirds, the lower part of the naked woman [another tattoo on the black soldier] had been ripped diagonally—to Tomekichi's hard gaze, it looked like a phantom."[57] This act of desecrating violence serves as symbolic retribution for the events of the Kokura Riots. It simultaneously, however, brings Tomekichi that much closer to the black canvas he so despises. Not only does he reek of death, but he is now responsible for the strokes of red that color the canvas—he is, in other words, now one of its painters. This gruesome act of corpse desecration makes him something other or less than human in the eyes of his peers, much like the "phantoms" of the Twenty-Fourth that haunt him. Even as his coworkers react to this gruesome scene, Tomekichi "didn't look back, as if oblivious to the panic happening right behind him."[58] This is almost a precise replication of the position Tomekichi inhabited during the Kokura Riots. The only difference is that now he is in the position of the black soldiers: he violates a racialized body in an act of symbolic violence that has no power to harm or resist the "eagle" itself.

The key here is that we shouldn't conflate "violence" with "potency." Given that the black soldier is already dead, even as Tomekichi desecrates the black body, he is just as impotent as he was during the Kokura Riots.

His outburst doesn't signify anything like justice, and his hopeless, violent protest is meaningless. The only "purpose" the conclusion of the text has is to bring Tomekichi's position closer to that of the Twenty-Fourth. As he reenacts the very violence of the Kokura Riots, it is almost as if Tomekichi has been possessed by the trauma of the event.

Moments of Silence, Moments of Blackness, and Ishikawa Jun's "The Legend of Gold"

Moments of Silence and the (Im)Possibility of First-Person Singular Narration

To read "Painting on Black Canvas" as simply silencing black voices, or to reduce it to an indicator of "the" Japanese representation of flat black characters in postwar literature, is to overlook the profound significance of blackness in the text. The story is ineffable without blackness, for the painting becomes visible only by virtue of its black canvas. It points toward the potential impossibility of narrating postwar trauma, and it is by virtue of blackness that this trauma, with all its contradictory nuances, becomes effable.

A similar concern—the impossibility of postwar Japanese narration and the necessity of black mediation—is at the heart of Ishikawa Jun's "Ōgon densetsu" (The Legend of Gold, 1946). "Legend" has been described by Noguchi Takehiko, one of the first and preeminent scholars of Ishikawa Jun's fiction, as "a narrative (*monogatari*) that conveys the new departure to the postwar world."[59] In this narratival depiction of the transition from war to peace, Ishikawa suggests that the instability of the narrating process itself must be supplemented if it is to aid the process of self-reconstruction. Within the context of the Occupation, the plausibility of self-formation based on the narration of a singular I, long a staple of modern Japanese literature, comes under assault. As Sharalyn Orbaugh contends, "One of the conspicuous elements of these stories is the radical split between the experiencing/transforming body and the 'I' necessary to speak or narrativize that experience/transformation."[60] From the very onset—that is, to borrow Noguchi's term, the "departure" (*shuppatsu*) of this period—silence supplements the narrating of the postwar Japanese self. It is only in the concluding moments of "Legend," when the narrator-protagonist, known to the reader simply as "I" (*watashi*), encounters a black soldier and the two share a silent dialogue, that "I" can begin the process of stable self-narration.

The onset of "Legend" bears witness to the paradox of a dethroned subject rewriting its subjectivity. Ishikawa wrote "Legend" in what is known as the *jōzetsu-tai* (garrulous style). The garrulous style, which employs the techniques of conversational narrative in written tales and is characterized by long, verbose sentences with minimal punctuation, came to prominence in Japanese literature in the 1930s.[61] When immersed in garrulous prose, the reader becomes entangled in a conversation with the narrator. The opening of "Legend" is perplexing insofar as, although there is undeniably a garrulous conversation taking place (between the protagonist *watashi* and a restauranteur), the text does little to orient the reader concerning the subjective positions of the interlocutors. William Tyler, who has produced a masterful English translation of "Legend," describes the opening of the text as follows.

> Who is speaking to whom in these opening lines is knowledge we acquire only as we read along. . . . Commencing in medias res, withholding identification of the initial speaker(s), and superimposing a narratorial voice that comments on the text like a talking head or a roving microphone. . . . Ambiguity is introduced to catch the reader off guard; and by commencing in medias res, Ishikawa prepares the way for the introduction of new and improbable imagery.[62]

Tyler's note provides two insights. First, language that might initially be misread as monologue is actually conversational narrative imbued with silence, hence Tyler's use of the term "speaker(s)." Moreover, this silent dialogue, Tyler continues, "prepares the way for the introduction of new and improbable imagery." For Ishikawa, silent silhouettes become speaking subjects by way of discombobulating encounters with the postwar present (and, as such, encounters with the lingering legacy of the wartime past). In "Legend," the realness of the postwar present is embodied in, among other entities, the "new and improbable" figure of an African American soldier, an amalgam of racial difference and Occupation might.

The Announcement and the Dialogics of Silent Desire

After being forced to evacuate his home due to the fire bombing of Tokyo, *watashi* embarks on a countrywide odyssey in a quest to fulfill "three secret desires" (*hitoshirezu mittsu no negai*): finding a repairman for his sporadically functioning watch, finding a hat to replace his wartime headpiece, and reuniting with the object of a former infatuation.[63] The secrecy surrounding these desires implies their ineffability; this narrative is the first telling of secrets that were heretofore unspeakable. As such, the stakes are doubled: *watashi's* sharing of these secrets embodies an urge to both fulfill said desires and tell the tale of this fulfillment to its completion. This is reminiscent of Peter Brooks's "exploration of the conjunction of the narrative of desire and the desire of narration," in which "narratives both tell of desire—typically present some story of desire—and arouse and make use of desire as dynamic of signification."[64]

This "conjunction" is explicitly embodied by *watashi's* first desire: to find a repairman for his broken watch. Just as the watch measures time in its staccato rhythm, *watashi* narrates a tale riddled with analeptic and proleptic shifts. *Watashi's* watch starts malfunctioning as he evacuates his house during one of the fire bombings of Tokyo that became a commonplace occurrence of the war's dénouement. The watch's unreliability is exacerbated on 15 August 1945 as *watashi,* now wandering throughout Japan in an attempt to realize his three desires, is struck in the chest by the sack of a fellow train rider who loses his balance on hearing news of the emperor's announcement of Japan's defeat.

Time is out of joint, broken in postwar Japan. Nowhere is a more haunting support of this conjecture to be found than in the Nagasaki Atomic Bomb Research Center, which houses a collection of mangled clocks frozen at 11:02—the time of the detonation of the second atomic bomb—that survived the onslaught. Or, as *watashi* articulates this shattered time, "These days, timepieces are broken pretty much everywhere; there is no way to find the standard of an exact time."[65] *Watashi's* proposed solution to this predicament is to set his watch by estimating the time according to the weather and his disposition (a task made difficult by his bodily ailments). In lieu of a standard from on high (the military, the emperor, and so forth), the human body and its desires take on a legitimizing function.[66] *Watashi's* broken watch, then, also indicates an opening and an opportunity to chart a new course on his own time.

> This can be read as the moment in which to resurrect the "time of individuality" (*"ko no jikan" wo yomigaeraseru*), which was undeniably swallowed up by the "the time of the collective/community" (*shudan/kyōdōtai no jikan*) under the wartime system. . . . Moreover, the watch is out of order. . . . This is an allegory: the out-of-order watch signifies that the self (*jiko*) has broken from the mad fascism that raged before the war. . . . In other words, the watch, which is the first desire, is an announcement of a break from the crazed time in which the individual was buried by the totality.[67]

In thinking about a resurrection of individualized time, Hwang's insight is the "announcement" (*kokuchi*). It is the sound of the watch that breaks the silence and motivates an enervated *watashi* to go on living. The watch is a messenger, the *nuncio* of the rejuvenating fall of fascism. Indeed, when *watashi* feels that the bleakness of the postwar landscape will overwhelm him, his watch breaks the silence, "as if it were saying 'not yet, it's not time for that [listlessness] yet.'"[68] The watch speaks to and encourages *watashi* in a language that is not his own. And yet, even though its semiotics are both punctuated by silence and profoundly different from those of the Japanese language, its announcement is communicative. In this regard, the watch adumbrates the presence of the African American soldier, who has yet to emerge and announce the life-sustaining miracle promised by the text's title.

Watashi's third and final wish—to be reunited with a war widow with whom he is infatuated—is the lynchpin of his triangulated desires. Approximately one year before the point at which the narrative opens, in December 1944, *watashi* spent an evening drinking sake with the woman, known to the reader only as *kono hito* (literally, "this person"), and her then husband in their house in the hills. The husband experiences a common side-effect of drinking too much sake: incapacitation. At this point, *watashi* decides to take his leave. As he descends the hill and attempts to navigate the dark and silence of the night, the woman guides him with gentle words: "'Please watch your step. Now turn to the left. Yes, now to your right,'—she spoke warmly to me in this manner. It was almost as if we were star-crossed lovers who, after exchanging our vows, were forced to part."[69] His relationship with the war widow remains shrouded in silence, however, as *watashi* can't muster the courage to confess his feelings to *kono hito*. His third wish, then, is to vocalize his heretofore silent desire.

Watashi acquires his opportunity to break the silence (and in so doing rejuvenate himself) thanks to a bit of serendipity that lives up to the moniker Legenda Aurea. After traveling the country in vain, *watashi* decides to abandon his quest to fulfill his third desire. His health has taken a miraculous turn for the better, his watch isn't as finicky, and he finds a hat worthy of a real human. With everything falling into place, *watashi* decides to turn his attention to finding a good cup of coffee. *Watashi*'s coffee odyssey is what brings him to the restaurant in Yokohama where the story begins.

As *watashi* sits in silence in the restaurant, a woman dressed completely in red takes the seat next to him. The woman, and now the legendary miracles begin to accumulate, is none other than the woman for whom *watashi* has been searching. The woman makes her voice heard before *watashi*'s by striking up a conversation with him, pulling both her body and her voice intimately close to him. Moreover, her tongue is polyglot; the woman quickly turns her attention to the storekeeper, whose monologue initiates the narrative and speaks to her in a "familiar" (*narenareshiku*) tone. The "familiarity" that the woman exhibits in her dialogue is juxtaposed with *watashi*'s silence. As the woman speaks with the storekeeper, *watashi* notices that her handbag is full of Lucky Strikes, chocolates, and "other goods that weren't produced in this country."[70] The woman's possession of foreign goods, the abundance of chocolates in particular—a trope of Occupation period fiction—is a sure sign of her affiliation with the demimonde.

Faced with his chance for wish fulfillment, *watashi* finds himself at a loss for words; the woman has never spoken to him with such startling intimacy. The woman has clearly undergone a metamorphosis—in a subsequent passage, the narrator will use the image of a butterfly to describe her new form—due to the war. Her new language (*kotobazukai*) produces and reproduces a caesura between her "now" (a war widow in what she calls 'Hama, Occupation period argot for Yokohama) and her "then" (being from a good family, having lost a husband to the war, and so on). After convincing himself that the woman who sits with him is the same women who occupies his memories, the couple "left the restaurant and, although we hadn't come to a verbal agreement, we set out toward Sakuragi-chō station as if we had."[71] As the pair head toward the station, *watashi*'s fulfilled wishes begin to unravel: "My new hat twisted awkwardly to the side, and the tick-tock crying of my watch fell silent."[72] *Watashi*'s silence is ultimately broken—and the text finally engages with the literary genre of its namesake, the hagiography—with the appearance of a black soldier.

> As we approached the station, she stopped clinging to me, suddenly pushed me aside, and started running away. I steadied my wobbly legs and, looking in the direction in which she had gone, I saw someone towering above the heads of the crowd. Magnificently tall, miraculously black—there was a single powerful soldier standing there. The black soldier (*kuroi heishi*) had a beautiful lightweight rose-pink muffler tied stylishly around his neck, and, when he shouted something or other I couldn't make out, the rows of his pristinely white, firm teeth glistened like gems. And the body of the woman dressed completely in red was clinging tightly to the thick chest of the soldier, just as a butterfly lands on the trunk of a tree. Her back was turned to me and it didn't even say "adieu," and [even without putting it into words, her silent back] indicated that she would never turn and look back in my direction.

What was I supposed to call out to her? Was I supposed to say, "Please watch your step?" Was I supposed to say "Turn to your left?" Was I supposed to say, "Now turn to your right?" There were no words that I could possibly say. All I had was a feeling of shame so strong it could kill me. Without comprehending anything, I ran at full speed toward the mixed crowd of people forming a whirlpool in the center of the plaza in front of the train station. As I ran, the blood in my body began to circulate vigorously, my breathing was regular, and my constitution was restored in an instant. And then at some point my warped hat straightened itself and the watch in my breast pocket began to sound pleasantly with a tick-tock. [73]

It is through the interconnection of the soldier, the woman, and *watashi* that the text makes good on the promise of miracle implied by the genre of the golden legend. Criticism of "Legend" tends to filter the text through *watashi*. Such reading fragments the interconnectivity of the three, making the presence of the black soldier a case of "adding insult to injury" ("and the extra fillip of the soldier's color *serves* to *underscore* the shocking, spectacular nature of the *narrator's experience*")[74] and the woman a vehicle in *watashi's* process of self-recovery ("this woman's existence . . . must always be grasped *within* (*ni oite*) the relationship she has with *watashi*").[75]

Such a reading, however, does not address two aspects of "Legend:" the way the text focuses on *watashi* precisely in order to expose the fragility of his subjectivity; and the fact that this fragility is stabilized only through mutual interdependence, the intersection between the self in flux and its others. Given her metamorphosis—as well as works such as Ishikawa's 1947 "Kayoi Komachi" (Visits to Komachi), in which a man analogous to *watashi* is rejuvenated after his discovery of Virgin Mary and Ono no Komachi in the person of sex workers—a strong case can be made for the centrality of the female character in "Legend."[76] Here, however, I want to focus on the black soldier as the vociferous cynosure of this holy trinity. Ishikawa's staging of the tripartite connection—the woman clings to the soldier, an entity who literally towers above the masses, and *watashi's* gaze locks on this same "central" point—is the first indication of such centrality. This is coupled with the narrator's diction. The soldier is described as *ayashii made ni iro no kuroi*, which I have translated as "miraculously black." A more literal translation of this description might read "his color so black it was uncanny." *Ayashii* is a multivalent word that encompasses the notions of the weird or the occult, as well as the questionable, suspicious, and unreliable, perhaps even the perverted. Etymologically, the word represents the adjectival embodi-

ment of the desire to make a sound when confronted with the wondrous or
the otherworldly, the "ah-some." That this adjective is used to describe the
blackness of the soldier places him in the realm of, to quote the Kōjien dictionary definition, the miraculous (*reimyō*). Perhaps the black soldier, even
in his silence, gestures toward something greater. Ik-koo Hwang describes
him as "an extremely effective sign" of the Occupation's ability to transform
"the interiority and individuality" of the postwar Japanese from subjects to
citizens.[77]

The final paragraph of "Legend" suggests that the soldier's transformative power extends to *watashi* as well. *Watashi's* physiology is intimately
connected to wish fulfillment; it is after repairing his watch, finding a new
hat, and abandoning his desire to find the woman that he experiences a
momentary reprieve from his ailments. The conclusion, then, with its miraculous depiction of animation—animation of *watashi's* hat, watch, and
self—suggests that his desire has been satisfied. If this is the case, *watashi's*
desire has been fulfilled not by direct, verbal communication with the embodiment of his past but by a nonverbal connection with the woman and
the black soldier. There is something restorative in such communion for
watashi, and it subsumes the need for a material connection to the past in
the ineffable miracles of life in the present moment.

All that is said between the three characters is said in a moment of silence. *Watashi*, the woman, and the black soldier never exchange words.
Nevertheless, this nonverbal exchange still speaks to *watashi's* desires. The
conclusion of "Legend" leaves unspeakable things unspoken, but this is not
to be confused with a negation of the communicative power of silence (and
blackness). In the words of literary critic Yokote Kazuhiko, the conclusion of
the story constructs an "undialogical dialogue" (*hitaiwateki taiwa*), and "it is
by way of these means that a collapsed self must support itself."[78]

The Legend of "The Legend of Gold": Silence, Dialogue, and Censorship

"Legend" was initially published in the March 1946 edition of *Chūō Kōron*.
This version of "Legend" was deemed suitable for publication by the SCAP
Civil Censorship Detachment (CDD). Later that year, however, the text was
reevaluated to determine whether or not it was suitable for inclusion as the
eponymous story in a collection of Ishikawa's short fiction. "Legend" did not
pass its reexamination unscathed. Judging from the marginalia of a "Legend" manuscript submitted for critique to the CDD before the publication
of the collection of short stories, the CDD didn't sanction the text's tacit

gestures toward international, multilingual, and interracial connections. The first red flag occurs on the first page, in which the storeowner refers to the "Chinaman across the way." Occupation censors flagged this phrase because it was "critical of China,"[79] one of the victorious Allied powers. The second interdiction replaces "Lucky Strikes," a reference that serves as a surefire sign of the woman's involvement with the Occupation-sanctioned demimonde, with the kanji characters for *tobacco* and elides any mention of American goods in the woman's handbag. This substitution and elision can be seen as an attempt to sanitize the particularity of the exchange of the (Japanese) female body for (an American GI's) goods. With "tobacco" the reader knows that the woman has acquired black market goods, but the source remains ambiguous—yet another attack on the multilingual aspect of Ishikawa's "undialogic dialogue."

The final act of censorship was to remove the black soldier from the penultimate passage. The CDD's explanation for such a critical deletion is simply "fraternization"; the CDD had a history of strictly proscribing depictions of relations between the Occupation forces and the Japanese citizens they were supposed to regulate. Given the aphoristic rationale for censorship—"fraternization"—it is difficult to pinpoint whether or not the soldier's race played a factor in this censorship, although we can speculate that an implicit critique of the Allied Occupation's segregationist policies would be a cause for concern. Whether we are more convinced by scholars such as Suzuki Sadami, who claims that it is the blackness of the soldier that drew the ire of the censors, or Tyler, who suggests that the depiction of fraternization is the target of censorship, it is unarguable that the removal of this scene, in concert with the deletion of the references to China and Lucky Strikes, would dismantle the multilingual, "undialogical dialogue" the text constructs.[80]

It is at this moment in the publication history of "The Legend of Gold" that a legerdemain by Ishikawa tacitly subverted the threat of censorship and brought about the legend of "The Legend." Although Ishikawa refused to publish the second, censored version of "The Legend of Gold" in his 1947 collection of short stories, the collection *itself* is entitled *The Legend of Gold*. Literary critics speak of the effect of Ishikawa's stratagem of publishing a short story collection in which the eponymous narrative is only paratextually present with the marvel that one typically reserves for legends. Yamaguchi Toshio describes *The Legend of Gold* as "the publication of a curious (*kimyō*) collection of stories in which the representative text has fallen out"; Takano Yoshitomo avers, "And thus a book the likes of which is rarely seen in this world (*yo ni mo mare naru tankōbon*)—a *Legend of Gold* in which the 'Legend of Gold' was not presented—came into the world"; and Tyler writes, "When the monograph *Ōgon densetsu* appeared early in 1947 sans the offensive story, the title called attention to the missing text by virtue of its "remaining absence."[81] The legend of "The Legend" does its mysterious work in a function analogous to that of "The Legend" itself: desire voiced even in (or, rather, precisely in) moments of silence.

Satirized Silence: Blackness, Linguistic Occupation, and Kojima Nobuo's "American School"

In *A Modern History of Japan*, Andrew Gordon writes, "The clinical word for exhaustion—*kyōdatsu*—was one defining term for the state of mind of Japanese people in these early postwar years."[82] Ishikawa's "Legend" is in many ways a story of the struggle to find the energy to break the somber silence of the postwar period. Kojima Nobuo's (1915–2006) "Amerikan sukūru" (The American School, 1954)—a text that one member of the thirty-second Akutagawa Prize selection committee described as "a powerful work of epochal significance"—is also interested in giving voice to the immediate postwar period, a moment that might otherwise be met with silence.[83] Compared to "Legend," however, the kinetic energy of Kojima's prose springs from a markedly different source: satire. Kojima's interest in satire is documented as early as his 1941 undergraduate thesis on the role of comedy in Thackeray. Kojima's satire is often focalized through the eyes of the enervated; his texts have been characterized as "satiric literature by the weak" (*jakusha ni yoru fūshi bungaku*) in which the weak are empowered by the sound of their laughter.[84] Here the power to narrate is intimately linked to the power dynamics of satire, with its emphasis on crownings and decrownings.

"American School" was published two years after the conclusion of the Allied Occupation of (mainland) Japan, yet it takes readers back to 1948, the meridian of the Occupation. The novella tells the story of three Japanese teachers of English and their varying responses to the encroaching colonialist threat of English as they visit an American school in Japan during the Occupation. Given Kojima's interest in the subversive power of satirical speech, here the term *occupation* includes but also gestures beyond physical occupation to the occupation of—to borrow Michael Molasky's articulation—memory, language, and expression.

In the eyes of the linguistic colonialist, Stephen Greenblatt writes, "The New World is a vast, rich field for the plantation of the English language."[85] A phenomenon analogous to Greenblatt's linguistic colonialism was born in postwar Japan; this might be called linguistic occupation. The language once regarded as the unspeakable tongue of the enemy (*teki no gengo*) was now the lingua franca between the occupier and the occupied, now the language of postwar best sellers such as the *Nichibei kaiwa techō* (*Pocket Notebook of Japanese-English Conversational Expression*).[86] The colonialist mechanisms that deracinate the linguistic landscape, Greenblatt continues, "reflect a fundamental inability to sustain the simultaneous perception of likeness and difference . . . [for] they either push the [Other] toward utter difference—and thus silence—or toward utter likeness—and thus the collapse of their own, unique identity," yet another brand of silencing. [87]

Take, for example, the opening lines of "American School."

> At the logistics meeting, the civil servant from the Supervisor's Department, who was to be the conductor of the observational tour of the American school, had . . . expressed several points of caution. Number one: adhere strictly to the designated gathering time. Number two: wear clean clothes. The second this second decree was given, a ruckus broke out among the teachers. Number three: be silent. On hearing this dictum, the ruckus gradually died down.[88]

There is something colonially (and satirically) bittersweet about the fact that Japanese teachers have been granted permission—that is, of course, assuming that they can follow the code of conduct suited to this colonialist exchange—to walk six kilometers to the American school in Japan. The silencing tug-of-war between "utter difference" and "utter likeness" is present from the very onset of "American School." As the text progresses, a satirical negotiation among silence, cross-cultural dialogue, and the reconstruction of postwar national identity occurs. One of Kojima's primary negotiators in the exchange between utter difference and utter likeness is an African American soldier. Moreover, the site of the negotiation is an American school in Japan, a space that not only makes audible the reverberating tensions of American race relations on the Japanese side of the Pacific but also suggests that the negotiation of postwar Japanese national identity must be done by triangulating Japan into those very race relations.

Satirical Silence and the Hauntology of Blackness

Although "American School" is populated with "thirty-some-odd" Japanese teachers of English, the story is focalized primarily through the eyes (and mouths) of three teachers: Yamada, a former imperial soldier turned English teacher; Michiko, the "sole woman" and most gifted speaker of English in the group; and Isa, the head English instructor, who has a seriocomic phobia about speaking English. Isa is, as head instructor, in many ways the fulcrum of the text. Although each of the three central characters provides idiosyncratic vantage points by which the American school can be viewed, the narrative gives privilege of place to Isa's encounters with the various manifestations of the Occupation forces.

Of these manifestations, there is an African American soldier who haunts Isa. For Derrida, the time of the ghost is marked by "the untimeliness of its present, of its being 'out of joint.'"[89] "And even if it is not *actually present*," Derrida proposes, "it affects *in advance* . . . and bereaves it in advance, like the ghost it will become, but this is precisely where haunting begins."[90] Isa's multiple encounters with the black soldier are narrated through temporal shifts that are both reminiscent and portentative. These out-of-joint encounters unhinge Isa's identity, his ontology unnerved and rearranged by the hauntology of blackness.

Indeed, Isa's first encounter with blackness precedes the beginning of the central narrative of "American School." At the logistics meeting, Yamada suggests a rule of his own: that the Japanese teachers speak only in English—a technique the text refers to as the "all method"—in order to show their English-speaking prowess. On hearing this, Isa "lets out a cry that sounds like a shriek" and says "that's preposterous, that's preposterous."[91] The narrative then flashes back to a period well before the beginning of the narrative proper in order to explain Isa's preposterous shrieking. Sometime before the logistics meeting (the reader can assume that, given the activity, the time is during the elections proctored by the Allies), Isa was delegated the task of translating for an African American soldier. The discrepancy between the story time and the narrative time of Isa's first encounter with blackness—Isa meets the soldier before the logistics meeting, and the narrative is obligated to take the reader back to that first encounter in order to explain Isa's response at the meeting—is revelatory. This serves as an index of the presence of blackness in "American School," which lingers even in absence.

Isa is given the task of translating for the black soldier "simply because he is the lead English teacher."[92] Being the head English teacher, however, does not qualify Isa to speak in English. He has "never once had a conversation in English in his life," "feels something like a ticklish embarrassment" whenever he has to speak it in class, and once feigned illness for two days in order to shirk his observational teaching requirement. Fearing what will happen if he dodges his responsibility with the military administration, Isa reports for duty. He greets the soldier with a phrase that he has practiced for days in advance: "My humble apology for keeping you waiting; this is truly an egregious offense."[93] The black soldier doesn't understand this "overly orthodox and polite" English,[94] which forces Isa to repeat the phrase several times. Isa subsequently gives up on the possibility of communicating in English and, with the exception of two words—"stop, go"—falls silent.

As Isa and the soldier ride together, Isa's frustration reaches a boiling point. Isa jumps out of the jeep and hides in the trees along the road. Upon being discovered by the black soldier, Isa articulates his frustration in Japanese: "Hey! . . . What if I made you speak Japanese. And said that there would be no mercy if you couldn't. How do you think that would go?"[95] Isa's expression of discontent with regard to this moment of linguistic occupation facilitates a literal face-to-face encounter with the black soldier.

> His partner [the soldier] brought his lonely-looking black face, with its neatly shaven mustache, right up to Isa's face and tried to hear what he was saying. Only his neatly shaven mustache had *an odd air of civilization*. It was almost as if he thought that if he could just get close enough he would be able to understand the meaning of Isa's rapid-fire Japanese. Isa deliberately repeated what he had said in this rapid-fire manner. Once he realized that the words coming from Isa's mouth were Japanese, the black corporal spread his arms and hunched his shoulders. If we *look at it from the black man's perspective*, the fact that Isa spoke hardly any *American English*—and, just when the soldier thought he was going to talk, he spoke in Japanese—was *probably* enough to make him [the soldier] feel a foolish sense of inferiority. His lonely face took on an even more lonely look and he drove.[96]

Diane Perpich suggests that the face of another human being "makes an ethical claim that compels the hearer without ever becoming audible."[97] This responsibility does not come about when or because the Other speaks up and makes a comprehensible claim. Rather, it is there from the very moment we look into the face of the Other. The face ethically compels—silently yet audible—in part due to its unrepresentablity: as Emmanuel Levinas begins "Ethics and the Face": "The face resists possession, resists my powers. In its epiphany, in expression, the sensible, still graspable, turns into total resistance to the grasp."[98] Isa's encounter shares a certain affinity with Levinas's articulation of the face-to-face, and it is crucial that any reading of this passage maintains the level of responsibility to the notion of the "ungraspability" of the face to which Kojima's text itself responds.

One can easily monologize Isa's depiction of the black soldier. Molasky, for example, suggests, "The choice of a black GI for this role could either be read as evidence of America's commitment to democracy or as proof of Japan's thorough fall from power (since the Japanese are now subjugated 'even to blacks'). The latter, less generous, interpretation is supported by the story's brief depiction of his . . . 'incongruously civilized air.'"[99] But what other interpretative possibilities exist "for the choice of the black GI" with his "odd air of civilization?" Perhaps Kojima is lampooning the irony of Jim Crow era African Americans proctoring free elections on this side of the Pacific; perhaps he intimates the failure of the Double V campaign; perhaps we are to read intertextually vis-à-vis works such as Fukuzawa's *An Outline of a Theory of Civilization* (*Bunmeiron no gairyaku*, 1875); or perhaps this evinces the fact that Isa is unreliable as a racialized narrator. The issue here is not whether Molasky's conjectures are right or wrong; indeed, both of Molasky's comments are insightful. Rather, the "issue" is how the logic of monologic reading gives critics a reason to stop reading critically—to, in short, fall *unproductively* silent—and how such silence potentially reproduces the kind of silence satirized by Kojima throughout "American School."

If, however, the reader continues to listen even in moments of silence, we are sure to hear something, and perhaps this something will resonate more clearly because of the silence. In Isa's first encounter with the black soldier, for example, the reader is reminded of the fractures within the English language. The reason the soldier has trouble deciphering Isa's stuffy English is that he expected a different variant of the language, namely, "American English." Here the narrator uses the term *beigo* (American English), which should be differentiated from *eigo* (English), which pervades the text. Indeed, the reference to *beigo* suggests, according to Yamamoto Yukimasa, "by way of the verbal exchange between the black soldier and Isa, the class difference within the English language" itself.[100]

To whom does language (American English, Japanese, or otherwise) belong, and from whose perspective should it be heard? The black soldier has brought to the text the expectation of an English that differs from the Occupation-sanctioned English that Isa has studied, an English imbued with race and class difference—the English of a black American soldier. Moreover, this expectation has been brought by way of free indirect discourse. The narrator delves into the thoughts of the black soldier and reproduces his portion of a *dialogue* that is occurring between him and the mute Isa: "*if* [*we*] *look at it from the black man's perspective*" (*kokujin ni shite mitara*).[101] The very act of narrating blackness has changed the perspective of the (presumably

Japanese) narrator. Now he (he is also presumably male) can see how Japan might seem threatening to a black male soldier.

Although their conversation was marked by several moments of silence, the exchange has left its traces on both Isa and the soldier. Their second encounter occurs as the teachers wait for the tardy ringleader. Isa is, of course, silent. On spotting the black soldier, Isa begins to eat his lunch because "There's no limit to the when or the who of being addressed in English in a danger zone like this, but Isa's intuition was something along these lines: if he could just manage to put food in his mouth, then they couldn't ask anything of him."[102] Just as Isa's silence is a testament to the mark his exchange with the soldier left on him, the soldier verifies that he is imbued with a trace of the silent Isa. Yamada, an imperial-turned-linguistic soldier in what he sees as the army of Japanese English teachers, zealously addresses any Occupation soldier within earshot in English. When he serendipitously addresses the black soldier, the soldier, puzzled by Yamada's combination of zeal and immobility, salutes him with the phrase he learned from Isa: "My humble apology for keeping you waiting; this is truly an egregious offense." Yamada is confused by the overly ceremonious English and assumes that the soldier is duplicating the speech of the absent supervisor.

This is a perfect Bakhtinian dialogue—indeed, the words in this carnivalesque dialogue are half someone else's. Isa's speech mingles with the soldier's, Yamada becomes the next link in the chain of interlocution, and Yamada assumes that these words befit a public servant, namely, the (still) absent supervisor. The dialogue here is also "double voiced"; not only is the moment dialogic, but it comes through a dialogic exchange between Yamada and the black soldier. It is difficult to continue the argument for monologism in the face of such textual evidence. If "American School"—again, a work that received the Akutagawa Prize and has been described as "in many respects the story of all Japanese after the war," a story that "will likely remain the most significant statement of the humiliated but determine [*sic*] Japanese psyche following the Second World War"[103]—must be dismissed, deemed "exceptional," or have certain sections censored in order to promulgate its representativeness, perhaps we should read for silence rather than silence the text itself.

Isa's next encounter with the soldier occurs as the teachers make the six-kilometer trek from the meeting place to the American school. Michiko, who has the foresight and adaptability to bring a pair of high heels and a pair of running shoes, uses her masterful English skills to negotiate a spot in an army jeep for Isa, who by this point is barefoot and hobbling. Now in its third haunting iteration, it comes as no surprise to the reader or Isa that the operator of the jeep is the black soldier; Isa "had a premonition that he would meet the black man again today."[104] Kojima utilizes this preordained moment to breathe dynamic life into the black character by providing the reader with information that precedes this current moment. After his election tour with Isa, the soldier is perplexed and tries to determine whether Isa's taciturnity was a sign of discrimination or of his lack of linguistic acumen. The soldier checks Isa's file in the Education Department and, with nothing to point toward the latter, assumes that the former must be the case. The soldier decides to exact his revenge on Isa by pulling a pistol and asking him, "So which is it? You not gonna speak English? 'My humble apology for keeping you waiting; this is truly an egregious offense.'—say it one more time!"[105] His revenge now chilled and served, the soldier laughs, reveals that the gun is a toy, and starts singing snatches of a jazz number.

Monologic reading requires downplaying the significance of this exchange because the passage devotes textual space to the creation of interiority and motives for the black soldier. Moreover, Isa's comments on the "oddly civilized" air of the soldier—a prime piece of ammo if one wants to read "American School" as a Japan-centered monologue based on stereotypes—have been satirically inverted. Now a barefoot Isa is being driven and bamboozled by modern inventions while listening to the soldier reproduce a brand of music almost synonymous with modernity: jazz. In the words of Kumagai Nobuko, "The black man, liltingly absorbed in jazz, and Isa are depicted contrastively. . . . Isa, the obstinate Japanese teacher of English, and the frank black American soldier symbolize the defeated Japanese and the victorious Americans."[106]

Moreover, the soldier has combated what he saw as disdain (*keibetsu*) with the subversive power of laughter. Kojima would write in *Contemporary Times and Satirical Literature* that "the upper class and the aristocracy are, just like the common people, ultimately nothing more than ridiculous people with weaknesses. The spectators [of satire] learn this and are relieved. This relief calls forth laughter from within the spectator."[107] Kojima has brought his readers into messy territory, for the black soldier is both emblematic of the victorious American regime and a master practitioner of the weapon of the weak—satire—in his self-defense of the narrator's commentary on his "inferiority." It is precisely such messiness that makes it difficult to incorporate "American School" into any representative mode of argumentation.

As the soldier and Isa are about to part, the soldier feels that their meeting was predestined (*innen asakaranu*) and prophesies that they will meet again. The soldier's prophecy is not actualized per se; with the exception of a brief passage in which the soldier finds his son and enters the school grounds, the soldier is not seen or heard from again. The soldier does, however, continue to haunt after his corporeal exit; Isa claims that the prophecy "sent a chill through his heart" (*kokoro no naka de gyo to shita*), a phrase that, particularly in the Japanese original, is befitting a haunting taunt.

The soldier drops Isa off outside the gates of the American school. This placement puts Isa in the proximity of "a flow of pure, beautiful words reminiscent of the murmuring of a small stream."[108] Although Isa can't decipher the meaning of the words, they "seemed not to be of this world,"[109] another phrase often associated with phantasmagoria. Isa realizes that the mellifluous voices belong to a group of schoolgirls who are conversing in English. Isa's spiritual response to this English is markedly different from what had been his characteristic visceral response of fear, aggression, and retreat. The difference, and this is a difference present in "The Legend" as well, seems to be located in the gender of the speakers. Kojima's women are marked with a certain fluidity that allows them to cross both physical and linguistic borders, hence Kojima's use of the conceptual metaphor of liquid—"small stream," "flow," and so on—to describe feminine language. In this phallocentric conception of reconstruction, enervated men depend on such flows of femininity for revitalization. Utilizing Brooks's notion of desire and narrative, Douglas Slaymaker articulates the relationship as follows. "Brooks' description of narrative maps exactly to what is found in postwar writing. The men write of women who structure the universe and who hold the key—indeed *are* the key—to the symbolic order. . . . The woman's almost mystical body takes on the source of universal power and knowledge; to master and possess the woman's body would then provide the key to the universe and to oneself."[110] Here the flow of feminine language is reproduced by Emily, a teacher who "is tall and beautiful like the ladies who appear in American movies," who tends to Isa's wounded feet. Much like the English of the schoolgirls, Emily's language is described as "words that flow on like the water of melted snow in spring."[111]

Isa is caught in this "feminine flow" of language because of the soldier, who is physically absent but continues to haunt Isa in silence. To continue the previous passage, Isa "finally realized, from the flow of the woman's conversation, which streamed like the water of melted snow in spring, that the reason he was in this predicament was thanks to the officiousness of that black soldier."[112] Moreover, Isa's response to his "predicament" is dictated by the absent soldier. Isa falls "silent like a mute" in the face of Emily's kindness because, "when he thought about what he should do if . . . he were showered with questions . . . by the large number of foreigners that surrounded him, the despondent feeling he had when he was in the jeep a while ago came back and resurrected itself again (*yomigaette kuru*)."[113]

Isa's despondence is rooted in a threat that often accompanies hauntings: possession. Here anxiety regarding possession refers both to the potential loss of possession(s) (e.g., the loss of his nationally/linguistically bound self-identity) and to the ghastly overtaking of the Other within the self, an Other who knows no boundaries. As Derrida articulates the phenomenon, "The difference between *inhabit* and *haunt* becomes here more ungraspable than ever. . . . Persons (guardians or possessors of the thing) are haunted in return, and constitutively, by the haunting they produce in the thing by lodging there their speech and their will like inhabitants."[114] Isa ponders his fear of possession, of losing himself to the voices that now inhabit him.

> He wondered why he had until that point so loathed, so feared the language that was this kind of flow of beautiful voices. Something whispered inside him (Japanese people speaking English like foreigners—ha!—what foolishness. If you speak like a foreigner, you will become a foreigner . . .) I will become a different person. That's the only thing I can't take.[115]

The "something" (*mono*) that whispers inside Isa is reminiscent of the "something" from *mono ni tsukareru*, a Japanese phrase for being possessed. This reminiscence is magnified by the parenthetical phrase that follows, which gives the impression of a separate entity, a "different person," talking in and through Isa. Insofar as Isa is inhabited, haunted by the words of the black soldier, the soldier's prophecy is fulfilled.

In the final passages of "American School," Yamada suggests that he and Isa conduct model teaching using the "all method," following which Isa decides he will either have to punch Yamada or quit his job. As a discombobulated Isa debates which solution he will employ, Michiko asks Isa to let her borrow his chopsticks—she has forgotten to bring her own. Isa hands her the chopsticks like "an unskilled relay runner who takes off before he has fully passed" his baton.[116] Michiko—the perfect picture of US-Japanese hybridity with her chopsticks in hand and high heels on foot—loses her balance and falls. After the debacle, the principal of the American school outlaws displays of the "kamikaze spirit" by disallowing Japanese teachers from taking the lectern, and he prohibits high heels just to be safe.

Yamamoto Yukimasa argues that Michiko's relay embodies "the possibility of [moving toward] bilingualism" (even if this possibility is ultimately occluded by the principal and the principal characters' fixation with Japanese identity).[117] This possibility can be heard, however, only when silence is not conflated with a lack of communication. The fact that the "possibility of moving toward bilingualism" is punctuated by silence does not nullify the movement. Or, as Kojima wrote in a key passage of his 1965 *Hōyō kazoku* (Embracing Family):

> Without uttering a single word out loud . . . Shunsuke screamed in the depths of himself as he was shopping: "We are companions. . . . Yes, I am a man shopping, but please try not to think of me just as a man shopping. I want to be with you as a human being; that's why I'm addressing you *in this way* right now. We are in a relationship even though we don't see or know each other. But it can't stay this way. This is precisely why we are friends.[118]

With this Kojima has resurrected Morrison's insight into the nexus of silence, trauma, and friendship: "And since the victim does not have the vocabulary to understand the violence or its context . . . friends . . . would have to fill those silences with their own reflective lives."[119] Even Shunsuke—an Isa-like figure who, unlike Isa, is also a professor fluent in American culture and literature—addresses his audience "in this way" (read: "in silence"), that is, through an appeal that makes a claim to interconnectivity even though it doesn't "utter a single word out loud." Although its expression is not definitive, Isa's silence at the conclusion of "American School" is most likely not the silent crescendo of a monologue but dialogic silence in the mode of Morrison, Bakhtin, and, Shunsuke.

Conclusion

"In any list of casualties of the Pacific War," Van C. Gessel writes, "on the Japanese side one would have to include the steadfast literary construct of self that had been forged by the prewar 'I' novelists. The novelists of this generation . . . have taken apart the central 'I' . . . bending and then breaking the vertical pronoun that had seemed so sturdy and unassailable in the *shishōsetsu*."[120] (To be sure, however, the dead and expired do return to haunt every now and again.) The fiction of authors such as Ishikawa, Kojima, and Matsumoto did a great deal of this bending and breaking. Okuno Takeo describes Ishikawa Jun as a literary figure "far removed" from the "binding curse of the I-novel" of "established Japanese literature."[121] Kojima's postwar works have been characterized as "an attempt at a new type of literature . . . a move from the so-called I-novel to what could even be called the relationship novel."[122]

This chapter presents one argument, one question, and one modest proposal concerning the way we read the "relationship novels" of Ishikawa, Kojima, and Matsumoto, which came to life in the postwar wake of the I-novel. The argument is that these texts, which were written or set during the Allied Occupation, exhibit a preoccupation with blackness. "As a metaphor for transacting the whole process of [in this case, the narration of Japanese racial identity in postwar Japan]," blackness "may be something [that Japan] cannot do without."[123]

The question I've posed is this: what are we to make of the translucent representations of blackness that appear and reappear in the texts of this era? "Blacks themselves," some might argue, "have been given practically no voice in shaping this racial discourse, other than by providing soundbites or stereotypical, disembodied images."[124] This is true, however, only insofar as it presents a truism: blackness can never be represented in all its plentitude, so any attempt at representation is always a kind of reduction or silencing—the literary counterpart never compares to "the real thing." In addition to this truism, there is the pervasive power of SCAP's censoring apparatus, what Marlene Mayo has called its "wholesale policing and censoring of Japanese media . . . in an attempt to 'end Japan's . . . racial consciousness and belief in divine mission.'"[125] Searching the ruins of occupied Japan for representations of blackness often exhumes a series of ghosts, the spectral remnants of censored voices, and what Jonathan Abel has recently called the blocks of black redaction ink that cross out the presence of cross-racial fraternization.

This chapter proposes that these spectral remnants may be meaningful; to adapt Abel's articulation, these remnants may be the "markers of silence that speak for silence."[126] My focus here has been on the spectacular visibility of disembodied images and the communicative power of silence. If we think in ontological ways, the disembodied image—the silent depiction—is insubstantial. If we think, however, in hauntological ways, the very fact that insubstantial black bodies appear and reappear in works of postwar Japanese literature is rich with hermeneutic possibilities. These spectral figures are significant *precisely because they are spectral.* That is to say, to argue that black soldiers written during the forced democracy of postwar Japan and under the watchful eye of Allied censors are insubstantial representations seems, to me, to miss the point. The fact that these black apparitions appear somewhere between the border of life and death and refuse to be banished is what makes them hauntologically significant. This haunting is a metaphor for what is left of Japanese racial identity in the wake of what Dower has called the Pacific War as a race war. Black ghosts serve as a reminder that race has long held the power to make one an insubstantial figure in the face of American power. Ontological readings—which dismiss insubstantial representations of blackness as insignificant—have no hermeneutic means with which to address this haunting power of representations of black soldiers in postwar Japanese literature.

In light of all this, I have proposed "overly imaginative" readings that run the risk of erring on the side of the speculative. I present such readings, however, to highlight the way in which representative readings of blackness can fall into the trap of being "underly imaginative," the way a focus on the black body short-circuits the scholarly imagination, giving visions of only the black skin that can be represented. A part of what is at work here is that representative readings by American East Asianists—a field that, since its inception, has had a dearth of black scholars—have erred on the side of definitive judgments of any text that might be read as inscribing antiblack racism. Although this sentiment is commendable, one of its by-products is readings that do not address the full interpretative possibilities of a text with fidelity, readings that are unable to see the hermeneutic forest beyond the judgment of the trees (not to mention the deforestation of those moments that challenge or contradict that which is "representative").

I have proposed here that representative readings are best done slowly and with an eye toward the danger of conflating "silence," "silenced," and "silencing." It has been argued that black authors "aren't given an opportunity to speak for themselves [in Japanese literary circles]; the other is narrated in the words of the self . . . it's a kind of literary imperialism (*bungakuteki teikokushugi*).[127] This argument, however, is in considerable tension with the members of the Japanese Association for Negro Studies, who were translating black literature at the very moment when works such as Kojima's "American School" and Matsumoto's "Painting on Black Canvas" were being published. One of the association's self-styled objectives was to "create something pure" by "hav[ing] [Japanese] people read only literature" "written by black authors and depicting black characters."[128] It is for this reason that the association didn't translate works in which white authors represented black characters or black authors represented white protagonists. The words of Ralph Ellison (words that would find a Japanese translation and readership due to the work of the association) might account for the discrepancy between the charge of "literary imperialism" and the association's objective. Ellison writes, "You often doubt if you really exist. You wonder whether you aren't simply a phantom in other people's minds," but in actuality, "I am an invisible man. No, I am not a spook like those who haunted Edgar Allan Poe; nor am I one of your Hollywood-movie ectoplasms. I am a man of substance, of flesh and bone. . . . I am invisible, understand, simply because people refuse to see me."[129]

In this chapter, I have focused primarily on representations of blackness. In the following chapters, I balance questions of representation with reconstructive questions that go beyond representation. Namely, I am interested in postwar Japanese literature's styling, translation (broadly defined), and intertextual and sociohistorical engagements with blackness. Each of these avenues provides new heuristics for thinking through the triangulation of race, literature, and Japan. It is to these new ways of thinking that the remainder of this book is dedicated.

CHAPTER 2

In the Beginning

Ōe Kenzaburō and the Creative Nonfiction of Blackness

God thought and thought, / Till He thought, / "*I'll make me a man!*"
— James Weldon Johnson, "The Creation"

Someday, I intend to write about my observations concerning this
issue in greater detail, but I think that contemporary Japanese
literature and black literature have qualitative similarities. . . .
Black American authors—Baldwin in particular—who have made
themselves through the means provided by the Western worldview are
a great stimulus vis-à-vis the sense of difficultly I have [regarding the
creation of literary works].
— Ōe Kenzaburō, "Konnan no kankaku ni tsuite: Wa ga sosaku taiken"

Toward a Rereading of Blackness in Ōe Kenzaburō

On 7 December 1963, the Tokyo branch of the Kokujin kenkyū no kai (Japanese Association for Negro Studies, (now the Association for Black Studies)
commemorated the issuance of the American Emancipation Proclamation
with a symposium of speeches, poetry readings, and movie viewings.[1] Ōe
Kenzaburō (1935)—not yet a Nobel laureate but by this point already an
Akutagawa Prize recipient and rising star of the literary world—took part
in the festivities by delivering a talk entitled "Negro American Literature
and Modern Japanese Literature." The seventh of December 1963, then, is
most likely the "someday" on which Ōe mused "in greater detail" about the
"qualitative similarities" between black and Japanese literature alluded to in
the epigraph.[2] "Negro American Literature" would seem to be an ideal place
to begin a study of Ōe Kenzaburō's 1960s nonfictional writing on blackness.
There is, however, no recording of Ōe's 1963 speech, and, according to my
personal correspondence with the writer, Ōe himself has no documentation
or recollection of what was said on that day.[3]

In lieu of "Negro American Literature and Modern Japanese Literature," perhaps we can begin by recalibrating our methodological approach to reading Ōe's creation of blackness. This recalibration addresses the fact that Ōe writes not black literature but black *literatures*, by which I mean that blackness in Ōe's texts has a wide variety of complex, conflicting manifestations. Insofar as blackness is, in the words of Marvin Sterling, characterized by the relationship between the "biological" "imagined fixity" of the identity of people of sub-Saharan African descent and the fluid "range of ideological agendas facilitated" by this imagined fixity, Ōe's vexed, multifaceted writing and rewriting of blackness is far from anomalous.[4] Doing justice to these facets—and, in so doing, doing justice to Ōe's rewriting of post–World War II Japanese American race relations—requires close reading of three intertwined moments in Ōe's oeuvre: first, the representation of the black, male body in Ōe's short fiction circa 1957; second, Ōe's creation of a black-Japanese analogy across his 1960s essays and reportage; and, finally, works such as *Kojinteki na taiken* (A Personal Matter, 1964) and *Sakebigoe* (The Cry, 1963), in which Ōe attempts to translate the program set in his 1960s nonfiction into fictional form.[5]

A considerable amount of scholarly ink has been spilled on the representation of blackness in Ōe's early fiction.[6] This chapter focuses primarily on that second facet of Ōe's writing of blackness and concludes with a prolegomenon of the third. This focus speaks both to my debt to previous scholarship and my concern that, when it comes to the question of blackness in Japanese literature, we have yet to articulate fully the way "nonrepresentational forces are always at work—forces that may produce representations but that cannot be explained by that logic." My concern is that previous scholarship has focused on the representations of race and "judgment of them [racial representations] in terms of their more or less accurate resemblance to reality and truth" without accounting for "the *emergence* of representations" or questioning how such racially charged texts "increase"—or, we might add, decrease—"the power of the subjects encountering [them] to act, to think, to move."[7]

Indeed, Ōe's 1960s nonfictional writing of blackness aims to add an avenue through which his readership can act, think, and move as racialized subjects in the postwar, post-Occupation era. The construction of this avenue is predicated on Ōe's sense of the affinity—to borrow Ōe's term, the "qualitative similarities" (*shitsuteki na ruiji*)—between both black and Japanese literature and the black and Japanese existential condition. Take, for example, Ōe's justification for his first trip to America: "I wanted to show the interest that I have in the way in which black authors (*kokujin sakka*) have continued to write a literature of their own even under the deep influence of European literature."[8] Throughout the 1960s, Ōe penned numerous essays, articles, and speeches in which he attempted to re-create himself as a kind of "black Japanese" author by resituating his literary techniques and thematic concerns in proximity to those of African American authors such as Richard Wright, James Baldwin, Ralph Ellison, and Chester Himes. This resituating exemplifies a fundamental shift in Ōe's engagement with black people, culture, and literature. He transitions from gazing at and representing black bodies—which characterized his writing of blackness in the late 1950s and, after he resituated his writing, became associated with the "white" or "western" gaze—to examining the world alongside black authors as a fellow "colored" (*yūshoku jinshu*) writer.

Over the course of this examination, Ōe began to envision a "qualitative" (*shitsuteki*, with *shitsu* here referring to "substance," "materiality," or "stuff") similarity between the Japanese literary worlds of his own creation and, to borrow the title of Richard Wright's haiku collection, this other world of African American literature. For Ōe, the "substantial"—or perhaps "essential" is more fitting—similarity between black and Japanese literature (and, by proxy, between black and Japanese characters and readers) is channeled through Ōe's studies of postwar French existentialism, with its foundational lesson on existence preceding essence. In other words, to return to the definition of *race* provided by Michael Hardimon in the "Introduction," Ōe's understanding of racial being posits socialrace—the intersubjectively formed concept of race created by virtue of one's existence in the social world—as more substantial than biological or phenotypical visions of race. And, for Ōe, Japanese existence in postwar, post-Occupation Japan shares a certain affinity with black existence in the civil rights era United States, which Ōe refers to as their "qualitative" or "substantial" similarity.

Ōe's nonfictional investigations of blackness are (figuratively and literally) creative; they create an analogy between the postwar Japanese and civil rights era African Americans, which, in turn, opens a space for shared stories—both factual and fictional—between African Americans and the Japanese. When I refer to the creation of this analogy as an act of creative nonfiction, I have two things in mind. I mean first to initiate an exploration of Ōe's nonfictional writings on blackness, which have been understudied due to the spectacular representations of blackness in his fiction. But I also want to highlight the stakes of Ōe's turn to an amalgamation of literary techniques and nonfictional facts in his writing of blackness. In "Situating the Beings of Fiction," Bruno Latour posits a quintessential difference between *Homo faber* and *homo fabulator*: whereas fiction has the capacity to create and re-create worlds and beings with no need for referential validation, nonfiction has the capacity to create chains of reference (the reader refers, for example, to the words on the page, which refer to the event in question, which refers to Ōe's lived experience as a "colored" author, which refers to the qualitative similarities of Afro-Japanese existence, and so on) that validate "a verifiable common narrative."[9] The author of creative nonfiction, of course, wields the capacities of both creative fiction and nonfiction. Ōe's turn to creative nonfiction, then, imbues his writing of race with an almost godlike authority. He can create racial subjectivities, utopias, dystopias, or whatever else he wills from dust even as his chains of reference lay claim to a verifiable common narrative of black and Japanese existence.

This chapter considers Ōe's self-styled re-creation as a "colored" author as it is articulated in his nonfiction written in the early to mid-1960s, the years in which he devoted himself to the project of constructing an analogical link between his own works and black literature. This analogical re-creation entails two gestures. Ōe begins with what I call the dialectics of the racial gaze—a phrase I borrow and adapt intentionally from studies of Jean-Paul Sartre to describe Ōe's positing of an analogous existential dilemma experienced by postwar black and Japanese people living under the disciplinary power of the white gaze. I also address the pitfall of Ōe's proposed solution, which has less to do with any logical fallacy on the part of Ōe than with the fallacies inherent to analogical thinking. The second gesture, in which Ōe stresses the pedagogic power of African American literature and its ability to assist all "minor writers" in overcoming the aforementioned existential dilemma, represents Ōe's discovery of "the greatest hint in regard to [the resolution of] not only the black problem (*kokujin mondai*) but all the problems surrounding Japanese people (*Nihonjin wo meguru subete no mondai*) as well" in African American letters.[10] I conclude with an analysis of Ōe's translation of the program set in his nonfictional works into fictional form, namely, by way of his 1963 *Sakebigoe*.

From Hauntology to Fictions of Race: A Preface to a Postcritical Reading of Ōe's Blackness (or, on the Absence of "Shiiku")

On an initial reading of Ōe's "Shiiku" (Prize Stock, 1957), the story of a black soldier who crash-lands and is subsequently captured and "reared" by Japanese villagers at the dénouement of the Pacific War, there is a passage that inevitably leaves a mark on the reader: after discovering that the soldier has a "magnificent, heroic, unbelievably beautiful penis," "Harelip [a young villager] strained to keep the goat's head down, and the black soldier labored mightily . . . but it simply would not work the way it did with a billy-goat."[11] This is the literal manifestation of the *shiiku* (animal husbandry) to which the title refers. This depiction of attempted black bestiality is spectacular in its repetition of the stereotypes bred by race-based fear and desire.

If the objective is to read for the representation of blackness in Ōe, this spectacular moment might serve as the fulcrum of a conversation on the ethics of cross-cultural representation. Perhaps such a conversation would begin where Ōe suggests it should. Ōe himself writes, "I can't forget the feeling of fear (*kyōfu* [a key term in Ōe's writing of blackness to which I will return momentarily]) and disgust, but in addition to those feelings the kind of reverence (*isshu no ikei*) that I felt the first time I saw a black soldier who represented the victorious army."[12] And perhaps such a reading would be done with an eye turned toward what Cornel West, channeling Kobena Mercer, has referred to as the "reflectionist argument," in which "the fight for black representation and recognition—against white racist stereotypes—must reflect or mirror the real black community, not simply the negative and depressing representations of it."[13] There would be, undeniably, insights to be gained from such a conversation.

I am more interested, however, in those moments in "Prize Stock" and Ōe that might be obfuscated by representational reading.[14] The narrator, a young village boy, for example, notices that the black soldier, who has been held captive and shackled in the boy's cellar, was "singing a song in a low, thick voice that mysteriously arrested us with its rawness, a song that tried to assail us with its lament and cry."[15] Although it cannot be said with any finality, it seems that the captive black soldier is singing a Negro spiritual. In chapter 1, I proposed that, when blackness is read representationally, such reading would be well served by the hermeneutics of a hauntology of blackness. Hauntology, much like the Negro spiritual, reverberates with life even when it is on the brink of death—it sings in the lower frequencies of the weight of historical baggage. A hauntological reading of "Shiiku" might account for both the spectacular and the spiritual, for the tension between a black soldier who is both "a nigger, so he can't be an enemy" and also a target of the "animosity (*tekii* [in Japanese, the term includes the character for 'enemy']) toward everything in the world that was churning and bubbling up inside me."[16]

But even such a reading would not be enough to begin a fuller account of Ōe's writing of blackness. For the remainder of this book, I want to suggest moving beyond representation-centered reading. The impetus for this suggestion resides somewhere at the intersection of my intellectual belief, hope, and intuition that blackness is ultimately irreducible to the content by which it is represented and that representation often belies the fact that—to borrow Sartre's articulation (and momentarily table the possibly racist implications of it, to which I return later in this chapter)—"the blacks are something other and more than what they are."[17] Representational reading might make us overlook the presence of any excess that cannot be fully represented; this approach has a set of tendencies that, in my mind, often misrepresent the complexities of the inscription of race.

Studies of Japanese representations of blackness, for example, tend to be synchronic insofar as they focus on a single ("representative") moment in a single text. But writings of race are often characterized by asynchronicity, by a messy pulling together of the past and the future into an inscribed presence. In the case of Ōe, this messiness means following the rhizomatic path that his writing of blackness runs from the 1957 "Shiiku" all the way through his 1997 "Toni Morrison and Ōe Kenzaburō (from the Shade of the Elm Tree)." Moreover, insofar as they delve into single moments of single texts, representative readings of blackness tend to be, for lack of a better term, intratextual. Here, too, the abundance of scholarly attention "Shiiku" has received is informative. Such readings tend to ignore the intertextual network that such representations plug into. This explains the dearth of scholarly attention paid to the interface between "Shiiku" and the other nodes of its intertextual network, for example, Ōe's 1958 "Kurai kawa omoi kai" (another short story that juxtaposes a black soldier and a Japanese boy and binds the two together with a Negro spiritual); the give-and-take between the crematorium imagery that begins and ends "Prize Stock" and Ōe's self-reported fascination with Huck Finn as an existential hero who "chooses a hell all his own . . . a free hero who wasn't collusively fixed to America";[18] or the affinities and disjunctures between "Prize Stock" and Itsuki Hiroyuki's (1932–) "Umi wo mite ita Joni."

I could continue. In short, however, what I want to say is this: reading for representation runs the risk of asphyxiating the critical imagination, leaving little room for the modes of reading proposed in the "Introduction" (translational, intertextual, experimental, and shared historical). Given the abundance of research on race and "Prize Stock," its absence here has already been addressed. What has yet to be addressed, however, is Ōe's writing of blackness beyond "Prize Stock." This absence is the primary concern of this chapter.

What I want to do here is complement representational readings of "Prize Stock" with what recently has been called postcritical commentary on Ōe's creative nonfiction. In *The Limits of Critique*, Rita Felski "reframe[s], reconsider[s], and in some cases refute[s] the . . . assumption" that "whatever is *not* critical must therefore be *un*critical."[19] For postcritical reading, Felski continues, "Interpretation becomes a coproduction between actors that brings new things to light rather than an endless rumination on a text's . . . representational failures."[20] I understand that dulling the critical edge runs the risk of what Jane Tompkins calls an "embrace of the conventional," which here refers to an intellectual complicity with the stereotyping, reification, appropriation, and misrepresentation that haunts any cross-cultural exchange.[21] I run this risk, however, in order to provide fuller readings of Ōe's coproductions, which in turn bring new things to light regarding Ōe's exchanges with Sartre, Baldwin, Wright, Ellison, and negritude. With this methodological preface in mind, I turn now to a consideration of the writing of blackness in what I call Ōe's 1960s creative nonfiction.

Ōe's Black-Japanese Analogy and the Dialectics of the Racial Gaze

In March 1961, the Asian-African Writers Conference, which saw itself as the literary wing of the more politically oriented Bandung Conference, held an emergency meeting in Tokyo. Ōe attended as a member of the Japanese delegation. He wrote that it was "around the time when the Asian-African Writers Conference was held that I began to carry black literature (*kokujin bungaku*) and works concerning Africa with me and nothing else and read them like a man who had been washed onto a deserted island."[22] Ōe's voracious reading of black literature was coupled with his contributions to both the *Kokujin bungaku zenshū* (The Complete Works of Black Literature)—a thirteen-volume collection of Japanese translations of the likes of Richard Wright, James Baldwin, Jean Toomer, and Langston Hughes published between 1961 and 1963—and the aforementioned Kokujin kenkyū no kai. As Yuichiro Onishi argues, the linguistic and cultural translation of the rhetoric of black liberation by the Kokujin kenkyū no kai fostered "colored-internationalism" and "Afro-Asian solidarity" rooted in a notion of race that "had less to do with personal identity than the politics of identification."[23] If personal identity politics is typically associated with embodiment and the ability to represent that which is embodied, Onishi's politics of identification is more interested in lived sociohistorical experiences and the ability to participate in political movements due to some (real or imagined) affinity between the participant and the movement. It is within this milieu that Ōe would begin to identify with black authors such as Wright, Ellison, and Baldwin.

The crux of Ōe's transpacific identification is what he sees as the shared fear (*kyōfu*) evoked by the white gaze in both civil rights era black Americans and postwar Japanese people. Kota Inoue proposes that postwar Japanese literature developed a number of motifs in response to the asymmetrical power dynamic between defeated Japan and the victorious United States. These motifs—which have been addressed, Inoue contends, in Ōe's writing—include humiliation at the emasculating loss of patriarchal power and a desire for individual freedom expressed through aggressive sexuality.[24] In reading Ōe's creative nonfiction of blackness, an additional motif becomes readily apparent: an arresting fear of another violent defeat at the hands of the Americans. Take, for example, the articulation of racial fear at the beginning of Ōe's "Jigoku ni yuku Hakkuruberī Fin" (Huck Finn Goes to Hell), the inaugural piece in a quintet of essays entitled "Dreams of a Traveler in America," which Ōe published in the left-leaning *Sekai* from September of 1966 to October of 1967. Somewhere between diary entries and political reportage, the five essays document Ōe's first trip to the United States in the summer of 1965. "Huck Finn Goes to Hell," and thus "Dreams of a Traveler in America," begins with extreme fear.

> America. I will never be completely free (*jiyu-ni naru koto wa nai*) from the mystical power that grips my chest whenever I hear the word "America." . . . The first and greatest feeling of terror (*kyōfukan*) in my life was brought about by the word "America." Our country fought with America. America might take my mother and . . . me—just a little boy—and make us lie facedown on the paved roads of our village and crush us with their tanks. And if the skin on my face wasn't hurt too badly by the shock, America might make a little lampshade with it as memorabilia of its trip to Japan. And if it managed to do a particularly good job and make it look really Japanese, America might give the lampshade to the president of the United States. . . . America might eat the flesh of a Japanese person.[25]

In this excerpt, America is represented as a bodiless actor—personified, yet bodiless nevertheless. The bodilessness of America is crystallized here both by the stylistics of the opening line, a sentence without appendages that begins and ends with a free-floating "America," and by the repetition of the phrase "the word America," (*Amerika toiu kotoba*). This is in stark contrast to the Japanese body. Ōe's Japanese body in pain is marked by its ethnicity: America "eats the flesh of Japanese people" (*Nihonjin no niku wo kuu*), makes lampshades that are "particularly Japanese" (*Nihonjin . . . rashiku*), and so on.

By highlighting the "Japaneseness" of the bodies within which America instills fear, Ōe opens a space for the interrogation of the heretofore disembodied "America" that elicits said fear. These American bodies turn out to be racialized à la their "Japanese" counterpart, with some races in proximity to their Japanese counterpart and others at more of a distance. The black body in white-black relations maintains a relationship with fear and pain analogous to the Japanese body in white-Japanese relations. The white body remains in a similar pose—instigator or agent that instills and commemorates fear and pain—even as Ōe's commentary shifts from white-black relations to white-Japanese relations and back again. In "Fukashi ningen to tayōsei" (Invisible Men and Diversity), the fifth and final installment of "Dreams," Ōe creates a fear that hangs ubiquitously over black Americans, that is, a fear reminiscent of the Japanese fear of whiteness with which "Huck Finn Goes to Hell" begins. Ōe writes:

> What many journalists saw even in the face of the heavyweight champion of the world before a bout . . . was the face of one young black boy that harbored a fear (*kyōfushin*) with the potential to erupt in insanity. . . . We don't have to stop at Cassius Clay; the reason we are humanely and deeply moved by the impression of a prebout black boxer captured by fear (*kyōfushin)* is that the fear (*kyōfushin*) he harbors regarding the violence (*bōryokuteki naru mono*) he is about to endure in a matter of minutes is connected to the gigantic fear (*kyōfushin*) that drenches the roots of his daily existence as a black man.[26]

Here in the closing essay of the quintet, Ōe returns to the first essay and constructs an analogue between Japanese and black fear of whiteness. The analogous diction of the two passages is unmistakable. The Japanese fear of American soldiers is referred to as "the greatest fear" (*saidai no kyōfu*) while the black fear recorded by American journalists is "gigantic fear" (*bōdai na kyōfushin*). The representation of fear in the two passages is also of a like kind. Both feelings of fear are evoked by phantasmagoric violence—the tank that has yet to crush the Japanese family, the punch that has yet to land on the pugilist's face. Fear arises in both cases from pain to be inflicted on young nonwhite males (Ōe as a child, Cassius Clay [later Muhammad Ali] as a "young man"). Both memories of fear are permutated into commemorative objects—Ōe's lampshade and the journalists' reports of Ali—by white American actors. Finally, these singular examples of black/Japanese fear of whiteness are deemed representative of a racial fear that pervades the daily existence of black and Japanese folks.

As such, Ōe's postwar Japanese fear finds its analogue in 1960s black America. On the following page of the essay, Ōe makes the link explicit for readers not familiar with the argument built over the series of essays: "Swollen fear of white people . . . lies at the heart of . . . fight[s] between . . . black brothers. Surely *we* can understand this violence if we compare it to the radicalization of the individual's violent crimes in states that are conducting large-scale wars."[27] Given that Japan was only two decades removed from the conclusion of its Fifteen-Year War and in the throes of the Vietnam War, the "we" here signifies the assumedly all-Japanese readership of *Sekai*. As the previous depiction of Muhammad Ali suggests, Ōe presents the ubiquity of the white gaze as a catalyst for black and Japanese fear and violence as the inevitable manifestation of that fear. In a move undoubtedly informed by his reading of Sartre, Ōe suggests that it is through this frightening gaze that Japanese people and African Americans acquire knowledge of themselves as Japanese/African Americans. Ōe's dialectic assumes that the postwar African American existential condition is the closest analogue to the postwar Japanese existential condition. As such, he cites examples of postwar black and Japanese existentialism almost interchangeably. During his time in the United States in the summer of 1965, for example, Ōe went to Atlanta to see Morehouse College and "visit the headquarters of the SNCC [Student Nonviolent Coordinating Committee] and Martin Luther King Jr.'s SCLC [Southern Christian Leadership Conference]."[28] The "first memorable scene" (*saisho ni mita inshō teki na nagame*) Ōe witnessed in Atlanta as he headed for the headquarters of SNCC was "the spectacle (*kōkei*) of two black people fighting on a street corner in a black neighborhood as if their lives depended on it."[29] As Ōe looks forward to the day when he can discuss this incident with black intellectuals, he begins to "see (*midasu*) not violence (*bōryoku*), but stark-naked fear (*kyōfushin*)" in the fighting men.[30] After his "discovery" of fear in the black Atlantans, Ōe "tastes a strange experience that goes beyond [seeing the spectacle of the fight]: what I actually experienced was the presence of the gargantuan eyes of white people (*hakujin no me*) on the backs of the two fighting men, and the eyes were gazing fixedly (*mitsumeteiru*) at the men."[31]

The fear of the white gaze Ōe posits in the "fighting brothers" episode finds its analogue in postwar Japan. Directly following his recollection of his childhood fear of America, Ōe rehearses the story of a young "idiot boy" from a village near his hometown who is convicted of sexually assaulting and murdering a young girl. Ōe's description of the murder is gratuitous in its violence; at one point the boy takes a bamboo spear and runs it through the girl's vagina to the base of her neck.[32] Ōe writes that the responsibility for such gruesome violence lies not with the hands of the youth but in the fear sown by "the illusion of America that exerted power over my village, the raping, slaughtering America," in the "homogenized (*jyunichi*) America that was the target of [his village's] fear (*kyōfushin*) and animosity."[33] Just as it is the fear crystallized by living perpetually under the white gaze that is responsible for black-on-black violence in Atlanta, Ōe's murderous youth living under the disciplinary gaze of the SCAP "has no choice but to revive the frightening illusion (*osoroshii gensō*) that once held all of Japan."[34]

Moreover, Ōe's nonfictional essays recount his own experience, that is, the lived "reality" of the analogous position shared by blacks and the Japanese in relation to the white gaze. During his first trip to the United States, Ōe spent most of his time at Harvard as a participant in the Kissinger International Seminar. After being mocked by four white students at Harvard Square on 15 August 1965—perhaps it is more than mere coincidence that Ōe's creative nonfiction places this event on the anniversary of V-J (Victory-Japan) Day—Ōe is reminded of Chester Himes's *If He Hollers Let Him Go*, particularly "Little Riki Oyana singing 'God Bless America' and going to Santa Anita with his parents the next day . . . I was the same color as the Japanese and I couldn't tell the difference. 'A yeller-bellied Jap' coulda meant me too. I could always feel race trouble, serious trouble, never more than two feet off." After falling under the white gaze, Ōe begins to comprehend the analogous position between the two, to "see himself as one and the same" with "the Nisei Japanese who were sent to internment camps and the black youth who begins to fear his premonition that he shares a like fate with the interned."[35] Ōe "began to see myself through the eyes (*me*) of those American cartoonists. I, the very same person who had until that time slipped into the hustle and bustle of Harvard Square without feeling the least bit out of place, now discovered myself alone standing there as a disgusting, bucktoothed, bespectacled Japanese like those in the comics . . . and felt something within the realm of fear."[36]

It is important to reiterate that it is not America per se, but the illusion (*gensō*) of a homogenized (*jyunichi*) American gaze that prompts such fear. In "Kyōdai na amerika-zō no kuzureta ato ni . . ." (After the Collapse of the Image of "Mighty America" . . .) Ōe writes that "Japanese people will be able to comprehend the real America for the first time only when we have been freed (*kaihō*) from the simplified, flattened (*ichimenka*) image of mighty America, if we . . . look (*mitsumeru*) at America as it actually is with new eyes (*atarashii me*)."[37] Ōe perpetually returns to this notion of an imagined homogenized America: "When we think of America and Americans . . . we think of a flat (*ichimenka*) America—America is the enemy; if an American

spots (*mitsukeru*) a Japanese person, he'll crush us to death with a tank . . .
we held a one-sided (*ichimenteki*) image of America."[38]

The Pedagogical Power of Black Literature I: The Power of Minor Literature

As the previous references to Himes and "invisible men" intimate, Ōe
contends that black literature posits possible worlds that provide alter-
natives to an illusory, homogeneous America; it is for this reason that
the literature of Baldwin and Ellison hold, for Ōe, the "greatest hint
in regard to [the solution of] not only the black problem, but all the
problems surrounding Japanese people as well."[39] In extrapolating Ōe's
interpretation of black literature, it might help us to think, as Ōe does,
of black literature as a "minor" literature in the sense suggested by Gilles
Deleuze and Félix Guattari. Minor literatures, whose language can be
"compared in another context to what blacks in America today are able
to do with the English language," are characterized by their "high coef-
ficient of deterritorialization" vis-à-vis "major" literatures.[40] Minor literatures' capacity to deracinate the (semantic, ontological, ideological,
and political) stronghold of major discourses makes minority "the revolutionary condition . . . for every literature within the heart of what is
called the great (or established) literature."[41] Given Ōe's assumption that
Japanese and African American people are analogously belittled by the illusions of power and homogeneity upheld by American racial discourse,
he turns to black literature as an "American 'minor' literature" that in-
jects "minority" with revolutionary potential; it "overthrows ontology,
gets rid of beginning, ends and origins . . . [and] a sense of fixity and
fixation."[42] Indeed, Ōe himself claims that black literature has a "destructive power" (*hakairyoku*) that "crushes the protective covering of naive
deception between white Americans and black Americans" and presents
the "truth of their intertwinement."[43]

Ōe deems black literature, the art form best equipped to free both black
and Japanese people from "the mystical power that grips [their] chest whenever [they] hear the word 'America.'"[44] "Among the black arts," Ōe writes,
"isn't the only field in which Japanese people can directly touch the spirit
and pathos of black people, can comprehend it and be moved by it without
losing the fact that they are Japanese, the black literature of Richard Wright
and Ralph Ellison?"[45] By arguing that it is only through black literature that
"I feel myself and, what's more, feel myself as a Japanese person, standing

side by side with black people and facing off against white people,"[46] Ōe places the potential solution to his analogous black and Japanese existential problems within the lines of African American prose.

In the following sections, I consider the potential solution that Ōe reads in and into authors such as Ellison, Wright, and Baldwin, three epochal figures in African American letters. It is important to note, however, that the germ of Ōe's notion of the power of minor black literature was planted by his engagement with African, rather than African American, writers. In his reports on the Asian-African Writers Conference, Ōe writes at length on his exchanges with the Cameroonian delegation. Ōe was drawn to the delegation's articulation of the writer's task, which was based on its advocacy of negritude. Ōe writes that the Cameroonian delegation's approach both served as his introduction to negritude and embodied the conference's "best discussion of politics, and, in the end, the most profound [discussion of] literature."[47] According to the Cameroonians' negritude-centered "image of the responsibility of the author," the author "is one who stands in the moment of the present while gazing steadily at the future, and thus, the author must always be the vanguard, the first line of defense against the . . . problems (*mondai*) that the people (*minshū*) consider essential (*honshitsuteki*)."[48]

Following what Sartre would call *littérature engagé*, both Ōe and the Cameroonian delegation see the writer as a kind of literary activist committed to alleviating sociopolitical ills by transforming the questions of the day into communicable narratives. In so doing, the writer crafts the channels of communication that in turn shape the avant-garde in the battle against oppressive ideologies, which is, in Ōe's case, the reductive gaze of an illusory American monolith. The writer's task, be it the black poet championing the value of negritude or the Japanese essayist assaying the illusion of monolithic American might, is a kind of discursive revolution in the face of reductive master narratives. "For me," Ōe writes in an article published some four months after the Asian-African Writers Conference in which he considers what he learned at the gathering, "the most important thing in my literature and my actual life is my intent to stir up discord in state power."[49] Following the program set by the Cameroonian delegation, Ōe goes on to suggest, "Whenever the image of a desperately brave student I saw on a newsreel . . . comes to mind, I remember that the most essential motif of my literary interest is my intent to stir up discord in state power. I realize this attempt in the form of novels and plays; I am obligated to turn it into a reality."[50]

Even with the self-styled "out of Africa" underpinnings of his conceptualization of protest literature, Ōe frequently reroutes his understanding of blackness through the United States and African American literature. Such a rerouting occurs, for example, in Ōe's assessment of negritude after his reading of Baldwin's *Another Country*. Now it is the exploration of black identity performed by the search for negritude in *Another Country*, rather than his conversations with the Cameroonian delegation, that catalyzes his vision of negritude as an embodiment of "the most fundamental (*mottomo kihonteki*) theme of literature."[51] This vacillation between engagements with African and African American embodiments of blackness is a familiar one to readers of Ōe's 1960s novels such as *Kojinteki na taiken*, *Sakebigoe*, and *Man'en gannen no futtobōru*, which swing between the intertextual activation of both African Americana and Africana. This vacillation, I argue, is strategic; the conclusion of this chapter considers the differing significance and signification of African American blackness and African blackness in *Sakebigoe*.

The Pedagogical Power of Black Literature 2: From the Homogeneity of Sartre and Mailer to the Diversity of Ellison and Baldwin

"Looking back on my student days," Ōe reminisces, "I realize now that my literary background existed on a delta surrounded by Sartre [and] Norman Mailer. . . . I was singing . . . in Sartre's voice, like a grotesque, red-cheeked puppet that belonged to a ventriloquist."[52] To be sure, Ōe's reading of Sartre and Mailer informs, among other things, his writing of Otherness and racial difference. What I would like to do here, however, is add a fourth node to Ōe's delta. Ōe's rechanneling of his writing of racial fear and existential ontology through his readings of African American literature alters his relationship with thinkers such as Sartre. The primary implication of this rechanneling is a change of allegiance in a game of racial politics; Ōe resituates himself alongside fellow "minority" (read: African American) authors in a show of transpacific racial solidarity. Our literary history of Ōe is incomplete insofar as it has yet to consider how reading the literature of Ellison and Baldwin teaches him, and opens new possibilities in his conceptualization and writing of blackness, Japaneseness, and racial difference.

As John Treat has persuasively argued, "The dark sketch of the human condition which Sartre draws prefigures the state of Hiroshima described in [*Hiroshima*] *Notes*," a collection of essays researched, written, and published concomitantly with Ōe's readings in African American literature.[53] Analogous to his mobilization of Sartre in *Hiroshima Notes*, Ōe reconfigures the template provided by Sartre to conceptualize the relationship between black and Japanese people and white Americans. Given that much of Ōe's discussion of race relations is in dialogue with Sartre's existential ontology, and that Ōe's disagreement with Sartre at a key juncture leads him to search elsewhere—namely, the work of Ellison, Baldwin, and Wright—for a solution to his existential dilemma, I briefly address the basic tenets of Sartre's existentialism as it is proposed in his *Being and Nothingness* before considering the foundation these tenets form for Sartre's and Ōe's respective philosophies of existential antiracism.

In *Being and Nothingness*, Sartre posits three kinds of being: the ontic "being-in-itself" (*etre-en-soi*) of the object world; the free being of human consciousness that must define its being for itself, hence "being-for-itself" (*etre-pour-soi*); and our being as it is gazed on by others in the world, our "being-for-others" (*etre-pour-autrui*). When "the look" of the other falls on us, Sartre suggests, we become objects defined by the Other.[54] It is "only for and by means" of "the Other's infinite freedom" that "my possibles can be limited and fixed."[55] Sartre, like Ōe, sees human exchange as inevitable—at times violent—conflict, the clashing of two freedoms trying to define themselves and the others around them. Many respond to the freedom of human being-for-itself with what Sartre calls "bad faith" (*mauvaise foi*). To be in bad faith is to live a life without, to borrow Sartre's term, authenticity; we are in bad faith when we conflate our refusal to choose with an inability to choose or, alternatively, when we essentialize either our own or the Other's being-for-itself in order to avoid the anguish of choice.

Sartre, who studied in Germany during the rise of Adolf Hitler, researched and wrote *Being and Nothingness* during the Nazi occupation of France, visited the Jim Crow South, and was the target of assassination attempts due to his role in the fall of the Fourth Republic, saw race and racism as classic examples of bad faith. Take, for example, Sartre's discussion of America's "peculiar institution" in his *Notebooks for an Ethics*. The slave owner presents himself, in bad faith, as a kind of "in-itself-for-itself" (*en-soi-pour-soi*), a being that is both conscious and the foundation of its own being. As a godlike figure, the slave owner "freezes the Other into an object" and now has a basis for the self-generation of his own subjective being.[56] Indeed, the slave owner's self-creation and justification come as the word of God.

> Noah, according to Genesis, condemned all the Blacks, the sons of Ham, to perpetual slavery. Here there is certainly an underlying bad faith. . . . When one is not yet certain about being in accord with the Bible, one says that the Black can be a slave since he *is not* Christian. . . . But since, at the same time, they [black slaves] were prevented from becoming Christians, they [slave owners] knew quite

well that Christian faith lay within their possibilities. In other words, that the Blacks are something other and more than what they are.[57]

Quoting *Being and Nothingness*, Jonathan Judaken extrapolates, "The objectification of your being, the designation of your essence by an Other, does not define who you are for-yourself."[58] The "objective conditions which structure our choices—class, race, place, the body, and the gaze of the Other" require "an interiorization and a subjectivizing" and "only have the meaning that an individual confers upon them," hence Sartre's claim that "Blacks" are "something other and more than what they are."[59]

Alongside Sartre's support of antiracism, however, came his Hegelian critique of the negritude movement and the prophecy of its demise: "This minor moment [of negritude] is not sufficient in itself. These black men who use it know this perfectly well; they know that it aims at preparing the synthesis or realization of the human being *in a raceless society*."[60] For Sartre, the path to racial good faith is homogeneous insofar as there is only one racial way of being—the synthetic, "raceless" society—that is in good faith, with race itself being both a creation and the creator of bad faith, as is the case in his slavery example. In light of the power Ōe reads into minor literature and negritude, however, it is clear that Ōe and Sartre have different visions of the power of "minor moments." For Ōe, the bad faith of race is engendered not by the notion of race itself but by the frightening imbalance of power in the economy of the racial gaze, an imbalance that evokes the fear, violence, and homogenized version of the racial Other discussed in the preceding section.

Ralph Ellison's literature, with its simultaneous positive affirmation of black identities and upheaval of American paradigms of static black identity, presents Ōe with an alternative to Sartre's "raceless society": diversity. Ōe first met Ellison in the summer of 1965 when Ellison was the final lecturer at the Kissinger International Seminar. After the lecture, Ōe and Ellison discussed their mutual support of the Ellisonian project of diversity. The exchange left a lasting mark on Ōe. In "Fukashi ningen to tayōsei" (Invisible Men and Diversity), Ōe follows an account of this meeting with Ellison by quoting the following excerpt from *Invisible Man.*

Whence all this passion toward conformity anyway?—Diversity is the word. Let man keep his many parts and you'll have no tyrant states. Why, if they follow this conformity business they'll end up by forcing me, an invisible man, to become white, which is not a color but the lack of one. Must I strive toward colorlessness? But seriously, and without snobbery, think of what the world would lose if that should happen. America is woven of many strands; I would recognize them and let it so remain.[61]

It is important to note that Ellisonian diversity, as well as Ōe's translation of it, is not synonymous with our contemporary use of the term—the two diversities have different resonances. Contemporary diversity is a call for (more often than not, institutional and statistical) equitable representation. As such, its antonym is along the lines of *homogeneity, tokenism,* or *disproportionate representation.* Ellisonian diversity, however, is more of a philosophical call for us to recognize an unspoken truth of American life: that one can be both fully black and fully American (and, for that matter, fully human) and that the true measure of the success or failure of the American project is whether or not we can make one out of the many while respecting the dignity of the one. It is a call, in other words, to recognize the existential validity of blackness given the historical American denial of its validity. Its antonym, then, is closer to *antimiscegeny, separate but equal,* or *black social death.* This is the sense of diversity Ellison has in mind when advocates in "What America Would Be Like without Blacks" for "an expression of American diversity within unity, of blackness with whiteness . . . [and] the presence of a creative struggle against the realities of existence."[62]

Following Ellison, Ōe, too, contends that diversity (*tayōsei*) is an answer to the fear and violence that comes with the denial of racial existences, in the plural. Keep in mind that Ōe presents the illusion of America as a monolithic source of power as the cause of Japanese Ameriphobia. Ōe mobilizes a matrix of terms to articulate and highlight the notion of the "monolithic": *ichimenka* (which I have translated as "flattened" or "one-sided"), *tanitsuka* (simplified or unified), *ichiyōka* (homogenized), and so on. The common denominators of these terms are readily apparent to speakers of Japanese. First, each includes the character that denotes singularity, "一" (read: in the previous terms as either *ichi* or *itsu*). In addition to this, all three end with -*ka* (化), a suffix similar to the English -*ization* that denotes the process of transformation. As such Ōe's "America" as an instigator of racial fear takes multifaceted racial identities and reductively transforms them (in addition to its suffixal duty, the character for *ka* also appears in the verb *bakeru,* "to transfigure," "appear in disguise," or "corrupt") into something monolithic and thereby "flattened," "simplified," "homogenized," and so on.

Although Ōe at times uses the English term *diversity,* his Japanese translation of the term, *tayōsei,* is telling; the prefix *ta-,* semantically in the vicinity of the English *poly-,* stands in direct protest of the monolithic treatment of Others implied by the *ichi-* of *ichimenka, ichiyōka,* and so on. Ōe's advocacy of "diversity" suggests that renewing a Japanese-American dialogue not doomed to repeat the violence and fear of the countries' shared past must be predicated on seeing each other as they truly are: diverse.

> Ralph Ellison tells us in that postwar novel [*Invisible Man*] that in order for America to survive from now on Americans will have to live with the diversity of Americans, the diversity that each human has, the diversity of white people, the diversity of black people. And isn't *this* the aspiration of America? I, too, think that diversity is the issue. . . . From now on us Japanese people, too, will have to acknowledge the diversity of the entire world, including America . . . and at the same time the diversity of Japanese people. It is from here that we must think about our future and our relationship with America. It seems that it is only when we do this that independence will become a possibility for Japanese people.[63]

Ōe will return again and again to "diversity" as a method of easing the psychological burden, the melancholy, of moving under such weight; it is Ōe's "hope that we . . . [will] use our imaginative power, and see [individuals] not as invisible men, but that we train our eyes (*me*) and see them as they *should be seen* (*miru beku*): as real people with diversity. This will be our safeguard from becoming 'invisible men.'"[64] To borrow Ichijō Takao's summation, we can "note the fact that Ōe was influenced by Ellison, that Ōe paid attention to their contemporaneous issue of diversity, and that Ōe took up [Ellison's project of diversity] as his central literary thesis."[65]

Ōe's summer trip to Los Angeles, which took place some five weeks after the Watts riots of 1965, solidified his commitment to the "project of diversity." Media coverage of the riots ensured that the spectacle of black violence was on full display. Viewing the coverage, Ōe wondered if the "all too vivid faces of individual rioters being displayed (*utsusu*) on television and in newspapers, magazines, and especially *Life* magazine will impede the civic life of Watts, which has now returned to normal."[66] After actually speaking with members of the Watts community, however, Ōe realized that the attention of national media outlets would not "impede" (*shishō*) life in Watts because such outlets don't see or show Watts. For Ōe, it is precisely in moments of spectacle that the actual people of Watts become invisible. "The cameraman of *Life* magazine who reports the violence (*bōkō*) of Watts in colorful pictures," Ōe contends, "saw the image of violence associated with people participating in the riots, which means he actually saw the conglomeration of fear (*kyōfushin*), but he did not see (*miru*) the actual individual faces of these 'invisible men,' black people."[67] Ōe clarifies this seeing that does not see as follows: "In other words, the white cameraman and the thousands of thousands of reader's eyes (*dokusha no me*) behind him . . . only viewed (*utsusu*) black people as they are seen in the minds of white people—that is, as a kind of graphic exposition of fear (*kyōfushin*), and fear here equals violence—and not their [the black people of Watts's] individual faces."[68]

Although Ōe initially posits that the gazing eyes of *Life* will not "impede" the rebuilding of Watts, he quickly shifts to a discussion of the way *Life* has not seen Watts at all. In so doing, *Life* sees, to borrow Ōe's articulation, "*nothing* but invisible men." Another way of putting this is to say that Ōe is a good reader of Ellison. *Invisible Man* begins with the narrator recounting his decision to end an altercation with a "tall blond man" on realizing that "the man had not *seen* me, actually."[69] This is followed by the battle royal scene, in which being blindfolded, a kind of pseudo invisibility, does little to stave off the narrator's fear of the gazing spectators; indeed, he "stood against the ropes trembling."[70] It is not until he begins to see through his blindness that his fear abates: "Everyone fought hysterically. It was complete anarchy. Everybody fought everybody else. No group fought together for long . . . [but] *with my eye partly opened now there was not so much terror.*"[71] Ōe's close reading of Ellison left an indelible and profound mark on him, one that catalyzed a divergence between Ōe and Sartre. I return to this divergence momentarily.

Concomitant with his rerouting of racial fear and existential ontology through Ellison, Ōe reroutes his notion of sexualized racial identities from a path that traverses Mailer to one through James Baldwin. Mailer and Baldwin went several rounds on the topics of black masculinity and sexuality from the late 1950s to the early 1960s. Although Mailer was and would remain one of the nodes of Ōe's "delta," Ōe sides with Baldwin throughout the debate. Keeping in mind Ōe's commentary on the March 1961 Asian-African Writers Conference, his advocacy of Baldwin followed his introduction to the negritude movement. The two events—Ōe's advocacy of Baldwin and his introduction to negritude—synergize. It is Ōe's understanding of the importance of negritude that ignites his support for Baldwin, and, reciprocally, it is through siding with Baldwin that Ōe expresses his support of negritude, which he understands to be the positive affirmation of black identity via literature.

Mailer's 1959 *Advertisements for Myself* included at least two essays that would have caught Baldwin's eye. In the first, "The White Negro," Mailer delineates the birth, life, and death of "white Negroes," American existentialist hipsters. Here there is a bit of Sartre and Ōe in Mailer, as each member of the trio provides an interpretation of black American being through the language of Sartrean existentialism and an explication of the significance of black existentialism to nonblack folks. In the face of a "human nature" that has culminated in world wars, the Holocaust, mutually assured destruction, and witch hunts, Mailer's "white Negroes" (read: American hipsters) realize that "the only life-giving answer is to accept the terms of death . . . [and] set out on that uncharted journey into the rebellious imperatives of the self. In short, whether the life is criminal or not, the decision is to encourage the psychopath in oneself."[72] Freed from the conformist values of (white) American society, hipsters turn to "Negro" values, culture, and language as a beacon in the search for the psychopath within. The template provided by the Negro, within whom "it is . . . no accident that psychopathy is most prevalent," has two pillars: violence ("the psychopath murders . . . out of the necessity to purge his violence, for if he cannot empty his hatred then he cannot love") and love ("not love as the search for a mate, but love as the search for an orgasm more apocalyptic than the one which preceded it. Orgasm is his therapy").[73] By "absorb[ing] the existentialist synapses of the Negro," white Negroes are able to live in good faith.

In addition to Mailer's image of "the Negro" as a hypersexualized, violent model of psychopathy, Baldwin also took umbrage with another piece *in Advertisements for Myself*, "Evaluations: Quick and Expensive Comments on the Talent in the Room." Mailer assesses Baldwin as "too charming a writer to be major" and "incapable of saying 'Fuck you' to the reader."[74] "Even the best of his [Baldwin's] paragraphs are sprayed with perfume," and his works amount to "noble toilet water."[75] It is important to note that Mailer's adulation of the hip Negro as the white Negro's heteronormative ideal of virility and violence is related to his critique of Baldwin as a "minor" writer. In "The White Negro: Superficial Reflections on the Hipster," Mailer notes that "of course one can hardly afford to be put down too often, or one is beat, one has lost one's confidence . . . one is impotent in the world of action and so closer to the demeaning flip of becoming a queer."[76] Following his put-down of Baldwin's "perfumed" prose in "Evaluations," Mailer offers the following apologia: "I have a terrible confession to make—I have nothing to say about any of the talented women who write today. . . . I do not seem able to read them. . . . Indeed I doubt if there will be a really exciting woman writer until the first whore becomes a call girl and tells her tale."[77] Baldwin, who is "impotent" and all too close to the "demeaning flip of becoming a queer," becomes in turn a minor writer only one step removed from the women writers elided in Mailer's "Evaluations."

Baldwin's response to Mailer's critique of his queer lack of virility and venom was staged twice, once in "The Black Boy Looks at the White Boy Norman Mailer" and once in *Another Country*. For our purposes, *Another Country* is of particular import. As the subtitle of "The White Negro"— "Superficial Reflections on the Hipster"—suggests, Mailer's borrowing of Sartrean existentialism is piecemeal. His freezing of black masculine (hyper) sexuality, essentialization of the valor of heteronormative sexual conquest over homosexual relations, and unidirectional appropriation of black sexual vigor in order to cure the existential strife of whites only can be described in Sartrean terms as a sadistic attempt to create a white in-itself-for-itself. *Another Country* is a two-pronged rebuke of Mailer's sadism, a search for an alternate realm in which love goes beyond the black-to-white heterosexual search for the next apocalyptic orgasm.

Rather than the static heteronormativity and effaced homosociality of the world of "The White Negro," *Another Country* provides a diverse network of homo-, hetero-, and bisexual relationships. Rufus Scott, a black jazz drummer and the central node in the network, commits suicide in the first fifth of the novel. With his death, the possibility of "absorbing" the "existentialist synapses of the Negro" through heteronormative emulation of his violence and hypersexuality is nullified. Vivaldo, a working-class man of Irish Italian descent and a friend of Rufus, begins to empathize with and understand Rufus posthumously via a relationship with Eric, a former lover of Rufus. With this Baldwin effectively turns the interracial, heteronormative sadism of Mailer on its head. If Mailer's estimation is that "to submit to another man—as Vivaldo does—is to be 'put down,' it enervates the hipster, sapping him of his heterosexual vigor and transforming him into a 'queer,'" then "In *Another Country* . . . Baldwin reframes this dynamic asserting that far from being debilitating, sexual submission produces the affective transformations and embodied identifications that Mailer is after in 'The White Negro.'"[78]

Ōe published commentary on *Another Country* throughout the early 1960s, his comments always lauding the transformative impact both the novel and Baldwin had on his own writing. Comments such as "I really love *Another Country*. I would keep this book by my side and try to think about my own problems" are indicative of Ōe's approval.[79] Mailer, however, was not as fond of *Another Country*. He deemed it "abominably written" and Baldwin an author who would never become a major figure in African American letters.[80] Mailer's disapproval of *Another Country* presents a significant dilemma for Ōe, effectively forcing him to choose between the novel that has inspired him and one of the authors he considered to be a part of the "delta" on which he built his authorial foundation.

Ōe went with Baldwin. He wrote *Sakebigoe* (The Cry) as he read *Another*

Country, and his satisfaction with *The Cry* was due to the fact that he surrounded its protagonist with an ethnically diverse cast of sympathetic semi-protagonists, "a new plan that I [Ōe] was taught by Baldwin" via *Another Country*.[81] Insofar as *The Cry* is informed by Baldwin's *Another Country*, Ōe contends, "I must admit that *The Cry* has a weakness akin to those Mailer pointed out in *Another Country*."[82] Although Ōe's essays don't comment specifically on the homophobia underlying Mailer's critique of Baldwin's "weakness," he aligns himself with Baldwin nevertheless, and the homosocial/sexual underpinnings of *The Cry* speak to this alignment. While conceding that following the teachings of Mailer "might have made *The Cry* a better novel," Ōe "places an extremely deep, even what can be called a personal trust, in Baldwin."[83] This trust is rooted in part in Ōe's investment in the negritude project of transnational racial solidarity. When Ōe writes, "Of course, I will never have an opportunity to sit at the same table with the kind of Americans whom Mailer writes about," he is alluding to the possibility of a black-Japanese imagined community where he *can* pull up a chair, hence his description of being "drawn in (*hikareteru*)" by the affirmative expression of negritude performed by black artists, "the first among them being James Baldwin."[84]

With this in mind, let's reconsider that divergence between Ōe and Sartre. To be clear, I am not arguing that Ōe's reading of Ellison is some kind of direct, purposeful rejection of Sartre. There is, however, an affinity—Ōe's illusory homogeny and Sartre's bad faith, and this affinity is followed by a divergence—Sartre's reading of negritude as aiming for a "raceless" society versus Ōe's Baldwinian interpretation of negritude, support of Ellisonian diversity, and "recognition" of race and desire to let it remain as it is. Ōe and Sartre have differing interpretations of "minor" moments. For Sartre negritude is to be synthesized. For Ōe, the bad faith of race is engendered not by the notion of race itself but by the frightening imbalance of power in the economy of the racial gaze, an imbalance that evokes fear, violence, and a homogenized vision of our racial Others. Ōe's divergence from Sartre stems in part from his concern with opening a space in which good faith and racialized, minoritarian identity can coexist. Ellisonian diversity as Ōe interprets it allows us to be our racial selves without sadistic—here in the Sartrean sense—appropriation of our racial Others.

After reading *Invisible Man* and *Another Country*, meeting with Ellison, and traveling to major metropolitan cultural hubs of black America, Ōe resets the origins of his creative nonfiction of race relations. The terms that were originally informed by Sartre's existentialism—or Ōe's existential antiracism—are now filtered through *Invisible Man*. This new beginning is indicative of both Ōe's valuation of Ellison and his desire to supplement the narrative of existential antiracism with Ellisonian diversity; Ōe suggests that the beginning and the end of racial bad faith can be read in *Invisible Man*. Allow me to translate at length an excerpt from Ōe's 1968 "On America," a speech given after Ōe's encounter with Ellison. This excerpt presents Ōe's narrative of race relations as it is channeled through *Invisible Man*.

> How is this type of Japanese person, the kind that has lived under the image of a unilaterally (*ichimenteki*) mighty America, going to fill in their psychological cavities (*anaboko*)? . . . I consider the words of Ralph Ellison, the black author (*kokujin no sakka*) . . . to be a remarkably clear hint. At the end of *Invisible Man*, Ellison provides us with a suggestion. The black youth who is the protagonist of the novel . . . secludes himself in a manhole all his own and tries to think about what America is. The impetus [for his meditation] is the Harlem riots. . . . During the riots, one crazed movement leader rides in on a steed while brandishing a spear. . . . The other black people [here Ōe is signaling the diegetic level of *Invisible Man*] who see this find it funny. . . . This kind of black violence, however, is not actually funny. When viewed through the all too sober eyes of black people (*kokujin no me*), they [this time the readers of *Invisible Man*], too, don't deem it simple comedy. It is something miserable, something dangerous. The youth determines that we must try to think of a way to rescue ourselves from this kind of comedy, from all this danger and misery. The youth concludes that Americans have to be rescued from homogenization (*ichiyōka*) and simplification (*tanitsuka*). . . . Homogenization (*ichiyōka*) . . . poisons Americans, and it is precisely diversity (*tayōsei*)—Ellison uses the word *diversity*—that we must protect, [so] we must preserve the varying attributes of humans. . . . If we protect diversity, tyrant states won't be born. . . . This is what Ellison says in his novel, which was published right after the war ended. I, too, think that diversity (*tayōsei*) is the central issue. . . . Japanese people must learn to recognize the diversity of America and the entire world.[85]

In this 1968 speech, the terms and themes we have traced from Sartre's *Being and Nothingness* are all filtered through *Invisible Man*. First, Ōe establishes his black-Japanese analogue by punning on the term *anaboko*. Ellison's *Invisible Man* begins (and ends) with the narrator "holed up," living underground. Ōe uses the same term—*anaboko*—to describe both the narrator's underground hideout and the pitfall in the postwar Japanese psyche. I have translated *anaboko* as "cavity" to reproduce the pivot of this pun; for Ōe, *anaboko* speaks to both the denotative, physical depression and the connotative, psychic depression of living underground. Next there are undertones of Sartre as Ōe attempts to overcome this cavity; the reverberations of Sartre are clear in Ōe's search for an exit from what he calls our dangerous comedy. Now, however, Ōe's exit traverses Ellison's *Invisible Man*. By citing the narrator's musing from the manhole, "Let man keep his many parts and you'll have no tyrant states," Ōe finds the "protection of diversity" to be a "remarkably clear hint" to the answer to Sartre's call for good faith.

Ōe's black-Japanese analogy is undeniably productive. Before turning to the conclusion—which provides a preliminary consideration of Ōe's translation of his creative nonfiction into fictional form—however, it is important to note one of the pernicious by-products of Ōe's analogical thinking because this by-product resides in both Ōe's nonfictional and fictional writing of blackness. For all their explanatory and sociopolitical potential energy, analogies, by definition, tell only how "X" is *like* "Y." The very grammar of the political analogy, as Janet Jakobsen reminds us, "reduces the relationship between various 'oppressions' to their similarities," which often submerges the historical "specificity of each experience" in "a generalized sense of oppression in which all oppressions are (generally) like each other."[86] To be sure, there is a genuine affinity between Ōe, who lived through the American-led Allied Occupation of Japan, and the black characters he encounters throughout the 1960s. It is also true, however, that Ōe's analogical thinking leaves little room for a discussion of how the singular historical baggage and contemporary trauma of the postwar Japanese *is not and can never be "like"* that of its singular African and African American counterparts. In his analogical rewriting of postwar Japanese identity, Ōe submerges the vexed, complex, historical specificity of the postwar Japanese in the similarity of a shared, transracial "oppression." Although Ōe's is no more or less of a false analogy than any analogy, it runs the risk of both historical amnesia and, particularly in his "black fiction," substituting questionable analogic logic for hermeneutic logic, a point to which I return momentarily.

In Lieu of a Conclusion: *Sakebigoe* between the *Authentique* and the Authentic

In lieu of a conclusion proper, I would like to consider *Sakebigoe* (The Cry), the story of a Zainichi Korean youth named Kure Takao and his obsession with the possibility of a life of Sartrean good faith for social minorities, as a text that translates the nonfictional narrative created by Ōe into fictional form. The vocabulary that anchors Ōe's creative nonfiction (fear, violence, gaze, cavity, depression, and so on) is literally and figuratively rewritten in *The Cry*. This analysis of *The Cry* functions in lieu of a conclusion insofar as the fictional text itself recapitulates Ōe's nonfictional commentary on the dialectics of the racial gaze and exhibits the pedagogical power of black literature. In fictional form, Ōe's studies of black literature informs *The Cry* in at least three ways: a shift from narratives focalized by Japanese boys to narratives focalized by ethnic, Baldwinian "semiprotagonists"; a shift from serpentine interior monologues to dialogues between those semiprotagonists; and a reconfiguration of the nodes of Ōe's intertextual network. In other words, Ōe's dialogue, characterization, and plots are now informed by his readings of black literature, culture, and history. He has significant stylistic debts to black writing.

As an aside, it is important to note that Ōe's 1960 novella *Kodoku na seinen no kyūka* (The Holiday of a Lonely Youth) is also a viable candidate for the kind of reading I propose for *The Cry*. After a near death experience, the eponymous youth of *Kodoku na seinen no kyūka* realizes that he is an invisible man. The young man claims, "There's a black author by the name of Ralph Ellison, and he wrote a novel about a young black boy. The novel begins with the line 'I am an invisible man.' There was something familiar and nostalgic about that oppressed, nameless rebel."[87] In light of the affinities of this work of fiction and the nonfiction discussed above, I provide a close reading of *The Cry* rather than *Kodoku na seinen no kyūka* with two things in mind. First, I am thinking of the excellent reading of *Kodoku na seinen no kyūka* and its relationship to African American literature provided by Ichijō Takao and the absence of a complementary reading for *The Cry*.[88] Second, the 1960 *Kodoku na seinen no kyūka* precedes Ōe's encounter with Baldwin's *Another Country*. A reading of *The Cry* facilitates a fuller understanding of Ōe's translation of his creative nonfiction of blackness into fiction and his engagement with Baldwin, and *The Cry* is particularly revelatory with regard to the results of Ōe's self-proclaimed experimentation with Baldwinian semiprotagonists.

The Cry begins just as Ōe's nonfiction writing of blackness does: with fear. The opening line of *The Cry* reads, "According to the pensées of a French philosopher who lived in an age of fear, in times of terror, when all humans are longing for a long overdue salvation, everyone who hears the distant cry of someone hoping for salvation loses faith in their hearing, wondering if the crying isn't their own."[89] Here Ōe's analogy goes sonic. The fearful cry of *Sakebigoe* is shared among three young men: a Japanese narrator; the Zainichi Korean Kure Takao; and half-black, half-Japanese Tora. All three live with their American benefactor, Darius. Reminiscent of the argument made in Ōe's 1960s nonfiction, *The Cry* presents the three young men, particularly Takao and Tora, as analogous figures who live in fear of the racial gaze. Both Takao and Tora are under the watch of "gigantic green eyes . . . that peer into them. . . . These are the eyes of the outside world."[90] Here the gaze is racialized by way of eye color; the gazer is, the reader assumes, white, and both Kure and Tora are phenotypically analogous and have brown eyes. As in his nonfiction, here, too, the "age of fear" is catalyzed by life under such racialized disciplinary gazes.

Ōe's nonfiction proposes that, given their analogous existential condition, Japanese authors and readers have much to learn from their African American counterparts. What I have called the pedagogical power of black literature manifests itself on both the textual and intertexual levels of *The Cry*. Textually, the amalgamation of black and Japanese literature in *The Cry* is embodied by its characterization of one of its semiprotagonists, Tora. He "was the mixed-blood (*konketsu*) child of an American Negro father and an immigrant mother of Japanese descent. He saw himself as a morass of black blood (*kokujin no chi*) and yellow blood (*ōshokujin no chi*) and called himself a racial 'tiger' (*tora*). . . . [He formerly] went by Tiger (*taigā*) . . . [and] we called him Tiger (*tora*)."[91] In this passage, the narrative completes the interpretive work for the reader, thereby ensuring that the notion of black-Japanese hybridization embodied by the moniker Tiger is clear. Moreover, Tora's name, Tiger, is presented as a signifier in motion. It begins in a neutral position bracketed by quotation marks, moves to the Japanese phonic approximation of the English *tiger* (the katakana *taigā*), and settles on the kanji (虎), thereby bestowing a Japanese name on Tora. Tora's entry into the Japanese linguistic system of signs reinforces the aforementioned racial hybridization with orthographic hybridization. Such mixings—of race and writing codes—both adumbrate the modus operandi of *The Cry* and are reminiscent of Ōe's nonfictional writing of blackness. Here Ōe's project of writing literary blackness in Japanese is less concerned with representation and more interested in cross-cultural analogy and confluence.

Takao, like Tora, "wants to go to Africa, . . . wants to go somewhere else"[92] to free himself from the cavity—here, too, Ōe uses the word *anaboko*, engendered by the frightful power of the racial gaze. Before he can make his escape, however, fear in *The Cry* culminates precisely as Ōe's nonfiction portends: in violence. Tora is shot and killed by two military police who cannot determine whether or not he is a "Negro." In death, Tora provides Takao with a path for escape. Takao imagines that "the blood that spills from Tora's body is carried away by the angels of the African jungle back to a heaven for black people. . . . Tora finally returned home to Africa."[93] After Tora's death, Takao "realizes that, if he . . . doesn't have an adventure so grand that it puts his own life in danger, then he will never be free, never feel the relief of living in a land that is all his own."[94]

It is at this juncture that the intertextual blackness of *The Cry* shines through. It does so, moreover, in a way that recalls two aspects of Ōe's creative nonfiction: the schism between African and African American blackness and the danger inherent in analogical thinking. To begin with the former, if, to return to Sterling's observation, the fluidity of blackness facilitates a range of ideological agendas, then Ōe has at least two agendas as he mobilizes blackness. For Ōe blackness signifies both the possibility of full membership in a transnational community and the possibility of protest against what he calls the illusion of monolithic American might. In *The Cry*, Ōe has delegated these two possibilities to different embodiments of blackness. Africa is, much like the continent itself, a capacious and multivalent signifier for Ōe.[95] One valence of Africa's significance, however, is its synonymity with an escape to a transnational, transracial homeland (think here of Bird in *Kojinteki na taiken*, who dreams of escape to Africa under a map of Africa, or of Majima Ichirō's assessment: "In his early endeavors in particular, from the late 1950s through the 1960s, Ōe's characters speak . . . of a longing for the African Continent, and Ōe himself . . . gazed at the Continent from afar as the terminus of a solidarity that goes beyond national borders."[96]) Pace his escapist view of Africa, African American literature becomes Ōe's source for blackness as protest, for what Amiri Baraka once called "poems that kill."[97] (Think here of the memories of black lynching that run alongside the rebellion narrative of *Man'en gannen no futtobōru*.)

With this we can begin to make sense of the climax of *The Cry*. As he searches for the "grand adventure" that will facilitate a return to his "Africa," Kure Takao turns (in)to Bigger; Ōe has written that his decision to thematize the existential crisis of a social minority, as well as the ethically and politically fraught murder that serves as the apex of Kure's crisis, is "ultimately rooted in Richard Wright, and that the novel's 'color' (*irodori*) has traces of" Wright's *Native Son*.[98] And here is the recrudescence of the danger of analogic: Kure Takao's murder of an innocent Japanese girl is supposedly analogous to or is "like" Bigger's murders of Mary and Bessie. What *The Cry* does not—and indeed cannot—address by way of its analogic is how Kure Takao's intentional murder is unlike the chain reaction of Bigger's accidental murder of Mary and subsequent intentional murder of Bessie. Nor will analogical thinking allow a questioning of the ethical, historical, and

Figure 1. Ōe Kenzaburō circa 1964, when he was writing *A Personal Matter*, holding a copy of *Stanford's General Map of Africa*. Note Ōe's skewed gaze, which asks readers to make eye contact with the cartography of Africa rather than the Japanese author who holds the map. (Reprinted with permission from Shinchōsha.)

postcolonial dilemma of Ōe, a Japanese author, writing of the victimization of an innocent Japanese person at the hands of a murderous Zainichi Korean. This line of questioning is effaced in an analogical analysis of how Ōe is "like" Wright and how Kure Takao—who "wasn't raised as Korean, wasn't raised as Japanese, wasn't raised as anything, so at least he wanted to become a killer"—is "like" Bigger.[99]

After positing a Sartrean existential analogue between black Americans and Japanese people, Ōe's nonfictional account of black/Japanese-white race relations diverges from Sartre's vision of a "raceless society" and turns to black literature in search of a solution to the shared existential dilemma of postwar African Americans and the Japanese. In *The Cry*, this divergence occurs at the juncture of Sartre's notion of the *authentique* and Baldwin's notion of the authentic. Sartre suggests that it is only by way of a raceless society that racial minorities can live *authentique*, good-faith lives. Ōe, however, "places an extremely deep . . . personal trust, in Baldwin" and his *Another Country*, and he wrote *The Cry* as he read it.[100] In *Another Country*, Baldwin "attempts to forge [an] . . . *authentic existence* in the United States" for black people by interrogating "the cultural landscape that defames, debases, and . . . destroys black . . . life, productivity, and genius."[101]

After the death of Tora, Takao's attempt to "avenge" his friend is also an attempt to forge an identity that is both *authentique*—that is, of Sartrean good faith—and authentic, that is, full of the complexity that Baldwin's *Another Country* attributes to human identity and not homogenized by racial or racist ideology.[102] Kure Takao articulates the intersection of the *authentique* and the authentic as follows.

> *Authentique*: authentic, right, certain, unmistakable, real, unmistakably of a certain land." Kure Takao wrote this in the notebook that contained his philosophical treatise and would sometimes invoke the French *authentique* [written in French in the Japanese original] as he pursued his feverish sickness. *L'homme authentique*, according to Kure, is one who lives in the real world with a firm grasp on his civil rights (*shiminken*). The authentic, the people of a country, the real people of a country, the people who are unmistakably of that land. I don't know why, but I know that he was not an *authentique* human and that this was the fundamental source of his anxious, thirsty, febrile disease.[103]

I agree with Michiko Wilson that Kure Takao is an "existentialist hero," that the murder he commits is both an exercise in existential freedom and a desperate bid to "secure the authentic life," and that his existential dilemma is rooted in the fact that he "had not been able to . . . live with authenticity in this world [from] the time his mother forced him to live as the fake Japanese Kure Takao, instead of the Korean Ochan," his Korean name.[104] I would add to Wilson's insights only the fact that the "authenticity" of *The Cry* has a second valence that is related to but not synonymous with the *authentique*: "authenticity" as a call to recognize the diversity and complexity of racial being and ensure that such being is not scathed by the reductive ideologies of racial oppression. This second valence is signaled in the previous passage by Ōe's references to Kure's desire for "civil rights" (*shiminken*) and the existential violence caused by a maternally imposed *sōshi kaimei*.[105] Ōe's "existentialist hero" looks less like those of Sartre's *Being and Nothingness* than like those of Sartre's *Notebooks for an Ethics*. For Ōe, existential freedom resides just beyond its ontological, sociopolitical, and racial limits; it is no coincidence that the story of Kure Takao, like that of Wright's Bigger Thomas, ends with our existentialist hero incarcerated and awaiting capital punishment.

In *Writing Selves in Diaspora: Ethnography of Autobiographies of Korean Women in Japan and the United States*, Sonia Ryang proposes two models of diaspora: the politico-classical and the personal-modern. The politico-classical model, exemplified by the Jewish and Armenian diasporas, is "premised on ethnic persecution as the cause of eternal dispersal and the loss of homeland."[106] This model typically includes a response to the trauma of losing one's homeland by way of collective action: the formation of collective memory, the writing of communal myths, a diasporic desire for homecoming, and so on. The second model, personal-modern, "is concerned with ontological insecurity and an ongoing crisis of identity, generally associated with modernity and the consequent rise of the reflexive self, but . . . more specifically related to the loss of the original homeland or home (real or imaginary)."[107] If the first model centers on collective traumata and their treatment, the second is more concerned with the solitary subject's struggle to find him- or herself when there is no way back home—think here, for example, of the "ontological insecurity" and "ongoing crisis of identity" of third-culture individuals. Although the polarity of these two models has a certain clarifying explanatory force, the reality of diasporas is usually somewhere between the politico-classical model and the personal-modern one. This is indeed the case, Ryang contends, for the Korean diaspora in Japan. The history of the modern creation of the Korean diaspora is such that even the conceptualization of a "Korean diaspora" is homeless and liminal, somewhere between the classical model and the modern.[108]

Ryang proposes an ethnography of autobiographical diasporic writing because, among other reasons, of the way in which autobiographical writing can function as a personal attempt to document the lived experience of diaspora. Autobiographical writing tries to provide a lasting, graphic testament to the otherwise liminal, sporadic qualities of diasporic life. Given the malleability of autobiographical writing—which always includes the possibility of writing and rewriting and therefore of "generat[ing], reconfigur[ing], and sometimes re-creat[ing]" the diasporic self—this genre is well equipped to, in the words of Ryang, "reveal [the] multiple authenticities" of diasporic storytellers.[109]

Although Ōe's writing of Kure's autobiography is decidedly fictional, this fiction records the "multiple authenticities" required to reestablish a sense of self in the face of the collective trauma of that first model and the ontological insecurity of the second. I have argued here that Ōe's second sense of authenticity, which combats Kure's ontological insecurity, becomes illegible without an intertextual reading of Ōe's creative nonfiction of blackness. Insofar as that second valence of authenticity is informed by Ōe's reading of Baldwin, Ellison, and Wright, *The Cry* enacts the program delineated in his nonfiction: a turning from the Sartrean dilemma of race to the pedagogical power of black literature. *The Cry* translates the same two movements— the dialects of the gaze and the revolutionary power of black literature as a minor literature—the same attending terminology (fear, the gaze, violence, authenticity, and so on), and the same positing of the pedagogical relevance and analogical applicability of black literature posited in Ōe's 1960s essays on the dialectics of the racial gaze into fictional form. Ōe's repetition of these two movements across literary genres exemplifies both his rich engagement with black literature and culture during the 1960s and the "great stimulus" black literature provided in relation to Ōe's creation of black characters and fiction.[110] This foundational moment in 1960s Afro-Japanese literary exchange, however, becomes more rather than less visible if we focus solely on Ōe's late-1950s fictional representations of blackness. In the 1960s, Ōe turned to writing a creative nonfiction of the existential analogy between postwar Japan and civil rights era black America, and this creative nonfiction situates its representations of black-Japanese affinity within a world of "nonrepresentational" affirmations (e.g., Ōe receiving intertextual tutoring from Baldwin rather than Mailer).

Chapter 3 turns to Nakagami Kenji's repetition and revision of the foundation laid by Ōe.

CHAPTER 3

Of Passing Significance

Pronominal Politics, Nakagami Kenji, and the
Fiction of Burakuness

Japanese people will be able to comprehend the real America for the
first time only when we have been freed from the simplified, flattened
image of mighty America, if we . . . look at America as it actually is
with new eyes.

—Ōe Kenzaburō, "Kyōdai na amerika-zō no kuzureta ato ni . . ."

For many Japanese people, the immediate postwar period was
certainly the first time they saw the real America . . . with their own
eyes. . . . As of late, it seems that we've finally come to the realization
that an "American" is not just white Jack and white Betty but also
black Tom and Indian Sue and Mexicans and Puerto Ricans and
Easterners too . . . the America of racial amalgamation . . . the real
America.

—Nakagami Kenji, "Amerika no hontō no koe."

Nakagami Kenji's (1946–92) rendition of "The Real Voice of America"
("Amerika no hontō no koe") shares an undeniable resonance with Ōe's
styling of America. Nakagami repeats many of the tropes—a "real" racially
diverse America over and against the illusory image of America held by the
wartime Japanese, the visible verifiability of American diversity with "one's
own eyes," and so on—established by Ōe. Even in the midst of such repetition, however, Nakagami includes moments of revision of Ōe's scheme.
Nakagami's verification of American diversity, for example, includes the audible (the "real voice") as well as the visible. And, whereas Ōe seems quite

comfortable and justified speaking as a representative of some Japanese "we," Nakagami first deploys the proper noun Nihonjin (Japanese people) and subsequently replaces it with the subject pronoun "we" (*wareware*), the very pronoun with which Ōe begins. Nakagami—an author who self-identified as a member of the *burakumin*, Japan's largest social minority—creates a schism between the proper nominalization of Japanese people and his own pronominal inclusion in the Japanese "we." In short, as Nakagami repeats the lexicon of Ōe, he also revises that very lexicon, first by separating the Japanese from the "we" that Ōe presupposes comfortably and justifiably, then by infusing a bevy of other proper nouns (e.g., Puerto Rican and Mexican) in the space between the Japanese and the "we," and, finally, by redeploying the "we" after the bevy such that we can no longer assume—comfortably or justifiably—who belongs in it.

Nakagami's discursive relationship with both Ōe and American race relations is of passing significance. By "passing significance," I mean two things. I mean this first with an eye turned toward the African American literary tropes and techniques that serve as a foundation for Nakagami's literary project. In a 1977 roundtable discussion, Nakagami interjected, seemingly apropos of nothing, "There's a literary term called 'passing.'"[1] Trudier Harris defines passing as "the act of moving *permanently* [keep this emphasis in mind as I return to it momentarily] from identification with blacks to identification with whites. . . . In the displays of power designed to keep black people 'in their place,' passing enabled them to subvert that power base and assume their own authority in naming and access."[2] Such movement is apropos of everything for Nakagami; passing, not to mention assumptions of one's own authority in naming and access, are maneuvers of profound significance.

As with passing, "significance" here takes on a valence informed by African American literature. "Writers Signify," Henry Louis Gates proposes, "upon each other's texts by rewriting the received textual tradition."[3] Signifyin(g) texts—with the dropped *g* noted here by way of parentheses, as Gates does, rather than with an apostrophe—are "written in the language of the tradition, employing its tropes, its rhetorical strategies, and its ostensible subject matter" and thus situate themselves in relation to literary traditions by way of repetition. Insofar as this repetition works, however, to create and assert the signifyin(g) writer's singular authorial voice by way of revision of the past—as, for example, in Nakagami's "The Real Voice," signifyin(g) texts repeat in the hope of breaking the template set by the iterations by which they are preceded. This is why Gates summarizes signifyin(g) as repetition with a signal difference.

"Passing significance," then, gestures first toward Nakagami's signifyin(g)—a term I want to revisit and introduce to Nakagami studies—on the "received tradition[s] from both African American and *buraku* writings."⁴ Through signifyin(g), Anne McKnight continues, Nakagami explores *burakumin* "identities through solidarities with minoritarian writers outside of Japan . . . as models for text-world relations unavailable in Japan."⁵ The possibility of *buraku*-black solidarity, present in Nakagami's oeuvre as early as his 1966 "Me, at Eighteen" (*Ore jūhassai*) and as late as works such as his 1985 *Yasei no kaenju* (The Wild Tree of Fire) and his 1988 *Buffalo Soldiers*,⁶ is foundational in Nakagami's search for alternative models of writing minority identity that he could repeat to the end of revising mainstream constructions of *burakumin* identity. Passing significance is Nakagami's radical rethinking of intertextuality. What might it mean for the *buraku* body to be read as composed of multiple texts in motion?

Passing significance might also be heard, however, in another register, one that gestures toward a second linchpin of Nakagami's writing. This is passing significance in the colloquial sense of the term, for Nakagami's works attenuate, downplay, and at times negate their foundational relationship with black literary tropes and techniques. Chapter 2 addresses Ōe Kenzaburō's identification with authors such as Wright, Baldwin, Ellison, and Himes. Nakagami, too, identifies with such authors. But Nakagami adds, or, perhaps more accurately, subtracts, something from Ōe. Indeed, Nakagami himself wrote about this subtraction, about the difference between his approach to writing blackness and Ōe's approach.⁷ Namely, Nakagami takes away the ease with which Ōe's black-Japanese analogy posits self-identicality within ethnic or racial groups (for Nakagami, "we Japanese" is not an easy thing to say). Nakagami also questions the static permanence Ōe supposes within the bonds of transracial affinity (even when Nakagami does manage to say that "we, in this moment, are now in this together, we are somewhere between blackness and *burakuness*," he constantly questions how long this new "we" will hold together.)

There is something of a paradox in Harris's description of passing as a "permanent move" to identification with a single racial group, and there is a subtle difference between signifyin(g) in a single voice versus signifyin(g) in a singular voice. Nakagami is acutely aware of this difference, particularly as it pertains to pronominal politics, both the way in which "pronouns show how different identity alignments work in real time," that is, how pronominal choices attest to political alignments and affiliations, and the way in which "each use of a pronoun constructs some part of the speaker's identity," that is, how pronominal choices create the very political identities to which we attest to align.[8] If *nominal* politics embodies what is typically an agonistic process of naming, identity creation, and political coalition building at the cost of excluding those parts that do not properly align with that which has been named, then *pronominal* politics reproduces this process while facilitating the speaker's circumvention of the power struggles and tedious deliberation that accompany acts of naming. Nakagami's literary project certainly works toward the creation of a "we," a literary network that stretches from the *buraku* in his hometown in Wakayama to the Bronx and with nodes all over the globe. But, compared to Ōe's, the mechanics of Nakagami's literary network is more quantum and less classical; it questions the erasures of acts of networking even as it builds a network.

Misidentification is Nakagami's blockade against the easy erasures that occur in the name of pronominal politics. By misidentification, I mean something akin to Judith Butler's articulation of it. In *Bodies That Matter*, Butler describes disidentification as the "failure of identification" that occurs when signifiers do not completely overlap with that which they signify and the subsequent "sense of standing under a sign to which one does and does not belong."[9] Misidentification names the inaccuracies, effacements, and omissions that inevitably arise during attempts to identify individuals whose complexity and excess outrun the simplicity of identifications. Nakagami posits such misidentification between both individuals and the terms that identify them—that is, first-person-singular misidentification—and between collectives and the banner that communally binds misidentified individuals—that is, first-person-plural misidentification. As such, pronominal politics becomes, for Nakagami, a fraught territory filled with the possibility of both fluid political motion and anesthetizing identitary violence.

In Nakagami's fiction and cultural criticism, any attempt to "identify" minorities and form solidarities based on the similarities between ethnically marked individuals—that is, any attempt to construct a minority "I" and "we"—is also simultaneously a misidentification, a case of mistaken/mis-taken identity. In this chapter, I consider the interplay between identification and misidentification in several key moments of Nakagami's literary career: his early short fiction such as "Me, at Eighteen" and *Nihongo ni tsuite* (On the Japanese Language, 1968), his 1977 *Asahi Journal* roundtable discussion on discrimination, the theory of jazz narration he experimented with throughout the 1970s, and so on. In each of these works, Nakagami's signifyin(g) "confirms an identity as it highlights its provisional, self-created nature . . . [for] his characters are suffocated by patterns of repetition from the past that also allow them to stay alive; they work to form an identity while struggling to shed it."[10] This vacillation between flowing identification and static misidentification both connects Nakagami with the transpacific discussions of civil rights for socially marginalized communities that were prominent when he began publishing in the 1960s and puts him in dialogue with thinkers such as Jean-Luc Nancy and Giorgio Agamben, who consider the possibility and ethics of communities based on something other than the presupposition of shared identity.

Part 1: Precedents of Passing Significance

Even Signifyin(g) Monkeys Fall from Trees: Nakagami's Entry into the Signifyin(g) Circle

Those familiar with the work of Gates will know that he posits the figure of the Signifying Monkey, "he who dwells at the margins of discourse, ever punning, ever troping, ever embodying the ambiguities of language" as "our trope for repetition and revision, indeed our trope of chiasmus."[11] Speakers of Japanese will be familiar with the adage *saru mo ki kara ochiru* ("even Homer nods" or, literally, "even monkeys fall from trees"). In defining literary signifyin(g) as a principle in which shared language serves as the adhesive of literary traditions, Gates's Signifying Monkey falls from the treetops, providing access to "our trope" (read: black American authors) to writers of all stripes. Although Gates begins by asserting that "whatever is black about black American literature is to be found in the identifiable black Signifyin(g) difference," he ends up with a theory of the sharability of language: "Signifyin(g), of course, is a principle of language use and is not in any way the exclusive province of black people, although blacks named the term and invented its rituals."[12] The implication here is clear: black (or *buraku*) authors are born not in the hospital but in the library. For Gates, "the blackness of black literature is not an absolute or metaphysical condition." Rather, by "blackness" he means "specific *uses of literary language that are shared, repeated, critiqued, and revised*."[13]

I argue in the following section that Nakagami shares, repeats, critiques, and revises the language of signifyin(g) in order to say that which he cannot signify in Japanese, his estranged native tongue. Before continuing down this line of inquiry, however, it is important to note that the affinity between Gates and Nakagami does not emerge simply because the two are both "minorities." Rather, Nakagami enters into what might be called the signifyin(g) circle precisely as Gates's theory portends: by way of shared reading and language.

The primordial soup for Gates's theory of signifyin(g) is the amalgamation of his extensive reading in African American literature, his knowledge of Yoruban folklore—particularly of Esu, the Yoruban trickster god—and his time at Yale circa 1975, during the apex of the Yale School. Recall from the previous chapter the influx of translated black literature in 1960s Japan, as well as the profound impact this newfound access had on authors such as Ōe Kenzaburō. Moreover, both primary and secondary sources attest that Nakagami was intimately familiar with the works of Richard Wright, Ralph Ellison, James Baldwin, Toni Morrison, and Ōe Kenzaburō. There is also Nakagami Kenji's relationship, both personal and working, with anthropologist Yamaguchi Masao. Yamagachi conducted extensive fieldwork in Nigeria on Yoruban folklore and the trickster deity Esu. In works such as "Folklore of the Jester," Yamaguchi Masao writes of what he calls the "ambiguity of Esu" (*Esu no ryōgisei*). There is something of Esu in Nakagami, for these two, to borrow Yamaguchi's summation of Esu, do their work "on the border between order and anarchy."[14] In "Written without Trickster Theory," a section of Nakagami's "Shoki no Ōe Kenzaburō: 'Shiiku' wo chūshin ni," Nakagami makes an argument about Ōe Kenzaburō's "Shiiku" that shares affinities with the one I posed in chapter 2. Whereas I suggest that the potential trappings of representational thought occur on the level of reading, Nakagami deems Ōe's writing itself as culpable for a limited imagining of blackness. Nakagami references Yamaguchi's scholarship on Esu as he critiques the lack of trickiness in the representations of blackness in the works of authors such as Ōe and Yamada Eimi. Finally, there is Nakagami's close personal and intellectual relationship with philosopher and cultural critic Karatani Kōjin. Karatani was a visiting professor at Yale in 1975, the same year in which Gates returned to Yale and began working in its Afro-American studies department. Karatani returned from Yale with a deepened interest in the very literary theorists, namely, theorists such as Jacques Derrida and the Yale School critics, whom Gates would address in his future work.

This, then, is the formation of interlocking signifyin(g) circles that, for example, connect Gates to Nakagami by way of Yamaguchi Masao and Wole Soyinka (who introduced Gates to Yoruban culture and mythology) or connect Nakagami to Gates via Karatani or—most germane to this conversation—in which a relationship between Gates and Nakagami is mediated by their shared reading of black literature. It seems safe to argue that the affinity between Gates and Nakagami is not coincidental, nor is it based simply on the fact that both are "minorities." Rather, it is based on a shared sociohistorical moment, shared readings, and a shared dialogue in real time; it is based on the fact that they both take part in the same tradition of literary and anthropological scholarship. It is because of this shared dialogue that Nagakami's engagements with African American literature are best read as signifyin(g) rather than intertextuality.

Alternative Discursive Universes: The "All Romance Incident" as Counterexample to Nakagami's Signifyin(g)

Gates sees signifyin(g) as the confrontation of "parallel discursive universes," as an "extended engagement between . . . separate and distinct yet profoundly—even inextricably—related orders of meaning."[15] In the twists and turns of semantic appropriation, dialogue, and intertextual linking manifested in signifyin(g), Gates continues, we "bear witness to a protracted argument over the nature of the sign itself."[16] The rationale behind Nakagami's signifyin(g) begins to emerge when it is juxtaposed with those "parallel discursive universes" with which it collides and argues over the "nature" of the signs *buraku* and *burakumin*.

The "All Romance Incident" (*Ōru romansu tōsō*) provides a telescopic view of these colliding discursive universes, for it set many of the postwar precedents for the "proper" literary handling of the *buraku* and the *burakumin*, which Nakagami writes against. In October 1951, *All Romance*, a pulp fiction magazine, published Sugiyama Seiichi's "Tokushu buraku," a story on the turbulent times and squalid conditions of life on the *buraku* streets.[17] The eponymous "*tokushu buraku*" is the Shichijō *buraku* of Yanagihara, Kyoto. At the time of the publication of "Tokushu buraku," Sugiyama moonlighted as a pulp fiction author and spent his daylight hours as an employee of Kyoto's sanitation and hygiene department. Sugiyama's portrayal of the Shichijō *buraku* was supposedly based on the "reality" of the squalor of *buraku* life that he witnessed during his day job; his short story was deemed an "exposé" (*bakuro shōsetsu*) by *All Romance*. The story's protagonist, Kōichi, is a practicing physician who lives and works in the Shichijō *buraku*. The plot whirls within a love quadrangle among Kōichi, Junko (Kōichi's love interest, a bootlegger's daughter from the *buraku*), a prostitute named Yasuko who propositions Kōichi (who is, unbeknownst to Kōichi, Junko's sister), and Yoshitarō (a low-level gangster engaged to Yasuko). The plot of Sugiyama's exposé of the "reality" of *buraku* life reads like a Japanese fantasy of the chain reaction of preordained calamity set off at *buraku* birth: two detectives charged with investigating the *buraku*-operated bootlegging industry are murdered in a *buraku* bar, the murders set off riotous clashes between the *buraku* and the police, the riots ignite a conflagration, the fire is followed by a monsoon (which floods the *buraku*), and the flood is followed in turn by a typhoid epidemic.

Sugiyama's "Tokushu buraku" contains a constellation of the recurring tenets of the "mainstream" Japanese literary discursive universe's construction of the *buraku* and *burakumin*: (1) both the *buraku* and *burakuness* (i.e., the identifying characteristics of the *buraku* and *burakumin*) are "realities" that exist a priori, fundamentally, and essentially; (2) this reality can be represented in language; (3) this represented reality is both communicable and transitive; and (4) communicability is followed by the desire to contain the *buraku* and *burakuness*. The reality of the *buraku* and *burakuness* of Sugiyama's "Tokushu buraku" exists a priori to "Tokushu buraku" insofar as the story is (supposedly) simply a re-presentation of the reality of the Shichijō *buraku*. Or, as the narrator describes Kōichi's sentiments on entering the *buraku*, "Kōichi, who owned a clinic in the Yanagihara *buraku*, had already heard the reality of it (*jijitsu no aru koto*), but he was still shocked severely when he really saw it with his own eyes (*genjitsu ni mokugeki*)."[18] Sugiyama's linguistic representation of the a priori reality promises a realist, one-to-one correspondence between the signifying words of his text and the signified reality on which it is based. In the case of Sugiyama's literary "exposé," such representational signs are what Watanabe Naomi calls *shirushi*, "marks" or "signs" that label the *buraku* and *burakumin* as such. *Shirushi* have much in common with the stereotype: both are literally signs that can be repeated across time *without* a signal/single difference. The children of Sugiyama's "Tokushu buraku," "pus-eyed, pockmarked, and snotty-nosed, frolic nearly naked in vacant lots"; the men are criminals, gangsters, and brutes who spend their days in bars where "a beer bottle might come flying your way if you didn't watch your mouth . . . [and] everyone spoke their mind and spoke it loudly—or just got drunk, fell over, and threw up wherever it ended up"; and the women are almost preternaturally alluring and willing to sell their charms for the right price (Yasuko "would do anything, even sell [her] body" to get out of the *buraku*).[19] The filthy, disease-ridden child, the ne'er-do-well, the licentious vixen—all these represent the formative synthesis of the *shirushi* (e.g., pockmarks) and the stereotype (filthy *burakumin* children).

By "communicable," I mean first Sugiyama's assumption that the aforementioned linguistic representations of the *buraku* and *burakuness* can be communicated to others, in this case, the readers of "Tokushu buraku." I also mean the assumption that *burakuness* is a kind of infection. From theories that posit *burakumin* status to ancestral links to impure occupations that contaminated (*kegare*) *burakumin* bloodlines to Sugiyama's implication that physical and marital entry into the *buraku* was tantamount to "transcending [read transgressing] race" (*jinshu wo chōetsu*), mainstream discourse on the *burakumin* often confronts the fear that *burakuness* itself might be communicable and overrun its predetermined borders.[20] In addition to being communicable, mainstream *buraku* discourse posits *burakuness* as transitive in the mathematical sense. If two children are *burakumin* children, then those two children are essentially identical in the a priori reality of their *burakuness*, in the *shirushi* that label them *burakumin*, in the communicability of their filth, and so on.

In tandem the communicability and transitivity of *burakuness* are the building blocks of a *buraku* community that travels over time and (national) space; the *burakumin* as imagined community is constructed, and individuals are included and excluded from said community, based on their relationship with communicable and transitive *burakuness*. In order to assuage fears of contamination, mainstream discourse on the *buraku* typically features a desire to contain the *buraku* and *burakuness*. As Timothy Amos argues, the "master narrative" of Japanese and *burakumin* history inscribes, as early as the Tokugawa period, "limitations . . . placed on [the] movement, residence, occupational change . . . marriage . . . even clothing and hairstyles" of early modern individuals based on their "status (*mibun*)."[21] Such containment, now in the sense proposed by Stephen Greenblatt, is also enacted in literary texts. Sugiyama's story, for example, in direct contrast to its claim to "transcend race,"[22] provides only two paths for the future of the *burakumin*: Kōichi and Junko's intra-*buraku*/*burakumin* marriage or Yasuko and Yoshitarō's exile (Yasuko attempts to abscond from the *buraku* only to be brought back into the fold; Yoshitarō takes the cultural trope of *burakumin* exile/emigration canonized in works such as Shimazaki Tōson's 1906 *The Broken Commandment* to its ultimate extreme: death). The containment of Sugiyama's fictional *buraku* is best summed up by Yasuko: "*Burakumin* will always be *burakumin*."[23]

In the 1951 All Romance Incident, the discursive universe of Sugiyama, who took up the tradition of writings on the *burakumin* by non-*burakumin* authors, collided with that of the National Committee for Buraku Liberation (Buraku kaihō zenkoku i'inkai, NCBL) and its Kyoto Branch, which was supposedly representative of *burakumin* en masse. Kyoto-born Asada Zen'nosuke (1902–83), the chairman of the Buraku Liberation Confederation of Kyoto (Buraku kaihō Kyoto-fu rengōkai, BLCK), and the BLCK launched a protest campaign against Sugiyama, *All Romance*, and the city of Kyoto. It is important to note that, even as Asada and the BLCK protested "Tokushu buraku" as a *sabetsu shōsetsu* (discriminatory story), they were actually in agreement with the first three tenets of Sugiyama's discursive universe. The BLCK, too, assumed that the *buraku* and the *burakumin* exist a priori to their creation in Sugiyama's story world and that the reality of the *buraku* and the *burakumin* could be signified in language with a one-to-one correspondence between the "reality" of the *buraku* and the "reality" of the story world. The problem with Sugiyama's story was that its reality was misaligned with the "truth" of the Shichijō *buraku*. The BLCK's official denunciation (*kyūdan*) aimed first at exposing the inaccuracies of Sugiyama's portrayal of the *buraku* by citing and deriding the text's stereotypical, derogatory depictions of the *buraku* and *burakumin*.[24] The opening of the denunciation amounted to a challenge to the aforementioned *shirushi*, that is, the signifiers, used to represent the *buraku* and *burakumin*, the signified.

Moreover, the BLCK—itself a branch of the NCBL, which was reformed in 1946 as a conglomerate of *burakumin* organizations disbanded during the wartime era—also assumed that *burakuness* holds within it the communicable and transitive marks of a community. The BLCK's denunciation posits two communities: the *burakumin* within the *buraku*, and the "Japanese" community, which contains the *buraku*, separately but equally, within its borders. The BLCK entitled its denunciation "How Are We to Fight the Municipal Government? The Central Tenets of the *All Romance* Discrimination Denunciation." The "we" here signifies and binds together the first community posited by the BLCK: the community of Shichijō *burakumin* and the larger *burakumin* community of the BLCK and NCBL, which transitively (here in the mathematical sense) represents and communicates on the behalf of the Shichijō community. In addition to this community, the BLCK denounced Sugiyama because his misrepresentation of *burakuness* is the foundation on which a discriminatory non-*buraku* Japanese community is constructed. The BLCK argued that the depictions of the *buraku* in Sugiyama's story "proliferated [anti-*burakumin*] discrimination to the thirty thousand readers" of the *All Romance* community and that the claim by the Kyūjō Public Health Department—Sugiyama's employer—that the incident was "a personal matter in the private life" of Sugiyama "tells the story" (*monogataru*) of the department's communal and systemic discrimination and apathy toward the *burakumin* community.[25]

The fundamental divergence of Sugiyama's and the BLCK's and NCBL's discursive universes occurs only with the fourth tenet: containment. Whereas Sugiyama and mainstream *buraku* discourse communicates to contain *burakuness*, BLCK/NCBL discourse aims to free it—the *L* in both acronyms stands for "liberation" (*kaihō*). In its denouncement, for example, the BLCK juxtaposes the opening of "Tokushu buraku," in which Kōichi gets off a train at Kyoto station and enters the sprawling Shichijō *buraku*, with the

Takayama municipal government's plan to plant trees around Kyoto Station. "Although a row of trees sounds nice," the BLCK extrapolated the logic behind the shrubbery as "the government's plan . . . to hide 'the sprawling *tokushu buraku* called Yanagihara' behind a row of trees . . . so it can't be seen from the windows of the train."[26] The embedded quotation in the previous passage is the BLCK's citation (a term that should resonate on multiple valences) of Sugiyama's description of the *buraku*. Connecting the story world to the real world, the BLCK argued that, rather than hiding (*mekakushi*) and containing the *buraku*, the government should invest in its renovation—just as Sugiyama should invest in ameliorating his fictional *buraku*. The remainder of the denunciation enumerates the ways in which the city should go about improving the *buraku*. Rather than containment, then, the BLCK called for activism that would correct the source of hyperbolic misrepresentations such as Sugiyama's: the dire reality of *burakumin* life.

The BLCK's denunciation of Sugiyama, which posited systemic origins and communal responsibility for anti-*buraku* literature alongside a call for activism, would set numerous precedents for postwar *burakumin* cultural protest. Nakagami's discursive universe, however, contests both mainstream, Sugiyama-style representations of *burakumin* and the precedents set by the NCBL. Nakagami did not deem the *buraku* and *burakumin* entities that exist fundamentally "in the world" a priori. Rather, he saw the *buraku* and the *burakumin* as *monogatari*—literally "narrated things." Here *monogatari* signals first Nakagami's fascination with the literary genre as such, particularly the emphasis the genre places on oral communication, complex familial structures, and the bizarre as a generative force. Following Karatani, however, Nakagami's *monogatari* also refer to "*monogatari* . . . in a more fundamental sense," one in which *monogatari* is not just a literary genre confined to antiquity but a mode of writing still viable in the modern era and constituted by the carnivalization of "a series of repetitive rituals."[27] Pace modern modes of storytelling such as the I-novel, with its imagined fixity of an authoritative "I" documenting a true story to a captive readership, the "ritual" of *monogatari*, for Nakagami and Karatani, is about the creation of a dynamic network of subjectivities and objectivities in flux. The "written discourse" of *monogatari*, Richard Okada proposes, "does not easily exist separately as a self-contained entity, but is always positioned vis-à-vis a multitude of 'intertexts,' whether linguistic stimulus . . . historical 'model,' genealogical imperative, narrator, and/or reader listener."[28] In the world of *monogatari* storytelling, the existence of the matter being narrated always vibrates somewhere within the network created by the act of storytelling, which connects listener to storyteller, storyteller to the past, and the past to other stories.

Nakagami's writings, particularly post-1977 works such as *Karekinada* (The Sea of Withered Trees), harness the power of the *monogatari* to destabilize the story of both a priori reality and a priori narrators and narratees of that reality. In direct opposition to the precedents and protocols set by the NCBL, Nakagami deemed "differentiating between good *monogatari* and bad *monogatari*—writing *monogatari* that enlighten us and decrying the ignorance of anti-*buraku* discrimination—unimportant."[29] Nakagami's objective, Yomota continues, is "an experimental attempt to borrow the form of the *monogatari* in order to . . . relativize all that has been narrated and believed by means of a . . . fabricated *monogatari*."[30]

Although Nakagami was a prolific author and saw the *buraku/burakumin* as narrated realities, he was also unconvinced that the *buraku* and *burakumin* could be fully represented in language with a one-to-one correspondence between the signifier and the signified. In the words of Nakagami, "Words are lies. Meaningless. Dubious from the very moment we bring them together like a pile of rocks."[31] For Nakagami, every linguistic representation of the world, every attempt to bind a signified to a signifier, is also a kind of misrepresentation. In the All Romance Incident, for example, what is elided in the back-and-forth between Sugiyama and the BLCK is the fact that the story is not about *burakumin* per se but resident Koreans who live in the Shichijō *buraku*: Kōichi, Junko, Yasuko, and Yoshitarō are all of Korean ancestry. The misrepresentation of the *burakumin* and Zainichi Koreans in "Tokushu buraku," Nakagami might argue, is a synecdoche for the misidentification that inevitably accompanies linguistic identifications.

Given his mistrust of language, Nakagami also questioned the communicability and transitivity of *burakuness* and whether a community, *burakumin* or otherwise, can be based on such tenets. Nakagami's writings, which ritualistically repeat and revise the space of the *buraku* and the *burakumin*, can be seen as Nakagami's attempt to communicate *burakuness* without the stereotypical connotations of (medical) communicability and (mathematical) transitivity that hamper the writings of his predecessors.

It is only on the fourth tenet that Nakagami—and then only partially— concurs with the BLCK; Nakagami was intimately invested in the project of contesting the containment of the *buraku* and the *burakumin*. However, he saw the assumptions of a priori *burakumin* identity, representative language, and communicability and transitivity *as* the discursive devices that contained the *buraku*; the NCBL's process of denunciation struck down single signs but did little to address the discursive system that generated such signs. Nakagami's dilemma, then, was to rewrite *buraku* and *burakumin* narratives that both resist containment and sidestep the linguistic and communal pitfalls of its parallel discursive universes. Another way of saying this is that Nakagami wanted to write *burakuness* not as mathematically transitive but as in transit, passing through, moving people from one place to another.

Nakagami's primary response to this dilemma: the writing of a chasm between the *buraku* and the *roji*—a fictional space in Nakagami's story world that is reminiscent of but never identical to the *buraku*—and a chasm between the "real-world" *burakumin* and the "I" of Nakagami's fictional characters, who are, like the *roji* they inhabit, reminiscent of but not identical to other (actually fictionalized) "flesh-and-blood" *burakumin* characters. McKnight has deemed this tactic Nakagami's writing of the *buraku* under erasure. "In other words, it is possible to read a suggestion of *buraku* identity through form, syntax, or allusion, without affirmation in semantic or positivist content."[32] Such erasure of the *buraku* and the *burakumin*, McKnight continues, "is interested in exploring what has constituted the historicity of *buraku* experience and discrimination but without making it a transcendental" and, in so doing, in prying *burakuness* from its containment without reification.[33]

This is of passing significance. Rather than signifying these alternative discursive universes, Nakagami turns to signifyin(g) in the space between the *buraku* and the *roji* left by his erasure. For the remainder of this chapter, I would like to make the following case: even as Nakagami turns to black literature in search of models of writing under erasure, he turns and turns and turns, never fully turning to a one-to-one correspondence between the *buraku* and those spaces "outside" Japan to which he turns, never penciling in the space opened by erasure or reproducing the tactics of those alternative discursive universes. As such, Nakagami's attempts to identify with other minority writers are accompanied by misidentifications of those writers, of the self, and of the communities that might be forged between them. Nakagami's signifyin(g) "dwell[s] at the margins of discourse, ever punning, ever troping, ever embodying the ambiguities of language."[34]

Part 2: Nakagami, Signifyin(g), and Identifyin(g)

Nakagami Kenji clearly identifies with minority writers around the globe. Eve Zimmerman, for example, writes that he "takes us beyond the borders of Japanese literature entirely . . . [for] he envision[s] his own place within Japan by cultivating a view from the outside, stressing his affinity to writers from other minority cultures."[35] Nakagami's 1966 "Ore, Jūhassai" (*Me, at Eighteen*) provides one of the earliest examples of Nakagami's "*buraku*" literature signifyin(g) and identifying with black literature. The title of the story hints at one of the text's primary concerns: the narration of a first-person singular identity. The narrator of "Me, at Eighteen," a Japanese youth referred to primarily as "I" (*ore*), is never identified as *burakumin*. The narrative begins, however, by situating the narrator's friends in a black intertextual network. Nishikawa, one of *ore*'s friends, "Loved Negro spirituals and modern jazz. Nishikawa had 'Swing Low, Sweet Chariot' and Bud Powell in his head, and this made his face look different from everyone else's."[36] Passages such as this provide Bakhtinian dialogue between the voices of *ore* and Nishikawa and the "reverberations of Thelonious Monk that . . . echoed throughout his room."[37] Nishikawa's participation in this dialogue marks his very identity; having "a head full of black music" alters the physical *shirushi* by means of which Nishikawa can be identified.

Although the narrator, whose name, Tooru, means "to pass," is never explicitly marked as *burakumin*, he does intimate his *burakumin* status by signifyin(g). On receiving a letter from Yuri, his girlfriend, *ore*

> slipped the letter between the pages of the novel I was reading. . . .
> I slipped the letter, still in Yuri's white envelope, between the pages
> where Rufus has relations with a white woman. I swelled up with
> laughter when I imagined the look of shock on her face if I were to
> run into Yuri like this and tell her "Your letter, look, it's in here," and
> have her read the page the letter was sandwiched between.[38]

The Rufus referred to here is Rufus Scott of James Baldwin's *Another Country*. Recall from chapter 2's discussion of Ōe's response to *Another Country*, which was translated into Japanese in 1964 by Takashi Nozaki as *Mō hitotsu no kuni*, that the novel sent tremors through the American literary scene when it was published in 1962 due to what was then considered graphic, radical representations of interracial sex. This is literal intertextuality, for by slipping a letter from his girlfriend between the pages where Rufus "has relations with a white woman," the narrator of "Me, at Eighteen" intimates his *buraku* identity by having a black voice, namely, that of Baldwin and his protagonist, reverberate dialogically within this work of *buraku* literature.

To read "Me, at Eighteen" and its representation of the narrator's "I," then, we also have to read black literature, namely, Baldwin's *Another Country*. This need for what McKnight calls parallax reading comes to a crescendo in a section of "Me, at Eighteen" entitled "Good Luck." In the previous section, "Love," Yuri and the narrator have a date on a boat. Yuri observes how "lucky" they are; the narrator is enthralled with how "sexy" Yuri is. In

"Good Luck," the narrator is assaulted by six men as he and Yuri leave the boat walking hand in hand. The beating is grotesque and gratuitous in its violence, and it makes the narrator wonder:

> Why are they punching me? They surrounded me after I got off the boat holding hands with Yuri and tried to lynch (*rinchi*) me. Had seeing me on a boat with a woman stimulated the frenzy of this pack of dogs? No doubt Yuri's crying as she watches me from beneath the shade of the Chusan palms of the high ground over there. Every time they hit me, her words—"We're lucky, aren't we?"—float to the top of my mind. Sexy, sexy, that's what I said. Sexy, sexy, we're lucky, aren't we? I repeated the mantra meaninglessly, like a cheap, skipping record. . . .
>
>   When the pack was convinced that I couldn't get up, they spat on me and left. I was shocked that, from the midst of pain so agonizing it might make me faint, the protagonist of that novel came to me again and again like something out of a dream. Sexy, sexy, the words are spinning. . . . Yuri's shocked face looks weird.[39]

The narrator's "lynching" clearly harkens back to the previous passage, in which he wonders how amusing Yuri's face would appear if she found her letter between the pages of *Another Country*. In order to identify the reason for the lynching, the reader must turn to the page in "that novel" where *ore* keeps Yuri's letter. In his first sexual encounter with Leona, *Another Country*'s Rufus frames his act of interracial sex as an act of violence: "Nothing could have stopped him, not the white God himself nor a lynch mob arriving on wings. Under his breath he cursed the milk-white bitch and groaned and rode his weapon between her thighs. . . . He beat her with all the strength he had and felt the venom shoot out of him, enough for a hundred black-white babies."[40] Although the sexual act between Rufus and Leona is consensual, their interracial sex brings with it the weight of the history of violence, both discursive and somatic, associated with the myth of the black rapist. Rufus is haunted by this myth. Rufus's violent assault of Leona is a failed attempt to beat this myth by way of a consensual penetration of her (white) feminine purity, hence the figuration of his penis as a weapon, his thrusts as a beating, and his ejaculation as ballistic. The violence of Rufus's assault is matched only by the metaphysical and physical lynching that awaits Rufus, "protects" Leona, and contains black masculinity on the proper side of a sexualized color line.

The actual lynching of *ore* is signifyin(g) on Rufus's impending lynching. Unlike Leona and Rufus, the narrator and Yuri have not engaged in any sexual activity. To answer the narrator's question as to why he is being assaulted, it is indeed the mere sight of the *burakumin*(?) narrator with Yuri that activates the history of violence associated with the *buraku* rapist, triggers the "frenzy of [the] pack of dogs," and instigates the lynching, a disciplinary measure intended to contain *burakuness*. In signifyin(g) (rather than signifying) the rationale for the lynching, Nakagami effectively resists the first three tenets of his competing discursive universes. The narrator of "Me, at Eighteen" has not been named a member of the *burakumin* and thus does not exist as *burakumin* a priori. (I discuss momentarily the generative power Nakagami ascribes to acts of naming.) There is no one-to-one correspondence between *buraku* "reality" and the "reality" represented in literary language. Rather, *burakuness* is mediated by blackness; the reader is obligated to read either English or Japanese in translation in order to surmise the identity of the narrator. *Burakuness*, as an entity that has yet to be named or represented, is not directly communicable or transitive. Nakagami has simultaneously upheld his fourth tenet as containment of *burakuness* has been subverted by its dispersion across multiple national literatures, by reading *burakuness* into literary locales beyond the borders of Japan and the *buraku*, for example, Rufus's Harlem.

African American music and literature are vital interlocutors for Nakagami, one of the foundations on which his signifyin(g) is built. Nakagami's setting of this foundation can be seen by moving from the 1966 "Me, at Eighteen" to his 1977 roundtable with Noma Hiroshi and Yasuoka Shōtarō and his 1978 *Kishū: Ki no kuni, ne no kuni monogatari*, which was inspired by the roundtable. Prompted by the unfolding events of the Sayama Incident,[41] in 1977 the *Asahi Journal* commissioned a series of roundtable discussions on discrimination in Japan. Noma and Yasuoka, who translated and introduced Alex Haley's *Roots* to the Japanese reading public in 1977, presided over the twelve roundtables. Nakagami Kenji was the fourth participant in the series, and he engaged with Noma and Yasuoka in a wide-ranging conversation on "the latent discriminatory mind-set of ordinary folks" at the root of anti-*burakumin* discrimination.[42] After the roundtable discussion, Nakagami was commissioned by Senbon Ken'ichirō—the roundtable series was the brainchild of Senbon—to write a series of essays for the journal. Nakagami was not satisfied with the tenor of the discussion, so he and Senbon decided that the essays would be documentaries based on actual fieldwork in the *buraku* areas of what formerly known as the Kishū province, which includes present-day Wakayama prefecture, where Nakagami was born, and Mie prefecture. The essays culminated in *Kishū: Ki no kuni, ne no kuni monogatari* (Kishū: Stories of the Country of Trees, Country of Roots).

The *ne* (roots) in the title is signifyin(g) on black literature. Senbon suggested that Nakagami model his historiography on that of Alex Haley's 1976 *Roots*. Concomitant with its wildly successful Japanese publication, TV Asahi broadcast the *Roots* miniseries on eight consecutive nights on 2–9 October 1977. As the *Asahi Shimbun*'s advertisement (fig. 2) for the broadcast suggests, *Roots*, a series about generational change among a family of black slaves, was billed as a story for "all humanity," including the Japanese. Senbon and Nakagami saw Haley's search for roots as an endeavor with importance that crossed linguistic and national barriers. Just as *Roots* challenged the writing of the black body in American history, *Kishū: Stories of the Country of Trees, Country of Roots,* was a salvo against the writing of the *buraku* body in Japanese history.

In *Kishū: Stories of the Country of Trees, Country of Roots*, Nakagami suggests that simply challenging the representation of the *buraku* body in Japanese history and letters is insufficient; there is a need to address the violence inherent in discursive constructions of identity itself. As he writes the *buraku* and *burakumin* in *Kishū* into Japanese history in the Japanese language, however, Nakagami encounters the Caribbean American critic and poet Audre Lorde's conundrum of the master's tools and the master's house.

Take, for example, the following musing on the grass in Ise, which McKnight has highlighted for its critical importance in articulating Nakagami's notion of imperial syntax. Nakagami writes:

> Grass is grass. That's what we think, but then again I wonder if the essence of grass is not the actual reality of grass in and of itself, but "grass," as in the word that we apply to it. . . . Words exist (在る) here. . . . If reigning over words is the work of the "emperor," a godlike figure, then calling grass by its given name, grass, writing and recording it by this name, is imperial syntax—it is to be subject to [imperial rule]. With that said, what is grass when it is displaced from the syntax of the "emperor?" . . . If I am to reject the syntax of the words of the "emperor," it can't be done in the gargantuan, written words of the country of *waka*; I will have to resist imperial syntax by bringing in some other language, some words that are of a different kind.[43]

Nakagami begins with a meditation on the arbitrariness of the relationship between the signifier and the signified. Indeed, "grass" could be signified by any array of signifiers; grass by any other name would smell just as sweet. It is what Nakagami calls "imperial syntax," which rules over and ties signifiers and signifieds together, giving them semantic order just as syntax gives sentences their "proper" syntactic order. In so doing, imperial syntax makes

Figure 2. Advertisement in the 1 October 1977 evening edition of the *Asahi Shimbun* for the Japanese television premier of *Roots*. Above the English title, the story is framed as "a message of the spirit for all mankind" or, as the superimposed Japanese over the English title suggests, a message of the spirit for men of all kinds.

grass grass (or, more significant, makes *burakumin burakumin*). In the process of solidifying relationships between signifiers and signifieds, Nakagami argues, imperial syntax privileges signifiers over signifieds, hence his claim that "words exist" and have a life that takes precedence over the things they signify.

Imperial syntax signifies many things for Nakagami, but here it is a metaphor for the relationship among language, power, and the oppression

Figure 3. Nakagami
Kenji with Bob Marley

of minority groups. As such it is a kind of shorthand for the legerdemain
of the first three tenets of the discursive universes with which Nakagami's
story world competes. We might say that Nakagami considered both mainstream representations of the *burakumin* and the response of the Buraku
kaihō dōmei (Burakumin Liberation League, BLL), the post-1955 incarna-
tion of the NCBL, to this representation as susceptible to the rule of imperial syntax. Nakagami suggests that challenging imperial syntax stipulates
"bring[ing] in some other language, some words that are of a different kind."
This imported language would have to be double voiced; it would have to
both speak to the *buraku* struggle against imperial syntax and go beyond the
sovereignty of imperial syntax's reign. One of Nakagami's imports is African
American literature and rhetoric. The 1977 roundtable book evinces Nakagami's reliance on two components of black language and literature: the
language of signifyin(g) and the trope of passing.

Throughout the discussion Nakagami borrows, or is signifyin(g) on, black
issues in order to discuss *buraku* issues. Take, for example, Nakagami's injec-
tion of the *mot d'ordre* "black is beautiful" into the roundtable discussion.

> Nakagami: By the way, there's a saying that goes "black is beautiful"
> (*burraku izu byutifuru*). That's how I feel. Just like the people who
> discriminate [against the *burakumin*], I think that we should have
> *buraku*. It's an extreme argument, isn't it? . . . But if "*buraku*"—
> not "black" but *buraku* is beautiful . . . then it doesn't matter if we
> have equality, it doesn't matter if there are differences. Taken to

the extreme, my argument would be exactly like that of the Black
Panthers—maybe we should make a separate *buraku* nation.
In my mind, that's how important the culture of the *buraku* is.
It's so important that that we should establish a separate *buraku*
republic. That's how I feel. Maybe we should make a separate
nation inside Japan, take Shikoku and designate it the land of the
buraku. (laughs)

Yasuoka: So now you're going to discriminate against us? (laughs)

Nakagami: Of course, that [the story of a *buraku* nation] was just
fiction. But this is the kind of ardor we must bring to [our view of
buraku culture].[44]

Here Nakagami crosses linguistic borders and breaks the rules of Japanese
signification, making the English word *black*—which in 1977 was typically
translated as *kokujin*—hold within it the word *buraku*, and thus a dialogue
between Nakagami and the black is beautiful movement emerges. By supplementing *buraku* language with black language, Nakagami attempts to
write "fictions" that are antidotes rather than poisons, that is, he tries to
write fictions that do not identify *buraku* in terms of imperial syntax but
still hold venom in the face of the reductive identifications of the *burakumin*
made in "imperial" mainstream discourse—think, for example, of the stereotypical precedents reinforced by *All Romance*. By supplementing *buraku*
talk with the language of black talk, Nakagami challenges the essentialist
writing of the *buraku* and *burakumin* in imperial syntax by signifyin(g) on it
rather than signifying in it.

Nakagami's most prominent act of signifyin(g) during the 1977 roundtable was his mobilization of passing. He introduces passing into the roundtable almost as a non sequitur: "By the way," he interjects, "this is a little removed from the *buraku* problem, but there's a literary term called *passing*."[45]
Yasuoka gives a brief definition of *passing*, and Nakagami responds with a
reference to Leila from John Cassavetes's 1959 film *Shadows* and a claim that
"it's easy to pass in Japan."[46] Noma substantiates Nakagami's claim by asserting that America, unlike Japan, faces the problem of "racial discrimination"
(*jinshu sabetsu*) and that racial difference is legible in a way that *burakumin*-
Japanese difference is not. Nakagami concurs: "And that's why it can hide. I
started with a reference to Tanizaki's *In Praise of Shadows*, but, in short, it's
easy to slip into the shadows [as a *burakumin* minority in Japan]."[47]

Nakagami juxtaposed his discussion of the ease with which one can pass
in Japan with a performance of that very passing. Throughout the roundtable, he makes several references to a young *burakumin* writer he knows.
This writer—even though he knows that there's "no sense in hiding" his

burakumin identity—passes, hiding half of himself from the *buraku*. This partially passing writer of Nakagami Kenji's acquaintance is none other than Nakagami himself; at the time of the roundtable, he had yet to "come out" as a *burakumin* writer. In his coda to *Kishū: Stories of the Country of Trees, Country of Roots*, Senbon divulges that Nakagami requested that his use of the first person to discuss aspects of his *burakumin* identity be changed to the third person. Nakagami is clearly playing a game of pronominal politics. In passing, he momentarily shifts the weight of narrating *buraku* issues as a *burakumin* from himself to a third person two degrees removed from the roundtable. This borrowing of passing allows Nakagami to resist imperial syntax. The "reality" discussed in the roundtable is a fiction that Nakagami focalizes at will, there is no reductive one-to-one correspondence between Nakagami's reality and his narration thereof, and there is not only no transitive equality between Nakagami and any other *burakumin*, but there is not even any transitive equality between Nakagami's narrating "I" and itself. In narrating *burakumin* identity in passing and under erasure, Nakagami's resistance counters the reductions common to both mainstream discourse on the *buraku* and the discourse of organizations such as the BLL, which was at times vocally critical of Nakagami's refusal to bind the signifier (his "I") to the signified (the "reality" of *burakumin* identity). Moreover, even as it resists imperial syntax, Nakagami's passing provides him with a trope with which to undermine containment. Much like Leila's tour de force, the performance in *Shadows* on which Nakagami's signifyin(g) repetition is based, Nakagami—who is in the company of Yasuoka and Noma as a member of an esteemed list of invitees to the roundtable series and in the similarly esteemed pages of the *Asahi Journal*—and his performance is an improvised subversion that exposes the arbitrariness of the demarcating lines of cultural containment.

Part 3: Nakagami, Signifyin(g), and Misidentifyin(g)

Nakagami identifies in civil rights era black language, literature, and music a mode of minority discourse with which *burakumin* can identify and subsequently mobilize in the struggle against imperial syntax. Such identification, however, runs the risk of positing the very kind of one-to-one correspondence between blackness and *burakuness* that Nakagami's signifyin(g) aims to undermine. As such, alongside Nakagami's signifyin(g) and identifyin(g), there are also moments of signifyin(g) and misidentifyin(g). Just as Nakagami writes a chasm between the *buraku* and the *roji* and refuses to bridge the gap between the "I" of his prose and the "I" of his lived experiences, he refuses also to identify completely with black language and culture. In a sense, then, Nakagami's works signify on themselves, repeating and revising the identifications made throughout in order to misidentify them. Such misidentification ensures that Nakagami's identifications with other minority groups don't replicate the discursive violence of the construction of *buraku/ burakumin* identity that he challenged. As Watanabe Naomi suggests, Nakagami would amount to just another "discriminator" if his critique settled for a power inversion; Nakagami negotiates a resistance to the "desire to be extraordinary" (*tsune naranu mono e no yokubō*), which happens by way of comparative identification, with a rewriting of the stereotypes of the *buraku* that is "peerless" (*hirui nai*) in its singularity.[48] Even as he identifies with black literature, Nakagami remains without peers, a subject who can never be identified in his plentitude.

There is extensive misidentification throughout both "Me, at Eighteen" and the 1977 roundtable—two of the texts that also evince Nakagami's identification with black language and literature. To begin with the roundtable, remember that Nakagami is identifying and signifyin(g) throughout the roundtable in order to say that which he cannot signify in Japanese without falling prey to the rule of imperial syntax. Even as he borrows terms from 1960s and 1970s black culture and literature (e.g., *black is beautiful* and *passing*), Nakagami posits black literature as a limited form of protest. He deemed "literature of denunciation" (*kyūdan no bungaku*) and "screaming novels" (*sakebi no shōsetsu*) acts of isolated protest that don't address the systematic depth and breadth of discrimination. Nakagami's refutation of the efficacy of such denunciations is a kind of scattershot, as he simultaneously addresses the shortcomings of the BLL's advocacy of denunciation, the limited scope of "screaming novels" of black Japanese literature such as Ōe Kenzaburō's *The Cry*, and the potential inefficacies of black protest literature by authors such as Richard Wright, who inspired Ōe's outcries.[49] In the words of Nakagami:

> There's this young author who was born in the *buraku*, and he's really unsatisfied when he reads novels about discrimination. They [the novels] are really shallow. Is the problem [of discrimination] really this shallow?—he thinks to himself. It's like, someone says you're smelly, so you lash out violently; is the *buraku* problem really that shallow? . . . It's deeper, thicker. . . . Take the black protest novel (*kokujin no kōgi no shōsetsu*), for example. Well, Baldwin is a little different, and Wright has some pieces that cut deep, but if you really think about it,

it's just minority literature. . . . Decrying discrimination, that's nothing but minority literature, it's boring.[50]

The irony of this claim is that Nakagami borrows a black literary technique—here, too, Nakagami is passing in his third-person discussion of "a young author born in the *buraku*"—in order to articulate the shortcomings of black literary techniques. A similar gesture occurs on the previous page, when Nakagami asserts that the logical endpoint of belief in the beauty of blackness is liberation from the demands of minority literature and realization that minority authors "think of themselves as more special than they actually are."[51]

The editing of "Me, at Eighteen" bears witness to the two-step of Nakagami's simultaneous identifying and misidentifying. *Ore*, the narrator of "Me, at Eighteen," identifies with Rufus, the protagonist of Baldwin's *Another Country*, and this is the reason why he recalls Rufus after his lynching. Nakagami's writing of the narrator's recalling of Rufus, however, varies depending on the edition of "Me, at Eighteen." "Me, at Eighteen" was first published in the March 1966 edition of the literary magazine *Bungei shuto*. It was republished in 1977 as one of the eponymous tales of a short story collection entitled *Jūhassai, umi e* (Eighteen Years Old, to the Sea). There is a conspicuous difference in the 1977 version's repetition of the 1966 lynching. The 1966 version reads:

> I was shocked that the protagonist of that novel came to me again and again like something out of a dream from the midst of pain so agonizing it might make me faint. Rufus's ridiculous words came and slipped nonchalantly from my mouth. "You mean, everybody ain't a animal like me? Hey, bitch, you mean everybody ain't a animal like me, or you mean ain't a animal like you?" If Yuri comes over, this is what I'll tell her: "This is good luck? Hey, bitch, am I the one with the good luck or are the punks beating me the ones with the good luck?" I feel my consciousness slipping away. Yuri's shocked face looks weird. Laughter swells up from the depths of my belly.[52]

Compare this to the 1977 version, which was published concomitantly with Nakagami's roundtable discussion.

> I was shocked that the protagonist of that novel came to me again and again like something out of a dream from the midst of pain so agonizing it might make me faint. Sexy, sexy, the words are spinning.

I feel my consciousness slipping away. Yuri's shocked face looks weird. Laughter swells up from the depths of my belly.[53]

The 1966 version is a perfect example of Gatesian signifyin(g). The narrator cites and repeats the words of Rufus with a signal difference: whereas Rufus addresses Leona and American race relations, *ore* repeats and signally reroutes his addresses to Yuri and anti-*burakumin* sentiment. The 1966 version's signifyin(g) on *Another Country* highlights *ore*'s identification with Rufus. With such identification, the reader can map a clear correspondence between Nakagami's work and Baldwin's; the narrator's questioning of who is "a animal" is a lucid translation of Rufus and Leona's final exchange.

In contrast, the 1977 version is signifyin(g) on a Baldwin under erasure. Whereas the 1966 version refers to Baldwin by name (e.g., after a verbal altercation with his sister, the narrator "picked up Baldwin's novel and flew out of the room, leaving my sister behind all alone"), the 1977 gestures toward a text similar to Baldwin's but never explicitly named as such (now the narrator "picked up the novel I was reading and flew out of the room, leaving my sister behind all alone").[54] With such misidentification, the reader can no longer pinpoint with authority the source of the original that the narrator repeats; the "novel I was reading," for example, may or may not be *Another Country*. In lieu of a search for the original, the indeterminacy introduced by signifyin(g) misidentification puts the onus on the reader and in so doing makes the reader cognizant of the fact that any act of identification and interpretation is an inherently political act. The reading I proposed earlier—that the narrator's lynching is akin to the preordained lynching that Rufus fears—for example, is an interpretation and identification of "Rufus" that I impose on the text at the expense of other interpretations and identifications. As such it is also a kind of misidentification that limits and mistakes the hermeneutic possibilities of the text. Indeed, "Me, at Eighteen" ends with a warning about the dangers of such identification. After the "lynching," *ore* and his friends decide to exact revenge on his assailants. As they prowl the night looking for the assailants, however, they inadvertently run over a police officer, only to discover that this "police officer" was a con artist impersonating an officer. The charlatan officer—himself a false authority figure charged with identifying and containing delinquents—is a synecdochal representation of the misidentification that accompanies any check of identification.

If the 1966 signifyin(g) and identifyin(g) version of "Me, at Eighteen" is a lucid translation of Rufus and Leona's final exchange, the 1977 signifyin(g) and misidentifyin(g) version obligates the reader to take responsibility for an opaque translation rife with the possibility of misidentifications. It also obligates the reader to take responsibility for our part in the politics of filling interpretative gaps and leaping the chasm between the *buraku* and black, between identities. Such opaque translation, which is, for Nakagami, a prerequisite for communication (cross-cultural or otherwise), denaturalizes the ease with which we might identify and build a community with "fellow minorities."

Signifyin(g) *On the Japanese Language*

Nakagami took up the issues addressed thus far—the possibility of signifyin(g) on black language and literature in Japanese, *buraku*-black identification/misidentification and the role such identification/misidentification might play in rewriting the fictions of *burakuness*, and, the point most recently introduced into our discussion, the opacity of translation and the difficulty of forging communal links in the wake of misidentification—in his 1968 novella *Nihongo ni tsuite* (On the Japanese Language). *On the Japanese Language* was both set and published during the Vietnam War. The narrator, a Japanese youth named Saitō but referred to throughout the narrative as *boku*, or "I," is hired ostensibly to introduce an African American soldier on leave, Ludolph L. Witt,[55] to the pleasures of postwar Tokyo nightlife. Beneath the veneer of altruistic hospitality, however, resides *boku*'s real job. He has been hired by a group of activist students to persuade the soldier to desert his duties by way of subtle inculcation of the (postwar) "Japanese" virtues of freedom (*jiyū*), democracy (*minshushugi*), and a pacifist constitution (*heiwa kenpō*).

On the Japanese Language is a crucible in which the affinity between a disillusioned Japanese student movement, dissatisfied with the Vietnam War and the American military presence in Japan sanctioned by the US-Japan Security Treaty, and a disillusioned African American nation still waiting on the promise of the Double V campaign to materialize and now shifting to a civil rights movement with teeth, is tested and mined as a potential source for black-Japanese transnational, transracial solidarity. As the novella's title suggests, however, this overtly political question is preceded by a questioning of the politics of language use, namely, the politics of ownership of a "native language," of communicating in translation, and of searching for a lingua franca with which to construct transnational, transracial solidarity.

Nakagami's Monku: Signifyin(g) in the Time of the Other

One of the most eminent aspects of the orthography of *On the Japanese Language* is its measurement of time. The story of *On the Japanese Language* occurs within the five-day period allotted to *boku* to complete his job. The passage of time in *On the Japanese Language* is marked by a kind of broken clock: the progression of each section of the story is signaled by the repetition of a single character: *natsu* (summer). The word *summer* appears twenty-three times throughout the novella. At each appearance, the character is offset from both the paragraph that precedes it and the paragraph it precedes. Moreover, this *natsu* is one of the few terms presented in bold type. This presentation gives the twenty-three "summers" the appearance of being transfixed, frozen between the rest of the text and the white space that marks it off from the narrative.

One response—perhaps the reader's initial response—to this presentation of time is to consider Ludolph's leave as a kind of liminal time. Between the stalemate war in Vietnam and the peace on American soil resides Japan, itself a liminal space of pseudo- and neocolonialism that enables the war with Vietnam but, as a country now reconfigured as a pacifist nation, does not "participate" in the war itself. This spatial liminality is juxtaposed with temporal liminality; *boku* and Ludolph are frozen in time between a spring that has ended and a fall that the text never shows the reader. This response, however, is one that reminds us of Johannes Fabian's writings on the "Other" and the politics of "time." Fabian argues that anthropology has cultivated a denial of coevalness in which the anthropologist puts the Other in his or her (temporal) place by denying the simultaneity of an Other who exists in real time and before our very eyes. The construction of a liminal space becomes a kind of defense mechanism in which, rather than encountering Otherness, it is contained and temporally asphyxiated.

In lieu of such a reaction, a second response, perhaps one that is more in tune with *On the Japanese Language*, is to think of the text as taking place in jazz time. It is "well known that Nakagami, who spent the late 60s in Shinjuku during the heyday of the jazz café, repeatedly referenced jazz music in his essays, interviews and writings on *monogatari*."[56] Nakagami makes no secret of this interplay with jazz.

> I should say this discreetly, but my early works, the length of my phrases, the extensive use of metaphor, the brevity of my phrases around the time I was writing *Misaki* [The Cape, 1975], the place-

ment of punctuation, the repetition of phrases in *Karekinada* [The Sea
of Withered Trees, 1977], all of this is extremely natural in jazz. . . .
Jazz is the great key to analyzing my novels and literary criticism.[57]

Given the opening of the story proper of *On the Japanese Language*—"It
was the beginning of summer. I was reading a short essay on bebop-era jazz
and waiting for Naoko [in a small modern jazz café called Monku]. I was
surrounded by the teeming . . . enveloping sound of the avant-garde sax; it
twisted around me like a coil"—it is clear that jazz might serve as a "great
key" to the time of the text.[58] Quoting Jelly Roll Morton, Gates suggests that
signifyin(g) repetition in jazz begins with a riff, with riffs seen as "a figure,
musically speaking."[59] The riff provides "'what you would call a foundation,'
'something you could walk on,'" and the signifyin(g) jazz improvisario walks
all over the riff as he or she repeats and revises it into a creation that is new
but also related to its foundation.[60]

Nina Cornyetz proposes that the staccato rhythm of Nakagami's sentence
structure is inspired in part by modern jazz syncopation.[61] In *On the Japanese
Language*, jazz serves also as an inspiration for the structure of the story and
the intertextual connections the story makes with works of African American
literature. Atsuko Ueda has described *On the Japanese Language* as a "*monogatari* with a circular structure" that, even as it circles in on itself, does not
preclude *boku* from undergoing change.[62] This structural repetition that allows for a signal difference can be read as the novella's riffing on jazz time.

The implications of Nakagami's jazz-inspired storytelling become apparent on reviewing his understanding of jazz's central features. Nakagami's
vision of jazz begins with the *kōdo*, a signifyin(g) term that refers simultaneously to the Japanese homophones *chord* and *code*. Eschewing a technical
definition, Nakagami proposes that the chord symbolizes that which defines
jazz as jazz. Whereas other musical genres (here Nakagami name-checks
Miles Davis and the blues) cling to the chords/codes by which their composition is legislated,

> jazz is different from other musical genres: the music that the black
> people who crossed [the Middle Passage] and came to America made
> is rooted in the law/system (chord/code and so on) held within jazz,
> yet jazz also realizes and stands in irritation at the fact that this very
> law and system is also a device used to oppress the development and
> rolling change inherent to the genre of modern jazz, which runs over
> in freedom.[63]

In its "irritation," jazz repeats the chords and codes at its foundation in order to overturn and destroy them by means of those very chords and codes. If, as Nakagami suggested, jazz is one of the keys to analysis of his literature and literary criticism, riffing repetition that longs for "development and rolling change" is one of the doors jazz unlocks.

Nakagami argued that the struggle against chords witnessed in jazz is feasible in both narrative fiction and the stories of our lives, thereby wedding his interest in narrative structure to identity politics. He writes, for example, "John Coltrane is more than a mere jazz artist; to me, he was a literary problem (*bungaku no mondai*) then [when Nakagami first encountered Coltrane in the late 1960s] and he is a literary problem now."[64] Nakagami also writes that what he calls jazz's fight to annihilate (*muka no tatakai*) chords/codes should be considered alongside the notion of chords/codes and law/system as "natural" (*shizen*); free jazz musicians such as Coltrane "blow to overthrow and twist backward the chords/codes, the 'nature' that, *from the moment people are born into this world*, they can no longer invade or even touch."[65] What is at stake in the struggle against chords/codes goes beyond the sonic and into the realm of the literary and ontological.

In writing his early works in jazz time, Nakagami is plotting an escape from the rhythms and foundations of *monogatari*. "I think that people can really understand quite honestly what I mean," Nakagami hints, "by '*monogatari* is my enemy' and 'the destruction of the fixed form of the *monogatari*' as a kind of extension of the free jazz movement executed in jazz by musicians like John Coltrane and Albert Ayler."[66] The "development and rolling change" of jazz, however, as sweet as the sound may be, provides no easy exit from the patterns of *monogatari*. Nakagami's outline of the difficulty of escape begins with the assertion that "chords/codes = nature, law/system = nature and *monogatari* = nature."[67] In the transitive logic of imperial syntax, that which is deemed "natural," the "essence" or "root" of an entity (be it a piece from the jazz repertoire, a work of literature, or a human identity) is equivalent to the way in which it is encoded, systematized, and narrativized. Insofar as jazz "struggles" (*tatakai*) against "nature," it also struggles against *monogatari*. In the face of the *monogatari* of jazz, "real" jazz searches for a singular reality that it can call its own. This search, however, faces a conundrum insofar as "reality (*shinjitsu*) itself is a lie. What I mean by this is that the word *reality* itself is in the midst of a *monogatari*."[68] The development and rolling change of jazz, insofar as it signifies on systematized chords/codes, is never fully released from those chords/codes, which are themselves equal to the narrated illusions of *monogatari*.

Although the possibility of escaping the prison house of chords/codes and *monogatari* is bleak, Nakagami does find one potential exit: exchange (*kōtsū*). Nakagami's *kōtsū*, which signifies on Marx's *verkehr* and the Japanese word for *transit*, "emphasizes relations between parts in a fluid system rather than fixed meaning" and as such is "useful for understanding how narratives stretch beyond one character, work or author."[69] Such riffing exchange is, in the words of Nakagami, "precisely what can annihilate jazz's equivalency to *monogatari*."[70] Nakagami hears in the rhythms of jazz the possibility of repetition that, even as it is rooted in the *monogatari* of some code/chord, still has the power to improvise, rearrange, and ultimately exchange one bit of the code (say, an aspect of "Japanese" identity) for some element of a new source code (say, an aspect of "African American" identity). This exchange imbues jazz with an energy that is literally creative, which makes jazz a possible exit from the codes of *monogatari*.

In *On the Japanese Language*, the repetition of the word *summer* can be read as Nakagami exchanging riffs with thinkers such as Baldwin and Ellison, two authors who figure prominently in the text's intertextual network, on the time that *boku* and Ludolph spend together. These riffs repeat the codes by which *burakuness* and blackness are written in the Japanese language with a Coltrane twist in the hope imbuing them with "development and rolling change." Analogous to his figuration of the blues, Nakagami claimed that "storytelling has its basic . . . fixed rhythm," which, if let to its own devices "will carry you through."[71] Repetition *without* a signal difference in these codes leaves one without "any progress . . . powerless," that is, with the blues.[72] Although it is "impossible to overturn these *monogatari*" completely, Nakagami's repetitions will "work closely with them, shift them a little, [and] try to rearrange them" by way of exchange.[73] Even though he is incarcerated in the prison house of *monogatari*, Nakagami continues, like Monk and Coltrane, to blow in jazz time, convinced—as he once wrote in response to Toni Morrison's *The Bluest Eye*—that when the "characters of a *monogatari*" are written "by an ethnic author as an ethnic author" there always remains the possibility that a "unique folklore (*dokuji no fōkuroa*) . . . will be born."[74]

This, then, is Nakagami's Monku, the jazz café in which *boku* and Ludolph spend the majority of their repeating summers. *Monku* signifies (is signifyin[g]) simultaneously Thelonious Monk, Nakagami's "entry point into a new world" of exchange between jazz and black culture; *monku* (文句), as in a phrase or expression; and the second meaning of *monku*, a complaint or verbal protest.[75] It is somewhere at the intersection of exchange, expression, and verbal protest that we are to understand the time of the story of *On the Japanese Language*, a story with repetitions that revisit in order to revise.

Signifyin(g), Identifyin(g), and Misidentifyin(g) On the Japanese Language

Initially, *boku* feels distant from Ludolph—at one point he describes the gulf between them as a *kiretsu* (fissure)—and sees him as nothing more than a tool to be used to complete a well-paying job. Members of the United Front of Students, an organization reminiscent of the Zenkyōtō, the "joint struggle councils" of the student movement of 1968, select *boku* as their "symbol of the youth of democratic, pacifist Japan" and pay him three thousand yen per day to spend five days with Ludolph.[76] *Boku's* primary responsibility during the five-day interim is to subtly inculcate Ludolph, corrode his fighting spirit with Japanese pacifism, and subliminally influence him to desert America's empire-building campaign in Vietnam. *Boku's* initial intuition is that he is not a good fit for the job, both because he is politically apathetic ("I have absolutely no interest in politics . . . [and] the outcome of Vietnam has nothing to do with me") and because the "fissure" between him and Ludolph might be too wide to traverse ("I didn't have the slightest idea how I was to . . . influence the black soldier and . . . make him . . . desert [the war effort]").[77]

As the exchanges between *boku* and Ludolph progress, the fissure between the two seems to close as *boku* purportedly gets to "know" and "understand" (*wakaru, rikai*) Ludolph. *Boku's* first inkling of his affinity with Ludolph occurs when he discovers their shared ambivalent sense of belonging to their native countries. *Boku* begins to "feel that I can understand (*rikai*) what the black soldier is saying. I can understand a black soldier who can't speak in English vociferously and frankly the way that white soldiers, burly as rugby players, do. Even if all of that is a lie cleverly constructed and wrapped up in the race problem, I can still understand it."[78] The burgeoning sense of identification that *boku* feels, that is, the closing of the "fissure" between them, is signified by their analogous position as readers of black literature. The members of the United Front of Students, for example, don't realize that Ludolph "is a black person, an invisible man" (the English "invisible man" is used in the Japanese original) and that his "psychological state" must be "understood" as such.[79] This is in contrast to *boku*, who—as he tries to persuade Ludolph to desert the war effort now out of a complicated concern for his well-being—worries that "maybe the black soldier can't hear my words. Just like black people lament that they are invisible men, maybe I have become an *inaudible man*."[80] Nakagami's signifyin(g) on Ellison's masterpiece simultaneously underscores the provisional social and thus ontological status of hyphenated being and posits a level of mutual understanding between those who reside in such provisional spaces. Reminiscent of the hauntalogy of blackness discussed in chapter 1, Ludolph becomes "a phantom . . . that dives into [*boku*]'s eye," an invisible entity made visible only from the vantage point of shared marginalization.[81]

Boku's identification with Ludolph, which is made legible through signifyin(g) on *Invisible Man*, is predicated on an epistemological shift, which is made legible through Baldwin's *Nobody Knows My Name*. Before Ludolph becomes visible to *boku*, the two ponder whether a youth who is putatively a symbol of democratic, pacifist postwar Japan can understand the Vietnam War from the perspective of a black American soldier. "To be honest," Ludolph admits, "I don't think you can understand my thoughts on the issue. Nobody knows my name" (the English "nobody knows my name" is used in the Japanese original).[82] In order to see Ludolph, *boku* must first know him. *Boku* recalls, "[I] thought that I understood the feeling of instability that the black soldier embraced; it was like losing your way at a dead end and only being able to flounder about. Nobody knows my name! I took the title of that novel by a black author, transposed it onto Ludolph L. Witt, and thought that I could shout: I'm the only one who knows who you are!"[83]

In intertextually invoking *Nobody Knows My Name*, however, this act of signifyin(g) also suggests a misidentification between *boku* and Ludolph. Much of Baldwin's essayistic project was devoted to destabilizing what might be called the segregation of American identity. The titular essay of Baldwin's *Nobody Knows My Name* is a case in point. It begins with Baldwin's musings on the "Northern Negro" revenant's vision of the South. The black traveler:

> sees the world, from an angle odd indeed, in which his fathers awaited his arrival, perhaps in the very house in which he narrowly avoided being born. He sees, in effect, his ancestors, who, in everything they do and are, proclaim his inescapable identity. And the Northern Negro in the South sees, whatever he or anyone else may wish to believe, that his ancestors are both white and black. The white men, flesh of his flesh, hate him for that very reason. On the other hand, there is scarcely any way for him to join the black community in the South: for both he and this community are in the grip of [an] immense illusion.[84]

The black traveler in another country is confronted with two phenomena. First, he encounters the inescapability of an identity defined by the intersection of his past and his present in a foreign land. This identity makes itself manifest only when we travel beyond the borders of our native communities and encounter individuals from other communities—when Baldwin's "Northern Negro" goes to the South, for example, or Nakagami's Ludolph goes to Japan. Baldwin reminds us that the traveler's state of namelessness is a kind of "inescapable identity" dependent on and intertwined with the Other. Second, this journey beyond the borders of our home exposes the contingency of communal belonging. For Baldwin "inescapable identity" is not followed by the formation of a community of people who identify with one another. Rather, this inescapable identity is actually a misidentification, for the "Northern Negro" is, "whatever he or anyone else may wish to believe" also a Southern Negro and a "white." As such, the namelessness of the revenant is also coupled with homelessness, and the traveler, now misidentified, can no longer join a community based on the "immense illusion" of identity. Nakagami, signifyin(g) on Baldwin through *boku*, concurs: "Oh Ludolph, you're even telling me that the United States of America is 'your country' ['my country' in English in the Japanese original]. The United States of America is an illusion (*gensō*). . . . I'm being manipulated by the illusion of a democratic, pacifist 'Japan' as a symbol of its youth, and he's being manipulated by an illusion of America many times more powerful than Japan's."[85] The parallelism of this last sentence suggests that it is precisely *boku* and Ludolph's act of finding their "inescapable identities," and thus identifying with one another, that also serves as the precursor to misidentification and awakening to the "immense illusion" of identity-based communities. The "asymmetry" (*hitaishōsei*) that Ueda reads between *boku*'s and Ludolph's respective relationships with their home communities even within the symmetry of their shared status as exiles from their respective home communities is a testament to the interplay among identification, misidentification, and precarious, itinerant belonging examined in *On the Japanese Language*.[86] Nakagami's admission in *Jazu to bakudan* (Jazz and Bombs, 1982) that *On the Japanese Language* is only "halfway based on a true story" (*hanbun jitsuwa*) and the "real" Ludolph was a white soldier (Nakagami writes Ludolph as a black character in order to make the story more "interesting") is another such testament.[87]

The very premise of *On the Japanese Language* is itself a kind of misidentification. *Boku*, literally a faux amis, presents himself as something he is not in order to gain a vantage point from which to "observe"—at times the text employs the English *observe*, at others the Japanese *kansatsu*—and perhaps persuade Ludolph. On reading Ludolph's diary, arguably another kind of black literature, however, *boku* realizes that he is not simply the observer but is also being observed. In a diary entry recorded on the day Ludolph first met the members of the United Front of Students, Ludolph notes his desire to become a "social scientist" alongside another reference to *Nobody Knows My Name*. *Boku* has misidentified Ludolph, a black man who is both a soldier and a budding social scientist. *Boku*, as an observer who is also observed, feels as though he has "been snared by the trick (*torikku*) played on him by the notebook."[88]

As the narrative progresses, such moments of peripetia begin to compile and magnify the intensity of the misidentification that runs alongside *boku* and Ludolph's identification. The United Front of Students, for example, takes a photograph of Ludolph and *boku* and plans to publish the it in a student paper with an article that claims that Ludolph has decided to desert the war effort. The article is, by the admission of the United Front, a "fictional *monogatari*."[89] The identification Ludolph and *boku* have made is not enough to break the codes/chords of the article and photograph's *monogatari*-like representation of the two. In an attempt to escape these codes/chords, *boku* suggests that the two get visas and abscond to some other country beyond the reach of the United States and Japan. Ludolph, however, does not believe that such a space exists. In Ludolph's bleak view, there is only one avenue to a space beyond the reign of American imperial syntax: death. The final moment of peripetia occurs with a suicide attempt by Ludolph. *Boku* implores Ludolph to desert so that his life will be spared, only to have his exhortations serve as a precursor to Ludolph's suicide attempt.

Baldwin wrote that "our passion for categorization, life neatly fitted into pegs, has led to an unforeseen, paradoxical distress; confusion, a breakdown of meaning. Those categories which were meant to define and control the world for us have boomeranged us into chaos; in which limbo we whirl, clutching the straws of our definitions."[90] Both Baldwin and Nakagami agree that it is only "within this web of ambiguity, paradox [that we] . . . can find ourselves and the power that will free us from ourselves."[91] Nakagami's tricky turn to black literature and music, his exchanges with the Other on the Other's jazz time—in short, the signifyin(g) present throughout *On the Japanese Language*—are done in search of a way of writing that can free him from imperial syntax and return him to the complexity of misidentifications. Or, in the words of Nakagami, "Free. I loved the word then and I love the word now; there's no changing that."[92]

The freedom that Nakagami seeks, however, seems to come at a price. If Nakagami's respite from imperial syntax occurs in the space opened by vacillations between the exchange of the chords/codes of *monogatari* and the new rhythms produced by misidentification's moments of discord/decoding, Ludolph's suicide attempt is an ominous omen. It portends that one cannot reside in the space opened by such vacillations and exchange in perpetuity, that the free jazz produced in such spaces must be silenced. In short, Nakagami's fiction might ultimately succumb to the containment it so vehemently challenged. Before accepting this implication, I would like to conclude by asking the following question: What comes after the near death experience of Ludolph?

Translating Signifyin(g) and Pronominal Politics

On the Japanese Language is framed by a narrative that asks questions. If and how we might be able to translate our "native tongues," how do these translations alter our ownership of languages, and how does the language of pronominal politics construct our individual and group identities? Insofar as Nakagami addresses these inquiries by way of a frame narrative, he addresses them through a kind of signifyin(g), a kind of repetition with a signal difference. The repetition of elements in the first paragraphs of *On the Japanese Language* in the story's concluding paragraphs is unmistakable. The first paragraphs read:

> If you came across a foreigner (*gaikokujin*) who couldn't comprehend a single word of Japanese, from which word would you begin to teach him Japanese? "See you," "How's it going," "liquor," "women." Or maybe you would show him a postcard colored in garish primary colors and teach him that this is the renowned FUJIYAMA, and maybe you would explain to him that the Japanese state and Japan itself brim with marvelous lyric poetry?
>   Courage, that's probably where I'd start.
>   That's what I wrote in his notebook. I can't imagine that the word I wrote in Japanese—courage—was comprehensible to a twenty-year-old foreigner who would have had desperate difficulties even telling Japanese apart from Swahili or Vietnamese. To this day, I still think all the time about the meaning of the Japanese that I taught him. Even I don't fully understand the meaning of this one word, "courage," and I'm talking to you in Japanese right now; can you picture a twenty-year-old foreigner headed to the battle front, surrounded by the hot stench of grass, mumbling now and again the one Japanese word that he remembers—"courage"? I want to know: if it were you, from which Japanese word you begin to teach him?[93]

Compare this passage to the closing paragraphs of *On the Japanese Language*. The narrator, now being interrogated concerning his role in Ludolph's suicide attempt, revisits the line of inquiry with which the novella begins.

"Courage," that's it, I think. That's what I wrote in the black soldier's notebook. *Help me!* That's what the black soldier cried.

The police officer stared at my face intently, ridiculing me with his glare. And what about you, could you understand the words that the black soldier cried—*Help me!* Can you translate the English "*Help me!*" into the Japanese that we use? I taught the black soldier the Japanese word "courage" without fully knowing what it meant.

A soft feeling of nausea suddenly struck me from deep within my body. In that small, hot interrogation room, I turned to the police officer, who was scorning and sneering at me, and asked him, "If it were you, and you met a foreigner who didn't know anything about Japanese, what words would you teach him first?" That's what I want to know. Faced with a foreigner who doesn't know a single thing about Japanese, what kind of Japanese would you teach him—that's what I want to know.

The police officer smiled condescendingly, as if my words, trailing off and unclear, were not Japanese but words heard in the vicinity of Thailand or Burma. I felt my entire body being twined by a fear that, in this room, the officer's derisive laughter would swallow my words, it might even make my body dissolve. I babbled repeatedly words that would hardly voice themselves deep in my body. From which word would you start teaching Japanese—that is what I want to know.[94]

The frame narrative's signifyin(g) is a double play on Nakagami's behalf insofar as the closing frame narrative repeats, critiques, and revises both the opening narrative and the logic of the essentializing readings of minority group solidarity with which some readers (maybe this can be called a BLL approach) might read *On the Japanese Language*, a work of "minority" literature. In the opening frame narrative, the reader is led to assume that the narrator, although he doesn't "fully" comprehend certain words of the Japanese language, is in control of his mother tongue. The narrator's mastery is evinced by the fact that he "is talking to you in Japanese right now." The responsibility for misunderstanding lies on the shoulders of the foreign youth, who can't differentiate "Japanese from Swahili or Vietnamese."

Nakagami's closing frame narrative suggests that the moment we begin to search for a translation of our "native languages" is the moment that we come face-to-face with the fact that we do not own our native tongues. After the reader has traversed the central narrative, which thematizes the cross-cultural dialogue between the Japanese *boku* and the black Ludolph, and arrived at the closing frame narrative, Nakagami shifts the responsibility for misunderstanding onto the narrator's (read the "native speaker's") shoulders. In stark contrast to the opening frame, it is now the narrator's "trailing off and unclear" Japanese that can't be differentiated from the "words heard in the vicinity of Thailand or Burma." Moreover, within the closing frame's syntactical repetition of "that's what I want to know," there is noticeable syntactical deviation. To mimic the syntax of the Japanese original, the narrator exclaims twice, "I want to know that (*boku wa sore wo shiritai*)," only to have the final sentence of the novel flip this syntax on its head, thus becoming "That is what I want to know (*Sore wo boku wa shiritai*)." Just as the narrator's fear that the he is losing control of his native language is twisting, twining, and making his body dissolve, so, too, is his syntactic control of language twisting and (over)turning. What I am calling *boku*'s loss of his native language has been articulated by Atsuko Ueda as the "slippage (*zure*) between *boku*'s singular linguistic system and 'Japanese'" and by Nakagami himself as the "distance (*kyori*) between 'Japan' and 'me.'"[95]

Derrida proposes that such babble "ruptures the rational transparency" of "the human community" in order to "interrupt colonial violence or . . . linguistic imperialism."[96] If syntactical imperialism can be added to this list, reading the opening frame narrative against the closing frame suggests that Nakagami would concur with Derrida. The opening frame narrative posits three versions of personhood: the first-person singular of the "I" (*boku*) of the narrator, the second-person singular of the "you" (*anata*) to whom "I" asks where to begin teaching Japanese, and the third-person singular of the "he" (*kare*). As a native Japanese speaker, *boku* supposedly belongs to the "we" of the Japanese state. It is this sense of belonging (to the Japanese state) that prompts *boku* to speak on behalf of Japan in search of a word that might "explain to him that the Japanese state and Japan itself is brimming with marvelous lyric poetry."[97] Note *boku*'s use of the third-person singular to refer to Ludolph. "He," that is, Ludolph, does not belong to the Japanese state. Ludolph's belonging to a different polity is signaled both by his unfamiliarity with the Japanese language and by the epithets "twenty-year-old foreign youth" and "foreigner," which occur four times in the two-page opening narrative. Between the "I" and the "he" is the "you" whom *boku* implores to answer his inquiry. Given that this "you"—an unspecified, ambiguous narratee whose position is superimposed on that of the reader—is a fellow Japanese speaker who might be able to answer *boku*'s question, we are to assume that the "you" of the narratee/reader, like *boku*, belongs to Japan by virtue of the adhesive of language.

The pronominal politics of the closing frame narrative, however, repeats such hasty assumptions in order to critique and implode them. We have already discussed *boku*'s loss of the Japanese language and subsequent loss of self and sense of belonging. By the closing frame narrative, *boku* clearly does not belong to the "we" (*wareware*) of the United Front, the connection between *boku* and Ludolph has been undermined by misidentification, and *boku* is left "shaking as if he has almost completely lost [his] ability to speak" a native language he no longer controls.[98] The closing frame also destabilizes and makes the reader misidentify the third-person singular. Ludolph, himself on the precipice of death after his suicide attempt, is referred to throughout the narrative as either "the black soldier" (*kokujin-hei*) or Ludolph. As such, when the closing frame reiterates the term *foreigner*—"Faced with a foreigner who doesn't know a single thing about Japanese"—the reader cannot be sure that this "foreigner" refers to Ludolph, a name that somebody—both *boku* and the reader—now knows. Rather than a reference to Ludolph in particular, the "foreigner" of the closing narrative seems to refer to a more general case—what is one to do when faced with a dialogue with a foreigner that requires translation? The closing frame narrative's shift from the particular to the hypothetical is highlighted by the elision of the "twenty-year-old youth" epithet, which was used to identify Ludolph. As such, the narrative has effectively split the third-person singular into multiple singularities.

This split in the third person is juxtaposed with an analogous split of the second person. Recall the opening frame's superimposition of the narratee and the reader and *boku*'s appeal to this narratee/reader to help him teach the Japanese language as a fellow representative of the Japanese state. In the closing frame narrative, the second person is occupied by both the narratee/reader and the police officer, a representative par excellence of the Japanese state whom *boku* directly addresses. This representative par excellence, however, not only has no answer to *boku*'s question, but his voice is the catalyst of *boku*'s loss of voice and self. After his exchanges with Ludolph—himself a figure who both does and does not belong to the United States—*boku* can no longer effectively communicate with the representative authorities of Japan and thus can no longer assume that he belongs to the Japanese community by virtue of the adhesive of language.

After Ludolph's suicide attempt, then, *On the Japanese Language* leaves the reader with an "I" that is "dissolving" (*yōkai*) and losing possession of its native language, a "he" that has been split into multiple singularities, and a divided "you" with which a first-person-plural solidarity can no longer be underwritten by means of a shared mother tongue. Even in the wake of such ruptures, however, *boku* continues to search desperately for a translation of the Japanese language so that he might speak with Ludolph. As the "I," "he," and first "you" dissolve, *boku* continues to implore the second "you," the narratee/reader, to answer his question: "If it were you, and you met a foreigner who didn't know anything about Japanese, what words would you teach them first?"[99] Indeed, the only potential community that *boku* has left is the one with a "you" who, like him, does not own a native tongue and will speak in translation, hence *boku*'s question: "Can you translate the English "*Help me!*' into the Japanese *that we use?*"[100] Note that *boku*'s native language is not something that he owns but something that he borrows, shares, and uses with other speakers.

Boku's perpetual search for translation is indicative of Nakagami's answer to the question of how we are to speak the Other's tongue without renouncing our own. *On the Japanese Language* posits "'English' and 'Japanese' [as] unequivocally designated language areas that are brought about only by way of translation."[101] As such the text provides a literary complement to Derrida's philosophical treatment of the necessity of translation. Derrida deems "the law of a translation" to be "both necessary and impossible . . . translation [as] duty, and debt, but the debt one can no longer discharge."[102] As a permanently insolvent debt, speaking in translation obligates *boku* to always search for the language of the Other while respecting the fact that he will never fully own that language. Such a search, Derrida suggests, will lead to two conditions: first, fissures in "universal tongue[s]," "unique genealogy," and the "peaceful transparency of the human community"; and, second, new forms of community in which we "belong without belonging."[103]

Conclusion

Nakagami's vacillation between identification and misidentification, his refusal to submit fully to any imperial syntax, his constant struggle to communicate via translation rather than originary language—in a word, his passing significance—exemplifies the act of speaking the Other's language in a state of permanent debt. Misidentification, Derrida and Nakagami would argue, the ability to "belong without belonging," is the critical starting point from which *boku* and "you" (the second you) might become a member of a truly inclusive "we," hence *boku*'s search for the place to begin teaching the Japanese language even after Ludolph's suicide attempt.

Judith Butler articulates the possibility of building miscommunities alluded to in the conclusion of *On the Japanese Language*: "Does politicalization always need to overcome disidentification? What are the possibilities of politicizing *dis*identification, this experience of *misrecognition*, this uneasy sense of standing under a sign to which one does and does not belong?"[104]

Nakagami's politicalization of misidentification asks us to see terms such as *black* and *buraku* as, to follow Butler again, a "permanent site of contest."[105] As a permanent site of contest, such terms never fully exhaust and define identities and thus never definitively dictate the terms on which others might join political communities. Such permanent contest requires a double movement: "to invoke the category [of black, of *buraku*, of anything], and hence, provisionally to institute and identify *and at the same time* to open the category as a site of permanent political contest . . . to interrogate the exclusions by which it proceeds, and to do this precisely in order to learn how to live the contingency of the political signifier in a culture of democratic contestation."[106]

Although such a double movement "open[s] up a difficult future terrain of community, one in which the hope of ever fully recognizing oneself in the terms by which one signifies is sure to be disappointed," Nakagami entrenches himself on this terrain as he struggles to repeat and revise the essentializing constructions of *burakuness* in imperial syntax.[107] His double movement obligates him to trade the stability of an essential identity and group solidarity for a vantage point from which to highlight the cursory nature of essential identities and group solidarities. Nakagami parlays the loss of an essentialized identity—he once claimed, for example, "I don't need to be in Japan; I don't need to be Japanese"—into the gain of a transient misidentity that can join communities situated well beyond the borders of Japan, hence Nakagami's claim, in the very same text in which he loses his "Japaneseness" no less, that "wherever I go, people mistake me for a native. It happened in Hong Kong, it happened in Macau . . . it happened in New York."[108]

I have tried to add the following to the scholarly consensus that Nakagami turned to a variety of traditions of minority writing in his global search for an alternative to imperial syntax: that his turn to black language, literature, and music in the late 1960s formed a foundation on which his future writings would build, that this informative engagement with blackness spanned the time from his early 1960s short fiction to his late 1970s *buraku* cultural criticism and 1980s speeches and reportage, and that he perpetually grappled with the problem of balancing his identification with blackness with his desire to guard against the formation of a *buraku*-black-based imperial syntax. The language and tropes of black literature provide Nakagami with a template for writing himself into and out of two communities simultaneously. Even as he forms solidarities with transnational minority groups in order to build an amalgamated language that won't buckle in the face of imperial syntax, he signifies on both the master('s) trope and the tropes of *buraku*/black cultural protest, both of which might ask him to identify essentially in a manner that is no less violent than that of imperial syntax to mitigate his first-person singularity.

I'd like to conclude by taking Nakagami up on his suggestion regarding the necessity of translation. The following is a translation of an excerpt from Nakagami's *Buffalo Soldiers*. The translated passage, the token's signifyin(g) in particular, synthesizes many of the arguments I have made here. In the excerpt, Nakagami recounts a story from his time in New York City circa 1988. A friend has invited him to watch a rehearsal of an all-black dance troupe. He writes:

> I watched the black men and women rehearse for an hour.
>
> And then I made up my mind.
>
> I would join their all-black group, dance with them as a black person who came from Japan.
>
> I am black.
>
> Inescapably black.
>
> Of course, this is me we're talking about, so I've never once thought about trying to escape my blackness.
>
> I know that black is beautiful.
>
> I know that black is purity.
>
> My knowledge of this, my sensibility regarding it, it is, in a word, the first salvo in the body's battle against language.
>
> No: keeping in mind that I'm a black person who came from Japan, this is language's first challenge to the body. . . .
>
> [On my way home, I] went down the stairs to get on the subway in the Bronx and was about to buy a token. When I pulled a dollar out of my wallet, a young black person standing next to the ticket gate said "You wanna buy a token?" and presented the tokens he had in the palm of his hand. A token's a token no matter if I buy it from the booth in the station or from the youth hanging out there. And I knew that, in Harlem or in the slums, subway tokens were used as currency. The youngster probably found the token in the back of a taxi or on the street and came here to sell it. And he's black. I'm black too. In other words, we're brothers.
>
> OK, I'll buy it from you. I bought two tokens from him for two dollars. . . . Those two tokens. When I put the tokens in, the turnstile's bar didn't budge. The coins were, in other words, fake. I'd been duped by the fake coins; the black woman in the booth who sold me a real token clicked her tongue in sympathy.[109]

CHAPTER 4

Genre Trouble

Breaking the Law of Genre and Literary Blackness in the Long 1970s

> As soon as the word "genre" is sounded, as soon as it is heard . . .
> a limit is drawn. And when a limit is established, norms and
> interdictions are not far behind . . . the law of genre. And this
> can be said of genre in all genres, be it a question of a generic or a
> general determination of what one calls "nature" . . . (for example, a
> biological *genre*) . . . or be it a question of a typology designated as
> non-natural and depending on laws or orders which were once held
> to be opposed to *physis* . . . (for example, an artistic, poetic or literary
> genre).
>
> —Jacques Derrida and Avital Ronell, "The Law of Genre"

Absent the framework of a conversation on blackness in Japanese literature, what would possibly bring the disparate collection of texts considered
here together? Given that the texts considered here are written in varying
styles and time periods and cover an array of thematic content, what else
might bind a text like "Kokujin no kyōdai" (The Black Brothers), Ema Shū's
(1889–1975) 1928 proletarian morality play in prose published in *Senki*,
with a text like *Kuronbō* (Darkie), Endō Shūsaku's (1923–96) 1971 satirical,
more-fiction-than-history historical fiction of Yasuke and Nobunaga? Or
what, for that matter, do Ishikawa Jun and Yamada Eimi have in common?
Or, in Derrida and Ronell's rephrasing of the question posed by Nakagami
in chapter 3, "For who would have us believe that we, we two for example,
would form a genre or belong to one?"[1]

This chapter addresses Derrida's inquiry by posing two questions of its
own.[2] First, how do various genres of Japanese literature, each with their

own generic conventions, think through blackness in ways that engage with the contours defined by those conventions? Generic difference, interestingly enough, ensures that various writings of blackness in Japanese literature are sui generis; the "blackness" of Yoshida Ruiko's (1938–) photojournalism, for example, engages with a different set of heuristics for the inscription of race than Morimura Seiichi's (1933–) murder mystery does. These differing generic conditions and end games lead to idiosyncratic constructions of race, and, symbiotically, race both reinvents and reinforces the conventions of the genres that attempt to contain it in singular ways.

The second question posed here is this. Are there shared affinities that cut across the generic borders of these disparate texts, thereby becoming "generic" to Japanese literary blackness? To be clear, I am arguing that if such affinities exist this would suggest not a *genre* of black Japanese literature, but evidence for *genericity,* that is, that there are *generic* aspects to the construction of black settings, characters, and stories in the works addressed here. Such genericity would speak to, among other things, the ways in which various authors—irrespective of generic guidelines—are engaged in and informed by larger, shared discourses of race and ethnicity. It also invites an exploration of how the tropes and stereotypes of blackness that circulate throughout Japanese literature become generic—an investigation of blackness in motion, the crisscrossing of blackness across the confines of genre, and its congealing and codification.

In tandem these two questions pose a larger set of inquiries common to genre studies: how does the individual become a part of the collective; how does the sui generis become generic; how much of the sui generis is effaced in reading for the generic; and in what ways does including the individual irrevocably alter the collective?

I ask these questions against the historical backdrop of a moment that I call the long 1970s. The period between the mid-1960s through the early 1980s saw a number of Japanese literary texts informed by events that carried transpacific significance with regard to race relations. Examples of such events include the escalation of the Vietnam War, the 1963 March on Washington, the Sayama trial mentioned in chapter 3, the Harlem Riots of 1964, the Tokyo Olympics of the same year, the assassination of Martin Luther King Jr. on 4 April 1968, the riots that surrounded the signing of the Civil Rights Act less than a week later, and so on. These events received spectacular coverage in the Japanese media. The reportage on black America by Honda Katsu'ichi (1932–) encouraged and sponsored by the *Asahi shimbun* is one pertinent example. Add to such media coverage the work done during this period by organizations such as Kokujin kenkyū no kai and the Afro-

NEGRO MONEY MEN

WOMEN WHO MAKE
STATE LAWS

JAPAN'S REJECTED:
Teen-age war babies
face bleak future

SEPTEMBER 1967 50¢

Figure 4. The cover
of the September
1967 issue of *Ebony*
magazine, which
features eight
photographs of black
Japanese "war babies"
entering young
adulthood in the long
1970s. They are, in
the words of *Ebony*,
"Japan's Rejected: Teen-
age war babies [who]
face [a] bleak future."

Asian Writers Association, which cultivated the circulation of literature and ideas throughout the Black Pacific. And add to that the "millions of dollars" that "paid for hundreds and perhaps thousands of promising young scholars brought from Third World countries to the United States on fellowships for the purpose of converting them to the new gospel" of the American world order.[3] This funding effectively subsidized the travel of Japanese authors throughout (black) America. Think here of Yoshida Ruiko's and Ariyoshi Sawako's (1931–84) funding from the Rockefeller Foundation, Oda Makoto's (1932–2007) and Yoshida Ruiko's funding from the Fulbright Foundation, and Ōe Kenzaburō's participation in Harvard's International Seminar during the directorship of Henry Kissinger. And, as if to embody the black-Japanese confluences of the era, the biracial children born during the Occupation came of age. *Ebony* magazine's special edition on Japan's war babies and Sawada Miki's (1901–80) *Kuroi jujika no Agasa* (Agatha of the Black Cross) were published in the same year, 1967.[4]

The ferment of the long 1970s gave birth to a black boom in Japanese literature. The period saw an explosion of black characters, settings, and motifs. From travelogues to murder mysteries and science fiction, its energy reverberated across genre lines. This chapter considers five works penned during this period (listed in the order they appear in this chapter): Yoshida Ruiko's *Hāremu no atsui hibi* (Hot Harlem Days, 1972), Honda Katsu'ichi's *Amerika gasshūkoku* (The United States of America, serialized in the *Asahi Shimbun* from 1969 to 1970 but published in book form in 1970), Ariyoshi Sawako's 1964 *Hishoku* (Not Because of Color), Morimura Seiichi's 1976 *Ningen no shōmei* (typically translated as "Proof of the Man" but referred to here as "Human Proof"), and an excerpt from Abe Kōbō's 1964 *Tanin no kao* (The Face of Another). I have selected these five texts in order to create a literary spectrum of generic approaches to the fact(s) of blackness. I begin with the work whose genre calls for the highest degree of fidelity between the written word and the blackness "out there in the world" (Yoshida Ruiko's photojournalism) and move gradually to the text from the genre that calls for the lowest (the science fictional elements of Abe Kōbō's *The Face of Another*). *Hot Harlem Days* is equal parts photojournalistic documentary, memoir, and political essay. Honda Katsu'ichi deals in political reportage. Ariyoshi Sawako's novel is a social realist depiction of Japanese war brides. Morimura Seiichi's *Human Proof* is, as the title intimates, a whodunit murder mystery. Abe Kōbō's *The Face of Another* is a polyvocal text that plays with multiple genres. With that said, the first genre among equals in this genre-bending text is science fiction.

This chapter addresses the "genre trouble" that the juxtaposition of these five texts engenders. I consider each individual text's sui generis contributions to Japan's writing of blackness. But I am also interested in the generic promises of cross-racial commonality and solidarity that cut across these sui generis texts and threaten to break the law of long 1970s American and Japanese racial ideology. Rather than focusing first on analogy (Ōe) or dynamic intertextuality (Nakagami), the texts of the long 1970s share a key generic mark: a characterization of Afro-Japanese relations as a kind of profound hybridity written in and on the body itself. Such hybridity, in turn, posits irrevocable, intimate intertwinement as the organizing principle of long 1970s racial existences.

Genre and the Sui Generis

Yoshida Ruiko and the Synesthetic Blackness of Hot Harlem Days

After graduating from Keio University and working as an interpreter/translator for the broadcasting company NHK International and an announcer for the Asahi Broadcasting Corporation, Yoshida Ruiko moved to the United

States in 1961 to pursue training in journalism. After studying at Ohio University, she began graduate coursework in broadcast journalism at Columbia University's School of Journalism under the auspices of the Fulbright Foundation. Shortly thereafter she met and married a fellow Columbia University graduate student. The newlyweds were encouraged by Columbia to participate in what Yoshida calls a housing experiment. The "experiment" was for Yoshida to live in subsidized housing in Harlem, the hope being that including members of the Columbia intelligentsia in the Harlem community would lead to cultural exchange and "edification" of the black residents. Yoshida's subsequent move to Harlem would turn out to be fortuitous. She spent the overwhelming majority of the 1960s as a resident of Harlem, and the sights and people there became the focal point of her life's work. By the time of her 1971 return to Japan, she had taken some thirty thousand photographs of Harlem. *Hāremu no atsui hibi* (Hot Harlem Days: Black Is Beautiful), which chronicles Yoshida's life in Harlem, is a companion piece to a Yoshida photo exhibition that opened in Tokyo in 1971, shortly after her return to Japan after a decade of life in Harlem and the United States.

In *Hot Harlem Days*, Yoshida articulates her rationale for transitioning from broadcast journalism to photojournalism. A part of her rationale was a generic "push" factor. Yoshida felt constricted by "'journalism,' which called for writing and speaking in English," her second language.[5] There was also, however, a generic pull factor: Yoshida found "a new world of wonders in 'the journalism of sight.'"[6] Yoshida saw in this wonderful new world the ideal medium for documenting life in Harlem. Recalling the photograph that marked her "birth as a camerawoman," for example, Yoshida remembers the subject of her photograph—a young black resident of Harlem celebrating her birthday—staring at her own face and, astonished, asking, "Is this me?"[7] In this moment of birth, both Yoshida and her photographed subject find a vision of black subjectivity that can be captured only through the lens of her camera. One operative term here is *her*. The beauty that Yoshida Ruiko sets out to record in *Hot Harlem Days: Black Is Beautiful* is one of familial belonging. Yoshida often plays the part of "big sister" or "mother" to her photographed subjects; one character in *Hot Harlem Days* even pulls out a picture of his mother to prove that she looks like Yoshida in spite of their racial difference. *Hot Harlem Days* frames Yoshida's collection of photographs as a kind of family album, and Yoshida's sororal/maternal connection to her photographed subjects facilitates her access to the intimate moments of the otherwise segregated communities of Harlem. Yoshida's vicarious inclusion in the "album" speaks to the possibility of a greater, transracial family, a point I will return to in the conclusion of this section.

On photographing the birthday girl, Yoshida "made [a] resolution: 'I'll record the faces and lives of those around me with my camera. My camera will capture everything, right down to that turpentine fragrance of black folks.'"[8] This resolution voices several of the signatures of Yoshida's photographic project. The first of these is her interest in the mundane aspects of everyday black life. For Yoshida black life is inseparable from the black folks who live it, making them the central subjects of her photography. A second signature is Yoshida's subscription to documentary realism, which is embodied in the passage above by her desire to "record (*kiroku*)" her black subjects. Two of Yoshida's self-proclaimed muses are Ishimoto Yasuhiro and Robert Flaherty; her photojournalism shows traces of the street photography of Ishimoto's "Chicago, Chicago" period and the narrative thrusts of Flaherty's documentary gazes at ethnic difference.

There is one other signature highlighted here that is of particular import: the synesthetic approach of Yoshida's photography. Yoshida's self-styled synesthetic aspirations are alluded to in the passage above by way of photography that captures turpentine fragrances. Although it reproduces a well-trod "smell of blackness" trope and metaphorically dehumanizes her subjects, here Yoshida attempts to articulate her intoxication with black beauty (and present her close-enough-to-smell-it black bona fides). I am not the first person to note that Yoshida's photography stretches beyond the visual as it attempts to record the sounds and smells and tastes and textures of Harlem. Kijima Hajime, a poet known for his arresting translations of Langston Hughes, made a similar argument in verse. In "For Ruiko and Her Pictures," one of the poems that accompanied the photography in Yoshida and Kajima's *Hāremu: Kuroi tenshitachi* (Harlem: Black Angels, 1974), Kijima writes that New York is a city where "distrust inhabits tall buildings, / No place where the senses aren't locked in."[9] Yoshida's photography, however, unlocks the senses: "You led me, clutching your camera, / To churches in Harlem, to midnight jazz bars. / You took photos, each photo a soft breath / Your lens groped through the labyrinth, the dark."[10] Just as the staccato rhythm of Kijima's verse strives to capture the feel and sound and soft aspiration of Yoshida's photography, Yoshida's photography attempts to exceed the limitations of visual representation, thereby facilitating her Japanese viewership's access to the full palette of the sensations of Harlem.

Yoshida Ruiko's sui generis contribution to the long 1970s writing of blackness becomes palpable when her text is juxtaposed with her images. If Yoshida's photography is synesthetic, her prose might be described as photographic. *Hot Harlem Days* is organized by way of prose episodes that might be called snapshots, each lasting approximately three to six pages. Many of these prose snapshots are paired with actual snapshots of the event be-

Figure 5. Harlem kids outside a jazz store. In each of these shots, angle, depth, and mise-en-scène replicate the sensation of sounds associated with various black urban spaces. (© Ruiko Yoshida.)

ing described, thereby enhancing the verisimilitude of the prose. Yoshida's writes in sepia tones, her detailed descriptions leaning toward the austere and avoiding moments of literary flourish. In lieu of flourish, there is photographic prose, or prose informed by Yoshida's time behind the lens. Take, for example, this sentence, which describes children smiling at Yoshida: "In a flash, their full, flesh-colored lips opened to show sparkling white teeth. The contrast between their sparkling teeth and chocolate skin left a profound impression on me; I've never seen teeth so beautiful, healthy, and white, I thought."[11]

The stark contrast between white and black spaces—a theme with obvious significance for Yoshida—recurs throughout *Hot Harlem Days*. In describing the development of "What's in the Poor Boy's Pocket," an award-winning photo that circulated throughout both Japan and the United States (and adorns the cover of *Hot Harlem Days*), Yoshida writes, "Immersed in the developing solution, the black space gradually expanded, and this was followed by white pupils. When they floated to the surface, I cried out, involuntarily, 'This is it!'"[12] Miura Masahiro notes that one signature of Yoshida's Harlem period is "macrophotography," shots from "point blank range, 50 centimeters from the face of the subject, which fills a 35 millimeter frame with the photographed face."[13] Ever the synesthete, Yoshida hears "some kind of plea" in eyes of the black children who fill her frames, "some kind of prayer, or perhaps some kind of protest, a doubt and a desire to believe and depend on me."[14]

The interplay between Yoshida's prose and photography helps her Japanese readership hear and see that plea. A vivid example of this occurs in "Black and White," a section of *Hot Harlem Days* in which Yoshida explores how the color line demarcates an impenetrable border in American sociopolitics and psyches. The section superimposes definitive statements such as "In America . . . blacks are seen as less than whites. That is the kind of country that America is," with photographs such as the one reproduced in figure 7.[15] An absolute border runs through the center of the image, separating the overwhelmingly white space, which dominates the top half of the image, from the underexposed dark space, which holds up its white counterpart. The photograph's narrative includes several moments of black and white integration, in which elements of the photograph appear precisely because of the contrast: the porcelain white fountain against its black backdrop, a placard that denotes the whiteness of this portion of the shared space in an authoritative font, and the thin black intrusion of a power cord that reaches up from the darkness to power the upper half are three examples of such contrast. The space designated for "coloreds," which is shot at an angle that

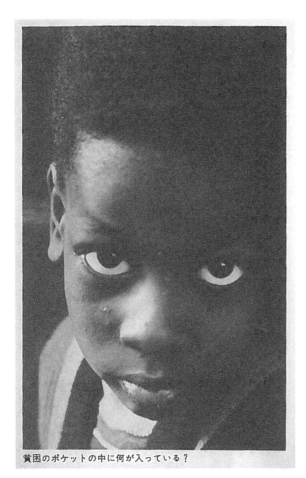

貧困のポケットの中に何が入っている？

Figure 6. "What's in the Poor Boy's Pocket?" (© Ruiko Yoshida.)

suggests this space is not shared equally, just barely squeezes into the left margin of the image. The contradictions of separate but equal are reflected in the image's inability to uphold the parallelism promised by features such as its central borderline and "equal" alignment of the white and colored plac-ards. A diagonal line—with (electrical) power on the top, the white fountain in the middle, and the blatantly belittled black fountain on the bottom—runs askew through the photograph. In both her prose and photography, there is little room for hyperbole; Yoshida's readers are obligated to come eye-to-eye and face-to-face with American discrimination.

Yoshida herself discovered the "plea in black children's eyes" during her time in Harlem. When she interviewed black musicians such as Art Blakey during her time as a broadcaster in Japan, all she could do was "wonder

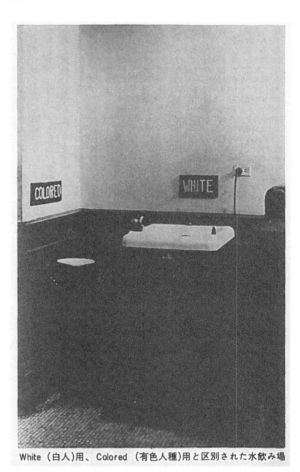

Figure 7. Yoshida's
visualization of the
contradictions of
"separate but equal."
(© Ruiko Yoshida.)

White（白人）用、Colored（有色人種）用と区別された水飲み場

why white people in America would discriminate against such courteous
black people."[16] After living in the United States, however, she could "feel
with [her] own skin the way that white people gaze at black people."[17] In
accounting for this change in racial consciousness, it might help to think in
photography's terms; the lived experience of life in Harlem allows Yoshida
to view the figures of blackness against its many backgrounds. In discussions
of topics such as the black family, poverty, violence, crime, sexuality, and
drug abuse, Yoshida rarely takes potshots at simple stereotypes. She instead
provides nuanced readings of the individual actors of Harlem against their
sociopolitical backdrops (the rise of the Black Panthers and black nationalism, the impact of the Vietnam War on black communities, the Kennedy
administration's antipoverty efforts, and so on).

Yoshida sees three things in these richly contextualized portraits of life in Harlem: the beauty of blackness, her own "yellowness," and the grotesqueness of Japanese discrimination. The final moments of *Hot Harlem Days* recapitulate these three discoveries:

> But why did I, a Japanese person, take photographs of American blacks with such devotion? Of course, a part of it was simply the environment I found myself in; I happened to discover beautiful images there. Now that I'm back in Japan, however, I've come to the undeniable realization that there was something more than just that. Theirs is a history of continual oppression and conflict. The image of them coming from that history and going to an awakening, full of dignity, to blackness was pulling at something within me. For me—as one who had been put in America, a racist nation-state with an amalgam of people of various races—it made visible my own identity as a yellow person. It happened subliminally. The photographs were an act of frantic resistance from a yellow woman who had been placed between black and white. Whenever I took photographs of their radiant skin, I felt a yellow liquid oozing from my pores like mustard.[18]

Yoshida begins by drawing a parallel between the condition of black Harlemites and her own, for they both "find themselves" (here Yoshida repeats the passive form to highlight a shared lack of agency) in the American environment and manage to create beauty under these conditions. Seeing this beauty is contingent on awakening and resistance to the conditions that attempt to undermine it: the invisible ideologies of a "racist nation-state." In Yoshida's case, this awakening is prompted by the *sugata* of black folks—a term that can mean "image," "picture," "figure," or "form" but also "state" or "condition." So her photographs provide pictures and images of the black condition. Moreover, on experiencing this awakening, Yoshida can see not only the beauty of blackness but the ugliness of Japan's own history of discrimination: "On the surface, at least, Japan is more peaceful than America. . . . But, on the other side of that surface, there is discrimination against the Koreans, who were once oppressed [by the Japanese], discrimination against the . . . *burakumin*," the "long history of discrimination against Okinawa" by mainland Japan, and the "pillaging of land from the indigenous Ainu, which bears a striking resemblance to the history of white Europeans pillaging the land of Native Americans with unfair means and prices."[19] Yoshida's awakening, then, means coming to terms with both the beauty and the ugliness done in the name of Japanese "yellowness," a "reject[ion]" of

"Western racial hierarchies, while criticizing her compatriots, particularly the Japanese intelligentsia, for their uncritical embrace of them and oppression of minorities at home."[20]

By juxtaposing synesthetic photography and photographic prose, Yoshida synergizes the respective claims to verisimilitude held by realist photography and journalistic prose, which gives her readers/viewers the impression of a documentarian recording of black life in Harlem with photographic accuracy. The overwhelming majority of Yoshida's panorama—both prosaic and photographic—depicts a beautiful struggle in the face discrimination, thereby evincing the "reality" of the titular beauty of Yoshida's Harlem. With this Yoshida entered a debate that stretches as far back as at least the Harlem Renaissance. In 1926 DuBois would propose that the "bounden duty of black American" and its artists was "to begin [the] great work of the creation of beauty, of the preservation of beauty, of the realization of beauty."[21] Yoshida agrees with DuBois: "If you don't think your subject is beautiful, if you don't love it, then you shouldn't photograph it. At least that's my photographic morality (*kamera moraru*)."[22]

From Objective Reportage to Reportage with an Objective: Honda Katsu'ichi's The United States of America

"As far as I know," Yoshida writes in *Hot Harlem Days*, "there is only a single (*ishoku*, literally 'of a different color') Japanese journalist who burst through the exoskeleton of his Japaneseness and lived with black people, traveled with them, and saw America through the eyes of black folks: the *Asahi shimbun*'s Honda Katsu'ichi."[23] Already a well-respected reporter due to his war correspondence from Vietnam, in 1969 Honda was encouraged by Tashiro Kikuo, who was at that time the chief editor of the main branch office of the *Asahi shimbun*, to conduct investigative reporting on the American "Negro problem." This assignment sent Honda to the United States, where he would, to borrow Yoshida's words, live, travel, and see the world through black (and Native American) eyes. Honda's six-month journey began in Harlem, which housed an American branch office of the *Asahi shimbun*, and included extensive travel throughout the South (the Carolinas, Georgia, Florida, Alabama, Mississippi, Louisiana, and Texas), the Southwest (primarily New Mexico and Arizona), and the West Coast (primarily California and Washington state). Although he did publish with *Asahi* while in the United States—this is the "Black World" (*Kuroi sekai*) series that *Asahi shimbun* ran from August 1969 through February 1970—Honda's 1970 *Amerika gasshūkoku* (The United States of America) compiles and chronicles his reflections on this period.

If considered generically, Honda's journalism shares a great deal of affinity with the photojournalism of Yoshida Ruiko. Indeed, Honda himself calls Yoshida's *Hot Harlem Days* "an account of what is most likely the most profound engagement of a Japanese person with Harlem."[24] One point of commonality between Yoshida's text and Honda's is that Honda includes and discusses several of Yoshida's photographs from *Hot Harlem Days* in his *United States of America*. It is precisely because of this affinity, however, that the nuances of Yoshida and Honda come into high relief. Take, for example, Yoshida's and Honda's different commentaries on an image shared between the two texts. Yoshida claims that the photograph captures the hostile solemnity that pulsed through black America in the days following Martin Luther King Jr.'s assassination. The photograph is of a Harlem bar and is shot from the far end of a bar counter, giving the image a surreal sensation of ongoing depth. Yoshida describes the scene as people eating in silence "with murderous intent in the air as if they themselves had just returned from a killing."[25] Compare this to Honda's portrayal of the same image. In a discussion of nightlife in Harlem, Honda includes the image alongside the following description: "The moment you set foot in the bar, [you're bombarded] by its teeming morass of people and sounds and voices. . . . Black skin gyrates violently in time to the record's rhythm. Women dance as they release explosive screams."[26] How is it that the same image can hold both solemn silence and explosive screams?

The difference here is indicative of the subtleties of Yoshida's and Honda's respective projects. Whereas Yoshida is interested primarily in recording the beauty of Harlem and its inhabitants, Honda is interested in a sociocultural anthropology of blackness and its political implications for his Japanese readership. Honda has a particular set of implications in mind (as does, of course, Yoshida and the other writers considered here), and his *United States of America* leverages the factuality of reportage to evince the interpretations of his anthropological data that he provides. That is to say, unlike Yoshida's, the self-styled objective of Honda's reportage is not "recording" or neutral reporting. Although his work is, according to Honda himself, "a report of the facts that I certainly saw with my own eyes and experienced with my own body . . . insofar as so-called objective reality is an illusion, I will say that my reportage is from the perspective of black people, who are on the side of the oppressed—they are the heart of my perspective."[27]

In this passage, which is a defense against claims that his reporting is biased and specious, Honda navigates the central conundrum of literary journalism, a genre that must counterbalance the myriad perspectives available to literary works with the single perspective—Archimedean—of objective journalism. In his *Reporutāju no hōhō* (Methods of Reportage), for example, Honda runs the following thought experiment. Suppose "we have five facts (*jijitsu*), or five documents—let's call them A, B, C, D, and E," which all explain the same phenomenon.[28] If D is the most likely to "draw the interest of the general public," Honda concludes, then we should focus 80 percent on D and leave the rest of the alphabet to supplement the remaining 20 percent of the story.[29] Honda's desire to "draw the interest of the general public" by emphasizing one fact (*jijitsu*, a term that also means "truth" or "reality") over others is a corollary of the value that he placed on reportage's ability to cultivate *mondai ishiki*, or "problem consciousness" (read: a sensitivity to and cognizance of the political woes of the day). As John Lie argues, Honda "became . . . critical of ethnography or any kind of reporting that ignored political context and power relations."[30] In 1970, that is, after his time in the United States, Honda wrote that "without problem consciousness, our materials will be used for evil rather than for good."[31]

In *The United States of America*, Honda turns his development of "problem consciousness" to the United States itself. The text begins with Honda highlighting what we might call Japanese problem unconsciousness. Japanese people, according to Honda, nurse a postwar myth of America as a land of perfect "democracy, freedom, and equality."[32] For Honda, this myth is indicative of a kind of myopia: "The United States of America that we [Japanese people] have been taught is entirely from the vantage point of white people (*hakujin-gawa*). . . . More than 99 percent of the deluge of news and information that flows from America has already been filtered, picked, and processed by the white point of view."[33] Aligning himself with his *Asahi* readership, Honda begins *The United States* with this view as his filter. One of his first reports was filed from South Carolina: "I should say it was my first time in the American *South*. But I didn't know the significance of that at the time."[34]

Honda comes to know its significance over the course of *The United States*; the lived experience of being a minority in America takes the things that Honda "couldn't comprehend when I first arrived" and transforms them into "things that I can now explain."[35] These newfound explanations hinge on the insights Honda acquired as he "spent more and more days and nights with black people."[36] Honda's reportage on black America can be divided into three sets of thematic episodes: reports on life in Harlem, pieces filed on the road from the "Deep South" (*shin-nanbu*), and interviews from an undisclosed town (most likely in the San Francisco Bay area) of the interracial families of Japanese war brides. In his reportage on Harlem, Honda focuses on the area's squalid, pernicious living conditions and the Harlemites' struggle against what Cornel West once controversially referred to as black nihilism. As an interlude between his reports on Harlem and the Deep South, Honda includes a brief history of American slavery. In the Deep South, he experiences a racial awakening. Under the watchful eye of the white gaze (which Honda refers to as *Nanbu no me*, literally "southern eyes"), Honda first experiences the perils of inhabiting a racialized body. In a central episode of this section, Honda is stopped by a police officer and has his race ("Oriental") recorded on a traffic ticket; this serves as official documentation of Honda's race and the proximity to black life—with its "constant, amorphous oppression"—that his race begets.[37] The final set of reports from black America, interviews with Japanese interracial war brides, provides firsthand accounts from "those Japanese people who have the most profound connection with black people."[38] Here Honda interviews families from a variety of socioeconomic backgrounds. Moreover, these families are, quite literally, on the other side of the continent from Harlem, where Honda's reportage begins. Insofar as the war brides' stories resonate with both the Deep South and Harlem tales that precede them, Honda implies that the limited access to the American dream that characterizes black life runs from high to low and coast to coast.

In moving from Harlem to the South to California, Honda engages in a mapping of blackness. Although this mapping is happening in the literal sense of the term—*The United States* includes extensive maps of Honda's travels—the mapping I'm interested in here is akin to the kind that Benedict Anderson develops through Thongchai Winichakul. In his consideration of the ways in which colonial technologies facilitate the imagining of post-colonial nation-states, Anderson writes of phantom states "named *after the map*," which are "to be imagined in quasi-logo form" (with, we might add, "negroid features").[39] The map projects (rather than records) boundaries that have yet to come into being.

The epicenter of Honda's map is Harlem. In his Harlem reportage, Honda delineates what we might call, in light of Hawthorne and James, the suffocating smallness of black American life, that is, the way racism undermines the grand American experiment. This smallness in Harlem is not anomalous but indicative of life in black America. From the poverty and crime of Harlem, Honda travels to and through the bodily dangers of racial oppression in the South and then to the difficulties of integration in the American West. Each of these are locations on the same map of black America, and, insofar as black America is also always America itself, each spot on the black American map is indicative of a nation united in (or divided by) its failing attempt to make good on its promises of "equality" and "democracy." "New York is," Honda writes, "the United States of America. Moreover, there is a sense in which New York is representatively American (*daihyōteki Amerika*)."[40] Honda asks his readers to imagine this community as sharing the same time(s) and conditions all over the map: "Becoming unnerved whenever you see a cop car, even though you haven't done anything wrong, just because you're traveling with black people—that's the South. And, ultimately, that's the United States of America."[41]

Honda also projects this vision of America across its dealings with a Global South. Honda was tapped for the *United States of America* project due to, among other reasons, his war correspondence from Vietnam between 1966 and 1968. As he traveled throughout the United States in 1969, Honda was astounded by what he saw as affinities between a war-torn Southeast Asian country and the world's most powerful democracy. Honda repeatedly interprets black American (read: American) phenomena through the lens of Vietnam: "Really, which one is more dangerous: New York or Vietnam?"[42] Here is another example: "I've walked all throughout a world made up overwhelmingly of black folks. This was, in one sense, a truly strange experience. The experience had something in common with my time traveling through and reporting on the liberated areas of South Vietnam."[43]

This "something in common" is a shared existence on what Honda calls the side of the discriminated (*sabetsu sareru gawa*) or, with more finality and verve, the side of those who will be killed (*korosareru gawa*). A concept that he would develop across his oeuvre, Honda's side of the discriminated posits American discrimination as having the same structures, techniques, and consequences no matter where it occurs on the map. As such this configuration also sows the seeds of transnational, transracial resistance. In a telling moment, Honda has one of his African American traveling companions serve as the mouthpiece of this possibility. After Honda himself asserts that "all [white American] children grow up being taught the lessons of the side of the discrimina*tor*. And then they grow up and become soldiers and go off to the Vietnam War," his companion claims, "This rotten, white cracker's America will fall only when the peoples of the third world and black Americans and other oppressed people band together and rise up together."[44]

Honda's interest in cultivating "problem consciousness" and telling American history from the African American perspective speaks to his view of the "side" on which Japan should reside. Honda was wary of Japan's reeducation during the American Occupation, which he deemed in large part responsible for "the United States of America as we [Japanese] have come to know it, that is, in other words, white America."[45] Problem consciousness and history from the black side serve as Honda's reminder and corrective. "We Japanese," Honda argued in *Korosareru gawa no ronri* (The Logic of the Killed, 1971), "must never forget the lesson we learn the moment we look in the mirror: we are, just like the Vietnamese and black people, a colored race."[46] Honda intends something bold in titling his work *The United States of America.*[47] According to him, viewing history from "the black side"— accounting for the ways in which racism and poverty undermine that postwar myth of America as a pristine democracy—is to see *the* United States and, in turn, to see where one stands with regard to the logic that underpins its union.

The Truth of Fiction and the Fact of Blackness: Ariyoshi Sawako's Not Because of Color

The arguments posed by Honda in *The United States of America* occur within the generic context of literary journalism. Recall, for example, Honda's claim that "more than 99 percent" of the American news that flows into Japan is representative of white America. Here Honda's technique leans more toward the literary end of literary journalism; "more than 99 percent" is hyperbole employed for rhetorical effect and flourish. Even—or perhaps particularly— when Honda's techniques lean toward the literary, their juxtaposition with the journalistic components of his text (e.g., his meticulous source citation and endnotes) ensure that his conjectures carry the weight of "objective" reportage. Moreover, Honda is a consummate stylist with a keen eye for detail; he once wrote that "when style has been perfected, careless fiddling will damage it, and cutting it will make it bleed. . . . Every single word has been hand-picked according to the author's singular rhythm and is therefore irreplaceable."[48] When Honda runs his meticulously calculated prose through the apparatuses of literary journalism, the cumulative effect is highly affective, rhetorically effective works.

Honda has literary journalism's multifaceted avenues to persuasion in mind when he writes, "Perhaps one of the weaknesses of the novel as a genre" is that "we read novels as 'works of fiction.'"[49] When Honda toggles between hyperbolic claims of "more than 99 percent" and actual statistics that have been researched, the verisimilitude of his reportage is heightened. Generically and generally speaking, however, the novelist must rely on other tactics as he or she makes claims of truth in texts that are read "as fictions." Or, in the words of Emiko, the narrator of Ariyoshi Sawako's *Hishoku* (Not

Because of Color), "Collecting numerical data and producing statistics is something that's well beyond my capabilities."[50]

And yet Honda's reportage and Ariyoshi's novel are rooted in shared experiences and like-minded questions. Like Honda, Ariyoshi's interest in American race relations and what these relations portend for long 1970s Japan was prompted in part by an extended stay in New York; a student and scholar of theater, Ariyoshi studied at Sarah Lawrence College in 1959–60 under the auspices of the Rockefeller Foundation. Another point of affinity between Ariyoshi and Honda is that, as if preempting Honda's claim that war brides are the "Japanese people who have the most profound connection with black people," Ariyoshi's *Not Because of Color* follows war bride Emiko from the black markets of Tokyo to the streets of Harlem.[51] However, whereas the verisimilitude of Honda's portrayal of black reality is vouched for by his interviews with flesh-and-blood war brides and their black husbands, Ariyoshi's is a fictional account of Emiko's marriage to a black American soldier that aims for social realism. The question becomes, then, how does Ariyoshi translate the concerns and experiences she shares with Honda into fictional form—what truths can be found in fiction?

This inquiry is best answered by addressing the two inquiries that reside just beneath the title of Ariyoshi's work: *What* is "not because of color," and if "it" isn't because of color, then what is its cause? The "what" under discussion here is nothing less than the conditions of black and racial being-in-the-postwar-world. Ariyoshi addresses the decidedly capacious topic of what it means to be black in the postwar world by way of scenarios that consider the interplay between setting (read: environment) and character development. In addition to the movement of racial characters as they trace the arcs of their character development, Ariyoshi's bodies are in actual motion. There is a bit of *The Jungle* in *Not Because of Color*, for, like Upton Sinclair's book, a variety of plot twists and subplots enable Emiko to traverse the various social strata of postwar Japan and the United States, color lines that might mark impenetrable boundaries according to the generic rules of nonfiction (be it literary or historical). With each character development that arises against the ephemeral backdrops of *Not Because of Color*, Ariyoshi adds another shade to her portrait of black life.

In taking race as the operative framework of this reading of Ariyoshi's *Not Because of Color*, I am straying a bit from one of the central focuses of Ariyoshi studies in order to add a layer to our understanding of the novel. Ariyoshi was one of the premier authors, if not *the* premier author, of social realism in the long 1970s. Many of her realist novels bring questions of gender relations into relief. The first novel that comes to mind here is *Akujo ni tsuite* (About an Evil Woman, 1978), in which the perspectives of no less than twenty-seven characters create a kaleidoscopic, realist representation of deceased businesswoman Tomikōji Kimiko. In turn Ariyoshi's depiction of the social reality of gender across several of her works has prompted scholarship that frames her literature by way of gender studies. Barbara Hartley, for example, has addressed the fact that representations of maternal bodies are central to the writing of transracial solidarity in *Not Because of Color*.

Although readings such as Hartley's are certainly insightful, the approach I take to *Not Because of Color* here considers Ariyoshi's writing of racialized bodies as central to the other thematic concerns explored in the text (war brides, maternity, class conflict and solidarity, national belonging and homelessness, and so on). This approach turns the text's title, as well as the interpretative logic that follows from this title, on its head. For the overwhelming majority of the novel, it is precisely because of color that the plot develops the way it does. Ariyoshi's interest in race is why she frequently consulted historian of African American culture Saruya Kaname, and attended a meeting of the kokujin kenyū no kai, during her writing of *Not Because of Color*. In taking this approach, I aim to enhance the focus on Ariyoshi's writing of the social reality of racial and ethnic difference—a central concern of not only *Not Because of Color*, but also Ariyoshi's *Geisha warutsu Itariano* (Italian Geisha Waltz, 1959), *Pueruto Riko nikki* (Puerto Rican Diary, 1964), and *Onna futari no Nyū Ginia* (Two Women in New Guinea, 1969)—in scholarly discussions of her work.

Not Because of Color is the (racial) coming-of-age story of Emiko. The novel begins with an adolescent Emiko, a girl from an impoverished, fatherless family who loses her home in one of the fire bombings of Tokyo, struggling to survive in occupied Japan. To make her way through the desolation of occupied Japan, Emiko takes a job in the cloakroom of an American-run cabaret. It is here that Emiko meets Tom Jackson, the man who will become her husband. Emiko's youthful naïveté gives her color blindness; although SCAP's diligent enforcement of the color line would have been conspicuous, Emiko sees the blackness of the cabaret's clientele (and, for that matter, Tom) as secondary to their Americanness. On their first date, for example, Tom and Emiko go to the Ernie Pyle Theater, the Occupation's repurposed version of the Tokyo Takarazuka Theater. In a setting that clearly implies the reconstitution of performed identities on American scripts and a putatively Japanese stage, Emiko notes, "There might be some people who find it odd that, at that time, I didn't feel anything out of the ordinary about the fact that Tom is black. . . . But, white people and black people mingled indiscriminately in that theater, and almost all of the soldiers were with Japanese women. . . . I didn't like the fact that we lost the war, but this wasn't a bad way to learn that the war was over and an alluring peace had arrived."[52]

Michael Molasky begins "A Darker Shade of Difference" with the reminder that "few images appear more often in Japanese literary accounts of the occupation era" than "A young GI on a street corner, towering over a crowd of children and playfully tossing out treats of chocolate and chewing gum."[53] "This soldier-cum-Santa Claus occupying Japan's postwar street corner" is, Molasky continues, "invariably, white."[54] Tom is the exception that proves Molasky's rule. (In the interest of gritty realism, however, Tom comes bearing provisions to be hawked on the black market rather than chocolate.) The power Tom holds as a member of the Occupation forces, in tandem with the buffer that the Pacific provides from the gravitational pull of American racism, allows him, like Emiko, to see Japan as a kind of postwar racial utopia. "I love Japan," Tom extols, "and I love its people . . . So let's forget all about the war. There is peace here [in Japan]. And there's something even greater than peace—greater than anything—here: equality. That's why I love Japan. There's equality. I don't want to go back to America; I want to stay in Japan for the rest of my life."[55] It is in the forced democracy of occupied Japan that Tom first experiences the ideals of American democracy.

Of course, the fact that Emiko mentions—directly to the narattee, no less, and from the temporal vantage point of her wiser, older self—that she "didn't find anything out of the ordinary *at that time*" about Tom's blackness adumbrates the racial awareness that Emiko will develop over the course of the novel. It also suggests that the Pacific is not enough of a buffer to nullify American racism. Emiko sees this truth at least twice during her time in Japan. The first time is during her pregnancy and subsequent motherhood. "The moment I realized I was pregnant, shock ran through my entire body and I saw myself as the wife of a Negro."[56] Emiko's body "responded viscerally to this reality [of impending black motherhood] faster than my mind could make a conscious decision: I did not want to give birth to that baby."[57] Even before experiencing the discrimination that awaits a black "mixed-blood" (*konketsu*) baby in postwar Japan, Emiko feels it—and practices it—viscerally with her skin. After the birth of her daughter and the (albeit vicariously) lived experience of racial discrimination, Emiko is now able to articulate cognitively the discrimination that she feels viscerally—a key moment in the development of her racial character. With this newfound revelation, she adopts and adapts Toni Morrison's haunting, *Beloved* (1987) rationale: "If I hadn't killed her she would have died, and that is something I could not bear."[58] Emiko decides to terminate her following pregnancies rather than endure racial discrimination's capacity, to channel Morrison again, "not just work, kill, or maim you, but dirty you. Dirty you so bad you couldn't like yourself anymore . . . she could never let it happen to her own [children]."[59]

Emiko's second encounter with this truth (in postwar Japan—she will encounter it every day after her move to the United States) comes in Washington Heights, the US Air Force housing compound where she serves as a maid. This is a job that Emiko can do "even with her black English," a sonic stigmata that bars her from other employment opportunities.[60] It is here that Emiko meets Mrs. Lee, who employs Emiko as a domestic worker. Trudier Harris writes that to be a black woman doing domestic work is to occupy "a role of invisibility," so much so that the employing "family may also discuss its most troubling affairs and assume that the entity which serves dinner is unthinking, incapable of communicating family secrets beyond the dining room walls."[61] Ariyoshi borrows the trope of the domestic worker as privy to the dirty laundry and skeleton-filled closets of their employers, in this case by airing Mrs. Lee's racial thinking. In reply to Emiko's questioning of the possibility of discrimination in democratic America, Mrs. Lee responses with this: "All American democracy did was emancipate them from slavery—no one knows whether that was a good thing or a bad thing."[62]

The first quarter of *Not Because of Color* is devoted to the construction and subsequent destruction of Japan as an equal-opportunity multiracial utopia. The remaining portion of the text turns a critical eye toward transpacific race relations as they are lived in the United States. It is important to note that Emiko's sea voyage to the United States—a moment that facilitates the introduction of the other war brides, who will become central characters in the second half of the novel—"was supposed to go eastward toward America from Japan, but instead it went in the opposite direction, westward and westward, on and on . . . grazing the northern tip of Africa and going out into the Atlantic."[63] This moment does double duty; it both ties *Not Because of Color* to the genre of war bride fiction and reminds the reader that Emiko's journey to America is irrevocably tied to the bloody history of black bodies coming and going to the United States.

During her time in Harlem, the place Tom calls home, both Emiko and Tom undergo transformations in their racial character. The Harlem apartment where they reside "sweltered just like the inside of that ship."[64] This is a bold play on Ariyoshi's part; her Harlem is an extension of the (metaphorical) slave ship.[65] Apropos of this extension, Emiko and Tom suffocate in Harlem. The charismatic, quixotic Tom of Tokyo is replaced by "a lethargic man completely unlike the one who lived in Japan."[66] Likewise, the "colorblind" Emiko of Japan is replaced with a mother of four black children (three pregnancies in Harlem, or, one child for each pregnancy she terminated in Japan) who comes to realize her own implicit biases against the inhabitants of Spanish Harlem, who reside "beneath" her in New York's racial geography.

A refrain runs alongside the novel's multiple reminders of these character transformations: that these metamorphoses—that is, the conditions of black life in Harlem and the social conditioning such life engenders—are not because of color. Emiko exclaims, "Just as I thought, the problem isn't skin color. Even if Negroes had white skin just like white folks, we'd probably still be living in Harlem."[67] In lieu of "color," there is something that—for Emiko (and Ariyoshi)—runs deeper than the racial divide: class consciousness. "Color is not the problem," she says, "American racial discrimination is class conflict!"[68] The black condition as presented in *Not Because of Color* is not about biology but the collisions of history, psychology, sociology, and economics or, as Emiko, channeling Marx, notes: "It seems to me that the reason Negroes are alienated from white society is not because their skin is black. . . . All humans want to think that they are better than they are, and they do this by establishing some group that is beneath them according to some standard."[69] With this, blackness becomes something that Emiko can participate in (like a class) rather than something that is written indelibly on the skin (like biological color). The novel concludes with a metaphor—Washington, DC, cherry blossoms that have taken on a different color than their Japanese counterparts due to American air and soil—and a simile—"I too have been transformed like the blossoms in DC. I am a Negro!"—which aestheticizes Emiko's shift in racial and class consciousness.[70]

It is true, as Honda Katsu'ichi proposes, that statistics are not at Ariyoshi Sawako's disposal in *Not Because of Color*. In lieu of statistics, Ariyoshi employs the techniques of social realist fiction—class-jumping plots and perspectives, environment-driven characterization, detail-rich internal monologues and descriptions of social conditions, and so on—to inscribe the facts of blackness. Ariyoshi's fictional intervention aspires to fill in the ellipses of Frantz Fanon in a way that may be beyond the capabilities of statistics. Fanon writes, "Understand, my dear boy, color prejudice is something I find utterly foreign. . . . But of course, come in, sir, there is no color prejudice among us. . . . Quite, the Negro is a man like ourselves. . . . It is not because he is black that he is less intelligent than we are . . ."[71] Ariyoshi's *Not Because of Color* has a certain kind of rhyme with Fanon's "It is not because he is black." Even if race is a kind of social construct, racism takes on a social reality that cannot be denied. And when this reality is denied, such denial is, more often than not, accompanied by the very protocols and procedures of racial prejudice. The claim that it is "not because of color" simply shifts the register of the conversation from race to intelligence (Fanon) or class (Ariyoshi). But, even with this shift, the conversation concludes in the same way as unabashedly racist conversations: with the exploitation of black labor and the oppression of blackness. In her critique of *Not Because of Color*, Yoko McClain suggests that Emiko's epiphanic transformation is a less than satisfying conclusion to the novel.[72] Be that as it may, the "cherry-blossom-colored glasses" with which Emiko views her newfound blackness is clearly Ariyoshi's attempt to end the novel with an uplifting acceptance of the undeniable facts and social reality of blackness, a point I return to in the final section of this chapter.

"Visit the Scene of the Crime One Hundred Times": Black Herrings and Human Proof

"Life, so they say, is made by chance encounters. Well, the reason this work came to be rests on two serendipitous meetings. The first was with Saijō Yaso's straw hat poem and the second with Kadokawa Haruki."[73] "The work" here is Morimura Seiichi's *Ningen no shōmei*, which is typically translated as *Proof of the Man* but, for reasons to be discussed momentarily, I refer to as *Human Proof*. Morimura penned *Human Proof* at the behest of Kadokawa, who was at that time an enfant terrible of the publishing world with a media-mixing vision best captured by the catchphrase "Read it and then see it or see it and then read it."[74] After taking over Kadokawa Publishing, Kadokawa shifted the house's focus to popular works. These popular texts were released almost simultaneously with media crossovers that were then packaged and promoted by the Kadokawa advertising machine. Kadokawa personally targeted Morimura to write for this machine, asking him to "compose a piece that would serve as proof of [his abilities as an] author."[75] Morimura responded with the 1976 *Human Proof*, a transpacific murder mystery. Both Kadokawa's vision and Morimura's *Proof* were wildly successful: *Human Proof* would go on to sell more than 7.7 million copies and produce equally profitable translations and adaptations (a film, several TV adaptations, and a hit song for Joe Yamanaka).

In order to unearth the significance of that second chance encounter—Saijō Yaso's "straw hat" poem—the reader, much like *Human Proof*'s Detective Munesue, will have to begin at the beginning and follow the protocols of literary forensics. *Human Proof* revolves around the death of Johnny Hawyard, an African American man in his twenties[76] who dies of stab wounds in the elevator of a high-rise hotel in Tokyo's Chiyoda ward. In his final moments, Johnny Hawyard leaves the reader with two clues: a tattered copy of a Saijō Yaso poetry collection and his dying words—"straw hat." These two clues are actually the overwhelming majority of the information needed to solve the mystery. That Munesue (and, by proxy, the reader) needs the remainder of the text to unravel its central enigma speaks to the interplay between the discursive assumptions of blackness in the literature of the long 1970s and the generic conventions of the murder mystery.

Two techniques, both highly informed by the poetics of detective fiction, obfuscate what would be an otherwise clear view of Johnny's killer. The first of these might be called *Human Proof*'s "black herring." I have in mind, of course, the red herring, a staple of detective fiction by which the attentive reader, precisely because he or she is attentive, is thrown off of the scent of the actual culprit. From its very first page, *Human Proof* works hard to convince the reader that Johnny Hawyard is a black man who is irrevocably foreign to Japan (or, technically, from even *before* its first page, as Johnny's skin tone in the cover art depictions of him seems to get progressively darker as the editions of *Human Proof* accumulate). Take, for example, the opening paragraph of *Human Proof*: "No one gave him any thought when he boarded the elevator. In a spot like this—a melting pot of people from all the world's places and races—the stranger wasn't a visibly noticeable presence."[77] The first chapter is titled "Etoranje no shi" (The Death of the Stranger), with *stranger* here a phonetic reproduction of the French *étranger*.[78] The pulling of the paratextual into the textual synergizes the word's power: the character being described (Johnny) is an *étranger*, an exotic alien just as foreign as the term that the katakana approximation attempts to bring into the Japanese language. With its insouciant tone, understated deployment of race, and deceptively simple style, the first paragraph, which ends with "wasn't a visibly noticeable presence" (*sahodo medatsu sonzai dewa nakatta*), establishes Johnny as simply and unquestionably foreign.

For *Human Proof*'s team of detectives (and the text's team of readers), the implication of Johnny's "unquestionable foreignness" works as a powerful piece of misdirection; it is a prompt to "change our line of investigation" and lends credence to the possibility that "because the victim is a foreigner . . . its highly likely that the perpetrator is a foreigner as well."[79] And Morimura's black herring slips in through this opening. On the very first page of the text, Morimura follows his declaration of Johnny's blackness with "He was black, but his skin color was diluted. It was almost a blackish brown. His hair was black and not too kinky. If made to choose one or the other, you could say that his facial features were almost Asian. He was a little short for a black person."[80] This passage begins with declaratives and nominalizations—Johnny "is a black man." These definitive statements and phrases, however, are juxtaposed with a series of ambivalent modifiers that suggest adulteration: *yaya* (somewhat), *amari* (not very), and *chikai* (almost) twice. Understated clues such as this—the "broken Japanese" that Johnny speaks, for example—pervade the text, serving as subliminal indicators that Johnny's relationship with Japan was not one of complete foreignness but one that had been somehow severed or broken.[81]

On a second reading, the reader can almost see Morimura smirk as his herring streams by. Johnny's "definitive foreignness," which is cosigned by his black skin, is in actuality an attempt to misdirect the reader from his true identity. Johnny is the product of a short-lived postwar marriage between Wilshire Hayward, a black GI stationed in Japan during the Occupation, and Yasugi Kyōko, who buries her past with Wilshire and reinvents herself as the wife of a powerful Japanese political figure. Johnny is raised in Harlem by Wilshire. His journey to Japan is an attempt to reunite with the mother and motherland that linger in his memory. A key component of Kyōko's postwar, post-Wilshire reinvention, however, is her status as an author, public persona, and expert commentator on parenting and family matters. Because the haunting recrudescence of Johnny would jeopardize her reinvention as an "all Japanese" good wife and wise mother, Kyōko decides to murder him, only to have him kill himself in a bid to protect Kyōko when her resolve wavers.

I wrote earlier that *Human Proof* is a more felicitous translation and interpretation of the title *Ningen no shōmei* than is *Proof of the Man*. I posit this retranslation for two reasons, the first of which is that the title *Ningen no shōmei* hinges on Morimura's black herring. The black body itself, insofar as it is also a Japanese body, is the human proof that underwrites Kyōko's culpability.[82] Until the final pieces of the mystery lock into place, Kyōko's importance to the narrative is that she is the mother of a central figure in one of the novel's subplots. Kyōhei, Kyōko's son from her second marriage, kills a woman in a hit-and-run accident, a fast-moving metaphor for Kyōhei's desire to escape feelings of abandonment caused by Kyōko's absentee parenting. Moreover, after the crime, Kyōhei absconds to New York. The moment the reader realizes that Johnny is biracial, an associative chain reaction is set off; it is a fairly simple operation to see Johnny as a mirror image of Kyōhei, reflected and inverted by the Pacific, which divides the brothers. The black herring technique is what contains this chain reaction; banking on a set of shared assumptions of his long 1970s Japanese readership, Morimura's mystery remains as such only as long as the black body is not seen as anything more than black. The moment that this assumption is shattered, that is, when the body can be seen as both black and Japanese, readers have what amounts to human proof of the identity of a Japanese woman spotted leaving the scene of Johnny's crime.

The other reason that I propose *Human Proof* as a retranslation recalls Morimura's second fortuitous meeting: the encounter with Saijō's straw hat poem. To commemorate the conclusion of his third year of college, Morimura made a trip to the hot springs of Kirizumi, a locale that would become a central topos of *Human Proof*. It was during this trip that Morimura himself—like Kyōko and Johnny—came across Saijō's "Boku no bōshi" (My Hat) printed on the wrapping paper of a bento box.[83] Saijō Yaso (1892–1970) was a poet known for his poetry for children, experimentation with French symbolist poetics, and the lyrics he provided for both children's and popular music. Saijō's "Boku no bōshi," a nostalgic lament of bygone childhood, was first published in 1922 in the second issue of *Kodomo no kuni*, a flagship publication of the Taisho period movement toward visually and literarily high quality, illustrated children's magazines.

The poem begins with the evocative "Momma, I wonder what ever happened to that hat, my hat."[84] This opening evocation turns into a refrain, each stanza beginning with a new call to and for "momma" (*okaasan*). As the poet searches his memory for "that straw hat that fell deep into the bottom of the valley along the path to Kirizumi," the refrain serves as a kind of punctuation, a series of verbal commas that insert successive layers of lost time between the poet and the hat.[85] By the poem's conclusion, which brings the listener to the poet's present, "the *Lilium medeoloides* have probably withered with the coming of winter" and the "snow has probably fallen quietly on that ravine / fallen as if it wanted to take that Italian straw hat, which once shone brilliantly, / and the initials 'Y. S.,' which hid under its brim / and bury them, silently, lonely."[86] Written with a nostalgia reminiscent of Ogawa Mimei's (1882–1961) claim that "children's stories are not meant for children alone but for all who have not lost the heart of a child," this poem laments more than the loss of a straw hat; it memorializes the loss of childhood and maternal companionship.[87] Morimura was undeniably affected by this poem; he once wrote that "everyone has a 'straw hat' from their mother" and that the hat, as a metonym of the "eternal mother," would become a central motif of *Human Proof*.[88]

The straw hat is an allusive presence throughout *Human Proof*, with *allusion* here taking on polysemic significance. The *Oxford English Dictionary* defines *allusion* as "an implied, indirect, or passing reference to a person or thing."[89] Much like the red herring, *allusion* in this colloquial sense is a key building block of the murder mystery: it rewards good readerly sleuthing with moments of epiphany. Here we should recall Johnny's final words ("straw hat"), the timeworn straw hat and Saijō poetry collection Johnny leaves behind as he makes his way from the crime scene to the Tokyo Royal

Hotel, and the reason Johnny selects the hotel as his final resting place: the light that shines through the windows of the ring of restaurants on the hotel's top floor is "just like a straw hat woven of light on the head of the night sky."[90] All this, particularly the Tokyo Royal Hotel, which intertwines Johnny's childhood and Saijō's poem with the very architectural foundation of Japan's national power,[91] is an "indirect reference" to Johnny's mother and motherland.

But *allusion* is also, as the *Oxford Definition of Literary Terms* suggests, "an economical means of calling upon the history or the literary tradition that author and reader are assumed to share."[92] Ever the close reader, Detective Munesue's asks, "What kind of relationship can exist between an exceptional lyric poet born in Japan and a black youth from the slums of New York? . . . Johnny Hayward–straw hat–Saijō Yaso, what could bridge the three? Whatever it was, it was hiding in that collection of poetry."[93] Here allusive poetry intertwines with the elusive prose that serves as the lifeblood of murder mysteries. The (Japanese) poetic voice that calls for *okaasan* (momma) speaks vicariously for Johnny as he calls for Kyōko, his yet to be identified (Japanese) mother. Kyōko confesses after Munesue reads a copy of Saijō's poem to her, and it is by acknowledging Johnny, the "human proof" of Kyōko's original sin of omission, that she revives misanthropic Munesue's faith in humanity and maternity (*bosei*). Given the text's questionable conflation of human fallibility and maternal responsibility, "proof of the woman" might be a closer translation of *ningen no shōmei*, but "human proof" is closer still to the text's multivalent use of the term.

As was the case with the black herring, the mystery hinges on, to adapt the definition provided by the *Oxford Dictionary of Literary Terms*, the reader's assumption that Johnny and Saijō *don't* share in the same literary tradition, that Saijō's call for "momma" can't ventriloquize Johnny's. And when the case is closed this transracial allusion provides the long 1970s Japanese counterpart to Aldon Nielsen's *Writing between the Lines: Race and Intertextuality*: "Intertextual readings pursue the diffusion of racial signification across the textual mappings of American consciousness."[94]

In the opening moments of *Ningen no shōmei*, Munesue reminds the reader of the detective fiction trope *genba hyakkai*: "Go over the scene of the crime one hundred times." This raises a question: what is it that this fiction searches for so compulsively? Ronald Thomas argues that detective fiction, as "a literary genre preoccupied with resolving questions of personal identity also speaks to questions about national identity" insofar as its deployment of the technologies of forensic science transform "the mysteries of individual anatomy and personal identity" into something with legibility, something that can "represent the general condition of the body politic."[95] With *Ningen no shōmei*, the proof is in the body itself. As the biracial children of postwar Japan came of age in the long 1970s (one of whom was Joe Yamanaka, who played the part of Johnny in the film adaptation of *Ningen no shōmei*), the "diffusion of racial signification across the textual mapping" of Japan's literary consciousness becomes apparent to any reader who can see past the red herrings of mythic homogeneity and the trappings of intranational intertextuality.

Abe Kōbō and the "Already Estrangedment" of Blackness

Abe Kōbō's 1964 *Tanin no kao* (The Face of Another) tells the story of a polymer scientist who, after a botched lab experiment leaves him with a disfigured face, attempts to reintegrate into his community in spite of the scarring and fragmentation of his face and his identity. To do so, he creates a lifelike mask—the eponymous "face of another," a second self that, when superimposed on the scarred self it hides, manages only to render visible the fissures in the narrator's psyche and community.

The Face of Another is composed of many genres. It is, quite literally, intertextual, a masterful weaving of discursive techniques and conventions informed by modes of writing ranging from the science notebook to the film scenario. The multiple discursive currents that run through *The Face of Another* are indicative of the tension between atomization and (chemical, social, marital, self, and so on) bonding thematized by the text. Or, to borrow Christopher Bolton's articulation, there is a dialogue of styles in *The Face of Another*, and "these languages alternate, intermix, and struggle with one another for control of the narrative. And in the course of the novel, the problem of constituting one's own personality as well as the challenge of reaching beyond oneself to communicate with others both emerge as problems of combining and balancing these different languages."[96]

I would like to build on two aspects of Bolton's insights. First, in the multigeneric dance of *The Face of Another*, science fiction takes the lead as one of the premier "languages" through which Abe conducts his experiment. This is perhaps most apparent in the several pages of *The Face of Another* in which Abe's faceless narrator builds an entire world around the science fictional novum of a face factory. Abe made both fictional and essayistic contributions to Japanese science fiction during its germinal years, and his roots in the genre are on display throughout *The Face of Another*. Second, Abe makes these "Others" toward whom his narrator must reach beyond himself to communicate with visible by giving them particular faces. *The Face of Another* brings postwar Japanese identity into dialogue with two of its constitutive others: Zainichi Koreans and African Americans. Or, as Ōe Kenzaburō wrote, "*The Face of Another* . . . leads the reader right to the door that opens us up to the problem at the heart of our engagement with Koreans. . . . And it is also, most likely, the first book-length novel produced in Japan to provide an essential avenue for approaching the black riots in the United States."[97]

Abe Kōbō's sui generis contribution to writing blackness at the onset of the long 1970s can be heard when these two notes are sounded simultaneously, that is, when we consider how the language of science fiction resonates with Abe's construction of racial and ethnic identity. The language of science fiction is one of estrangement, with "a representation which estranges" defined as "one which allows us to recognize its subject, but at the same time makes it seem unfamiliar."[98] The "look of estrangement," as Darko Suvin continues his classic definition, "is both cognitive and creative," and it is one of the "necessary and sufficient condition[s]" of science fiction; the genre's "main formal device is an imaginative framework alternative to the author's empirical environment."[99] Although science fiction has spawned a plethora of definitions as far-reaching as the many universes the genre covers, these definitions share the common denominator of fictional world building rooted in the (hard or soft) scientific imagination, a process that estranges us from our nonfictional world building. This is an invitation to see the world in brave new ways. Arthur C. Clarke once quipped that science fiction "is something that *could* happen—but you usually wouldn't want it to," whereas "fantasy is something that *couldn't* happen—though you often only wish that it could."[100] Abe's definition shows a certain affinity to this line of thinking, or, as Bolton writes, Abe found science fiction interesting "precisely because it combines truth and fancy. . . . Abe says the best science fiction employs science to establish a 'hypothesis'—a creative premise that is then used to investigate some other theme."[101]

Consider, then, the estranged creative premises of Abe as he investigates race and ethnicity in *The Face of Another*. In a passage toward the end of the novel, the narrator turns on the television to distract himself from his worries, but "when things aren't going your way, you can't just change the channel: I was just in time for the foreign news, which was right in the middle of a report on the Negro riots in America."[102] *The Face of Another* was published first in abridged form in *Gunzō* magazine in January 1964. This was followed by a book-length version published by Kodansha in September 1964, some two months after the 1964 Harlem riots. Although the abridged version of *The Face of Another* does include a passing reference to racial discrimination, this version does not include the narrator's serendipitous encounter with the news coverage of the Harlem Riots.[103] The Harlem Riots scene was added to the full-length version, which was published after the actual riots. This addition to the novel's concluding moments suggests that Abe's science fictional text is engaging with his (to borrow Suvin's articulation) "empirical environment," which, at the dawn of the long 1970s, spans the distance from Japan to Harlem.

As the faceless narrator thinks through both the affinities and discontinuities between his predicament and the black rioters, Bolton's dialogue of styles begins, with the narrator slipping into one of his science fictional/ metaphysical musings. These musings, which lead ultimately to the possibility of like-minded, riotous revolution by the defaced, are qualified with a striking assertion: whereas the narrator's predicament is a science fictional anomaly, an estrangement (supposedly) defined "by me and me alone," the predicament that the narrator calls the *kokujin mondai* (Negro problem) is long-standing, pervasive, and cyclical. This is why Abe's newscaster comments that the riots are reminiscent of "the summer of 1943," the date of another riot in Harlem ignited by the killing of an African American by an officer of the New York City police department.[104]

In other words, here is the burgeoning of a writing of blackness that can make itself visible only in works that engage with the notion of estrangement, one of the building blocks of science fiction. Abe writes the lived experience of blackness as *already* estranged, as already deviant from that which is deemed normal, as already defamiliarized and defamiliarizing. The estrangement that the narrator of *The Face of Another* experiences only by virtue of the accidents of technological intervention—his disfigured face and the novum of a mask that is almost but not quite human enough—is made analogous to the everyday life of black Americans. Here Richard Calichman's reading of *The Face of Another* is particularly informative. In "The Minority as Structure of Social Formations," he writes that "what can be seen" in *The Face of Another* is "a phenomenon that is in fact extremely widespread in racial and ethnic discourse . . . a *remarking whose force is such as to reatroactively create the original mark*."[105] "Such marking" (e.g., the scared face of the protagonist), Calichman continues, "allows us to better understand society's negative remarking on Korean residents of Japan and blacks in the United States on the basis of the categories of race and ethnicity precisely by the retroactive force of the remark."[106] Here we might recall Fanon's remark in "The Fact of Blackness": "Look Mom, a Negro!"[107] There is, of course, no originary mark on the newborn that could possibly live up to the difference buried deep within that "fact." So "society's minoritarian remark-ing comes to retroactively furnish the existence of such mark[ing] at the level of projective fantasy."[108] Abe's narrator suggests that there are individuals for whom the remarks of the Other become remarkable only when the self has been similarly marked.

As a genre rooted in estrangements extrapolated from the far reaches of the scientific imagination, science fiction is particularly primed to make the estrangement of blackness visible. We should note here that the majority of the "naturally born" Japanese minorities of *The Face of Another* are marked by external technological intervention: the tattoo ink of the *yakuza*, the ke-loids of the *hibakusha*, the bandages and polymerized facelessness of the narrator, and so on.[109] The non-Japanese minorities, resident Koreans and African Americans, are simply born; it is through the remarks of the narrator and the newscaster that they become minorities. What Abe has done, then, is highlight the space between the invisible men of H. G. Wells and Ralph Ellison. For Ellison, invisibility is not "a matter of a biochemical accident to my epidermis. That invisibility to which I refer occurs because of a peculiar disposition of the eyes of those with whom I come in contact. A matter of the construction of their *inner* eyes, those eyes with which they look through their physical eyes upon reality."[110] There is no need for technological or science fictional interventions to make social minorities invisible because invisibility is acquired the moment the minority falls under the gaze of the majority. In this sense, a social minority is already estranged, already un-like the majority. By juxtaposing science fictional estrangement and social alienation, Abe makes visible the already estranged nature of blackness (or of "Zainichiness" or of anyone deemed the Other).

The Genericity of Blackness in the Literature of the Long 1970s

By reading and writing race through their respective generic conventions, each of the texts addressed above compose sui generis portraits of black-ness in the long 1970s. The synesthetic black beauty of Yoshida Ruiko's *Hot Harlem Days*, Honda Katsu'ichi's negotiations between objective reportage and his self-styled objective (rewriting American history from a black per-spective for a Japanese readership), Ariyoshi Sawako and the racial character development of *Not Because of Color*, Morimura Seichi and the discovery of the black body within the Japanese body politic, Abe Kōbō and the already estrangedment of blackness, each of these is a singular contribution.

And yet readers can't help but hear resonances across these texts, as each singular voice contributes to the emergence of a larger conversation. What I am suggesting here is, of course, a risky proposition, for the soldering of collectives always runs the risk of incinerating the nuances of the singular. Nevertheless, the second question with which this chapter began remains: "For who would have us believe that we, we two for example, would form a genre or belong to one?"[111] It is not my intention to answer this question by proposing a "genre" of literary blackness in the long 1970s. If, as John Frow writes, "The law of genre is a law of purity, a law against miscegenation," it is clear that the genre-hopping blackness of Japan's long 1970s breaks this law, for there is a limitlessness, a refusal to be detained in this blackness, that shatters such purity.[112]

What I am proposing, however, is that there is something *generic* about the blackness that runs across these texts. I understand that the distinction I want to make between considering the works of the long 1970s generic and considering them a genre may seem like semantic quibbling. But I think there is something more than semantics at stake. This seems to me to be a place where the reading of literature can inform the living of life, namely, the larger issue of how "readers" navigate a world with "characters" of various races. The biological notion of genus and the literary notion of genre share a common etymological source, and there is a degree of overlap in the way these two terms contain blackness. A genre of black literature is not that far removed from stereotypical notions of a "genus" of black people, as both assume a limited set of texts/people with members that/who can be included in that set according to their possession of certain identifying marks. Something in the jump from a single text to its inclusion in a closed genre is reminiscent of the stereotypical jump from a single individual (a black person, a resident Korean, an immigrant, or what have you) to a static notion of group identity ("the blacks," "those Koreans," "immigrants," and so on). In suggesting genericity or the generic rather than a genre, I want to slow down that jump and consider the possibility of irreducible singularity alongside commonality. Japanese literature of the long 1970s suggests that a generic approach to blackness might have emancipatory potential. This potential becomes particularly viable if the sui generis can disseminate generically. *What if everyone thought about blackness with the nimble, imaginative singularity of our best creative writers?* It might be that the recognition of racial and ethnic difference is not an impediment to a shared vision of the commons but the recognition on which any project of shared commonality must begin.

Whereas, more often than not, genre gestures toward the closing of sets, genericity might be read as a concern with the possibility (and costs) of endlessly iterative engagements between the individual and the collective or as the structural principle that upholds such a possibility. Here, too, I am thinking, in more or less Derridean terms, that genericity is akin to Derrida's consideration of the impure genre of genres, that principle on which genre itself functions. Insofar as the marks of genre (e.g., black skin) can be remarked on again and again (as it is illuminated by Yoshida's brilliant flashes, as it is amalgamated by Morimura's herring, as its sociological and psychosomatic scarring is juxtaposed with Abe's technological scarring, and so on), genericity gestures toward the ways in which blackness participates without belonging. It does "not *belong* to any genre" but "*participates* in one or several genres . . . yet such participation never amounts to belonging."[113] A consideration of the genericity of blackness, that is, a consideration of blackness as both participating in the conventions of the literature of the long 1970s and always stretching beyond the limits of those conventions, opens an inquiry that a consideration of a genre of black Japanese literature would not. In light of the social power and purchase of genre (genres "actively generate and shape knowledge of the world,"[114] thereby putting bodies in their place), the mobilization of the generic black body in the literary imagination of the long 1970s, rather than the "genred" black body, reaches for something beyond the era's discursive conventions of thinking through race even as it participates in them.

Although they cannot be reduced to a single genre, there is indeed something generic about the black bodies of Yoshida, Honda, Ariyoshi, Morimura, and Abe. As was addressed in the "Introduction," a part of the impetus here is that these authors are contemporaries and, as such, are responding to the same set of historical contingencies. Another factor, however, is that these contemporary authors are reading one another's work and remarking, synergistically, on the generic marks of their cohort. Over the course of this chapter, for example, I have already noted Yoshida's commentary on Honda, Honda's commentary on Yoshida, and Ōe's commentary on Abe. Another noteworthy example of this is an exchange among Yoshida, Honda, and Morimura. Yoshida's photography circulated throughout Japan and ended up, among other places, on the cover and in the pages of Honda's *United States of America*, now serving the objective of Honda's reportage. Her photography would appear yet again in Morimura's *Human Proof.* Rather than actual photography, however, there is the photographer's fictional doppelgänger, a "petite, svelte" Japanese photographer living in Harlem named Mishima Yukiko.[115] Yoshida certainly fits the description, right down to the parallel rhythm of their names. It is Yoshida/Mishima's photography that ultimately exposes the black herring; whereas her photograph of Johnny's father is of "a pure black man," Johnny himself "doesn't seem completely black . . . his facial features closer to Asian."[116] From photojournalism to political reportage to murder mystery, each iterative passing of the trope of photographed black skin as representative evidence of black identity adds genericity to this technique.

The iteration of such generic techniques leads to the creation of a generic narrative of transpacific race relations across these texts. This narrative begins with an assertion reminiscent of Ōe's illusion of monolithic American might and right discussed in chapter 2—keep in mind that Ōe, too, is a contemporary of the authors discussed here. The texts of the long 1970s are predicated on the assumption that American democracy keeps its promises. In the first chapter of *Hot Harlem Days*, for example, Yoshida recounts one of her first encounters with an African American. In an attempt to uplift the downtrodden man, Yoshida tells him that he must "chin up and fight racial discrimination."[117] This "pull yourself up by the bootstraps" quixotism is summarily glossed by the older, wiser, narrator, who says, "Looking back on it, I see now that my expression was like something from one of those textbooks on American-made democracy used in Japan."[118] Honda, too, writes of "democracy, freedom, and equality—the image of America that we Japanese were taught after the war."[119] Alongside Honda, Ariyoshi's Emiko has no trouble translating Tom's speech on equality in occupied Japan because "I already knew 'equality' and the other big words he used; the very first page of my textbook [a conversational Japanese textbook distributed to GIs by SCAP] read 'The Allied Forces have occupied Japan in order to bring its people peace and equality.'"[120] There is, of course, a metaphoric thrust to these generic references to the inculcating power of textbooks and education. But this should not obfuscate their historical grounding. As Sheldon Garon writes in *Molding Japanese Minds: The State in Everyday Life*, "Advising SCAP to promote adult education in March 1947, the Allies' Far Eastern Commission broadly defined education as a 'preparation for life in a democratic nation, and as a training for the social and political responsibilities which freedom entails.'"[121]

The next moment in this shared narrative is one of epiphany, an awakening to the broken promises of American democracy. In *Democracy in Black*, Eddie Glaude writes that black Americans' lives exist "in the gap between who America said it was as a democracy and how we actually live."[122] Glaude's argument builds on a line of thinking in black theology that can be traced to Martin Luther King Jr. (a monumental figure of the long 1970s): that the intersection of Matthew 25:40 and the lived experiences of black American citizens might cut through the very foundation of American democracy.[123] That is to say, the measure of a democracy is its treatment of its most vulnerable citizens. As Japanese authors received first- and secondhand accounts of the experiences of black Americans throughout the long 1970s, the view of democracy from black America effectively served as a sort of "reeducation," an undermining of the perfect union written of in Allied textbooks. In other words, authors such as Abe Kōbō both see and write about Glaude's gap. In Abe's words, "There exists one myth in America: a unique kind of legend of a liberated and free 'people.' . . . It seems unnecessary to explain what blacks signified to Americans in the past: they were merely putty in sealing up the gaps in this cracked 'myth of the people.'"[124]

Harlem, as a topos that is both firmly within and utterly removed from the cracked myth of America, becomes a central locale in this epiphany. In his reading of Yoshida's *Hot Harlem Days,* the historian Saruya Kaname writes:

> Harlem is a symbolic neighborhood. It is a neighborhood like a mirror—it takes all of the traits of American society, condenses them into a single point, and reflects them in their totality. The moment you step into Harlem—no, you don't have to actually enter its space, just by saying a word about Harlem, listeners can hear what kind of person you are, they can see into your inner depths. That's the kind of place Harlem is.[125]

Saruya's notion of a symbolic Harlem is on full display in each of the texts addressed here. Honda posits a tension between American ideals and American racism. Harlem—insofar as Honda sees it as both like the "capital of an independent [black] nation" and yet "not so different from the 'regular' parts of New York as to be severed" from that "representatively American" city—symbolizes that tension.[126] Ariyoshi's war bride, too, wonders if "Harlem," with its "ash-gray buildings," "is really America at all. The New York in the postcards has rows of beautiful buildings, wonderful structures that look like sweet confections."[127] "No one can imagine," Emiko continues, "a life this wretched and this low right in America, the winner of the war, in the middle of a city that's the world's greatest financial hub. But Harlem, the black city of New York, is such a place."[128] In a language a bit more hardboiled, Morimura's detective reiterates the questioning of Harlem as both off-center and central to America's vision of democracy. "One of the roots of New York's—no, America's—deep, underlying illness is here."

The entire city of New York is a pal to the rich. It's a city that grins only at the folks with money. The people with money are treated like humans; the ones without it are tossed like garbage. The best proof of that is Harlem.

To the west of Central Park, there's a place where, unlike Harlem, humans are supposed to live. A place where there are rows of deluxe apartments on spacious green lawns. A place where seasonal flowers bloom like crazy and you could feed thirty mouths in Harlem on the money set aside for pet food.

The people here never go above 100th Street. For them, anything north of 100th was New York, but it wasn't *New York*. In this world, heaven and hell are just a stone's throw away.[129]

The generic, paradoxical relationship between Harlem and the American landscape is least apparent with Yoshida Ruiko. For the authors discussed above, Saruya's symbolics of Harlem are predicated on the projection of a reified Harlem in disarray. John Russell, for example, has noted that in Japanese travel guidebooks "all accounts are virtually identical in their representation of present-day Black Harlem as a dangerous, decaying reservation populated by not particularly friendly natives."[130] For a reason to be discussed momentarily, Yoshida wants to eschew reductive representations of Harlem. But even she notes "the scraps of paper and half-eaten food and empty cans and bottles that littered the streets of Harlem," observing that "there was ten times more litter here than what you would find in an upscale area like Park Avenue."[131]

At this juncture, we should revisit Honda via Ōe. I posited earlier that Honda was interested in a map of Harlem that connects this symbolic site to long 1970s Japan. The concern here is that the history of something like the Three-Fifths Compromise bleeds into something like the three-to-five compromise of the Washington Naval Treaty.[132] That is to say America's legacy of domestic racism inevitably colors its militaristic engagements abroad, in which post-Anpo Japan is now complicit. Such bleeding fosters, as Takuma Hideo argued, a kind of transpacific racial consciousness that makes it impossible for the Japanese to "sit idly by . . . and say with a careless face that it is like this in America and like that in England."[133]

This biracial Tokyo to Harlem connection, a generic motif of the texts under discussion, is embodied by the biracial children who populate these works. It is here that Ōe is informative: "For mixed-blood children and their mothers, the race problem is not an issue that can be solved without getting their hands dirty."[134] Rather than focusing first on analogy (Ōe) or dynamic intertextuality (Nakagami), the texts of the long 1970s characterize Afro-Japanese relations as a kind of profound hybridity written in and on the body itself. This tactic is reminiscent of Elaine Scarry's insight into the anchoring capacity of the body in pain, in which reading "the hurt body of another person" as it is "juxtaposed to the disembodied idea" allows for a "belief [that we have] experienced the reality of the second" by "having sensorily experienced the first."[135] The black-Japanese bodies in pain generically interspersed throughout these texts—Yoshida's photographs of biracial children protesting on the streets of Harlem, Honda's interviews with bullied and bruised biracial families, the verbal torment that prompts Ariyoshi's Emiko to move her biracial child to Harlem, the serrating body blow that serves as the impetus of *Human Proof*, the associative connection between James Powell (the boy whose death ignited the 1964 Harlem Riots) and Abe's scarred and faceless narrator, Ōe's biracial "Tiger," who is gunned down by military police, and on and on—attempt to anchor the disembodied cultural reality of black-Japanese hybridity.

Moreover, this anchored intertwining is written in a generic grammar in which African Americans and Japanese are "on the same side" insofar as both are (passively) discriminated against by the (active) discriminating American powers that be. See, for example, Honda (who writes of the "logic of the *discriminator* and the logic of *those who are discriminated against*," with the emphasis between the active and the passive form in the Honda original), Ariyoshi ("Now I can say it with perfect clarity: in this world, there are only two races—the users [*tsukau ningen*] and the used [*tsukawareru ningen*]), and Abe Kōbō ("There is next to nothing shared in common between black folks and me, with the exception that we both are discriminated against [*henken no taishō ni sarete iru*]").[136]

Once the blood ties between black and Japanese life are made irrevocable by the anchoring of generic grammar and hybrid bodies, these texts turn to their shared conclusions. These conclusions (here suggested in both the colloquial and literary sense of the term) are reminiscent of Baldwin in *The Fire Next Time*, a text that was translated into Japanese in 1963, the same year as its English publication and two years after the scholarly journal *Kindai bungaku* singled out Baldwin for critical attention in a special issue on black literature. Here Baldwin explores two avenues for cleansing the sins of racism: self-affirming water ("You can only be destroyed by believing that you really are what the white world calls a *nigger*") and incendiary social fire ("Neither civilized reason nor Christian love would cause any of those people to treat you as they presumably wanted to be treated; only the fear of your power to retaliate would cause them to do that").[137] The conclusions that Japanese authors propose to the "Negro problem"—now envisioned as a dilemma anchored in a shared concern for hybrid, Afro-Japanese bodies—begin to reflect the firsthand, secondhand, and lived experience of such Baldwinian thought.

Yoshida, who had documented familiarity with the works of Baldwin, subscribes to the self-affirmative power of celebrating black beauty (a maneuver that underpins the aforementioned downplaying in Yoshida's *Hot Harlem Days* of the aesthetic differences between Harlem and the "real" United States). Hence Yoshida's recapitulation of her work: "I have watched, through both my camera and my bodily experiences (*taiken*), the people of Harlem transform from enervated Negroes to beautiful Blacks."[138] Ariyoshi's Emiko, too, leans toward such beautiful self-affirmation. After her realization that the cherry blossoms of Washington, DC, must change their color, so, too, does she realize "I, too, am a Negro . . . so I have to work with everything I have in the Negro world. Anything else is a lie."[139] So, too, does Honda, who, essaying against the colonization of the mind, writes:

> The crown jewel in the processes of oppression, discrimination, colonization, and enslavement is an enslavement of the mind that makes itself manifest as the slavery of aesthetic sensibilities. . . . The Japanese are quite far along in [this final mode] of colonization
>
> When African Americans opened their eyes to the idea that America . . . in all its organizations, institutions, and values, has been designed with whites (or, more specifically, a certain subset of whites) in mind and not blacks, their revolutionary work went so far as to overthrow that [enslaved] aesthetic sensibility. "Black is beautiful"—the words that capture that work—is, in a sense, a more radical movement than "all power to the people," the motto of the Black Panthers.[140]

The conclusions of Abe and Morimura gesture more toward the Baldwinian perils and promise of the fire next time. Abe's insertion of the Harlem Riots of 1964 into the final notebook of *The Face of Another* adumbrates his conclusion. The faceless narrator, stalking his wife as he carriers a pistol, warns that "this time, the mask that's coming to get you will be a wild beast."[141] The fire "this time (*kondo*)" portends that it is by way of the interruption of violence that the disenfranchised break the cycles of effacement upheld by the law. What is intriguing here, however, is the way Abe, in his Abe way, has the narrator undermine this very possibility even as he posits it. In reading this conclusion against the previous passage on the

Harlem Riots, it is clear that the narrator's position has been inverted. He is now, pistol aimed at an unarmed woman, the faceless embodiment of murderous authority, that gatekeeper who determines—under the threat of punishment—who can and can't enter a given social space. As such this violence, which emphasizes the difference of "this time," becomes yet another iteration of the very violence that scarred the narrator and set the gears of effacement in motion.

The grooves and contours of Abe do not lend themselves to generic reading; it is with Morimura that there is a more generic encounter with Afro-Japanese resistance as violent protest. Alongside its hybrid body—embodied here by Johnny, the novel's "human proof"—a series of subplots that suggest Afro-Japanese parallelism run through *Ningen no shōmei*. One of these is the aforementioned maternal abandonment of both Johnny and Kyōhei, his transpacific reflection. Another is the parallel tracks shared by Johnny and Detective Munesue. The detective, like Johnny, was abandoned as a child by his mother during the Allied Occupation. He also loses his father, who dies after he intervenes and is subsequently beaten by a group of American GIs who are harassing a young Japanese woman (who turns out to be Johnny's mother). This moment serves as the impetus of both Munesue's loss of faith (*fushin*) in humanity and his desire to "get revenge, slow revenge, one-by-one."[142]

The conclusion of *Human Proof* returns to this pivotal moment. The penultimate section has Munesue's faith in humanity restored by Kyōko when she provides her human(e) proof by confessing that Johnny is her son. Munesue's slow revenge fills the final pages of the text. This revenge, however, occurs on the streets and by the hands of Harlem. The transpacific scope of this murder mystery requires Munesue to team up with Ken Shuftan, a Manhattan detective. *Human Proof* concludes with Detective Shuftan's stabbing at the hands of an unnamed assailant in Harlem. As the detective searches for a motive, he claims that "there was no justification . . . just as there was no clear justification for why, in a faraway time when he went to Japan as a soldier, he had urinated on a defenseless Japanese man," Detective Munesue's father.[143] The "justification" for this stabbing, as Shuftan himself realizes, is that his debt to Japan "will be written off if I die here."[144] Here, the violent power of Harlem ensures that American racism—which divides child from mother and citizen from motherland—repays its debts both at home and abroad. And so the text ends with Harlem, now a breathing organism with a will of its own, basking in its victory; Shuftan has a scar on his arm that looks like a vulva (a heavy-handed metaphor/identifying mark) that he received during his time fighting on the front lines of an island in the South Pacific during World War II. And:

Figure 8. A photograph by Yoshida Ruiko of a third-world unity rally held in Harlem in December 1970. The multicolored third-world solidarity championed at the rally speaks to the long 1970s desire for Afro-Japanese hybridity. (© Ruiko Yoshida.)

At that very moment, a single beam of light from the late-day set-ting sun streamed through the buildings of Harlem and took his old, blackened scar and painted it raw and fresh, as if the stabbing and bleeding had just begun. That little slice of Harlem where Ken Shuftan breathed his last breath sank eternally to the bottom of an unbelievable silence, as if it had been severed from the workings of New York.[145]

With the scars of the Pacific War literally brought to light by Harlem and its residents, Morimura's conclusion imagines the violent power of Afro-Japanese hybridity in the long 1970s.

Conclusion

Adhering to the tools and techniques of their respective genres, each of the five texts considered here makes a singular contribution to the writing of blackness in Japan's long 1970s. Yoshida Ruiko's *Hot Harlem Days* provides a Japanese complement to Ann McGovern's *Black Is Beautiful*. Like McGov-ern, Yoshida's juxtaposition of visual imagery and the imagery of the written word function as a kind of ambassador to the beauty of blackness for Yo-shida's readership. Honda Katsu'ichi's *The United States of America* presents reportage with an objective (rather than objective reportage), a rewriting of American life from the perspective of African Americans. Ariyoshi's *Not Be-cause of Color* investigates the ideological infrastructure of American racism and classism, which she deems the two great facts of black American life, by way of social realist fiction. Morimura's *Human Proof* detects and discovers the black body hiding within the Japanese body politic. Abe Kōbō's science fictional approach to the *kokujin mondai* (Negro problem) is, like Ellison's invisible man, a reminder that there is something already estranged about the black American experience.

Abe's articulation, which places a discussion of blackness within a broader, transpacific conversation on identity and community formation, also serves as a reminder of the generic concerns that underpin this shared turn to black characters and settings throughout the long 1970s. The contradic-tion inherent to Japan's postwar reeducation—a promotion of the ideals of an American-style democracy stewarded by second-class citizens—became palpable given the events of the long 1970s. The literary response to this contradiction reverberated across genre lines, with Japanese authors imagin-ing a new racial politics that spoke for both Japanese and black bodies, or

Afro-Japanese bodies, as it struggled to redefine the limits of government "by the people, for the people" at home and abroad. With Harlem serving as its symbolic capital, this biracial community and commonality confronted the broken promises of American democracy with an aesthetic of racial self-affirmation and a threat of violent protest.

By way of transition to the final chapter, which moves from the long 1970s to the hip hop performances of blackness in Japanese literature that began in the 1980s, I will conclude by stating explicitly what has been implicit thus far. In stirring up "genre trouble," I am thinking—as Judith Butler did and Derrida did before her—of the way in which considerations of genre, which are interested fundamentally in the way the singular might become the plural, might provide some insights that reverberate generically. This is the avenue where Carolyn Miller, who writes in "Genre as Social Action" that genre might be viewed as "conventions of discourse that a society establishes as ways of 'acting together,'" meets Derrida.[146] For Derrida, the "participation-without-belonging of the mark creates the possibility that future instances may fall within the genre."[147] Derrida sees in such participation without belonging—to rearticulate his insight through the terms of Miller—a powerful way for people to act together and "casts the relationship between a genre and its instances into the language of democracy."[148] In other words, in a multiethnic democracy becoming an American is not an issue of belonging to a particular group (being black or white or Asian or whatever). Rather, one is "American" insofar as one participates in the American project. And, insofar as one's mode of participation can change, there is a kind of openness and endless possibility about what it means to be an American—this is participation without belonging. I agree with Derrida and see how something like participation without belonging might alleviate some of the essentialist genre trouble we have gotten ourselves into.

But it is precisely because I agree with Derrida that I find the devil's advocate that plays out in the authors of the following chapter intriguing. Unlike their long 1970s predecessors, hip-hop-inspired Japanese authors such as Itō Seikō and Mobu Norio see themselves as participating in hip hop culture without belonging to it, their race barring them from belonging to a music and movement rooted in black culture. Indeed, for those who wish to argue according to the terms of Japanese appropriation of black culture, the problem becomes the very fact that Japanese hip hoppers participate without belonging. Moreover, this argument is a reminder that African Americans (I should say it in the language of Derrida I suppose) have "always already" participated in American democracy without fully belonging and deferral might not sound as appealing if what is being put on hold is a dream. And it is for this reason that, again, for those who wish to argue over cultural appropriation, cultural appropriation is worth arguing over in the first place. With our belonging already jeopardized, now our modes of participation no longer belong to us as they drift through the United States and across the Pacific. This is what Rey Chow gestures toward when she notes, "Contemporary uses of poststructuralist theory have tended to adopt poststructuralism's solution, differencing, without sufficiently reflecting on its flip side, its circumvention of exclusion. . . . [H]owever permanently the issue may be deferred, the originary differential of inequality will not and cannot go away."[149]

I turn now to the final chapter, which invites conversation about the "participation without belonging" of authors such as Itō Seikō, Mobu Norio, and Yamada Eimi.

CHAPTER 5

Japanese Literature in the Age of Hip Hop

A Mic Check

> Junpei's stories were well written—everyone could agree on that.
> But there was no denying that they strayed from the current literary
> trends. His style was lyrical, and there was something about his plots
> that made them feel antiquated. Your average, contemporary reader
> wants to see fresher styles and bolder stories. This is, after all, the age
> of computer games and rap music.
>
> —Murakami Haruki, "Honey Pie"

Mic Check: Blackness and Japanese Literature in the Age of Hip Hop

Murakami's musings in his 2000 *Hachimitsu pai* (Honey Pie), a metafictional tale of author Junpei, invite a series of inquiries. What are the fresh styles and bold stories that readers seek in an age of rap music? What is, for that matter, the age of rap music and when did it begin?[1] Does this age alter our expectations of what "Japanese" literature is and how it might function? And here are two questions that are both effaced and embodied by Murakami's articulation. What happens to blackness when the artists who construct it are not black? What possibilities and pitfalls open for the writing of blackness in an age when rap, which once had inextricable ties to black people and communities, has gone global, when it has become the source music for *our* age, when the readership of Murakami's Junpei (whose namesake points toward the work of another author stuck in the sandpits of transnational homelessness, Abe Kōbō) is expecting Japanese literature informed by the cadences of hip hop?

This chapter explores these questions by way of a mic check, that is, by listening to the lyrics and musical criticism of Itō Seikō (1961–) and the novels of Yamada Eimi (1959–) and Mobu Norio (1970–). Imani Perry suggests that Americans have a preference for sonic blackness and visual whiteness (think of Paul Whiteman, Elvis, and Eminem).[2] Riffing on Perry, this chapter addresses the interface of sonic blackness and Japanese narratives in the works of Itō, Mobu, and Yamada.

There is a great deal of shorthand in this formulation, so let me be clear about what I mean by "sonic blackness" and "Japanese narratives." In the context of hip hop, *sonic* is a loaded term that includes sound, aurality, orality, rhetoric, trope, style, cadence, and, we might add, performative swagger. As for "sonic blackness," there is no essence, nothing absolute, biological, or pure about so-called black sound. If "blackness" is the social fiction that delineates the constellation of ascriptions that describe the commonalities of people of sub-Saharan African descent, then "sonic blackness" is the chapter in that fiction that defines its sound. There is indeed, however, *a social fiction* about how blackness sounds. This is what Zora Neale Hurston underscores when she says, "The American Negro has done wonders to the English language. . . . No one listening to a Southern white man talk could deny this." This is also what Nina Eidsheim hears as she listens to what she calls the "micropolitics of timbre," the "persistence of the metaphor of vocal timbre as the unequivocally unmediated sound of subjectivity means that qualities which are believed to be essential, such as race, are also believed to be heard in vocal timbre."[3] This social fiction, moreover, takes on a cultural reality through the processes of public performance. As hip hop has gone global, artists across the globe have open-source access to "sonic blackness" as it is performed in and through hip hop. Insofar as the sounds of hip hop have been *coded as black*, Japanese authors fluent in the styles and tropes of hip hop can remix "sonic blackness" in and into Japanese.

By "Japanese narratives," I do not mean to suggest some Nihonjinron-esque claim of monolithic singularity, some smoking gun that unites all Japanese narratives uniformly. Nor am I referring solely to thematics or diegetic indices—characters, settings, and so on—that point toward "Japaneseness"; readers of Yamada Eimi, for example, will know that several of what I call her "Japanese narratives" are set in (black) America and feature black characters. By "Japanese narratives," I mean works that are narrated in Japanese and consumed primarily by a Japanese readership. These narratives cater to an imagined Japanese readership—they are "for us (Japanese readers), by us (Japanese writers)"—and carry with them the assumption of a shared horizon of linguistic, cultural, geopolitical, and historical expectations that tie writer to reader.

In longhand, then, by "the interface of sonic blackness and Japanese narratives," I mean an exploration of how hip hop provides a social fiction of the sound of blackness that has global currency and how authors such as the trio considered here translate and repackage that fiction as Japanese narratives for an imagined Japanese readership.

In this chapter, I consider the writing of blackness in Japanese literature in an age in which the signs and techniques of the "postracial" exist side by side with the legacies and realities of the racial. There is a great deal of tension at the nexus of sonic blackness and Japanese narratives. On one turntable, there is the very fact that sonic blackness can travel and be translated, localized, and internalized in the first place. This intimates the fictionality of sonic blackness as a social fiction; we cannot help but question the essentialism of black sound in the face of hip hop's border-crossing sonic ventriloquism. Implicit to this loosening of the grip of racial essentialism is the possibility of expanding its cast of characters, extending the community of folks who speak with, to, and in black tongues. On the other turntable, however, there is the very real possibility that when sonic blackness meets Japanese narratives, it simply becomes the sound system that reifies the borderline of Japanese communities, identities, and cultural nationalism. Insofar as "Japanese narratives" are built on the assumption of a shared language and horizon of expectations, every importation of fictionalized sonic blackness from the outside runs the risk of factionalizing the "Japaneseness" that binds the narrative itself. This makes Ian Condry's reminder critical: "Generally in Japan, corporate support has flowed more quickly either to those who accommodate the marketing world's fetishization of blackness . . . or to those who deemphasize blackness in favor of aligning themselves with Japan's [tradition]."[4]

This tension at the nexus of sonic blackness and Japanese narratives gives rise to a dance that I call the postblack two-step. It is a fumbling little dance—set to a staccato rhythm—that makes dancers contort as they try to balance themselves with the two steps it proposes: a step toward the possibility of experimental voices that imply antiessentialist and transracial visions of racial and ethnic identity and affinity and a step toward potentially narcissistic narratives of racial and ethnic identity predicated on (and at times policed by) the ethnic and racial paradigms of yesteryear. It is easy to dismiss the possibility of postblackness as so much naïveté—to see postblack two-steppers as simply stumbling over themselves—if the term *postblack* is taken as synonymous with *color blindness* or "a world in which racism no longer exists." But what happens when we take David A. Hollinger up on the challenge he proposes in "The Concept of Post-racial: How Its Easy Dismissal Obscures Important Questions" and define the postracial as "*a possible future* in which ethnoracial categories central to identity politics would be more matters of choice than ascription."[5] In turn postblackness would see blackness, in Touré's words, "not as a dogmatic code worshiping at the altar of the hood and the struggle but as *an open-source document, a trope with infinite uses.*"[6] In short, what happens when blackness is seen as a fiction even as we remain painfully aware of the power that fictions can hold over us? We come face-to-face with the "Dolezal Dilemma."[7] Is this a new way of racial being or a new way of racial appropriation? In this light, postblack two-steppers appear much less naive, or, rather, they appear naive only insofar as no one really knows what the future of race holds.

This chapter considers the postblack two-step as it is performed by Itō Seikō, Mobu Norio, and Yamada Eimi in their hip-hop-informed cultural productions. I begin by reading the creation of sonic blackness in the early hip hop of Itō Seikō against his musings on blackness in his music and cultural criticism. The contrast between his sound and the streak of cultural nationalism that runs through his criticism provides a precedent-setting blueprint for the interface of sonic blackness and Japanese narratives. From there I turn to Mobu Norio and his Akutagawa Prize–winning *Kaigo nyūmon* (An Introduction to Nursing, 2004), a novel that translates the precedent set by Itō Seikō into fictional form. The final section listens to the stylings of Yamada Eimi's 2003 *Payday!!!* I read in *Payday!!!* an attempt to add a new interpretation of the postblack two-step to an oeuvre that has opened Yamada to charges of stereotyping and racial (racist?) appropriation and commodification. Chapter 3 considered Nakagami Kenji's exchanges with blackness as they were mediated by, among other things, jazz. Shifting from explorations of Japanese writings of blackness in the jazz age, which privileged musicality, to those of the age of hip hop, which privilege verbality, occasions a new inquiry: how should (or, for that matter, can) Japanese authors articulate the blackness of which their writings are composed?

Mic Check: Itō Seikō and the Postblack Two-Step

Rapping in Japanese with Itō Seikō: "Clever Vernaculars" and the Felicitous Translation of Sonic Blackness

Itō Seikō's literary bona fides are impeccable. His work has garnered him a pair of nominations for the Mishima Yukio and Akutagawa prizes, and his 2013 *Sōzō rajio* (Imagination Radio), for which he won the Noma Prize for New Writers some twenty-five years after his first nomination, has been deemed an instant classic of post 3–11 literature. But Itō Seikō is just as nice on the mic: he was a seminal member of the first generation of Japanese hip hoppers. His 1989 *Mess/Age* was a pioneering album that proved the possibility of rapping in Japanese, and his recent work with Kuchiroro has proven that the established author still has a few rhymes left.

"It started," Itō Seikō reminisces on the 2009 track "Hippu hoppu no shoki shōdō" (The Initial Impulse for Hip Hop), "with a Far East Network American military broadcast / listening to Sugar Hill Gang—a blast from the past / the bumping beat had my heart in a pinch / heard Bob Marley, been puffing in admiration ever since / mimicking the lyrics, English gibberish / had to chew on it for years to spit out Japanese like this."[8] These lyrics tell the tale of a young Seikō, his Waseda University well within the radio broadcast range of the Yokota Air Base, mimicking the lyrics and delivery of American rap, which he did to entertain his Waseda peers. This play, however, gradually transformed into (to borrow the Teriyaki Boyz's tagline) "serious Japanese"; his fascination with the rhythm and rhyme of hip hop fused with his study of English poetry and sparked his interest in producing such poetry in Japanese.

This interest, however, presented Seikō with a kind of lyrical and linguistic conundrum: how does one translate "English gibberish" into Japanese that is felicitous to the spirit of the English of hip hop? In the early days of Japanese hip hop, there was the belief that such translation simply couldn't be done. The linguistic and poetic characteristics of the Japanese language seemed to collude against the formal possibility of rapping in Japanese. Noriko Manabe notes that first-generation Japanese rappers "originally started rapping in English, believing that their own language lacked the ability to make rhymes and rhythms."[9] The second hurdle was more about sociolinguistics. The first generation of Japanese hip hoppers—Itō Seikō, Tinnie Punx (Takagi Kan and Fujihara Hiroshi), Chikada Haruo, DJ Krush, Crazy-A, and so on—were listening to and inspired by the first generation of American rappers and their precursors—Grandmaster Flash, the Sugar Hill Gang, Chuck D and Public Enemy, KRS-One, Run DMC, and so on. Remember, too, that, as Tricia Rose writes, "From the outset, rap music has articulated the pleasures and problems of black urban life in contemporary America. Rappers speak with the voice of personal experience, taking on the identity of the observer or narrator."[10] If rap is seen as expressive of the black condition, with black rappers telling black narratives for black audiences, then the question of "whether or not you can rap in Japanese" takes on a second meaning: is rap still rap when it is expressive of other (Japanese) conditions?[11]

Itō Seikō saw these two problematics, Japanese rhyme and voice, as intertwined. As such he also saw the solution to the problem (read: the creation of felicitous Japanese translations of hip hop English) at their nexus.
For Seikō, the solution stems from his understanding of the power of black
English. He characterizes black English as having dynamic, what Henry
Louis Gates might call signifyin', power. Every word is hypercharged and
holds within itself the potential energy to transform and signify something
new. In a March 1988 dialogue with Saeki Kenzō entitled "'Ai shiteru' wo
kowasanakya Nihongo wa kaerarenai" (We Can't Change the Japanese Language until We Crush 'I Love You'), Seikō claims:

> There are these unthinkable words that seem to come from the bot-
> tom and burst to life, like a grassroots movement. It won't work un-
> less we have words like that. Take black folks today. They have words
> like "bad" and "def." They take everything and they're constantly
> changing its meaning like a grassroots movement, right?[12]

Two things here are important for Seikō: the perpetual motion in the meaning of the English language prompted by black usage and the fact that the
impetus for this motion doesn't come from on high. Rather, this linguistic
revolution comes from the ground up, à la a grassroots movement. Without
this grassroots movement of meaning from the bottom, Seikō says, "it won't
work."

The "it" under discussion between Seikō and Saeki Kenzō is *umai hōgen*,
which can be translated as "a clever vernacular." Seikō's self-styled need for a
clever vernacular was rooted in part in his work as a rapper. He agrees with
Noriko Manabe, who writes, "Rap is unique: perhaps no other genre is as
highly dependent on language. Without the distraction of a melody, rap
leaves the words exposed, pounding its . . . message into one's ear."[13] Seikō
is discomfited by such exposure: "Rapping 'I love you,' that's tough. It'd
be alright if I had a melody. But with rap, you're throwing raw words out
there, just like an ordinary conversation. So it'd be just like what happens
when you tell someone you love them in a regular conversation."[14] And
what happens when you tell someone "I love you"? For Seikō, nothing, for
"The melody is meaning; the beat is meaningless, right? So you can arrange
certain lyrics with the melody for emphasis. But, with rap, all the lines are
equal, so you can't emphasize a given line . . . [and] that's the hardest part [of
rap]: the word you want to highlight just gets washed away."[15]

The dilemma he faces as a rap lyricist is, for Seikō, a metaphor for sociopolitical participation and communication in turn-of-the-era Heisei Ja-

pan. With no melody to adorn or obfuscate their impact, there is a kind of equality between every lyric; every lyric has the opportunity to have its voice heard. This is why Seikō posits rap as "apposite for political speeches and things like that."[16] If, however, every voice can be heard equally, there is the risk that no voice can rise above the noise. As the rap lyric goes, so goes contemporary political and cultural discourse. Equal in the eyes of the law, just as every lyric is weighed equally in the measure of the beat, we (or, rather, the listenership of Japanese hip hop) have equal access to both a language that is "apposite for political speeches" and, because of that very equalizing force, the risk that "the words we want to highlight will just get washed away" in the churning of the discursive currents. The Japanese rapper's lyrical dilemma becomes, then, a musical, metaphoric microcosm of the dilemma of communication in Seikō's Japan. Or, in Seikō's words:

> The Japanese that everyone speaks these days—the Japanese you hear on the news and whatnot—I get the feeling that it's an incredibly artificial language. I mean, if you took black people's rap from the South Bronx and exported it to, say, the West Coast, no one would be able to make out what was being said, right? That would never happen in Japan. . . . The language is incredibly artificial. It's like we're singing in this artificial language so that anyone else can follow along. When it's like that, when you don't know who's the object of what's being said, then there's no subject, and really no purpose to what's being said. So it just goes out into the world and gets washed away.[17]

It is clear here that Seikō deems the risk of equal communication more potent than its promise, and this is why his metaphors overlap, with both meaningless communication and rap lyrics on meaningless beats being "washed away." This is also why he refers to Japanese as *jinkōteki* (artificial or man-made) and *jinkōgo* (an artificial language). *Artificiality* here is a near synonym for *equality*, with the distance between the near synonyms representing the fine difference between everyone having an equal *voice* and everyone having an *equal* (and thereby nullified) voice. With that in mind, Seikō's rendition of the power of rap and black English comes to the fore; the grassroots power of hip hop English signification and the need for such power in Japanese become a kind of baseline for Seikō's rap theory. Unlike Japanese—a language of "artificial equality," Seikō sees clever vernaculars as the lifeblood of hip hop signification. In his contribution to the 2014 essay collection *Rappu no kotoba 2* (Japanese Rap Words 2), for example, Seikō claims that the appeal of the soundscape of *Wild Style*, the catalytic film that ushered in the Japanese "age of rap music," was "in its chaotic amalgamation." The film featured not only African Americans but also "a Hispanic protagonist [Zoro, played by "Lee" George Quiñones] . . . Chicano accents, Jamaican English, Latin music like boogaloo, and then you had some Funk too."[18] The task that Seikō sets for himself as a hip hop translator, then, is to "interpret all that Tokyoically (*Tokyo-teki ni*) with the means provided by hip hop."[19]

I noted earlier that Seikō considers the problems of Japanese rhyme and voice to be intertwined. It is at this juncture that the two meet; the grassroots vitality of black English signification is activated by hip hop means, and the means that most fascinates Seikō is rhyme. By rhyming in Japanese, by having "artificial" Japanese fall into sonic symphony like the "clever vernacular" par excellence, Seikō hopes to activate a similar vitality in Japanese. In his contribution to a special issue of *Eureka* entitled *The Poetics of J-Pop: On the Frontline of Japanese*, Seikō writes that rapping in Japanese was akin to "presenting the results of an experiment: I can twist Japanese like this. . . . I thought it would be interesting to shackle Japanese with rhyme. . . . I thought: with rap, maybe I can destroy the Japanese language."[20]

It is with his 1989 album *Mess/Age* that Seikō would display his rhyming experimentation.[21] The album announces this experiment before it sounds a single lyric: the compact disc (CD) is flanked by a "rhyming bible" and liner notes that describe the CD as "a grand adventure in the Japanese language."[22] Condry writes that "the double entendre of the . . . title" of Seikō's *Mess/Age* announces his hypothesis: "that a creative reworking of an era (*age*) that had become a 'mess' could arise through the serendipitous cross-language fertilization in his "message.'"[23] If the "mess" is born of "subjectless, meaningless" expressions in an artificial language, then rhyme is a kind of incubator for a Japanese that has been cross-fertilized with a "clever vernacular," the sonic blackness of hip hop, with all its grassroots vitality.

Take for example "Mess/Age," one of two eponymous tracks on the *Mess/Age* album. The track opens with pure rhyme.

Mess!

Mayakashi, ayakashi, amayakashi, sukashi	Deceive, hard to perceive, pamper and pacify with make believe
Katasukashi, gomakashi, hagurakashi	Sumo-style subterfuge, a ruse to confuse and lose 'em

Mukashinatsukashi shikashi aiso tsukashi   Nostalgic but choleric
Himitsu akashi, bakashi, hito no akashi   Exposé, metamorphic play, this
is who we are today[24]

Rapping over a minimalist, percussion-driven beat, Seikō pushes the listener's attention to the verbal acrobatics of his repetitive, rhyming Japanese. He begins with an assessment of our age—"Mess!"—thereby reminding the listener of the border that impedes his "message": this "mess/age." From there he dives into a verse that is subjectless, which, given his musing on subjectless Japanese, means that everyone (and no one) is listening. Pure rhyme, however, holds this subjectless message together. In the first four bars, Seikō takes advantage of the rules of Japanese grammar and pronunciation to make his rap flow. He selects verbs that end in *-kasu* and conjugates them to the *renyōkei* (conjunctive form), which allows for a series of linked rhymes with nouns, adjectives, and adverbs that end in *shi*. Take, for example, the opening bar. Seikō pairs *mayakashi* (from *mayakasu*, "to cheat or deceive") with *ayakashi*, a term that, insofar as it holds multiple meanings (either a classical Japanese variant of "unclear" or a sea specter reminiscent of a Kraken looking to sink our collective ship), meets Seikō's criterion for clever vernacular. In turn this pair is matched with *amayakashi* (to pamper), a term that, due to simple etymological happenstance, looks like an amalgamation of *mayakashi* and *ayakashi*. Moreover, in Japanese onomatopoeia, sounds from the *sa-* line—*sa, shi, su, se,* and *so*—are associated with a lack of friction or slipping from one moment to the next. Add to this the fact that the Japanese vowels *i* and *u* are weak vowels that are dropped when placed between or behind a final voiceless consonant such as *s*. So not only do his listeners hear sounds that imply a lack of friction, but they also slide from one moment to the next, eliding many of the vowels that might act as sonic intermediaries. This sliding motion sends the listener careening into the fourth bar's lyrical endgame: that the rhyming morass of lyrics that have come before, many of which are true rhymes, serve as *hito no akashi* (a testament to or proof of who a person is). In a song in which Seikō refers to Japan's "slumbering media," his rhyming messages bear witness to the possibility of a linguistic alternative to the soporific, artificial language of "standard" Japanese. Or, to quote the penultimate line of "Mess/Age:" "Waking you up, shining rhythm's light / here's the message, it's got bite / take the flow of things and stop 'em midflight."[25]

For Seikō, clever vernaculars wake the people from such slumber. They allow for unconventional expression, give birth to new modes of signification, and cut through the noise of "equal voices." The next four bars of

"Mess/Age" are a case in point. Here the *shi*-based rhyme scheme switches to one rooted in *-riai*, which Seikō forms by creating a series of compound verbs between (*godan*) verbs that end in *-ru* and the verb *au*, which, when serving as the suffix of a compound verb, suggests "coming together to do X." A central theme of *Mess/Age* (both the track and the album) is an exploration of what happens when the masses (*gunshū*) come together in an information age. The second four bars make that exploration rhyme.

Masaguri-ai, saguri-ai, naguri-ai	Grabbing each other, tabbing each other, jabbing each other
najiri-ai, majiri-ai, soshiri-ai	Objurgate, congregate, incriminate
mushiri-ai, ibiri-ai, ibari-ai	tear into them—they're in tears and putting on veneers
shaberiai, takariai, chikau ai	people talking, crowds gathering, promises of loving[26]

Here the rhyme scheme pushes toward the final phrase: promised love. This phrase is conspicuous in its break from the rhyming rule set by the other three bars. Here, rather than the "compound verb plus *ai*" formula, there is a verb, *chikau* (to vow or promise), modifying the noun *ai* (love). Given that this phrase is preceded by *takaru*, a verb that can mean either "to flock" or "to extort," the promise of love that the verse ends on seems to be another *ayakashi*, a spectral promise of a mess/age. Be that as it may, what is important here is that we remember the claim that Seikō posits in "We Can't Change the Japanese Language until We Crush 'I Love You'": a Japanese person would be hard-pressed to rap about love. Seikō's clever vernacular is already making good on its promise to expand the boundaries of Japanese discourse.

Playing in the Background: Postblack Two-Stepping through the New Cultural Politics of Affiliation

Insofar as Itō Seikō's search for hip hop rhymes and a clever vernacular is inspired by a self-proclaimed affinity with the likes of the Sugar Hill Gang, Run DMC, and KRS One, his interest in the "grassroots movement" of "black talk" like "bad" and "def" is indicative of an affinity for the fiction of sonic blackness. I should, however, be just as clear as Seikō is concerning what I mean by the term *affinity*. *Affinity* here refers to a "liking for or attraction to a person or thing."[27] This affinity is not to be confused with any of the other definitions of *affinity*, including "similarity of characteristics or nature; resemblance; common ground," "the state of being closely connected or mutually dependent," an "alliance or association between people," or even "sympathy and understanding for something."

Again, Seikō speaks for himself on this issue. In describing the rationale for his early 1990s turn away from hip hop and toward spoken-word performance, Seikō writes:

> Well, from the very start, I was susceptible to the flows of Malcolm X, the Black Panthers, and [black] Muslims. (Laughs.) Although I can understand where they are coming from, there was a part of me that couldn't sympathize with them. I couldn't express solidarity with their words of black supremacy—that's the obstacle I ran into. First off, I'm not black. And second, even if I wanted to put a fist in the air, the reality of the matter is I've never experienced discrimination.[28]

There is a certain tension between Seikō's hesitant laughter at his "susceptibility" and his inability to overcome the "obstacle" of racial imagining. This is the same tension that resides within the definitions of *affinity*. There are many ways of reading this tension.[29] The most productive reading, however, occurs when it is considered in light of Condry's "new cultural politics of affiliation."[30] Condry begins with the premise that certain frames of analysis invoke "notions of cultural authenticity that may prove ill-suited to . . . transnationally oriented productions."[31] Building on Cornel West's new cultural politics of difference, which aims to "inspire alliances without essentializing," Condry asks that we "reorient our attention away from questions of whether the Japanese 'get it' or 'don't get it' when it comes to race and hip-hop" and focus instead on "questions of what Japanese hip-hoppers are doing with the music *in their own worlds*."[32] Such focus stems from Condry's insight that "the criticisms of Japanese appropriations of blackness reinforce essentialized notions of blackness and Japaneseness."[33] By "examining the fraught debates *within Japan* over the appropriateness of using" hip hop identity markers and modes of performance (rather than co-opting them as salvos for a preexisting American debate), we begin to see both how Japanese hip hop "creates a space for questioning race and power by *laying bare the constructedness of racial identity*" and the "*signs of an emerging transnational cultural politics of race*, in the sense of promoting action on racial issues that transcend national borders and of doing homework to share the burden of history."[34]

I agree with Condry that the power of Japanese hip hop is best heard by way of consideration of the cultural work that it does "in its own world."

When I take him up on this insight, however, I see the postblack two-step. On the good foot, the very fact that Itō Seikō has rhythm, rhyme, and a clever vernacular (in Condry's words) "lays bare the constructedness of racial identity" and (to revisit my summation) "intimates the fictionality of blackness." Seikō is living proof that there are no racial barriers to the reproduction of the technical and formal aspects of hip hop performance.[35] Given that a part of what is being performed in black poetry and black music is the black poet and the black musician, "transracial" performances have the potential to radically undermine essentialist notions of race and gesture toward new ways of racial being and belonging.

But on the off foot, there is the very real possibility that, insofar as the prefix *trans-* can suggest, rather ambivalently, moving both through and beyond race, such performances can leave us not with the "improvisational sensibilities," "protean identities," and "international perspectives" of West's new cultural politics of difference but reifications of the racial paradigms of yesteryear.[36] There is nothing inherent in the postblack two-step that demands that the second step will move toward "transracial politics." This aspect of that second step becomes particularly visible when viewing, as Condry suggests, the work that hip hop discourse does within Japanese cultural circuits. Certain hip-hop-informed cultural productions show, Condry says, "signs of an emerging transnational cultural politics of race." The postblack two-step, however, is a reminder that what we are seeing may be precisely that: signs. Signs show no natural affinity for any given signified. Although the translatability of the signs of hip hop's "blackness" does imply the mutability of race, it does not necessarily follow that these translated signs will engender narratives of "flexible sensibilities" and "protean identities." I am reminded here of Azuma's database animals, who devour all the signs without a need for any narratival garnish.

Indeed, depending on how they are deployed, these signs may even reify the (racial) ties that bind. Itō Seikō's "affinity without association" is a case in point. His clever vernacular is rooted in a kind of cultural nationalism that solidifies rather than loosens race-based "truths." For Seikō *the* Japanese are X ("a [Japanese] man and a woman who love one another can't say 'I love you,'") and *the* blacks are Y ("Take black folks today. . . . They take everything and they're constantly changing its meaning like a grassroots movement, right?").[37] What Condry finds "most promising is not the identity per se, but rather [the] signs."[38] As long as the rhyming signifiers (here in the double sense proposed by Gates) remain rooted in identities colored by what Joe Feagin would call a racial frame, however, the rhythm of the postblack two-step is set on an infinite loop; some dancers will lead with the right foot, others with the left, and we will prefer some interpretations to others, but it is, inevitably, a variation of the same song and dance.

Here I should highlight a crucial caveat: the importance of the sample. Artistic interpretations of the postblack two-step, as well as the critical interpretations they inspire, vary significantly depending on the sample under investigation. The sample is, of course, much more than mere evidence for a given argument. Rather, samples determine the trajectory of a given argument in intractable ways. The "signs of an emerging transnational cultural politics of race" would be much more difficult to see given a sample that "highlighted the neo-nationalist rhetoric and racism (against Koreans and Chinese) behind some [Japanese] hip-hop."[39] Conversely, the possibility of a transnational cultural politics of race becomes more apparent the more progressive the sample.

Let me play that back: the sample is of paramount importance—it should shape, in intractably ways, how we read signs. In the musical sense of the term, sampling occurs when an artist references or repeats the verbal and sonic phrases of another artist. Although it can be argued that all musical production begins with sampling broadly defined, this argument is particularly true for hip hop, a genre whose origins reside in the isolation and looped repetition of the breaks composed by other musicians. If the hip hop track can be seen as a kind of dialogue between the lyricist and the producer, the conversation that occurs between them is, in theory, irrevocably colored when the lyricist raps with or over a sample. Take, for example, Imani Perry's assertion, "When Dr. Dre lays lyrics of gangster destruction over mellow soul, his composition signifies on that earlier music's interpretation of the black experience and yet uses it as a vernacular for creating the contemporary meaning he articulates."[40] All this is simply another way of saying that sampling is a synecdoche for the importance that "signifyin(g), dialogism, and intertextuality" should play in any "understand[ing of] hip-hop's borrowing practices."[41]

I say, however, that the sample "should, in theory" function in this manner because the conversations that occur in Dr. Dre's vernacular are not analogous to the conversations that occur in Itō Seikō's vernacular. Seikō's *Mess/Age*, which was produced by Yann Tomita, relies on a dizzying array of samples that includes the works of Donald Byrd, Pharoah Sanders, Kool & the Gang, and Mighty Sparrow. One of the most fascinating targets of Seikō's sampling is Sun Ra. Sun Ra and his Arkestra performed in Tokyo in 1988, the year before the release of *Mess/Age*. Itō Seikō remains inspired by Sun Ra.

On 6 April 2015, he tweeted that when he is "writing lengthy pieces" the music of Sun Ra provides him with "nourishment."[42] The interstellar theme of the cover art of *Mess/Age*, as well as the name of the label under which the album was released (Astro Nation), is most likely an homage to Sun Ra. Moreover, two tracks on *Mess/Age* sample Sun Ra, including the aforementioned "Mess/Age," which samples "Interstellar Low Ways." In addition to rapping over the sounds of the Arkestra, the lyrics of *Mess/Age*'s "Verbalien" are inspired by Sun Ra's visions of Afro-futurism. In "Verbalien," Seikō raps that he is a "verbal alien" whose intergalactic lyrics transport him to, among other destinations, Swaziland, Kenya, Ghana, Namibia, Ethiopia, Nigeria, and the Sudan. In "Message"—the eponymous track with which *Mess/Age* concludes (this is not to be confused with "Mess/Age" the eponymous track with which the album begins)—Seikō's rhymes have mended our "mess/age" into a viable message. His work done, Seikō blasts off into outer space: "So, I guess it's about that time for me to jump up on my [space]ship / burning out on tailwinds, jump on in and take a trip / I guess it's about that time for me to go to yet another planet, salutations to all of you who happened up on my orbit."[43]

This sampling should present Seikō with a cosmic dilemma: he should hear a great deal of cacophony between his lyrics of affinity without association and the Sun Ra riffs that he samples, which aspired to channel improvisation as a kind of sonic and spiritual guide toward transcendence from mundane trappings. Although the cosmic themes and references to space that populate Sun Ra's performances have often been deemed "eccentricities," John Szwed, Sun Ra's biographer, writes that these can be read as "part of a shared vision of a black sacred cosmos . . . where the pilgrim is comfortable wherever he or she may travel. . . . This black cosmic vision is easily seen as part of the theme of travel, of journey, of exodus, of escape which dominates African-American narratives: of people who could fly back to Africa, travel in the spirit, visit or be visited by the dead; of chariots and trains to heaven."[44] If Sun Ra is Seikō's "nourishment," then rapping about jumping on Sun Ra's spaceship should give Seikō an allergic reaction. Seikō, by his own admission, is not comfortable navigating the space of post-Public Enemy rap, and his space-based lyrics borrow all of the metaphor with none of the substance of African American narratives of salvation. Reminiscent of DJ Ark, the primary narrator of Seikō's *Sōzō rajio* (Imagination Radio), who "specialized in American literature on a whim and for no particular reason, but really did most of [his] studies by reading in [Japanese] translation—ha ha ha," there is a kind of discord between the sonic blackness and the Japanese narratives of Itō Seikō.[45]

"Hip-hop songs," of course, "can textually signal their borrowing overtly or not do so, and both approaches can be manifested in a number of ways."[46] It is not my intent to prescribe or proscribe how Japanese hip hop(s) can engage with their American counterpart(s). I can see, in Noriko Manabe's summation, the cultural work performed by "distorted sampling or pro-longed juxtapositions of different tempos" as "products of hip-hop related technologies" that give rise to "innovations in the rendering of [Japanese] musical nationalism" even as I remain skeptical of the imagined identities broadcast by sonic nationalism and distorted samples.[47]

What I am noting, however, is the way in which Seikō's sampling speaks to a broader current in the Black Pacific. (And, in the conclusion of this chapter, I note the possibility that there might be another dance available to us. Moreover, insofar as he represents a single current, I do not mean to suggest that Seikō is representative of "the Japanese" approach to hip hop. But his thoughts are revelatory in regard to a crucial facet of contemporary Afro-Japanese cultural exchange.) The current I am speaking of is along the lines of the one identified by Nina Cornyetz, who writes, "The attraction to blackness must not be confused with a deep identification . . . [for] it is a metaphoric valorization of blackness as such . . . an appreciation for African American hip hop and other music, and not a desire for a closer relation with 'real' black culture, or of course, black folks for that matter."[48] I would like to sample Cornyetz's insight—that "blackness is a sign that means exactly what it signs, and not a symbol to be interpreted, by which I mean, there is nothing, really, to *read* beneath, or encoded with this blackness"—and arrange it for a literary studies beat (Cornyetz here is interested in *gyaru* and visual studies): the "signs" of sonic blackness sampled by the likes of Seikō are, in turn, repackaged for Japanese nar-ratives.[49] Sampled and divorced from their black roots, they now carve routes through a Japanese system of signs that is not beholden to any black origin myth. In other words, while I agree with Condry that we do not need to "judge foreign artists primarily in terms of their contribution to African American struggles," this does not absolve us from the need to think through the fact that Japanese hip hop heads do not see an obliga-tion *to judge themselves on these terms.* For this would be a primary dif-ference between Afro-Japanese exchange as interaction and Afro-Japanese exchange as transaction. This difference is particularly pressing given the discussions in the preceding chapters, which consider the historical prec-edents set by Ōe's black-Japanese analogy and Nakagami Kenji's experi-mentation with passing.

The Logic of Itō Seikō's Sampling

Lawrence Grossberg has written on the ascendance of a "neoeclectic main-stream" that "operates with a logic of sampling in both senses of the term (that is, 'sampling' as both a production technique and a habit of listening)."[50] This neoeclectic mainstream "refuses to draw and empower generic distinctions as meaningful."[51] "Good music is good music" might be its motto. Even with this motto in mind, however, the sampling of the neoeclectic mainstream still attempts, Grossberg continues, "to hold onto its 'territorializing function.'"[52] There is a line between numbers 40 and 41 of the Top 40: 40 is in while 41 is not.

What all this—a logic of sampling that refuses to make meaning of genre even as it marks its territory—sounds like to me is the building blocks of the postblack two-step, a dance that both grooves with antiessentialist notions of black sound and brings Japanese listeners together by telling stories in Japanese. And the term *sampling* is particularly apt, for just as sampling (I am thinking here of the grocery store) is, by definition, a noncommittal act that does not imply full endorsement, Seikō's hip hop combines samplings of black sound with narratives written for Japanese audiences.[53] The "discord" heard between his nonengagement with black narratives even as he raps in a "clever vernacular" inspired by the stylings of black artists over samples of black music is the logic of sampling in motion. Whether or not such sampling moves toward the erasure of the problems of racial difference or the kinds of virtuosic remixing that can occur only when the problems of racial difference have been erased is, it seems to me, dependent on the sample and how interactive/transactional it may be. No two iterations of the postblack two-step are the same or, for that matter, different moments in the same iteration of the postblack two-step are not necessarily identical in execution. With that in mind, I turn to two iterations of the postblack two-step in contemporary works of Japanese literature.

One: Mobu Norio and the Postblack Two-Step

The Sonic Blackness of Kaigo nyūmon

Mobu Norio, a graduate of the literature department of Osaka University of the Arts, is a DJ/musician/music critic who moonlights as a novelist. He burst onto the literary scene with his 2004 *Kaigo nyūmon* (An Introduction to Nursing), which was awarded both the Bungakukai New Writers Award and the Akutagawa Prize. *An Introduction to Nursing* tells the semiautobiographical tale of a twenty-nine-year old private musician who becomes the primary caretaker for his eighty-eight-year old grandmother. With the exception of brief, interstitial excerpts of an introductory nursing handbook—the eponymous "introduction to nursing"—the story is narrated from the perspective and in the voice of the twenty-nine-year old "*ore*" (I). It is this voice that caught the attention of the Akutagawa Prize committee members (for better or worse). Although the story is set in Sakurai—the city in Nara prefecture that Mobu calls home—the narrator's monologues are delivered in the voice of a passionate rapper.[54] As committee member Miyamoto Teru wrote in his assessment, "As soon as you start reading Mobu Norio's *An Introduction to Nursing*, the text conveys the fact that the young narrator's rap-style tough-guy tone is one of the novel's stratagems. It seems to me that without that style *An Introduction to Nursing* would have been nothing but a run-of-the-mill, commonplace novel."[55]

Let me begin with the sonic blackness of *An Introduction to Nursing* (I will return to Miyamoto's claim momentarily). The overwhelming majority of *An Introduction to Nursing* is dedicated to the narrator's freestyle, stream-of-consciousness rapping of his days and nights nursing his grandmother. Almost every page of the text flaunts hip-hop-inspired sonic blackness. With some sentences running on for the length of an entire page, the narration gives the reader the sensation of eavesdropping on a rapper in midflow at a private concert. Mobu's sentences are flavored by the very hip hop techniques that rappers such as Itō Seikō employ when on the mic. Take, for example, an excerpt from the narrator's self-introduction.

"YO, FUCKIN, 朋輩（ニガー）俺がこうして語ること自体が死ぬほど胡散臭くて堪らんぜ、ニガー。夢か、リアルか、コマーシャル・ビデオか、麻の灰より生じた言い訳か、悟っては迷う魂の俺からニガーへ、どうしたって嘘ばかりになるだろうから、聞き流してくれ。俺はシャイなおとこだ。

YO, FUCKIN, nigga, the fact that I'm even tellin' it to ya like this is so lugubriously dubious, it makes me furious, nigga. Is this a dream, is this real, is this a commercial, or is this just an excuse born from the bud? This comes from me—a soul who once was lost and once was found—and goes around to my niggas. Either way, it's bound to be full of lies, so just let my words drown. I am a shy guy.[56]

Every line here plays with rhythm and rhyme. In the first line, the substandard conjugation *tamaran* allows for a rhyme with *usan*, which I have translated, in order to preserve the rhyme, as "lugubriously dubious, it makes me furious." In the second line, as the narrator questions himself, the repetition of embedded questions and the interrogative *ka* makes for a rhythmic bassline—"is this a dream, is this real, is this a commercial." This is followed by the rhyming of *e*-family sounds in the third line: *nigaa e, doushitatte,* and *shitekure*. And we can almost hear the cadences of snare drums in the final line. This ten-syllable sentence can be broken into three phrases: "*ore wa,*" "*shai na,*" and "*otoko da.*" The final syllable in each phrase ends in *a*, giving a 1-2-3, 1-2-3, 1-2-3-4, sequence with a series of internal rhymes: "I am a shy guy." The passage's most audible engagement with the fiction of sonic blackness as it is refracted by hip hop is its use of the term *nigaa*. I return to the function of the term *nigga* in *Kaigo nyūmon* momentarily.

Diction, rhythm, and rhyme are the primary markers of *Kaigo nyūmon's* hip hop sound. The text does, however, exhibit other techniques sampled from hip hop's soundscape. Take, for example, *ore's* reply when he when is lauded by a professional health care worker for his dedication to his grandmother. He claims that his filial piety is "*ata, ata, atarimae na no da yo, nigga.*"[57] Here Mobu highlights his recurring return to his grandmother's side by emulating the turntable technique known as a stutter. If hip hop music originated in the isolation and repetition of danceable breaks, then the stutter technique, in which an isolated musical moment is repeated in rapid succession as if the turntable is stuttering ("here-we, here-we, here we go now"), is at the very heart of hip hop sound. Mobu Norio works the sampling machine for the band the Ultrafuckers, and *An Introduction to Nursing's ore* "has occasions when [he] wears out the rubber keyboard of the sampling machine."[58] It comes as no surprise, then, that *ore* deems his devotion to his grandmother "natch, natch, natural my nigga," his voice emulating a fundamental sound of the hip hop soundscape. Here the stutter technique acts as a kind of sonic metaphor for *ore's* rhythmic returns to his grandmother's side.

Another example can be found in *ore's* reaction to his discovery of a negligent nurse's uninspired care for his grandmother: "Oh, what a fuckin' shit. And that last 'shit,' make sure you punch the 'i,' stretch it out a little bit, turn your mouth up and lift its butt up in the air when you pronounce it, like this: 'sheeiiit'—you feel me?"[59] This "oh what a fuckin' shit," including the g-droppin' reduction, is produced in English in the Japanese original. In *Hip Hop Japan*, Condry writes that the Japanese hip hop recording studio is "a place of learning through repeated performance and intense scrutiny" where rappers work toward a "kind of rhythmic nuance that shows that the paradox of being hip-hop in terms of rap, flow, rhyme, and originality leads lyricists to a deeper sensitivity to the potentials of the Japanese language."[60] Here, *ore* turns his living room into a kind of hip hop recording studio, with *ore* acting as the veteran producer and the narratee serving as the apprentice emcee in the recording booth. In so doing, Mobu's narrator pushes everyone who cares for his grandmother to approach their job with the intense scrutiny, rhythmic nuance, and deep sensitivity that the space requires.

The Sound and the Fury and the Postblack Two-step: Kaigo nyūmon as "Japanese" Narrative

In concert, these techniques—the flow, diction, rhythm, rhyme, cadence, and delivery of *ore*'s narration—imbue *An Introduction to Nursing* with a hip-hop-flavored sonic blackness. With this in mind, we can turn to the significance and signification of this sonic blackness. I am interested, actually, in what this sonic blackness *does not* signify, for *ore*'s hip hop voice in no way suggests either Afro-Japanese hybridity or antiessentialist experimentation with new ways of racial being. *An Introduction to Nursing* is interested in telling a "Japanese" story; namely, the text attempts to give a voice to the lived experiences of a generation of Japanese youths who came of age during a time of contracting economic opportunity and population aging. It simply performs that story in "black-voice"—a kind of narratival ventriloquism that throws voices across the color line.

Mobu's hip hop style signifies at least four aspects of his narrative. First, the narrator's hip hop delivery highlights the age difference between himself and his grandmother. Whereas the narrator prefers hip hop, his grandmother prefers that "slow dope . . . like *Nodo jiman*."[61] First broadcast via radio on 19 January 1946 by the Japanese Broadcasting Corporation, *Nodo jiman* (Proud of My Voice) is now a weekly, televised amateur singing contest. The implication here is that *ore*'s grandmother has preferred the genres sanctioned by the contest—Japanese popular songs and folksongs—since at least the postwar period. As such her musical sensibilities were born in an age that precedes the birth of both the narrator and hip hop by some four decades.

Second, playing on the "angry rapper" image cultivated by gangster rap, *ore*'s hip hop sound has affective significance. The title *An Introduction to Nursing* derives from a nursing guidebook that *ore* cites and recites at length. Whereas *ore*'s hip hop approach to nursing is laced with affective pepper, the guidebook is filled with formalized bromide. *Ore*, for example, bases his ethics of care on a kind of selflessness; he, to borrow his colloquialism, "kills himself" as he puts his grandmother's well-being above his own. Or, as *ore* articulates this ego death, "Yo, nigga, have you ever killed somebody? Every night, when I go in to help Grandma take care of business, I go in with a killer instinct. And I do it with a smile, you feel me?"[62] Compare this to the language of the nursing guidebook, which offers practical platitudes such as "one must not (*bekarazu*) nurse in silence" in punctilious Japanese.[63]

With his hip hop approach on one turntable and the "official" guide on the other, the narrator's mixing of the two styles makes the passion of his style audible. In contrast, the "official" approach—which requires reminders to communicate with those who need care—is presented as inorganic and metallic. "Inorganic and metallic" are the operative terms. In "Robot Rights vs. Human Rights: Forecasts from Japan," Jennifer Robertson writes that the Japanese state imagines robots as a replacement for human workers, which is why the Abe administration "earmark[ed] $24 million dollars toward the development of urgently needed nursing and elder-caregiving robots" in June 2013.[64] *Ore*'s affected hip hop voice signifies his belief that there is no robotic replacement for human care. In response to seeing a prototype of a robot nurse at a robotics exhibition, *ore* quips:

> Researchers see the body in need of care as nothing more than an engineering problem, and it shows in the design of their [nursing] machines, and their business-as-usual approach is shit, and it shows in the pieces of scrap metal they develop. You want me to show you a blueprint for the nursing robots of the future? Strive for a phenomenal robot, the kind you would make if you knew it would nurse you, jerk. Make a nursing robot in the image of a grandchild you adore, you know what I'm saying?[65]

Third, the narrator's hip hop style serves as a reminder of his search for his production value. Perhaps the premier irony of *An Introduction to Nursing* is that the text, which is typically read in solitary silence, is essentially a silent rap set to a silent beat. In hip hop parlance, the instrumental is the realm of the producer, and a track without an instrumental would have no production value. As such, the time that *ore*—who once was single-mindedly devoted to music—spends silently recording his days with his grandmother is time in which he must search for and redefine his notions of "production" and "value." Hence lines such as this one: "Every day, the CDs scattered across my room accumulate a thin layer of dust, and, just like that dust, every day I accumulate a thin layer of defeat."[66] Moreover, *ore* is unemployed, financially dependent on his mother, and engaged in invisible labor in the domestic sphere, giving his search for production value a gendered vector. The masculine bravado of his hip hop voice embodies the narrator's attempt to redefine what it means to be a productive man; this is why one of the narrator's hip hop fusillades begins with this salvo "I bet you're thinking that I'm halfheartedly taking care of Grandma just because I'm unemployed and have nothing better to do and don't have anything productive to contribute to society."[67] In its hip hop voice, *An Introduction to Nursing* attempts to rewrite the terms on which nursing is evaluated, arguing that the value of nursing stems from an ethics, rather than economics, of caregiving.

Fourth, the hip hop language of *An Introduction to Nursing* embodies a search for a community that extends beyond the home. Although caring for his grandmother is the connective tissue of his immediate family, *ore* is left with a question: who cares about the caretakers? *Ore* is reminded of this concern whenever he has an opportunity to care for his grandmother with a professional nurse. "Anytime I get a chance to work with a nurse," *ore* asserts, "our house gets a taste of the reassurance that comes with sharing labor with a phenomenal colleague. 'My mom and I aren't alone, we're saved,' that's how I feel."[68] The term that I have translated as "anytime"—*hyōshi*—is telling. In this idiom, *hyōshi* means "whenever I have the chance to," but the term itself comes from music and suggests musical time, tempo, beat, or rhythm. This coupling of musical time and nursing time is reminiscent of Cornel West's claim that the "kinetic orality" of black music, its incorporation of techniques such as call and response, for example, facilitates the formation of communities.[69]

In concert, the four facets signified by *An Introduction to Nursing*'s hip hop style—age difference, passionate care, the search for the production value of caregivers, and a concomitant search for community—sound the central theme of *An Introduction to Nursing*, an attempt to give voice to the lived experiences of a generation of Japanese youths who came of age during a time of contracting economic opportunities and an aging population. Indeed, given that *An Introduction to Nursing* is semiautobiographical, we might consider the text as a kind of *ore-shōsetsu*, a twist on the Japanese I-novel that gives voice to the experiences of Mobu's generation. I provide this admittedly simplified articulation of the text's theme as a transition to our next step; the hip hop narration of Mobu Norio, like the hip hop of Itō Seikō, pairs "sonic blackness" with "Japanese narratives" as it does the postblack two-step.

It is on this note that we can return to one of the two issues that were previously tabled: Miyamoto Teru's claim that *An Introduction to Nursing* would be a "commonplace novel" without its hip hop stylistics. Miyamoto's review of *An Introduction to Nursing* was titled "Yokei na kyōzatsubutsu," which can be translated as "superfluous impurities" or "foreign objects." The "impurity" or "foreign object" here is the hip hop narration that "gives this novel its value." This impurity is "superfluous" insofar as it adulterates an otherwise "commonplace" story about the relationship between the nurse and the nursed.[70] There is an unspoken, nationalist underpinning to this critique, for "commonplace" here is synonymous with "Japanese." What Miyamoto leaves unspoken (does it go without saying?) is that *An Introduction to Nursing* tells a commonplace *Japanese* narrative. Fellow Akutagawa Prize committee member Ishihara Shintarō writes in the same invisible ink when he speaks of the "inevitability" of "contemporary social customs" such as "unemployment and nursing homes" in the stories of young (Japanese) authors.[71]

An article from the 28 July 2007 issue of *The Economist* asks, "As Japan ages and shrinks, workers must support an ever larger proportion of retirees. By 2030 . . . Japan will have just two working age people for each retired one . . . [so] can a working population support such a number of future retirees?"[72] This article serves as a reminder that *An Introduction to Nursing* is "commonplace" to those who came of age during Japan's "lost decades." Mobu Norio and *An Introduction to Nursing* provide *The Economist* with a precarious answer: *ore* asks for a measurement of the toll of Japan's shifting demographics in human, rather than economic, terms. Or, in *ore's* words, "When I assess my performance in either absolute or relative terms, I receive a perfect score if the metric of assessment is my grandmother's smile."[73]

Maria Roemer proposes an investigation of "precarity as a literary motif, or perhaps a literary mode" whose interest is "not the construction of a new class of literature, but . . . a theoretical framework to discuss representations of cultural and socio-economic change and its repercussions for individual lives."[74] Given that precarity is a literary mode that would find good readers all around the globe, I can imagine a version of *An Introduction to Nursing* written with Condry's "emerging transnational cultural politics of race" or the "international perspectives" and "improvisational identities" of West's "New World *bricoleurs*." *An Introduction to Nursing*, however, voices hip hop bricolage without the bricoleur; the text is the fiction of sonic blackness in the service of a "Japanese narrative," the postblack two-step in action. Like Itō Seikō before him, even as Mobu Norio raps in a black voice and searches for a larger community, he expresses little interest in explorations of transracial affinity or improvisational identities. As *An Introduction to Nurs-*

ing moves toward its conclusion, *ore* recapitulates with this: "the way I feel when I take care [of my grandmother] has nothing to do with race or . . . continent."⁷⁵ Compare this to bell hooks's claim that "many other groups now share with black folks a sense of deep alienation, despair, uncertainty, [and a] loss of sense of grounding . . . [and these] shared sensibilities which cross the boundaries of class, gender, race, *etc.* . . . could be fertile ground for the construction of empathy . . . and serve as a base for solidarity and coalition."⁷⁶ hooks argues that hip hop might serve as a lingua franca of this shared sensibility.

Although their rhetoric appears to be parallel, the border crossing suggested by hooks is not synonymous with the border patrol implied by Mobu. *Ore's* disinterest in the kind of black-Japanese coalition intimated by hooks is apparent throughout *An Introduction to Nursing*. One case in point is a section of the text that recounts Ore's first trip to New York. After rapping through the entire story, *ore* travels to the birthplace of rap but does not speak to or hear a single black voice during his time in New York. Another case in point is the text's mobilization of sampling. *An Introduction to Nursing* samples only one work of music: the 1998 "Cabin Man," by the Minneapolis-based noise rock band Cows. That is to say, although *ore* creates a black voice of his own, he does not recite or discuss the words of any black musicians.

And, on that note, it is at this juncture that we should consider the use of the term *nigga* in *An Introduction to Nursing*. The book employs American hip hop's controversial tactic of co-opting the term *nigga* and redeploying it as a term of racial camaraderie. In the complete version of *An Introduction to Nursing*, the narrator says the word *nigga* some thirty-six times. Syntactically, the epithet often occurs at the onset of sentences and is preceded by the English *yo*. Take, for example, the last sentence of the text. Mimicking a phrase that hip hop artists use to note the end of their verses when rapping collaboratively, the story ends with "Yo, my nigga, I'm out."⁷⁷ Breaking the fourth wall and addressing the narratee and reader directly, here the language of hip hop speaks to *ore's* search for community. This argument also holds on the level of orthography. Challenging the standard practices of the Japanese language in a way reminiscent of Itō Seikō's "clever vernacular," Mobu writes kanji characters that mean "comrade" and are typically read as *hōbai* and glosses them with *nigaa*, a Japanese transliteration of the word *nigga*. It is for this reason that I have translated *ore's* usage as "my nigga," a marker of companionship often employed in hip hop. The word *nigger* has always been about evoking race-based quarantine, about demarcating mobility (or the lack thereof) into and out of spaces based on race. The word is a discursive policing of the color line—and it is hypervigilant. This remained true even after the word was co-opted by hip hop, hence the debate within hip hop circles about who has the authority to use this term and who doesn't. Mobu Norio officially entered that debate in a September 2004 interview in *Bungakukai*. When asked when he decided to incorporate the "yo, nigga appellation" into the narration of *An Introduction to Nursing*, he replied:

> I have this friend, a real bad boy, and whenever he calls me, the first thing out of his mouth is "nigga." Well, it's a discriminatory term, isn't it? But [in reply to that charge], he says that, in the West, there's no one who faces as much discrimination as the Japanese do. 'I mean, we're Asians. That's enough to get you discriminated against.' That's what he said. 'And living in Thailand or Cambodia is cooler than living in Japan. Japan's not cool.' I guess you could say that's his delinquent sensibility.
>
> It's the same with words that have been deemed discriminatory: I use them unwaveringly because that's my sensibility. That's what he thinks, and he's been a major influence.[78]

There is a clear schism between the rationale of Mobu Norio and that of his "influential friend." Although the friend's racial logic is decidedly convoluted, it is nevertheless a "racial logic" of sorts: the Japanese have shouldered the highest degree of western discrimination and, as such, have the authority to use the term as a salutation of racial camaraderie in, we are to assume, a way analogous to African Americans. Moreover, since the Japanese are "Asian," use of the term *nigga* works some kind of racial alchemy, transforming Japanese people into Thais or Cambodians, who are—again, we can only assume—closer to black than "uncool" (*dasai*) vanilla Japan. It is a serpentine and fallacious argument, but this argument places *nigga* as the fulcrum of a game of racial identity politics.

Compare the logic of his "influential friend" to that of Mobu Norio himself, who employs the term "because it works" both for the stylistics of *Kaigo nyūmon* and for his own "unwavering . . . sensibility." It is the friend who is considering questions of race, a topic on which Mobu Norio has nothing to say. Mobu is simply sampling the "major influence" of the sounds he's heard both in American rap and over the phone. This is a clear distillation of the vexed maneuver I call the postblack two-step. Step one: Mobu Norio's tale is a case of what Marvin Sterling has called *jibun sagashi*, a search for Japanese voice and self through blackness.[79] Mobu's search reads like a hip hop diary in Japanese and includes some thirty-six *niggas*—reifying the racial boundaries that the term implies with every deployment—but not a single black voice. Step two: this search is conducted through a fictional sound system that managed to migrate from the Bronx to Nara and permeate the Japanese language, thereby exposing the permeability of language. Given that, to quote *ore*, "YO, nigga, humans are made up of words," there is both risk and potential in the attempt to balance the reification of one step with the fluidity of the other.[80]

One-Two: Yamada Eimi and the Two-Step to a Different Beat

The Critique of Yamada Eimi and Yamada's Style Lately

There is one other member of the Akutagawa Prize committee whose commentary on *An Introduction to Nursing* is germane to this discussion: Yamada Eimi. Yamada both deemed *An Introduction to Nursing* "a very solid novel" and gave Mobu Norio a piece of advice. Stop glossing the kanji for "companion" (*hōbai*) with "nigga," she said, "because that's provincial."[81] By deeming Mobu's approach provincial, Yamada promotes the putative cosmopolitanism of her approach to writing blackness, which is anchored by the "authenticity" of her previous marriage to Craig Douglas, an African American soldier formerly stationed in Yokosuka, and her time in New York, Douglas's hometown. Since the 1985 debut of her *Beddo taimu aizu* (Bedtime Eyes), Yamada has been regarded as the self-styled dean of black culture in Japan, her literary landscape spanning thousands of pages of short stories, novellas, novels, manga, literary criticism, dialogues, and essays that feature African Americans and African Americana. One testament to her "deanship" is Itō Seikō's claim that Yamada's creation of terms such as *pon shite iru* exemplifies the kind of black-inspired "clever vernacular" that he searches for in his lyrics.[82]

The irony here, of course, is that the very Yamada Eimi who is lauded as dean and chided Mobu for his approach has been derided for her own reductive (at best) or stereotypical and racist writings of blackness. Three critiques recur in readings of Yamada: first, that Yamada's texts are stereotypical/reifying/fetishistic; second, that her fixation on the black Other is ultimately self-serving; and, finally, that her challenge of heteronormativity actually reinforces traditional gender roles. Yamada's black Other, it has been argued, is a male placeholder of sorts, a means by which the Japanese female self is actualized. In the words of Satō Ai, Yamada does not traffic in "stories in which an 'I' loves a . . . black person" but "stories of the self-awakening and growth of an 'I' by means of belittling and loving a black person."[83] "In short," as Richard Okada concludes, Yamada's narrator's "desire to preserve an uncomplicated stance of heterosexual innocence continually deflects the narrative from the realm of the genuinely radical."[84]

I hear in these critiques a push to make the multiplicity and singularity of the lived experience of blackness audible. This section addresses Yamada's reply. I am not particularly interested in defending Yamada. I am interested, however, in presenting a reading of blackness that accounts for the textual evidence in its entirety. The critiques presented above become less applicable to Yamada's later novels, particularly *Animal Logic* and *Payday!!!*, the novel I consider here. Take, for example, John Russell's claim that Yamada produces "masturbatory" narratives that are "recreational and (pro) creative (though seldom producing bicultural offspring)" and that "privilege discourse about blacks while effectively precluding any dialogue [with blacks] . . . [thereby] silencing the Black Other."[85] Russell's is easily one of the most persuasive recapitulations of Yamada's shortcomings. But what are we to make of Robin and Harmony, the black and Italian biracial twins who focalize *Payday!!!*? Or, for that matter, of the three generations of black voices that serve as the axis of *Payday!!!*? And, even if this text represents an anomaly in Yamada's oeuvre, isn't the point of Russell's critique to advance a reading of Yamada that respects the importance of plentiful representations of minority voices?

If these critiques of Yamada have lost some (though certainly not all) of their argumentative force, I suggest that this is because of what we might call, punning on Edward Said's notion of "late style," Yamada's "style lately." Compared to her debut works, it is clear that Yamada's later novels move toward a new idiom for the writing of blackness. She once wrote, "There are some young [Japanese] folks who . . . are still infatuated with rap and scratching. . . . They claim to be rappers, but they have no idea what [black] rappers are actually saying. . . . They'd be better off if they just listened more normally."[86] Here, rather than imitate *what* we hear—a sonic blackness of which we have only a tenuous grasp—Yamada advocates that we mimic *how* it is heard. She refers to this as "normal listening" (*futsū ni kiku*), which asks us to hear blackness both as and within the mundane. Insofar as she is interested in the everyday sound(s) of black life, it becomes impossible to reduce or equate "sonic blackness" with "hip hop." This is in part what Yamada means when she deems Mobu "provincial." Yamada's writing of blackness aspires to—even when it doesn't reach—a kind of literary translation of the sounds of blackness in all of its plenitude.

The Displacement of Hip Hop and Amanuentic Narration in **Payday!!!**

An attempt to make good on the promise of "normal listening" is at the crux of Yamada's style lately.[87] Here I consider the gravitational pull that normal listening exerts on Yamada Eimi's 2003 *Payday!!! Payday!!!* is the coming-of-age story of Harmony, an aspiring musician who moves with his black father to South Carolina after the divorce of his parents, and Robin, Harmony's twin sister, who remains in Manhattan with her Italian American mother. The story revolves around the death of Robin and Harmony's mother on 9/11; the loss of their (white) mother is the catalyst that reunites the (black and interracial) family.

In *Payday!!!* normal listening informs both the text's thematic displacement of hip hop and its use of what I call an amanuentic narrator. As the preceding section suggests, Yamada's critics have made a strong argument that her early works do not make good on the promise of "normal listening." I read in *Payday!!!*, however, an attempt by Yamada to transition from her old stylistic approach to writing blackness (which typically meant black masculinity)—in which the biologically bound essence of black masculinity exists a priori as an object to be subsequently identified by the subject (typically a Japanese female) through the sensual—to a new "postracial" idiom in which the narration of black subjectivity takes precedence and black identity and sexuality are seen as a kind of social and linguistic performance. In *Payday!!!* this new idiom plays out thematically by way of the displacement of hip hop; it plays out narratologically by way of amanuentic narration.

To begin with the displacement of hip hop in *Payday!!!*, a central motif of the text is Harmony's search for self-expression in the blues. Although Harmony is trained classically in piano, he "doesn't wanna play Brahms"; he wants to become a bluesman.[88] His search for the blues prompts both his move to the South and his donning of a new name (Harmony was born Robert). During what Murakami calls our "age of rap music," Harmony's friends have difficulty comprehending his preference for the blues. They ask, "'The blues? Why in the hell do you like the blues? It's doesn't have any beat or flow (the rhythm and expression of rap music). You're crazy."[89] They answer, "The only people who appreciate that kind of music [the blues] are old people and white folks, right?"[90] This response to the blues presents a dilemma for the teenage Harmony. He is not old, and he does not identify as white; it is his decision to play the blues rather than classical piano that "demarcated the moment in time when his relationship with his [white] mother began to gradually degrade."[91]

The solution to Harmony's dilemma is the introduction of a kind of postracial, identitarian freedom. Harmony's father, a music teacher, encourages Harmony to "try placing value only on the things that honestly make you shake, Harmony. There's no need for a black teenager to like hard-core rap just because he's a black teenager."[92] Robin, Harmony's twin sister, hears a similar message in her Manhattan upbringing. I translate this passage at length because it encapsulates Robin and Harmony's postracial freedom.

> Mom and Dad intentionally raised Harmony and me to be unaware of interracial problems. That's what Robin thought. Even though the majority of the students he taught were black (*Afurika-kei*), he sent his own children to a school downtown where students of various races mingled. Most of the kids at the school downtown were getting to know their roots even as they were being liberated from those very roots. It was there that his children, Robin and Harmony, were raised to believe that they could only be themselves. No one can teach you your style; it's something you're always choosing on your own. That's the guideline he set for his children. Jazz and classical music flowed from their home, but if they took one step out of their home and went to the other side of the street, there was salsa, there was hip hop, and there was rock and roll. They had the freedom to choose whichever one they liked.[93]

Reminiscent of Grossberg's neoeclectic mainstream, the racial world constructed in *Payday!!!* is rooted in terms such as "freedom" (*jiyū*), "liberation" (*kaihō*), and "choice" (*erabu*). This (in concert with Robin's color blindness) is a hallmark articulation of freedom from the burden of carrying the historical baggage of race that the postracial promises.

In sounding this freedom, *Payday!!!* produces a soundscape in which hip hop—that is, music that might otherwise be deemed synonymous with black sound—is actively displaced. In presenting hip hop as one of many sounds, *Payday!!!* suggests that there is no single sound that is synonymous with the multifaceted possibilities of blackness. Harmony says as much to Kate, his father's girlfriend, when he explains to her why he plays the blues even though "most young black boys don't listen to jazz and the blues." It's because "I'm half white . . . that's what my friends say when they tease me. But man, I don't even care about that. You can't explain people's taste. I just want to be free from having to like X kind of music because I'm race Y. As long as you pay respect to your roots, isn't it all good?"[94] Japanese readers should take note of the phrase *raku ni naritai*, which I have translated as "be free from." The kanji for *raku* resonates in the term for music, *ongaku*, and musical performance becomes a venue at which Harmony can literally play and perform his identity with ease, without paying homage to hip hop's (or any other) vision of what blackness is "supposed to be."

A revelatory example of the displacement of hip hop in *Payday!!!* occurs in the fourth chapter. This is after Robin and Harmony have tacitly acknowledged that their mother, who worked at a brokerage firm, died on 9/11. Robin finds her Uncle William and Shirlene, his partner, dancing not to "Who am I," from Snoop Dogg's 1993 *Doggystyle*, but to "the song that Snoop Dogg (a famous rapper) sampled": "Atomic Dog," from George Clinton's 1982 *Computer Games*.[95] As Robin joins the dancing, Harmony realizes that his mother was not the stricture he imagined her to be: "He got the sense that she was the kind of person who, if he would have continued studying the piano the way she wanted him to, would have said something like this: Robert, you come and dance with us too."[96] Here Yamada has turned the approach of Itō and Mobu on its head; rather than dancing to samples, she dances to that which has been sampled. In so doing, hip hop is displaced by that which came before it; here Yamada's turntable attempts to turn back the clock of Afro-Japanese cultural connections. If, as David Morris reminds us, hip hop's dark side is "the essentialism and tactics of exclusion that have sometimes underlain its rhetoric of antiracist empowerment," then this coming together of a black family and the memory of a white mother speaks to the significance of Yamada's displacement of hip hop.[97]

In *Payday!!!* the thematic displacement of hip hop works in concert with Yamada's amanuentic narration. Yamada has long positioned herself as a kind of amanuensis. As early as the epilogue to her 1987 *Soul Music Lovers Only*, Yamada infamously declared herself "the only sista [*kokujin-jo*, literally "black woman," a term Yamada glosses with "sista"] in the world who can handle Japanese beautifully."[98] Yamada writes, she continues, on the behalf of black men who would never have the literacy to read her writing.[99] She doubled down on this mantra in her 1988 "The Near Black Freshness and Appeal that Comes Because We're Japanese," a dialogue with musician Kubota Toshinobu that appeared in the same issue of *Music* as Itō Seikō's treatise on clever vernaculars. Yamada claims, "When you live with black folks, there's no need for proper English. So much so that they tell me that my English is blacker that black people's English. It's habitual now."[100] The fact that I have translated Yamada's assertion into English should not obfuscate the fact that she is positioning herself as an amanuensis; she speaks of her better-than-black black English *in Japanese* for the Japanese readership of *Music*.

Within the context of African American literature, the position of the amanuensis, which rose to critical importance as abolitionists wrote slave nar-ratives as or for those who could not, is contentious. On the one hand, the amanuensis facilitates the act of storytelling and bridges the divide between speaker and listener and in so doing brings stories that might otherwise have never been heard to new audiences. On the other hand, we should ask corol-laries to Gayatri Spivak's inquiry. Can the subaltern speak for themselves, can the amalgamated voice of the amanuentic story ever capture the voice of the original storyteller, and how are we to gauge if and when the amanuensis mis-represents the stories and characters on whose behalf he or she speaks?

In considering how this dynamic plays out in Yamada's *Payday!!!* it is helpful to think of amanuentic narration in the novel as it occurs on three levels: the level of the word, the level of the sentence, and the level of the intertext.[101] The interweaving of these three levels is on full display in a key passage from the first chapter of *Payday!!!* Robin, visiting Harmony in South Carolina for the first time since the divorce of their parents, recalls an exchange she had with her brother as they witnessed the unraveling of their parents' marriage. Harmony tells Robin that he "wishes he didn't have any Italian blood" and he "doesn't love that woman [his mother], can't love that woman."[102] In reply, Robin

> surveyed her brother's room as she searched for a retort in her discom-bobulated head—I have to say something. Hip hop and old school CDs and LPs were piled haphazardly next to turntables and CD play-ers. She picked one up and pretended to examine it as she fought back the tears that blurred her vision. Busta Rhymes, Timbaland, Lucy Pearl, Ann Peebles—a little old, a little new, all a mess. Jay-Z, Nelly—and who's Charlie Patton? And these really old records, is this what you call the blues? Then she picked up the magazines and books that were scattered about on the floor. *XXL*, that's a hard-core rap magazine. *Vibe* and James Earl Hardy's *The Day Eazy-E Died*, Maya Angelou and Nikki Giovanni. . . . She felt like somebody was watch-ing her, so she spun around. There was a poster on the wall from the recently released *The Hurricane*, and Denzel Washington was scowl-ing in her direction with frightening eyes. This . . . Robin said to herself. This is the room of a black (*Afurika-kei*) boy.[103]

On the level of the word, the narrator's descriptive lexicon is peppered with terms that signal (supposedly) the lived experience of everyday black life. These signals are informed by hip hop technology and parlance: "old school" (*ōrudo sukūru*), "turntable" (*tāntēburu*), "hard-core rap" (*hādokoa rappu*), and so on. Yamada's technique is reminiscent of the insights of Roland Barthes and Cornyetz. Playing with Barthes's claim that the "narrative luxury" of descriptive minutia "finally [says] nothing but this: *we are the real*," we can say that the hip hop minutia that populates Harmony's room aspires to achieve the "black reality effect."[104] And Cornyetz proposes that Yamada's katakana-rich vocabulary is "lifted from its context [and] slipped into Japanese syntax, which gives it the appearance and atmosphere of American slang, while, in fact, it remains Japanese."[105] This reminder makes visible Yamada's amanuentic work as she packages and converts the "reality" of black stories into a form palatable for Japanese consumption.

On the level of the sentence, Yamada mobilizes two techniques: free indirect discourse and parenthetical narration. The narration of *Payday!!!* relies on the liberal use of free indirect discourse, in which the distance between the narrator and the text's black characters thins and creates the illusion of black characters "directly" expressing themselves without the mediation of an amanuentic narrator. The passage above, which narrates Robin's discovery of the signs of Harmony's black masculinity, is a case in point. The epiphanic time that elapses while the pair of questions in the middle of Robin's survey ("who's Charlie Patton?" and "is this what you call the blues?") and the second set of ellipses ("This . . . Robin said to herself. This is the room of a black boy") bracket Robin's "discovery" of Harmony's black masculinity, a performance Harmony fine-tunes through the means of blues and hip hop.[106] The reader accesses the thought process that leads to Robin's epiphany by way of free indirect discourse; the repetition of "this," in tandem with the phrase "Robin said to herself," highlights this technique, which otherwise works in stealth.

Moreover, Yamada's Japanese narrator, which converges with but never occults black characters by way of free indirect discourse, interjects parenthetically whenever she needs to play the part of editor. There are no parentheticals in the passage quoted above; here katakana serves in lieu of parentheticals, translating English words phonetically rather than semantically. *Payday!!!*, however, provides a bevy of parenthetical notes explaining references to Americana—amanuentic support for readers engaging with a "black story" that masquerades as a kind of Japanese translation. The first example of such parenthetical interjection is a sign of what's to come: the narrator pauses parenthetically after "AA" to tell Japanese readers that the term refers to "(Alcoholics Anonymous)."[107] In the Japanese original, AA is glossed parenthetically twice, once as "Alcoholics Anonymous" and once as "断酒会," a Japanese neologism for AA. Such support ensures that the Japanese readership of *Payday!!!* can fully comprehend this "black story" without reaching for a dictionary.

On the level of the intertext, Yamada's narrator weaves a world informed by a network of black texts. In the passage cited here, the narrator takes note of *XXL*, *Vibe*, *The Day Eazy-E Died*, Maya Angelou, Nikki Giovanni, and *The Hurricane*. What the narrator's "black" lexicon achieves on the level of the word, the noting of black intertexts brings to the level of the text—there is a kind of "black reality effect" that dissipates throughout the entire text. Moreover, such Afro-Japanese intertextuality signals the bona fides of our amanuentic narrator. Reminiscent of Yamada's claim that her black English is blacker than black, when free indirect discourse lets the reader hear Robin ask "is this what you call the blues," the assumption is that the narrator, situated in the space between Japanese and African American texts, already knows the answer. And, as such, this narrator is qualified to play the part of amanuensis/translator.[108]

The techniques of amanuentic narration congeal around the central requirement for a text written by way of amanuensis: the amanuensis must write someone else's story. *Payday!!!* does not feature a single Japanese character. For *Payday!!!* Japan is in the past; the only reference to Japan is Uncle William's one-liners about his visit to Japan during the Gulf War. Moreover, *Payday!!!* is divided into five chapters. Chapters 1 and 3, entitled "Robin," are both focalized by Robin and present her as the central character, while chapters 2 and 4, by Harmony, and the dual narratives converge in chapter 5, "Robin, and Harmony." The narrative's vacillation between Robin's and Harmony's stories works in conjunction with Yamada's amanuentic technique to create the illusion of black characters "directly" expressing themselves without the mediation of a narrator. *Payday!!!* belongs to Robin and Harmony; their story just happens to be told in Japanese.

Payday!!! *and the Same Old Two-Step*

I argued in the previous section that Yamada's search for a new idiom for the writing of blackness plays out in her thematics (the displacement of hip hop) and her narratival technique (amanuentic narration). We might argue, however, that it is ultimately just played out. There is an unresolved contradiction yet to be addressed in Yamada's new "postracial" idiom: her lingering subscription to the tropes of race as a biologically determined category. Depicting a postracial world inhabited by people of essentially biological races, Yamada's new idiom for the styling of blackness falls into many of the tropic pitfalls of her old idiom.

Payday!!! presents blackness as a kind of freestyle postracial performance.

I read in *Payday!!!*, however, a dilution of Judith Butler, who writes, "Performativity is neither free play nor theatrical self-presentation; nor can it be simply equated with performance. . . . I would suggest that performativity cannot be understood outside a process of iterability . . . and this repetition is not performed *by* a subject; this repetition is what enables a subject."[109] Yamada equates the performance of black masculinity with the performativity of black masculinity. This equivocation occurs, moreover, against the backdrop of a burgeoning postracial paradigm of identity construction.

In her equivocation between performance (read "free play" and "theatrical self-presentation") and performativity, with its "ritualized production . . . reiterated under and through constraint, under and through the force of prohibition and taboo, with the threat of ostracism and even death controlling and compelling the shape of the production but not . . . determining it fully in advance," Yamada attempts to transition to postracial performances of black masculinity in which the "fact of blackness" would not serve as an absolute determinate of how one performs one's singular blackness. In order to make such an a transition, however, Yamada would first need to address the requirement of "one identification at the expense of another," a requirement that, Butler continues, "inevitably produces a violent rift, a dissension that will come to tear apart the identity wrought through the violence of exclusion" that accompanies the inscription of racial identities.[110] That is to say, the unresolved contradiction of *Payday!!!* (and this might also be one of the unresolved contradictions of the postracial age of hip hop itself) is that it performs blackness without first addressing the "violent rift" and contradiction inherent in the creation of racial identities and racial frameworks themselves.

The discourse of race mobilized throughout *Payday!!!* intimates this contradiction. There is, for example, the juxtaposition of "wanting to be free from having to like X kind of music because I'm race Y" with "ethnicities" (e.g., *Afurika-kei*, the term *Payday!!!* uses to denote black characters) whose personalities are determined by their "blood" (*chi*). Take Michelle, for example, a Chinese American girl whose acerbity is due to the fact that "she has kanji in her DNA"—a jest that harbors a bit of the truth of Yamada's writing of race.[111]

It is in the romantic relationships of black males, however, that this contradiction manifests most vividly. *Payday!!!* portrays the love lives of three generations of black men: Harmony, a representative of the postracial era; his grandfather, a spectral remnant of the age of intraracial romance; and Harmony's father, Ray, and Uncle William, two figures of the generation of "interracial" relationships. Although the representation of three generations of black men is engineered to signal the progression from the intraracial to the postracial, all three generations are remarkably similar in their failed attempts to build sustainable relationships. (The only "successful" relationship is Robin's; it seems that Yamada Eimi's black men, to borrow an expression from black slang, "can't get no love" in the postracial era). Moreover, each failure is framed in terms of absence and addiction, the selfsame framing of failed black masculinity seen in Yamada's early works.

Harmony lives with his grandmother, and it is primarily through her memories of her late husband that the reader learns of the grandfather's failed marriage. Harmony's grandfather was "lazy and good for nothing, drank all day, and got in and out of women like he was changing clothes."[112] That is to say, he was a composite of several stereotypes of black masculinity. His fast life, moreover, led him to an early grave. The absence of Harmony's grandfather, whose death occurs well in advance of *Payday!!!*'s story, signals both the death of the intraracial age and, supposedly, the death of Yamada's stereotypical writing of blackness.

The grandfather's memory is kept alive and unwell, however, in Uncle William, a doppelgänger whose alcoholism is "inherited from his father. And he looks just like his daddy too—he was a handsome man, and loose with his booze and his women."[113] If the absence of the grandfather signals both the death of the intraracial age and the death of Yamada's essentialist tropes of blackness, Uncle William signals their lingering specter, an unsurprising recrudescence given the lingering adherence to the "biology" of race and bloodlines. Uncle William, for example, "hates Chinese people, because I married one and that was something terrible."[114] The reader need not worry about the fact that his ex-wife was actually Japanese because "it's all the same—they're both Asians."[115] In Uncle William we see the tension and unresolved contradiction between Yamada's old idiom and her new one. The signature Japanese love interest is now present only in her absence, and Uncle William does indeed add a new facet to Yamada's addicted/alcoholic black man stereotype—an interest in recovery—but it does seem that the more things change the more they remain the same.

Ray, Harmony's father and the other representative of the age of experimental "interracial" romances, also engages in a failed interracial relationship framed in terms of lack and addiction. Ray loses Harmony's mother, Sophia, twice: once when the two divorce and once again on 9/11. After this second loss, to quote Sophia's father, Ray becomes "just some African American."[116] Although the loss of the (white) mother serves as the impetus for the reunion of the black family, it also reignites Ray's addiction: "jungle fever." Ray begins a second relationship with Kate, a white woman who was once married to a black man and is thus "good at handling black men."[117] Ray's relationship with Kate is narrated in terms of lack. Kate has no voice and is referred to as *ano hito* (something like "you know who") until the latter portion of the final chapter, when Kate and Ray's clandestine relationship is revealed. The absence of the voiceless, nameless Kate is a testament to the fact that she is a substitute for Sophia, whose body is never found. In the words of Kate, "Ray and I are just alike—we've both lost someone we can't replace. We've come this far, aimless really, clutching the pillow next to us that no longer has an owner. Don't you think it's about time we end that lonely game?"[118] As such, both Ray and Kate become not two singular post-racial individuals in a relationship but the next item in a collection of lovers spurred on by, to borrow the phrase used in *Payday!!!*, "jungle fever"; indeed, the reader, much like Harmony, can't help but "think, perhaps a little mean-spiritedly, 'I see: you and Dad have a taste for the same [stereo?]type."[119]

Harmony's grandfather, Uncle William, and Ray all exemplify the "violent rift," the lack and subsequent addiction, born of intra- and interracial relationships between racialized individuals who subscribe to a biological paradigm of race and its requirement of "one identification at the expense of another." Because Yamada has yet to absolve her writing of this paradigm, Harmony's postracial performance of black masculinity, although it attempts to progress beyond the boundaries set by the performances of his forefathers, is ultimately trapped somewhere within the contradictory space of black masculinity as it is performed by them.

Harmony is initially defined by his attempt to distance himself from the whiteness of his mother—both literally when he moves to South Carolina and figuratively when he renames himself in the blues tradition and eschews his mother's desire for him to become a pianist. As the narrative progresses, Harmony gradually closes this distance and comes to terms with his biracial identity. The primary substitute for his mother is his lover, Veronica, an older, married black woman who "consoled him, stroked his hair for a long time. [She made] the tragic spectacle of New York go away. She made him cry and feel all better."[120] There is clearly something maternal about Veronica, and their relationship ends when Veronica can no longer play the role of (white) mother; the two separate when Veronica refuses to see Harmony on his birthday, which happens to coincide with her husband's birthday. Moreover, Harmony, addicted to Veronica, refuses to pursue a relationship with the aforementioned Michelle, a Chinese American girl who is both attracted to Harmony and, unlike Veronica, a member of his "postracial" generation. In Harmony, then, there is both a failed intraracial relationship and an inability to begin a postracial one. Harmony is the representative par excellence of Yamada's unresolved contradiction, and Yamada, in turn, is not unlike Harmony: trapped between two contradictory modes of thinking through blackness.

In *Racism without Racists*, Eduardo Bonilla-Silva maintains that "most sociological writing on races gives lip service to the social constructionist view" only to "proceed to discuss 'racial' differences . . . as if they were truly racial."[121] This song and dance, Bonilla-Silva continues, with "its 'we are beyond race' lyrics and color-blind music will drown the voices of those fighting for racial equality . . . and may even eclipse the space for talking about race altogether."[122] Yamada's transition to a "racism without racists" paradigm for the writing of blackness speaks to one of the truths of our postracial age: racial identities are beginning to dissipate even as the institutions and ideologies that sustain racism ossify, and our desire for the postracial is moving much faster than our framing tropes, stories, and conceptualizations of race are.

After the passage in *Payday!!!* that describes Harmony and Robin's postracial freedom, Yamada writes that the twins have this freedom because their parents raised them such that "they didn't feel a single bit of the pain of being born to parents of different races . . . [as for the twins] reality was always in some faraway place."[123] On reading *Payday!!!* I can see at least two ways to read this "reality." One would be the essential reality of biological race—and all its concomitant stereotypes—as it is portrayed in Yamada's earlier works. That second reality would be the realities of postrace. The *post* of *postracial* does not mean that race magically evaporates. If race is a fiction, its genre is creative nonfiction; even as a construct, race, to follow Bonilla-Silva again, "has a social reality . . . [that] produces real effects on the actors racialized."[124] Moreover, the central theme of the fiction of race is essential immutability. Race is a fluid fiction of immovable essence, an iterative fiction that, in its telling, claims a single fact as its constitutive element. As such, the "real effects" that Bonilla-Silva highlights cannot be performed away. This is the reality of postrace. This is the reality that Stuart Hall suggests when he says, "I think we can't turn to the reality of race"—by which he means "the stories and the anecdotes and the metaphors and the images which . . . construct the relationship between the body and its social and cultural space"—"because the [false] reality of [biological] race itself is what is standing in the way of our understanding."[125] In *Payday!!!* Yamada, even as she turns the hip hop down, dances between these two realities of race.

One-Two One-Two: The Dance We're Doing Today and the One We Might Do Tomorrow

Itō Seikō, Mobu Norio, and Yamada Eimi all do renditions of a dance that I have dubbed the postblack two-step. This dance is characterized by a mastery of the style and sound of, in the cases considered here, hip hop expressions of blackness. For Itō Seikō, this means the creation of a "clever vernacular" by way of translation and sampling of hip hop sounds. Mobu Norio effectively translates the techniques of Japanese hip hop into prose narrative. Yamada Eimi, in an attempt to let blackness speak for itself, positions hip hop as one sound among many. Yamada translates black voices into Japanese in a way that Lawrence Venuti has called invisible and I have called amanuentic, which produces "black" voices that read as flawlessly "Japanese." These techniques—clever vernaculars, sampling, hip hop, and amanuentic narration—allow sonic blackness to be heard in and through Japanese. The very creation and hearing of this sound expose the fictive element of sonic blackness and, by proxy, of the blackness to which this sound gives voice.

With this sonic blackness, however, there is a second step: the pressure exerted by the telling of Japanese narratives packaged for consumption by a Japanese audience. For Itō Seikō, there is a streak of Japanese cultural nationalism in his music criticism that leads to sampling without affinity, which Lawrence Grossberg argues is part and parcel of the logic of sampling itself. For Mobu Norio, it is only the sound of blackness that travels, as hip hop's historical interest in initiating open discussions of racial being and belonging has eroded. (This is—to be sure—an argument that one could make about hip hop on both sides of the Pacific). The "blackness" in his works registers not on the level of semantics but the level of stylistics, his black-Japanese exchange characterized by the internalization of a free-floating transnational blackness that is hardly weighed down by historical baggage. For Yamada Eimi, the second step of her postblack two-step at times reverts to the tropes and stereotypes of racial thinking. Yamada's faux pas are to be expected if David Goldberg is correct in asserting that racism *precedes* race, which, as the *post* of *postracial* suggests, precedes postrace in turn.[126]

In each of these artists, then, there is a dilemma: they exhibit mastery over the social fiction of sonic blackness even as the content of their discourse drifts toward reifying Japanese narratives. These authors sound, to borrow that problematic Americanism, "blacker than ever," even when they reify the borders of Japanese reading communities. I have referred to this dance as the postblack two-step.

I would like to address two notes—one for each step considered here—in closing. First, following Murakami Haruki's summation, I have framed the texts considered here as written in "the age of hip hop." This periodization, however, should not obfuscate the other time markers that might frame the work of Itō, Mobu, and Yamada. That is to say, the "age of rap music" is also the age of burst bubbles and database animals. Andre Craddock Willis has called hip hop "an expression of the complexity of post-modern African-American life."[127] Writing against what she deems Willis's romanticization of jazz, the blues, and rhythm and blues, Tricia Rose writes that rap and hip hop should be seen as "linked . . . to the processes of urban deindustrialization" in the 1970s and 1980s and that "hip hop culture emerged as a source for youth[s] of alternative identity formation and social status in a community whose older local support institutions had been all but demolished."[128] The temporal context of hip hop in Japan seems to lie somewhere between Willis and Rose. Itō Seikō's 1989 *Mess/Age* dropped just before the Nikkei Stock Average and the economic malaise of the Lost Decades did, and Azuma Hiroki writes that *otaku* subculture congealed "from the 1970s to the 1980s. This period, moreover, coincided almost directly with the coming into vogue of the intellectual trend known as 'postmodernism.'"[129] Insofar as the age of hip hop might also be viewed under this broader aegis of the age of the postmodern precariat, it should come as no surprise if the postblack two-stepping of writing blackness in Japanese literature in the age of hip hop steps beyond the boundaries of hip hop to inform the articulation of blackness in other Japanese media and modes of discourse.

Second, I wrote earlier of not feeling a pressing need to predict or prescribe the direction of that second step of the postblack two-step. Japanese hip hop can provide, as Condry and West proffer, a soundtrack for moves toward a transracial politics of difference. It can just as easily, however, provide a soundtrack that moves toward racial and ethnic essentialism. Think here of the New Tōjōists of Hikita Kunio's *Kyōki no sakura*, who become involved in a plot to erase "black rap graffiti"—and black bodies—from the streets of Tokyo even as they are spurred on by the hard-hitting lyrics of rap group King Ghiddra.[130] My decision to anchor the analyses of this chapter in a metaphor that borrows terminology from dance—the two-step—is strategic. Just as highly choreographed productions can engender dramatically idiosyncratic performances (not to mention missteps), I have tried to address both the patterns and the singularities of the performances of blackness by these three authors.

What I can predict, however, is this: we cannot postblack two-step our way out of the postblack two-step. The first step of the postblack two-step is, ironically enough, firmly rooted in race. Itō Seikō's clever vernacular is predicated on the existence of a monolithic black vernacular with mystical signifying power, Mobu Norio's hip hop narration is validated by a self-sanctioned identification with blackness, and Yamada Eimi's normal listening and amanuentic narration presuppose the existence of essentially black people out there in the world. This is simply a reminder of Paul Gilroy's conjecture that even "dedicated antiracist and antifascist activists remain wedded to the most basic mythologies and morphologies of racial difference."[131]

There is only so far one can move when yesteryear's racial frameworks are the initiating step toward postracial maneuvering. The end of the postblack two-step has to begin with a more radical break in the thinking of race, both subjectively and intersubjectively. This may look, as it did for Nakagami Kenji, like Butler's disidentities, that "experience of *misrecognition*, [that] uneasy sense of standing under a sign to which one does and does not belong."[132] This may look like the Gilroy of *Against Race*, whose planetary humanism urges "a fundamental change of mood upon what used to be called 'antiracism'" and "terminat[ion of] its ambivalent relationship to the idea of 'race' in the interest of a heterocultural, postanthropological, and cosmopolitan yet-to-come."[133] It may look like Giorgio Agamben's lovable singularities, in which the "lover wants the loved one *with all of its* predicates . . . [and] the lover desires the *as* only insofar as it is *such*. . . . Whatever singularity (the Lovable) is never the intelligence . . . of this or that quality or essence, but only the intelligence of an intelligibility."[134] If it doesn't look like this, it might continue to look like the postblack two-step, ad infinitum, ad nauseum.

Conclusion

Parallax Vision and Playing in the Shadows—
Elsewhere and Otherwise

Single vision produces worse illusions than double vision or many-headed monsters.

—Donna Haraway, *Simians, Cyborgs, and Women*

Over the course of this book, I have discussed two visions of the blackness in postwar Japanese fiction. The first of these is concerned primarily with the problem of how to represent that which has a sustained history of misrepresentation. This vision critiques the representation of black (typically male, GI) bodies in postwar Japanese literature and questions what the implications of such representations might be for both the sense of self of Japanese bodies and the body of postwar Japanese literature. I have argued that this first vision—which has dominated studies of blackness in Japanese culture to date—runs the risk of registering only that which has been represented by the text.

It is for this reason that I have attempted to supplement it with a second vision of the blackness in postwar Japanese literature. This second sight seeks Japanese literary engagements with black people, literature, thought, and culture that go beyond that which has or can be represented. Although this approach, when compared to representative studies, is inevitably inconclusive, I have summarized its vision as primarily interested in translational, intertextual, experimental, and shared historical moments of contact between postwar Japanese literature and blackness. These four modes of engagement provide new avenues for thinking about the messy postwar intersections of race, blackness, Japaneseness, and Afro-Japaneseness.

In tandem, these two visions provide a much clearer picture of what we might, following DuBois, call the double consciousness of postwar Japanese literature. And it is here that I would like to return to the claim with which this book begins. I wrote in the "Introduction" that "the history of blackness in postwar Japanese literature is the history of postwar Japan and its racial thinking, and this transpacific view of blackness is, in turn, also a chapter toward understanding a global history of blackness in its plentitude." This is, of course, a lofty claim. But I believe that the first half of this claim (that the history of blackness in postwar Japanese literature is the history of postwar Japan and its racial thinking) is one that is instantiated by the texts addressed in this work.

David Morris, playing with Slavoj Žižek's political parallax, has referred to "Japan's world-historical position" as one best seen as a "history of the parallax."[1] One vision of Japan is a "view [in which], despite its development and wealth, Japan is best understood as a victim of exploitation and repression from the moment of its entry into the modern world."[2] But, with a slight shift in parallactic position, Japan's history can just as easily be seen as one of "elite-driven modernization, with resistance to external imperialism often deployed to justify various forms of dominance and exploitation."[3] To call for a history of the parallax, then, is to propose that the trajectory of modern Japanese history—from Commodore Perry's forced opening of Japan to contemporary debates on American military bases on Japanese soil—is best seen as a negotiation between a sovereignty made fragile by violent encounters with the American state on the one hand and the pain—inflicted on both Japanese and non-Japanese bodies—of state-sponsored violence justified by that encounter on the other.

If postwar Japanese history is best read in the parallax space between visions of lost sovereignty and state-sponsored violence on racialized bodies, to trace the blackness of its literature is simply to consider its history in one of Ralph Ellison's lower frequencies. This is reminiscent of Nahum Chandler, who writes in "Introduction: On the Virtues of Seeing—at Least, but Never Only—Double," "If one brings this discussion into view with a certain kind of attention," we see that "matters of 'blackness' . . . and matters 'Japanese' have long been implicated in one another."[4] This "new parallax," Chandler continues, might provide "another sense, or senses, of world, including another sense of Japan."[5]

In each of the historical moments addressed in this book—be it the wake of Japan's lost race war, the post-Occupation/civil rights 1960s, the "new race" experimentation of the long 1970s, or the problem of where Japan ends and begins, which arose anew during the age of globalization and hip hop—blackness, particularly in its literary manifestations, has served as a key negotiator in the writing of Morris's parallax history of Japan. This is what I mean when I say that the history of blackness in postwar Japanese literature is the history of postwar Japan and its racial thinking. This is simply an adaptation of Toni Morrison's claim that blackness was an invaluable resource in the postwar Japanese literary imagination, one that functioned as a crucial mediator in the reimagining of race and "Japaneseness" in the wake of the Pacific War. Or, rather, it is simply an update of the methodology of John Russell, an addition of the texts, techniques, hermeneutic nuances, and scope of literary studies to his critical insight that blackness "serve[s] the reflexive function of allowing Japanese to mediate on their racial and cultural identity in the face of challenges by Western modernity, cultural authority, and power."[6]

As for the second half of the claim made in the "Introduction" (that considering the history of racial thinking in Japan affords us an opportunity to consider the machinations of race in other spaces and places), I mean simply that parallactic visions of Japan might, in turn, provide insights into the contours of racial thinking writ large. I mean this both theoretically and empirically. To begin with the theoretical implication of parallax visions of Japan, Rey Chow has noted that the "potential, and hence danger" of racial thinking is in its ability to conflate formulaic, conventional representations of people with creative, original representations of them.[7] In other words, the basic formulas and conventions of stereotypical depictions of racial difference often prove to be quite malleable and exhibit an uncanny ability to create a range of new stereotypical iterations in a variety of locales: "an X, a Y, and a Z can walk into a bar" in Japan or the United States or wherever. So there is, in theory, the possibility of creative local instantiations of racial thinking that exhibit the conventional patterns of this thinking as it is seen elsewhere and otherwise.

This theoretical possibility has its empirical counterpart in what Chandler has called "another archive."[8] I am interested primarily in the blackness of the Japanese literary archive, but there is just as much play in the shadows on the other side of the Pacific, as African American authors, concomitant to and often in dialogue with their Japanese counterparts, imagine new ways of racial being through "Japanicana." An exploration of that other archive, refracted through the archive considered here, might look like the following.

This manuscript begins by suggesting that even the most ethereal black presence in Japanese literature can be haunting in its hermeneutic power. A study of the "Japaneseness" of modern African American literature might very well begin on the same note. As Gerald Horne writes, "We must take into account the specter of Japan, particularly in the first four decades of the twentieth century," as a kind of catalyst for the black racial imagination, as an "alternative" to the "herrenvolk democracy of the United States."[9] Pioneering writers of Afro-Japonisme, thinkers such as George Schuyler and W. E. B. DuBois, often initiated experiments in racial thinking with gestures toward Japan. A case in point is *Black No More*, a quintessentially Schuyler-style send-up of America's racial pathologies. *Black No More* features a procedure that can "turn darkies white" concocted by a Dr. Crookman.[10] Although Crookman's discovery is rooted in German science, in the preface to *Black No More*, Schuyler attributes the birth of the procedure to Japan.

> With America's constant reiteration of the superiority of whiteness, the avid search on the part of the black masses for some key to chromatic perfection is easily understood. Now it would seem that science is on the verge of satisfying them.
>
> Dr. Yusaburo Noguchi, head of the Noguchi Hospital at Beppu, Japan, told American reporters in October, 1929 that as a result of fifteen years of painstaking research and experiment he was able to change a Negro into a white man. While he admitted that this racial metamorphosis could not be effected overnight, he maintained that, "Given time, I could change the Japanese into a race of tall blue-eyed blonds."[11]

Even if this is the only reference to Japan in *Black No More*, it seems to me that the hermeneutic possibilities and stakes become more—not less— intriguing when the possibility of "racial metamorphosis" hinges on a singular encounter with Japan.

I am reminded here of the haiku to which Richard Wright turned during his final years, poems like "An empty sickbed: / an indented white pillow / in a weak winter sun" and "An autumn sunset / casting shadows of tombstones / over mounds of graves" and "I feel autumn rain / trying to explain something / I do not want to know."[12] It is the spectrality of Japan in these poems—the passing nod to the trope of the self-memorialization of the dying haiku poet, the seasonal words that suggest the poet has no more seasons left, in short the engagements with Japan that go beyond the representable—that is intriguing. Those explanations that "we do not want to know" might be just on the other side of that which has been represented.

The very grammar of the analogy suggests that Ōe's black-Japanese analogic, the central focus of the second chapter, will have its African American counterpart. Ōe himself is aware of this, hence his citation of Chester Himes's

If He Hollers Let Him Go. One impetus for *If He Hollers* is the wartime removal and internment of some ninety-four thousand Japanese Americans from California. Bob Jones, the protagonist of *If He Hollers*, is one of the many African Americans who filled the void left in the housing and labor markets of Los Angeles after the forced removal of Japanese Americans. In filling this void, both Himes and Jones become painfully aware of the existential analogy articulated by Ōe. Kevin Allen Leonard proposes that "the Japanese American internment encouraged some blacks to perceive themselves as participants in a larger struggle for worldwide democracy," which prompted black writers to "blur the distinctions between African Americans, Africans, Latin Americans, and Asians."[13] This "blurred distinction" is the analogy that Ōe has in mind when he cites the following passage of *If He Hollers*: "Little Riki Oyana singing 'God Bless America' and going to Santa Anita with his parents the next day. . . . I was the same color as the Japanese and I couldn't tell the difference. 'A yeller-bellied Jap' coulda meant me too."[14]

Just as Ōe is thinking "Japaneseness" through a blurry black-Japanese analogy, wartime and postwar black authors such as Himes are thinking "blackness" through a Japanese-black analogy. This is most palpable in a moment in *If He Hollers* that Ōe does not cite: its conclusion. The text concludes with the imprisonment—or, we might say, internment—of Bob Jones due to a false accusation of interracial rape. Even when his name is cleared, Jones must still pay the price required to keep the integrity of his white accuser intact: he is given the "choice" of either incarceration or participation on the front lines of World War II. With this, Jones's premonition has been actualized—his predicament is indeed that of "Little Riki Oyana." In having his full citizenship predicated on the "no-no boy" dilemma of choosing between either giving up his freedom or fighting in a global race war, *If He Hollers* ends precisely where it begins: with "blackness" occupying the space once held by "Japaneseness." The fungibility of these two positions speaks to the black-Japanese analogy that circumnavigated the Pacific in the postwar era.

Although Nakagami, the focus of chapter 3, gestures toward Ellison and Baldwin, I sense in Amiri Baraka a kindred spirit. Having been transformed from bohemian to black nationalist, from black nationalist to third-world Marxist, and from Everett LeRoy Jones to Amiri Baraka, Baraka is, like Nakagami, a protean figure. The two are also contemporary travelers. Nakagami's study of black literature and music spans the period from the mid-1960s through the 1980s while Baraka's interest in Japan extends from his 1950s readings in Zen Buddhism to his 1998 creation of an African American variant of haiku. Both authors also have a shared interest in—to return to the argument posited in the chapter—the performance of improvised ethnic identities. In *Hunting Is Not Those Heads on the Wall*, Baraka would propose "art-ing," a creative process of art and self that "emphasize[s] the spontaneous and the improvisational, privileging the verb . . . while criticizing the noun."[15] And both engage in the signifying, punning practices of the black oral tradition (remember, for example, Nakagami's double entendre with the Japanese *kōdo* [chord/code]) in search of a vocabulary that might go beyond the confines of national language. Baraka's punning coincides with his cosmopolitan turn; Nakagami's comes in search of a break in and from imperial syntax.

But for our purposes the most significant affinity between the literary projects of Nakagami and Baraka can be seen in Baraka's "low coup," an African American, politically charged, down-home variant of the "*hai-ku*." According to Baraka, the low coup, which sprang from his "long reading of the Japanese Haiku form" can be characterized as having "no fixed amount of syllables like the classic, just short and sharp."[16] In characterizing the low coup in this way, Baraka has produced an almost pitch-perfect resonance with Nakagami; indeed, Nakagami turns to black literature and music precisely in order to "unfix" classic Japanese forms—be they literary or identitarian. Moreover, the "sharpness" of Baraka's low coup, much like the hard edge of Nakagami's coup in the face of imperial syntax, signifies the power of literary language to challenge, revolutionize, and redefine that which has been reified by the ruling discursive regime. When Baraka writes in *Un Poco Low Coups* that "we are trying to figure out where we are and we aint gonna ask you!," he is speaking the language of Nakagami.[17]

Nakagami's work began at the forefront of what I call the long-1970s, a period defined by experimentation with the lines drawn by genre—both literary and biological. The result of this experimentation is the creation of a black-Japanese hybrid body, with *body* here referring both to the biracial characters who populate these texts and the literary offspring—the body of literature—engendered by the mingling of black and Japanese literary language, tropes, topoi, and historical events. These bodies serve, to borrow the title of a text discussed in chapter 4, as "human proof" of the false promises of American democracy, a topic of considerable import for Japanese authors who came of age during and following the American Occupation of Japan. Although these hybrid characters supposedly have dual citizenship and hence access to both Japanese and American spaces, they are ultimately sequestered to the spaces of second-class citizenship. Think here of the Washington Heights of Ariyoshi Sawako's *Not Because of Color* or the Harlem of Honda Katsu'ichi's *The United States of America*, Morimura Seiichi's *Human Proof*, Abe Kōbō's *The Face of Another*, and Yoshida Ruiko's *Hot Harlem Days*. And it is this immobility that belies the promise of life, liberty, and the pursuit of happiness enshrined in both the American and postwar Japanese constitutions.

Although not a work of African American fiction per se, Neal Stephenson's *Snow Crash* reads like a response to the legacy of the works of the long 1970s. *Snow Crash* features an America in which the regulatory power of the federal government has all but collapsed. This makes for unadulterated American freedom: "This is America. People do whatever the fuck they feel like doing, you got a problem with that? Because they have a right to. And because they have guns and no one can fucking stop them."[18] Playing with the conventions of genre fiction, Stephenson projects the question of the long 1970s into the future: will such American freedom apply to someone like Hiro Protagonist, the aptly named hero of *Snow Crash*? "It is possible," Stephenson writes, "to see Hiro's eyes, which look Asian. They are from his mother, who is Korean by way of Nippon. The rest of him looks more like his father, who was African by way of Texas by way of the Army."[19]

The first crash of the novel is an automobile accident, which occurs with our Hiro on his way to deliver a pizza to a burbclave (a portmanteau for the suburban enclaves that organize middle-class life in *Snow Crash*), White Columns. White Columns is "Very southern, traditional, one of the Apartheid Burbclaves. Big ornate sign above the main gate: WHITE PEOPLE ONLY. NON-CAUCASIANS MUST BE PROCESSED."[20] Written in imposing orthography, which performs the phalanxlike impenetrability that it inscribes, this passage leaves the reader wondering if Hiro, with his eyes from his Zainichi Korean mother and skin from his black American father, has free access to this America. Because he has been rendered immobile, a "kourier" who's "got a White Columns visa . . . has a visa to everywhere," delivers the pizza for Hiro. In having Hiro's first delivery be one that he cannot make due in part to his race, Stephenson challenges the science fictional trope of reading Japan as "our" shared projection of a global future—the "future perfect" of William Gibson—while eliding the questions of race, which just might undermine the possibility of a shared Japanese American future.

The long 1970s were followed by an age of hip hop, a cultural phenomenon that has had an undeniable impact on the global writing and reading of blackness. In this book, I have focused on what I call the postblack two-step, a dance that takes the stage with the open-source sharing of blackness in hip hop. In Japan this dance both features experimentation with the aurality and physicality of blackness and retreats into hip-hop-flavored cultural nationalism.

Because hip hop is (and, I argue, always has been) a transpacific movement, the conversation in chapter 5 is reflected on the other side of the
Pacific—something like Japaneseness in black literature in the age of hip
hop. Take, for example, Junot Diaz's *The Brief Wondrous Life of Oscar Wao*,
a novel by and about a self-described black American immigrant from the
Dominican Republic (DR). *The Brief Wondrous Life* is a family history of
the *fukú*—a curse that doubles as a metaphor for the lingering legacy of the
sexual and colonial violence that haunts the DR—of Oscar's family. The
chronicling of Oscar's history coincides with and is mediated by the age of
hip hop. As the narrator sets the stage and the clock, "The only things that
changed in those years were the models of the cars, the size of Maritza's ass,
and the kind of music volting out the cars' speakers. First freestyle, then Ill
Will-era hip hop."[21] Moreover, in a move reminiscent of Mobu Norio, it is
through the languages and cadences of hip hop that our chronicler, Yunior,
finds the words to articulate the at times ineffable violence of this tale.
Michiko Kakutani has referred to this as the novel's "bilingual b-boy flow."[22]

The *fukú* leaves its mark on every member of Oscar's family. It scars them
both physically and psychically, irrevocably altering their bodies, sexualities,
and identities—in short, their humanity. For Oscar this means a masculinity that does not meet the standards of Dominican machismo. Oscar's
cursed deviance from the "Dominican norm" is made legible in part by the
Japaneseness of his identity. Oscar is unable to "hide his otakuness," and the
"Japanese mall on Edgewater Road" is "considered part of [his] landscape,
something to tell [his] children about."[23] Oscar even measures his very life
itself in "hit points," a standard of vitality he has internalized in part by way
of Japanese video games. Moreover, the interplay between Dominican bass
lines/baselines and Japanese flows is highly visible in Oscar's sister, Lola.
Lola, with her "manga eyes," is nursing a dream of going to Japan.

> I'm teaching English in Japan next year, she said matter-of-factly. It's
> going to be *amazing*.
> Not *I'm thinking about* or *I've applied* but *I am*. Japan? I laughed,
> a little mean. What the hell is a Dominican going out to Japan for?
> You're right, she said, turning the page [of *Introduction to Japanese*]
> irritably. Why would *anyone* want to go *anywhere* when they have
> New Jersey?[24]

In the narrator's laughter, there is something akin to the second maneuver
of the postblack two step. Due to his friendship with Oscar, an aficionado
of fantasy role-playing games, the narrator is able to imagine Dominicans
otherwise, and yet he is unable to imagine them fully integrated in Japan.

This limited imagination is something like the post-Japanese two-step, or the post-black-Dominican two-step being played out by way of the post-Japanese two-step. On the one hand, Japan offers a promise of escape from the *fukú* of Dominican cultural nationalism and the haunted legacy it carries with it. But, on the other hand, there is no greater proof that the homeland is still cursed by the *fukú* than our attempts to escape it. Diaz himself has suggested that this dynamic is the central problem explored by *Oscar Wao*, a novel in search of a way out of the infinite loop of the postblack two-step or, in Diaz's summation, an attempt to write about racial reality and logic without reductively endorsing that logic.[25]

In presenting the arguments of the five chapters of this study from the other side of the Pacific, I hope to put this book in dialogue with works such as Bill Mullen's *Afro-Orientalism* and Yunte Huang's *Transpacific Imaginations: History, Literature, Counterpoetics*. It is precisely this kind of conversation that I have in mind when I say that the history of blackness in postwar Japanese literature is a chapter in a greater history of racial thinking.

Given that this book comes at a moment when the systematic devaluing of literary studies coincides with violent misreadings of black bodies, I would like to conclude with an observation. The Japanese authors who produce the richest readings of blackness—the Nakagami Kenjis and Yoshida Ruikos—are those who had the time, means, support, and intellectual will to travel, meet, and break bread with black people and digest their encounters slowly, carefully, and thoughtfully. Their engagement with black cultural and literary studies transformed the grammar and aesthetics of their existences. Perhaps these authors and the models of reading race they propose can serve as a kind of philosophy, with philosophy here understood to be a love of wisdom with the power to transform the way we see the world.

Notes

Introduction

1. Tanaka Minoru, "'Genbun' to 'katari' saikō: *Kami no kodomotachi wa mina odoru* no shinsō hihyō," 9. "Black ships" (*kurofune*) refers generally to European trade vessels, which had black hulls, and specifically to the coal-powered steam engines, which emitted black smoke, of the Perry Expedition, which entered Japanese waters during Japan's isolationist Edo period (1603–1868). Because the Perry Expedition forcibly ushered in the opening of Japan, *kurofune* is also used as a metonym for the conclusion of Japanese isolationism and the beginning of Japan's reckoning with western powers. All translations, unless noted otherwise, are my own. As a rule of thumb, I cite the Japanese title when the translation is mine, and the title in English translation when the translation belongs to someone else.

2. See John Dower, *Black Ships and Samurai: Commodore Perry and the Opening of Japan (1853–1854)*.

3. Matthew Calbraith Perry, *Narrative of the Expedition of an American Squadron to the China Seas and Japan Performed in the Years 1852, 1853, and 1854 under the Command of Commodore M. C. Perry, United States Navy*, 295.

4. Quoted from a program printed for the 1894 performance by the Japan Expedition Press.

5. Victor Yellin, "Mrs. Belmont, Matthew Perry, and the 'Japanese Minstrels,'" 266–67.

6. Toni Morrison, *Playing in the Dark: Whiteness and the Literary Imagination*, 46.

7. Morrison, *Playing in the Dark*, 47.

8. For an introductory survey of studies of Japanese literary representations of blackness, see John Russell, "Taishū bungaku ni miru Nihonjin Kokujinkan"; John Russell, "Race and Reflexivity: The Black Other in Contemporary Japanese Mass Culture"; Tetsushi Furukawa and Hiromi Furukawa, "Nihon no sengo shōsetsu ni okeru 'kokujin'"; Ted Goossen, "Caged Beasts: Black Men in Modern Japanese Literature";

and Michael Molasky, "A Darker Shade of Difference," in *The American Occupation of Japan and Okinawa: Literature and Memory.*

9. Toni Morrison, "On the First Black President."

10. "Race and Human Variation."

11. David Barash, "Race (Part 1)."

12. Antonio Damasio, *The Self Comes to Mind: Constructing the Conscious Brain,* 204.

13. Martha Nussbaum, "Fictions of the Soul," 245–46.

14. In *Freud and Philosophy,* Paul Ricoeur proposes that "the contrary of suspicion . . . is faith. . . . No longer, to be sure, the first faith of the simple soul, but rather the second faith of one who has engaged in hermeneutics, *faith that has undergone criticism, postcritical faith. . . .* It is a rational faith, for it interprets; but it is a faith because it seeks, through interpretation, a second naïveté." Paul Ricoeur, *Freud and Philosophy: An Essay on Interpretation,* 28, my emphasis. Sharalyn Orbaugh's *Japanese Fiction of the Allied Occupation: Vision, Embodiment, Identity,* Anne McKnight's *Nakagami, Japan: Buraku and the Writing of Ethnicity,* and Ichijō Takao's "Ōe Kenzaburō to roku jyū nendai no 'Amerika': Rarufu erison no iwayuru 'tayōsei' wo megutte" are three examples of productive readings of blackness beyond its representation in postwar Japanese literature. My approach here is informed by the methodology established by these scholars.

15. John Russell, "Race and Reflexivity: The Black Other in Contemporary Japanese Mass Culture," 6. I should note that Russell's writing on blackness in Japanese culture is prolific, and that his thinking has shifted over the course of three decades of scholarship. Even given the nuances and contours of his work, however, there does seem to be a through line. Take, for example, Russell's concluding thoughts in his 2012 "Playing with Race/Authenticating Alterity: Authenticity, Mimesis, and Racial Performance in the Transcultural Diaspora": "In the end, racial performance and mimicry leave us with a recycling of old racial clichés, not their destruction" (80).

16. Russell, "Race and Reflexivity," 4.

17. I say "reiterate" because Nina Cornyetz and I address this significance in William H. Bridges and Nina Cornyetz, eds., *Traveling Texts and the Work of Afro-Japanese Cultural Production: Two Haiku and a Microphone,* 14–15.

18. Gayatri Spivak, "Can the Subaltern Speak?," 275.

19. Rachael Hutchinson and Mark Williams, "Introduction," 7.

20. Almost every page of this manuscript has been enriched by engagements with anonymous readers. But my articulation here is particularly indebted to their insights.

21. Michael O. Hardimon, *Rethinking Race: The Case for Deflationary Realism,* 2–3.

22. Hutchinson and Williams, "Introduction," 5.

23. For more on Giorgio Agamben's notion of the example as "pure singularity," see "Example" in his *The Coming Community.*

24. I have in mind here Jacques Derrida, *The Gift of Death*, 65. As Geoffrey Bennington proposes in his genealogy of this expression, however, "the instant of decision is a madness" functions as "a kind of watchword or password or slogan" across several of Derrida's works. For more on this, see Geoffrey Bennington, "A Moment of Madness: Derrida's Kierkegaard," 104.

25. Perhaps something like this is what Gayatri Spivak has in mind when she proposes in "Can the Subaltern Speak?" that certain "aspects of Derrida's work . . . retain a long-term usefulness for people outside the First World" (87). Even if Derrida's "real object of investigation is classical philosophy," Spivak continues, his approach to reading texts provides a way to address the potential pitfall of becoming a "first-world intellectual masquerading as the absent nonrepresenter who lets the oppressed speak for themselves" (87).

26. Tanaka Minoru, "'Genbun' to 'katari' saikō," 9.

27. Tanaka Minoru, "'Genbun' to 'katari' saikō," 10; Tanaka Minoru, "'Yomi no hairi' wo toku mittsu no kagi: Tekusuto, 'genbun' no kage, 'jikotōkai,' soshite 'katarite no jikohyōshutsu'," 11.

28. David Palumbo-Liu's *The Deliverance of Others: Reading Literature in a Global Age* begins from a similar premise, that "great works of literature deliver difference, otherness, that which is nonsimilar to us, all with the effect of making us better, richer, more moral" (12). Palumbo-Liu differs from Tanaka, however, in that his study also asks if it is possible to have too much Otherness; at what point does "irreducible otherness" become unintelligible and unhinging? In this study, I follow Tanaka's line of reasoning and address the implications of Palumbo-Liu's insights in a separate study.

29. Tanaka Minoru, "'Yomi no hairi' wo toku mittsu no kagi," 11.

30. See Tanaka Minoru, "'Jikotōkai' to 'shutai' no saikōchiku: 'Bishin,' 'Daiichiya,' 'Takasebune' no tajigen sekai to 'Rashōmon' no koto." I translate *jikotōkai* as "deconstruction," rather than "self-destruction," in order to follow the translation suggested by Tanaka.

31. Marielle Macé, "Ways of Reading, Modes of Being," 222, 216.

32. For more on *zuihitsu*, see Linda Chance, *Formless in Form: Kenko, Tsurezuregusa, and the Rhetoric of Japanese Fragmentary Prose*.

33. Tanizaki Jun'ichirō, *In Praise of Shadows*, 48–49. The quote is from the translation by Thomas J. Harper and Edward G. Seidensticker.

34. Cornel West, "The New Cultural Politics of Difference," 104.

35. Tanizaki Jun'ichirō, *In Praise of Shadows*, 63.

36. Morrison, *Playing in the Dark*, 17.

37. Morrison, *Playing in the Dark*, 17, my emphasis.

38. Marvin Sterling, "Searching for Self in the Global South: Japanese Literary Representations of Afro-Jamaican Blackness," 56.

39. Jared Sexton, "The Social Life of Social Death: On Afro-Pessimism and Black Optimism," 6–7.

40. Fred Moten, "Blackness and Nothingness (Mysticism in the Flesh)," 778.

41. E. Taylor Atkins, *Blue Nippon: Authenticating Jazz in Japan*, 42, emphasis in original.

42. John Dower, *War without Mercy: Race and Power in the Pacific War*, 4.

43. Dower, *War without Mercy*, 4.

44. Kanagaki Robun, *Aguranabe*, 273; *Seiyō dōchū hizakurige*, 254.

45. Natsume Soseki, *Sanshirō*, 79; Nagai Kafū, *Amerika monogatari*, 209–10. The translation of Soseki is Jay Rubin's.

46. Rotem Kowner, *From White to Yellow: The Japanese in European Racial Thought, 1300–1735*, 31.

47. Fukuzawa Yukichi, *An Outline of a Theory of Civilization*, 17. The translation of Fukuzawa here belongs to David Dilworth and G. Cameron Hurst III. Rachael Hutchinson, *Nagai Kafū's Occidentalism: Defining the Japanese Self*, 30, emphasis in original.

48. Michael Green, *Black Yanks in the Pacific: Race in the Making of American Military Empire after World War II*, 45.

49. General Douglas MacArthur served as Supreme Commander for the Allied Powers (SCAP), from the conclusion of World War II to 1951. (The post was held from 1951 until the conclusion of the Allied Occupation of mainland Japan in 1952 by General Matthew Ridgway.) MacArthur and his staff supervised the Occupation.

50. Eiji Takemae, *Inside GHQ: The Allied Occupation of Japan and Its Legacy*, 130–31.

51. Mary Louise Pratt, "Arts of the Contact Zone," 37.

52. John Russell, "Consuming Passions: Spectacle, Self-Transformation, and the Commodification of Blackness in Japan," 130, my emphasis.

53. Dower, *War without Mercy*, 4.

54. Ōe Kenzaburō, "Sengo sedai no imēji," 17.

55. Originally signed in 1952, the Treaty of Mutual Cooperation and Security between the United States and Japan (often abbreviated in Japanese as ANPO) effectively wed Japanese security to American interests in Asia. Prime Minister Kishi Nobusuke's initiation of the revision and reratification of ANPO in 1958 was the sparkplug for a series of protests that would rock Japan in the 1960s. The ranks of protesters included the All-Japan Federation of Students' Self-Governing Associations, often abbreviated as the Zengakuren, a conglomerate of (at times violent) student revolutionaries, radicals, communists, and anarchists.

56. Ali is quoted in Nathaniel Deutsch, "'The Asiatic Black Man': An African American Orientalism?," 194.

57. Ōe Kenzaburō, "Ryūkeisha no dokusho," 2–3.

58. See Wendy Matsumura, *The Limits of Okinawa: Japanese Capitalism, Living Labor, and Theorizations of Community*. Michael Molasky, Mitzi Uehara Carter, and

Ariko Ikehara have done exemplary work for scholars interested in considerations of race and blackness in Okinawa.

59. The translation here is Molasky's in *The American Occupation of Japan and Okinawa: Literature and Memory*, 97.

60. Susan Hamaker, "Nago Mayor Says US Bases 'A Legacy of Misery' in Okinawa."

61. Mitzi Uehara Carter, "Nappy Routes and Tangled Tales: Critical Ethnography in a Militarised Okinawa," 10.

62. Chinen Seishin, *The Human Pavilion*, 236. The translation is by Robert Tierney.

63. Andrew Gordon, *A Modern History of Japan: From Tokugawa Times to Present*, 289, 292.

64. Gordon, *Modern History of Japan*, 289–90.

65. Ian Condry, *Hip-Hop Japan: Rap and the Paths of Cultural Globalization*, 29.

66. A decorated haiku poet, Lenard Moore is, among the other accolades he has received on both sides of the Pacific, the first African American to be elected to the post of president of the Haiku Society of America.

67. In *Otaku: Japan's Database Animals*, Azuma Hiroki suggests that postmodern consumption as it is witnessed in *otaku* culture is characterized by a disregard for a product's place in relation to some grand narrative and a fascination with selecting whatever catches one's eye/I. This mode of consumption, for Azuma, is akin to a primal dive into and out of databases.

68. Murakami Takashi's self-styled "superflat" artwork—which Cornyetz's "Murakami Takashi and the Hell of Others: Sexual (In)Difference, the Eye, and the Gaze in ©*Murakami*," describes as the culmination "of traditional planar Japanese art forms and contemporary, globally circulating, non-realist, nonhumanist anime-manga chimerical life forms" (182)—found two of its many global homes in sartorial collaborations with rapper/fashionista Pharrell William and the cover art of the 2007 Kanye West album *Graduation*. Although such transracial collaboration is supergenerative, perhaps the "flatness" of such exchanges is crystalized by the lingering memory of a battery of unfortunate comments made by Japanese politicians. In 1986, for example, Prime Minister Nakasone Yasuhiro told some one thousand young members of his Liberal Democratic Party (LDP) that the average intelligence of US residents was lowered by the inclusion of blacks, Puerto Ricans, and Mexicans. In 1988 Watanabe Michio, then chief of the LDP Policy Affairs Research Council, claimed that, whereas bankruptcy would besmirch the honor of any upright Japanese citizen, blacks would revel in the levity of having no financial responsibilities. And in 1990 Kajiyama Seiroku, justice minister and member of the LDP, compared foreign prostitutes in Tokyo to African Americans crossing the red line into white neighborhoods.

69. Michael Keevar, *Becoming Yellow: A Short History of Racial Thinking*, 143.

70. "translation, n." *OED Online.*

71. Walter Benjamin, "The Task of the Translator," 255.

72. Aldon Nielsen, *Writing between the Lines: Race and Intertextuality*, 22, 24.

73. Julia Kristeva, "Word, Dialog, and Novel," 37.

74. Hans Robert Jauss and Elizabeth Benzinger, "Literary History as a Challenge to Literary Theory," 12, my emphasis.

75. Nahum Chandler, "Introduction: On the Virtues of Seeing—at Least, but Never Only—Double," 5.

Chapter I

1. Russell, "Playing with Race/Authenticating Alterity," 44, my emphasis.

2. Russell, "Playing with Race/Authenticating Alterity," 44.

3. Russell, "Consuming Passions," 130.

4. Molasky, *American Occupation of Japan and Okinawa*, 72; Theodore Goossen, "Tasha no sekai ni hairu toki," 429.

5. Russell, "Race and Reflexivity," 4.

6. The Army Reorganization Act of 1866 established several African American regiments of the US Army. Known colloquially as "buffalo soldiers," the all-black regiments preempted the spirit of *Plessy v. Ferguson* by establishing "separate but equal" units of the army according to race. De jure segregation of the US Army would continue until the middle of the Allied Occupation of Japan when President Harry S. Truman officially desegregated the country's armed forces with Executive Order 9981 in 1948. In occupied Japan, segregation typically occurred in labor, recreation, facilities, and in-quarters social activities. African American soldiers were often assigned to service units irrespective of their training and talents. Off-base recreational areas were subject to de facto segregation, with "black districts" catering to black soldiers and "white districts" catering to white soldiers. Racial enclaves formed on base as well, with soldiers, depending on the base, either using the same facilities at different times or using separate, racially designated facilities. African American newspapers from this period include interviews with black soldiers complaining of the "honorary whiteness" of Japanese American soldiers, who often worked in military intelligence alongside white soldiers. For more on this, see Michael Green, *Black Yanks in the Pacific: Race in the Making of American Military Empire after World War II.* For more on SCAP, see the "Introduction," n. 49.

7. Russell, "Race and Reflexivity," 4.

8. Moten, "Blackness and Nothingness (Mysticism in the Flesh)," 744.

9. Moten, "Blackness and Nothingness (Mysticism in the Flesh)," 744.

10. Jacques Derrida, *Specters of Marx: The State of Debt, the Work of Mourning, and the New International*, 10; Russell, "Playing with Race/Authenticating Alterity," 83.

11. Colin Davis, "Hauntology, Spectres, and Phantoms," 377.

12. Rey Chow, "The Old/New Question of Comparison in Literary Studies: A Post-European Perspective," 305.

13. Dower, *War without Mercy*, 16.

14. David Danow, *Models of Narrative: Theory and Practice*, 119, second emphasis mine, others in original.

15. Tessa Morris-Suzuki, "Lavish Are the Dead: Re-envisioning Japan's Korean War," 8.

16. Morris-Suzuki, "Lavish Are the Dead," 8.

17. Given SCAP censorship of Japanese media at the time of the riots, it is difficult to specify the exact number of soldiers who escaped. The *Fukuoka-ken keisatsushi* (History of the Fukuoka Prefectural Police) estimates that approximately two hundred armed soldiers escaped, but, according to William Bowers, William Hammond, and George MacGarrigle in *Black Soldier, White Army: The 24th Infantry Regiment in Korea*, a formal complaint filed by the police force in the immediate aftermath of the riots "alleg[ed] that approximately one hundred black deserters from an unknown unit had killed a Japanese citizen, seriously injured another, and committed acts of rape" (80). At the time of the riots, the regiment counted more than three thousand members in its ranks.

18. Pertinent documents can be found in Boxes 4469, 5550, and 5551 of Record Group 338, Entry 37042, of Archives II of the National Archives at College Park, Maryland. Copies of approximately seventy of these reports are housed at the Matsumoto Seichō Memorial Museum in Kitakyushu, Japan.

19. Bowers, Hammond, and MacGarrigle, *Black Soldier, White Army*, 80. These statistics are also recorded in Fukuoka-ken Keisatsu Honbu, *Fukuoka-ken keisatsushi Showa zenpen*, 857.

20. "Tōbōhei wa hōkoku wo, Kokura kenpeitai kara."

21. Kitakyushu shiritsu Matsumoto Seichō kinenkan, *Kuroji no eten: kizamareta kioku*, 15.

22. Molasky, "Darker Shade of Difference," 84.

23. Molasky, "Darker Shade of Difference," 84.

24. Molasky, "Darker Shade of Difference," 90.

25. Molasky, "Darker Shade of Difference," 83.

26. Molasky, "Darker Shade of Difference," 89.

27. Morris-Suzuki, "Lavish Are the Dead," 8.

28. Matsumoto Seichō, "E no gu," 79. The impetus for Matsumoto's commentary is the murder of a Kokura family at the hands of James L. Clark, an African American soldier, on 4 July 1950. This tragedy occurred both prior to and distinct from the Kokura Riots.

29. Toeda Hirokazu, "Matsumoto Seichō to shimbun shōsetsu," 30.

30. Matsumoto Seichō, "Kuroji no e," 71.

31. Matsumoto Seichō, "Kuroji no e," 74–75.

32. Junko Hayakawa, "Spatial Complexity: Musically Urbanized Kokura Gion Festival," 70.

33. Matsumoto Seichō, "Kuroji no e," 77–78.

34. Matsumoto Seichō, "Kuroji no e," 82, 83, 84, 89.

35. Matsumoto Seichō, "Kuroji no e," 85.

36. Matsumoto Seichō, "Kuroji no e," 100.

37. Matsumoto Seichō, "Kuroji no e," 89–90.

38. Matsumoto Seichō, "Kuroji no e," 90.

39. Matsumoto Seichō, "Kuroji no e," 85.

40. Matsumoto Seichō, "Kuroji no e," 98, 99.

41. Matsumoto Seichō, "Kuroji no e," 99.

42. Matsumoto Seichō, "Kuroji no e," 81.

43. Matsumoto Seichō, "Kuroji no e," 100.

44. Morris-Suzuki, "Lavish Are the Dead," 3.

45. Matsumoto Seichō, "Kuroji no e," 110.

46. Matsumoto Seichō, "Kuroji no e," 111, my emphasis.

47. Matsumoto Seichō, "Kuroji no e," 111.

48. Matsumoto Seichō, "Kuroji no e," 122.

49. Matsumoto Seichō, "Kuroji no e," 124.

50. Molasky, *American Occupation of Japan and Okinawa*, 91.

51. Matsumoto Seichō, "Kuroji no e," 107.

52. Matsumoto Seichō, "Kuroji no e," 107.

53. Matsumoto Seichō, "Kuroji no e," 115.

54. Matsumoto Seichō, "Kuroji no e," 125.

55. Toake Endoh, *Exporting Japan: Politics of Emigration to Latin America*, 135. For readers seeking more background information on the *burakumin*, Timothy Amos's *Embodying Difference: The Making of Burakumin in Modern Japan* provides a comprehensive introduction.

56. Matsumoto Seichō, "Kuroji no e," 105.

57. Matsumoto Seichō, "Kuroji no e," 129.

58. Matsumoto Seichō, "Kuroji no e," 129.

59. Noguchi Takehiko, "Ishikawa Jun," 96.

60. Orbaugh, *Japanese Fiction of the Allied Occupation*, 327.

61. William Tyler, "On 'The Legend of Gold' and 'The Jesus of the Ruins,'" 271–72.

62. Tyler, On 'The Legend of Gold' and 'The Jesus of the Ruins,'" 204, 273. Ishikawa employs a similar tactic in "The Jesus of the Ruins" (*Yakeato no iesu*, 1946), a critically acclaimed short story often anthologized with "Legend" in which an intellectual has an epiphany due to his encounter with Jesus, a derelict, lice-infested street

urchin in a black market. "Jesus" begins with narration such as, "Under the blazing sky of a hot summer sun, amidst choking dirt and dust, a cluster of makeshift stalls has sprung from the land. . . . For today is July 31, 1946, and come tomorrow, the first of August, official notice has been served that the market is to be closed for good." William Tyler, *The Legend of Gold and Other Stories*, 72. This narration leads the reader to the false assumption of third-person, "objective" narration. It is only after approximately ten pages of such narration that the narrator presents himself as an "I."

63. Ishikawa Jun, "Ōgon densetsu," 327. The translations of works by Ishikawa Jun and Kojima Nobuo in this chapter are mine. My work, however, was made much easier by the existence of masterful translations of Ishikawa by William Tyler and of Kojima Nobuo by Lawrence Rogers.

64. Peter Brooks, *Reading for the Plot: Design and Intention in Narrative*, 37, 48.

65. Ishikawa Jun, "Ōgon densetsu," 326.

66. For more on this, see Douglas Slaymaker, *The Body in Postwar Japanese Fiction*.

67. Ik-koo Hwang, "'Senryō' to no sogū: Ishikawa Jun 'Ōgon densetsu' ni okeru sengo jyūyo," 129. The word *kuruu* is used to describe both a watch that is out of sync and insanity or senility. The "madness" of the watch, as well as, by proxy, the madness of time/the times, is a central facet of the excerpted passage.

68. Ishikawa Jun, "Ōgon densetsu," 327.

69. Ishikawa Jun, "Ōgon densetsu," 332.

70. Ishikawa Jun, "Ōgon densetsu," 331.

71. Ishikawa Jun, "Ōgon densetsu," 333.

72. Ishikawa Jun, "Ōgon densetsu," 333.

73. Ishikawa Jun, "Ōgon densetsu," 333–34.

74. Orbaugh, *Japanese Fiction of the Allied Occupation*, 459, my emphasis.

75. Takano Yoshitomi, "Ishikawa Jun sengo no shuppatsu: 'Ōgon densetsu' ni okeru zetsubō ni tsuite," 69–70, my emphasis.

76. See, for example, Andō Hajime's *Ishikawa Jun ron*.

77. Ik-koo Hwang, "Senryō to no sogū," 140–41.

78. Yokote Kazuhiko, "Ōgon densetsu wa ni do to tsukurareta," 24.

79. This manuscript is housed in the Gordon W. Prange Collection of Occupation Censored Materials, University of Maryland, College Park.

80. Suzuki Sadami, "Kaidai," 764. For Tyler's commentary, see his "On 'The Legend of Gold' and 'The Jesus of the Ruins.'" Although her "Literary Reorientation in Occupied Japan: Incidents of Civil Censorship" addresses Ishikawa Jun in passing, Marlene Mayo's research is a highly informative resource for those interested in the censorship of fraternization in postwar Japan.

81. Yamaguchi Toshio, *Ishikawa Jun sakuhin kenkyū: "Kajin" kara "Yakeato no Iesu" made*, 12; Takano Yoshitomo, "Ōgon densetsu ron: Zetsubō kara no saisei ni tsuite," 125; Tyler, "On 'The Legend of Gold' and 'The Jesus of the Ruins,'" 221.

82. Gordon, *Modern History of Japan*, 226, 229.

83. Hirose Masahiro, "Neitibu supīkā no inai eikaiwa: Senji sengo no renzoku to 'Amerikan sukūru,'" 6.

84. Rizawa Yukio, "Kojima Nobuo ni okeru fūshi to chūshō," 13.

85. Stephen Greenblatt, "Learning to Curse: Aspects of Linguistic Colonialism in the Sixteenth Century," 16.

86. See Cho Jung-Min, "Kojima Nobuo 'Amerikan sukūru' ron." Cho notes that the notebook sold some four million copies in September 1945 alone.

87. Greenblatt, "Learning to Curse," 31.

88. Kojima Nobuo, "Amerikan sukūru," 228–29.

89. Derrida, *Specters of Marx*, 161.

90. Derrida, *Specters of Marx*, 161.

91. Kojima Nobuo, "Amerikan sukūru," 230–31.

92. Kojima Nobuo, "Amerikan sukūru," 231.

93. Kojima Nobuo, "Amerikan sukūru," 231.

94. Kojima, "Amerikan sukūru," 232.

95. Kojima Nobuo, "Amerikan sukūru," 233.

96. Kojima Nobuo, "Amerikan sukūru," 233, my emphasis.

97. Diane Perpich, *The Ethics of Emmanuel Levinas*, 54.

98. Levinas, *Totality and Infinity*, 197.

99. Molasky, *American Occupation of Japan and Okinawa: Literature and Memory*, 198.

100. Yamamoto Yukimasa, "Hisenryōki-ka ni okeru kotoba no fūkei: Kojima Nobuo 'Amerikan sukūru' wo megutte," 128.

101. Kojima Nobuo, "Amerikan sukūru," 233, my emphasis.

102. Kojima Nobuo, "Amerikan sukūru," 246–47.

103. Van C. Gessel, *The Sting of Life: Four Contemporary Japanese Novelists*, 210–11.

104. Kojima Nobuo, "Amerikan sukūru," 255.

105. Kojima Nobuo, "Amerikan sukūru," 257.

106. Kumagai Nobuko, "Kojima Nobuo 'Amerikan sukūru' imejarī ni miru 'shishōsetsu,'" 114, 115.

107. Rizawa, "Kojima Nobuo ni okeru fūshi to chūshō," 14.

108. Kojima Nobuo, "Amerikan sukūru," 258.

109. Kojima Nobuo, "Amerikan sukūru," 259.

110. Douglas Slaymaker, *The Body in Postwar Japanese Fiction*, 31–32.

111. Kojima Nobuo, "Amerikan sukūru," 261.

112. Kojima Nobuo, "Amerikan sukūru," 261.

113. Kojima Nobuo, "Amerikan sukūru," 261.

114. Derrida, *Specters of Marx*, 158.

115. Kojima Nobuo, "Amerikan sukūru," 259.

116. Kojima Nobuo, "Amerikan sukūru," 281.

117. Yamamoto Yukimasa, "Hisenryōki-ka ni okeru kotoba no fūkei," 133.

118. Kojima Nobuo, *Hōyō kazoku*, 156–57, my emphasis.

119. Toni Morrison, "Unspeakable Things Unspoken: The Afro-American Presence in American Literature," 259.

120. Gessel, *Sting of Life*, 3, 5.

121. Okuno Takeo, "Ishikawa Jun no shōsetsu no gainen," 152.

122. Makibayashi Koji, "Kojima Nobuo no hōhō: 'Americkan sukūru' no bunseki wo tooshite," 10.

123. Morrison, *Playing in the Dark*, 47.

124. Molasky, *American Occupation of Japan and America*, 72.

125. Mayo, "Literary Reorientation in Occupied Japan," 135.

126. Jonathan Abel, *Redacted: The Archives of Censorship in Transwar Japan*, 166.

127. Goossen, "Tasha no sekai ni hairu toki," 429.

128. Hashimoto Fukuo, "Atogaki," 256.

129. Ralph Ellison, *Invisible Man*, 3.

Chapter 2

1. See "Kaihō," 38.

2. Ōe Kenzaburō, "Konnan no kankaku nitsuite: Wa ga sosaku taiken," 94.

3. Ōe, ever the writer, communicates primarily by way of handwritten letters. I wrote to him in August 2010 to inquire about "Negro American Literature and Modern Japanese Literature," which is referenced in a program for the 1963 symposium. Ōe replied on 21 September 2010. Although he has no recollection of the speech, in his letter he wrote that he "feverishly" (*nechū*) read the works of James Baldwin, Richard Wright, Ralph Ellison, and Chester Himes in the early 1960s. My thanks to Professor Michael Bourdaghs for facilitating my correspondence with Ōe.

4. Sterling, "Searching for Self in the Global South," 56.

5. The narratives of Ōe's 1957 "Shiiku" (Prize Stock) and 1958 "Kurai kawa, omoi kai" (Dark River, Heavy Oar) and "Tatakai no konnichi" (Today the Struggle) are propelled primarily by the Japanese narrator's gaze and the author's representation of the black male body. Several of Ōe's post-1961 works—primarily *Sakebigoe* (The Cry, 1963) but also moments in *Kojinteki na taiken* (A Personal Matter, 1964) and *Man'en gannen no futtobōru* (The Silent Cry, 1967)—are highly informed by Ōe's reading of Wright, Baldwin, and Ellison.

6. Scholarship that takes up the representation of blackness in Ōe's "Prize Stock" includes Russell, "Taishū bungaku ni miru Nihonjin Kokujinkan"; Russell, "Race and Reflexivity"; Norma Field, "Neitibu to eirian, nanji to ware: Ōe Kenzaburō no shinwa, kindai, kyokō"; Furukawa and Furukawa, "Nihon no sengo shōsetsu ni okeru 'kokujin'"; Goossen, "Caged Beasts"; Molasky, "Darker Shade of

Difference"; and Reiko Tachibana, "Structures of Power: Ōe Kenzaburō's 'Shiiku' ('Prize Stock')."

7. Marco Abel, *Violent Affect: Literature, Cinema, and Critique after Representation*, 74, 58, 85.

8. Ōe Kenzaburō, "Amerika no yume," 184. "Amerika no yume" (American Dream), which Ōe penned before his inaugural journey to the United States, is not to be confused with *Amerika ryokōsha no yume* (Dreams of a Traveler in America), a series of essays written in commemoration of his travels in America.

9. Bruno Latour, *An Inquiry into Modes of Existence: An Anthropology of the Moderns*, 251.

10. Ōe Kenzaburō, "Fukashi ningen to tayōsei," 35. I use *minor* here in the manner suggested by Deleuze and Guattari.

11. Ōe Kenzaburō, "Prize Stock," 152, 153. The translation here is John Nathan's.

12. Ōe, "Sengo sedai no imēji," 16.

13. West, "New Cultural Politics of Difference," 104.

14. For more on representative reading as it is defined here, see the "Introduction" and chapter 1 of this volume or the introduction to Bridges and Cornyetz, *Traveling Texts and the Work of Afro-Japanese Cultural Production*.

15. Ōe Kenzaburō, "Shiiku," 135.

16. Ōe Kenzaburō, "Shiiku," 92, 133. The translations of Ōe here are mine.

17. Jean-Paul Sartre, *Notebooks for an Ethics*, 563.

18. Ōe Kenzaburō, "Jigoku ni yuku Hakkuruberī Fin," 240.

19. Rita Felski, *The Limits of Critique*, 2, emphasis in original.

20. Felski, *Limits of Critique*, 174.

21. Jane Tompkins, *Sensational Designs: The Cultural Work of American Fiction, 1790–1860*, xvi.

22. Ōe Kenzaburō, "Ryūkeisha no dokusho," 2–3.

23. Yuichiro Onishi, *Transpacific Antiracism: Afro-Asian Solidarity in Twentieth-Century Black America, Japan, and Okinawa*, 100.

24. Kota Inoue, "Postwar Japanese Fiction and the Legacy of Unequal Japan-US Relations," 157.

25. Ōe Kenzaburō, "Jigoku ni yuku Hakkuruberī Fin," 229.

26. Ōe Kenzaburō, "Fukashi ningen to tayōsei," 140.

27. Ōe Kenzaburō, "Fukashi ningen to tayōsei," 141.

28. Ōe Kenzaburō, "Fukashi ningen to tayōsei," 142.

29. Ōe Kenzaburō, "Fukashi ningen to tayōsei," 140.

30. Ōe Kenzaburō, "Fukashi ningen to tayōsei," 140.

31. Ōe Kenzaburō, "Fukashi ningen to tayōsei," 140.

32. Ōe Kenzaburō, "Jigoku ni yuku Hakkuruberī Fin," 230. Initially used as training weapons at military academies, Japanese civilians, Okinawans in particular, were issued and trained in the use of *takeyari*, bamboo spears, for civil defense purposes

in the case of an Allied invasion. The use of this wartime relic in a postwar homicide between Japanese civilians, in conjunction with the homicide taking place in an air raid shelter, is indicative of the lingering and liquid fear and violence Ōe attributes to prolonged war.

33. Ōe Kenzaburō, "Jigoku ni yuku Hakkuruberī Fin," 230.
34. Ōe Kenzaburō, "Jigoku ni yuku Hakkuruberī Fin," 230.
35. Ōe Kenzaburō, "Jigoku ni yuku Hakkuruberī Fin," 237.
36. Ōe Kenzaburō, "Jigoku ni yuku Hakkuruberī Fin," 236.
37. Ōe Kenzaburō, "Kyōdai na amerika-zō no kuzureta ato ni . . . ," 31.
38. Ōe Kenzaburō, "Amerikaron," 99.
39. Ōe Kenzaburō, "Fukashi ningen to tayōsei," 39.
40. Gilled Deleuze and Félix Guattari, *Kafka: Toward a Minor Literature*, 17, 16.
41. Deleuze and Guattari, *Kafka*, 18.
42. Mary F. Zamberlin, *Rhizosphere: Gilles Deleuze and the "Minor" American Writings of William James, W. E. B. DuBois, Gertrude Stein, Jean Toomer,x and William Faulkner*, 10.
43. Ōe Kenzaburō, "Gendai bungaku to sei," 371.
44. Ōe Kenzaburō, "Jigoku ni yuku Hakkuruberī Fin," 229.
45. Ōe Kenzaburō, "Kokujin no suijaku to katsuryoku: Āto Bureikī to sono gakudan," 22.
46. Ōe Kenzaburō, "Kokujin no suijaku to katsuryoku," 22.
47. Ōe Kenzaburō, "Ajia Afurika ningen no kaigi," 339.
48. Ōe Kenzaburō, "Ajia Afurika ningen no kaigi," 340.
49. Ōe Kenzaburō, "Kyōken ni kakushitsu wo kamosu kokorozashi," 64.
50. Ōe Kenzaburō, "Kyōken ni kakushitsu wo kamosu kokorozashi," 64.
51. Ōe Kenzaburō, "Dosutoefuskī: *Hakuchi* to Bōrudouin," 603. Ōe's use of *negritude* is idiosyncratic and does not fully signal the history that scholars of black literature would typically associate with the term. Given that Ōe's *negritude* refers primarily to Baldwin and Ellison rather than Senghor and Césaire, his usage is closer to the literal meaning of the word *blackness* than it is to that of negritude intellectuals. The parenthetical gloss that often accompanies the use of *negritude* in Ōe's works, *kokujin de aru koto* (literally "the fact that X is a black person"), attests to his literal rather than literary historical use of the term. There is, however, an (albeit uncritical) sense in which Ōe follows the negritude movement's positing of universal, transnational blackness among all black artists by cross-applying *negritude* to black authors en masse, including Baldwin and Ellison.
52. Ōe Kenzaburō in *Genshuku na tsunawatari*, 155, quoted in Yasuko Claremont, *The Novels of Kenzaburo Ōe*, 4–5.
53. John Treat, *Writing Ground Zero: Japanese Literature and the Atomic Bomb*, 234. Ōe conducted fieldwork in Hiroshima from the summer of 1963 to 1964 and published his findings in installments in the journal *Sekai*. The 1965 *Hiroshima Notes*

compiled the *Sekai* essays. Ōe published *Sakebigoe* in 1963 and the aforementioned "American Dream," in which he discusses his interest in black literature, in 1965, the same year as the publication of *Hiroshima Notes*.

54. Sartre's "look" (*le regard*) is occasionally translated as "gaze." I employ the "gaze" translation for the remainder of this excerpt.

55. Jean-Paul Sartre, *Being and Nothingness: A Phenomenological Essay on Ontology*, 362.

56. Sartre, *Notebooks for an Ethics*, 563, emphasis in original.

57. Sartre, *Notebooks for an Ethics*, 563.

58. Jonathan Judaken, "Sartre on Racism: From Existential Phenomenology to Globalization and 'the New Racism.'" 27.

59. Judaken, "Sartre on Racism," 27.

60. Jean-Paul Sartre, "Black Orpheus," 327, my emphasis.

61. Ōe Kenzaburō, "Fukashi ningen to tayōsei," 139–40.

62. Ralph Ellison, "What America Would Be Like without Blacks."

63. Ōe Kenzaburō, "Amerikaron," 102, emphasis in original.

64. Ōe Kenzaburō, "Amerikaron," 102.

65. Ichijō Takao, "Ōe Kenzaburō to roku jyū nendai no 'amerika,'" 11.

66. Ōe Kenzaburō, "Fukashi ningen to tayōsei," 144.

67. Ōe Kenzaburō, "Fukashi ningen to tayōsei," 145.

68. Ōe Kenzaburō, "Fukashi ningen to tayōsei," 145.

69. Ellison, *Invisible Man*, 3–4, emphasis in original.

70. Ellison, *Invisible Man*, 18.

71. Ellison, *Invisible Man*, 19, my emphasis.

72. Norman Mailer, *Advertisements for Myself*, 339.

73. Mailer, *Advertisements for Myself*, 346, 347.

74. Mailer, *Advertisements for Myself*, 471.

75. Mailer, *Advertisements for Myself*, 471, 472.

76. Mailer, *Advertisements for Myself*, 352.

77. Mailer, *Advertisements for Myself*, 472.

78. Brandon Gordon, "Physical Sympathy: Hip and Sentimentalism in James Baldwin's *Another Country*," 92.

79. Ōe Kenzaburō, "Konnan no kankaku ni tsuite," 92.

80. Norman Mailer, "Norman Mailer vs. Nine Writers," 60.

81. Ōe Kenzaburō, "Konnan no kankaku ni tsuite," 93.

82. Ōe Kenzaburō, "Konnan no kankaku ni tsuite," 93.

83. Ōe Kenzaburō, "Konnan no kankaku ni tsuite," 94.

84. Ōe Kenzaburō, "Amerika no yume," 184; Ōe Kenzaburō, "Modan jazu to boku jishin," 542.

85. Ōe Kenzaburō, "Amerikaron," 100–101.

86. Janet Jakobsen, "Queers Are Like Jews, Aren't They? Analogy and Alliance Politics," 67.

87. Ōe Kenzaburō, *Kodoku na seinen no kyūka*, 56–57.

88. See Ichijō Takao, *Ōe Kenzaburō: Sono bungaku sekai to haikei*.

89. Ōe Kenzaburō, *Sakebigoe*, 7.

90. Ōe Kenzaburō, *Sakebigoe*, 77.

91. Ōe Kenzaburō, *Sakebigoe*, 24.

92. Ōe Kenzaburō, *Sakebigoe*, 29.

93. Ōe Kenzaburō, *Sakebigoe*, 144.

94. Ōe Kenzaburō, *Sakebigoe*, 144.

95. For a synopsis of these valences, see Majima Ichirō, "Kūhaku no chi kara: Ōe Kenzaburō to Afurika," especially 332.

96. Majima Ichirō, "Kūhaku no chi kara," 331.

97. Amiri Baraka, "Black Art," 106.

98. Ōe Kenzaburō, "Ryūkeisha no dokusho," 3. Ōe also suggests that the title *Sakebigoe* is a translation of the trope of lamentation that Ōe reads in Wright's *Native Son* and *Uncle Tom's Children*.

99. Ōe Kenzaburō, *Sakebigoe*, 169.

100. Ōe Kenzaburō, "Konnan no kankaku ni tsuite," 94.

101. Charles P. Toombs, "Black-Gay-Man Chaos in *Another Country*," 105, my emphasis.

102. By "full of the complexity that Baldwin . . . attributes to human identity and not homogenized by racial or racist ideology," I refer to what might be called the identitarian desegregation advocated in Baldwin's nonfictional works. For one example among many, consider his "Here Be Dragons," one of his later essays in the 1985 *The Price of the Ticket*. Baldwin reminds us, "Each of us, helplessly and forever, contains the other—male in female, white in black, black in white. We are a part of each other. Many of my countrymen appear to find this fact exceedingly inconvenient, and so very often do I. But none of us can do anything about it." James Baldwin, "Here Be Dragons," 690.

103. Ōe Kenzaburō, *Sakebigoe*, 144. My emphasis is in bold.

104. Michiko Wilson, *The Marginal World of Ōe Kenzaburō: A Study in Themes and Techniques*, 41. The translation of Ōe here is Wilson's.

105. I read in Takao's mother's decision to bestow a Japanese name on her Zainichi Korean son reverberations of the *sōshi kaimei* policies, which in the years 1939–45 obligated ethnically Korean subjects of the Japanese empire to adopt Japanese-style family names. Even after the United States Army Military Government in Korea's 1946 issuance of the Name Restoration Order, some Zainichi Koreans opted to keep their Japanese-style names in order to—to borrow the term from black literature— "pass" and avoid discrimination.

106. Sonia Ryang, *Writing Selves in Diaspora: Ethnography of Autobiographies of Korean Women in Japan and the United States*, xv.

107. Ryang, *Writing Selves in Diaspora*, xv.

108. Although Korea was well within Japan's sphere of influence as early as 1904, the Japan-Korea Treaty of 1910 marked the official beginning of Japan's annexation of Korea. After annexation, one of the first policies implemented by Japan's governor-general of Korea, Terauchi Masatake (1852–1919), was to make good on Japan's 1906 law permitting Japanese landownership in Korea. The upshot of land reform policies was the gradual and steady transfer of landownership from Korean owners, who didn't have "legal proof" of their ownership, to Japanese owners. This literal, collective loss of homeland—particularly when considered alongside the forced emigration, labor, and conscription of Koreans by the Japanese during the Pacific War—aligns with the politico-classical model. On the other hand, the events of the postwar era included several building blocks of the personal-modern model. After repatriation, some 650,000 Koreans remained in postwar Japan. The United Nations–backed elections of 1948 and the inconclusive outcome of the Korean War in 1953 would replace a unified Korea with the two Koreas, the Republic of Korea (South Korea) and the Democratic People's Republic of Korea (North Korea). With their homeland (unified Korea) now no longer on the map, postwar Koreans in Japan experienced one impetus for the "ontological insecurities" of the personal-modern model of diaspora in 1952, when the San Francisco Peace Treaty nullified the Japanese nationality of Zainichi Koreans who received their status as nationals by way of Japanese colonial rule. A second impetus came in 1965, when Japan normalized relations with South Korea. Normalization made permanent residence in Japan contingent on gaining South Korean nationality but created no avenue for full Japanese citizenship (not to mention the creation of a stateless status for individuals who identified with North Korea).

109. Ryang, *Writing Selves in Diaspora*, xliii.

110. Cf. Ōe Kenzaburō, "Konnan no kankaku ni tsuite," 93.

Chapter 3

1. Nakagami Kenji, Noma Hiroshi, and Yasuoka Shōtarō, "Shimin ni hisomu sabetsu shinri," 34.

2. Trudier Harris, "Passing."

3. Henry Louis Gates, *The Signifying Monkey: A Theory of Afro-American Literary Criticism*, 124.

4. McKnight, *Nakagami, Japan*, 135. McKnight's *Nakagami, Japan* presents a cogent analysis of Nakagami's *buraku*-black signifyin(g) circa 1968, the year in which Nakagami's *Nihongo ni tsuite* (On the Japanese Language) was published. I argue here

for expanding the time frame of Nakagami's engagement with the black arts to cover the two-decade period from 1966 to 1988.

5. McKnight, *Nakagami, Japan*, 135.

6. For more on this, see Nishida Kiriko's exegesis of self-articulation and the kinetic friction among the terms *nigger, native,* and *mixed-blood* in Nakagami's *Yasei no kaenju*. Nishida Kiriko, "Nakagami Kenji *Yasei no kaenju* ni okeru ekkyō no kanōsei to fukanōsei: 'Kuronbo,' 'dojin,' 'konketsu,' to mizukara wo kataru koto."

7. See Nakagami Kenji, "Shoki no Ōe Kenzaburō: 'Shiiku' wo chūshin ni."

8. Jennifer Cramer, "'Do We Really Want to Be Like Them'? Indexing European-ness through Pronominal Use," 620.

9. Judith Butler, *Bodies That Matter: On the Discursive Limits of "Sex,"* 219.

10. Alan Tansman, "History, Repetition, and Freedom in the Narratives of Naka-gami Kenji," 258.

11. Gates, *Signifying Monkey*, 6, 52.

12. Gates, *Signifying Monkey*, xxiv, 90.

13. Gates, *Signifying Monkey*, 121, my emphasis.

14. Yamaguchi Masao, *Dōke no minzokugaku*, 204.

15. Gates, *Signifying Monkey*, 45.

16. Gates, *The Signifying Monkey*, 45.

17. From the interwar to the early postwar period, the *buraku* was often referred to using the moniker *tokushu buraku* (specially marked *buraku*).

18. Sugiyama Seiichi, "Tokushu buraku," 561.

19. Sugiyama Seiichi, "Tokushu buraku," 570. The term used here is *Pansuke*, a derivation of *pan pan*.

20. Sugiyama Seiichi, "Tokushu buraku," 559. This is from the blurb introducing Sugiyama's story, which claims that the "flower of humanism" can always blossom and overcome even racial difference (between *burakumin* characters and non-*burakumin* protagonists and, by proxy, readers).

21. Amos, *Embodying Difference*, 41.

22. Sugiyama Seiichi, "Tokushu buraku," 559.

23. Sugiyama Seiichi, "Tokushu buraku," 570.

24. Unconvinced that the legal system would provide them with an opportunity to air their grievances, the NCBL often resorted to *kyūdan* (糾弾), extralegal "denuncia-tions" of discrimination. These denunciations typically consisted of publications and/or public gatherings in which offenders were verbally chastised.

25. Buraku kaihō Kyoto-fu rengōkai, "Wareware wa shisei to ika ni tatakau ka: *Ōru romansu sabetsu* kyūdan yōkō," 541, 542.

26. Buraku kaihō Kyoto-fu rengōkai, "Wareware wa shisei to ika ni tatakau ka," 546.

27. Karatani Kōjin, *Origins of Modern Japanese Literature*, 163.

28. Richard Okada, *Figures of Resistance: Language, Poetry, and Narrating in the 'Tale of Genji' and Other Mid-Heian Texts*, 29.

29. Yomota Inuhiko, *Kishu to tensei: Nakagami Kenji*, 104.

30. Yomota Inuhiko, *Kishu to tensei*, 106.

31. Nakagami Kenji, "Toki wa nagareru," 239.

32. McKnight, *Nakagami, Japan*, 73.

33. McKnight, *Nakagami, Japan*, 73.

34. Gates, *Signifying Monkey*, 52.

35. Eve Zimmerman, *Out of the Alleyway: Nakagami Kenji and the Poetics of Out-caste Fiction*, 4.

36. Nakagami Kenji, "Ore, Jūhassai," 10.

37. Nakagami Kenji, "Ore, Jūhassai," 10.

38. Nakagami Kenji, "Ore, Jūhassai," 10.

39. Nakagami Kenji, "Ore, Jūhassai," 23–24.

40. Baldwin, *Another Country*, 22.

41. In 1963 a sixteen-year-old girl, Nakata Yoshie, was abducted and subsequently raped and murdered in Sayama, Japan. Ishikawa Kazuo, a member of the *burakumin* community near Nakata's home, was convicted of the murder. Given the circumstantial evidence used to convict Ishikawa, procedural concerns that suggested a coerced confession, and Ishikawa's claims of innocence, the Sayama Incident became a flash point for debate on *burakumin* criminality and justice.

42. "The latent discriminatory mind-set of ordinary folks" is a translation of the title of the *Asahi Journal* roundtable discussion featuring Nakagami.

43. Nakagami Kenji, *Kishū: Ki no kuni ne no kuni monogatari*, 189.

44. Nakagami Kenji, Noma Hiroshi, and Yasuoka Shōtarō, "Shimin ni hisomu sabetsu shinri" [The Latent Discriminatory Mind-Set of Ordinary Folks], 40–41.

45. Nakagami Kenji, Noma Hiroshi, and Yasuoka Shōtarō, "Shimin ni hisomu sabetsu shinri 34.

46. Nakagami Kenji, Noma Hiroshi, and Yasuoka Shōtarō, "Shimin ni hisomu sabetsu shinri," 34.

47. Nakagami Kenji, Noma Hiroshi, and Yasuoka Shōtarō, "Shimin ni hisomu sabetsu shinri," 34.

48. Watanabe Naomi, *Nihon kindai bungaku to "sabetsu,"* 140.

49. Nakagami Kenji, Noma Hiroshi, and Yasuoka Shōtarō, "Shimin ni hisomu sabetsu shinri," 51.

50. Nakagami Kenji, Noma Hiroshi, and Yasuoka Shōtarō, "Shimin ni hisomu sabetsu shinri," 51.

51. Nakagami Kenji, Noma Hiroshi, and Yasuoka Shōtarō, "Shimin ni hisomu sabetsu shinri," 50.

52. Nakagami Kenji, *Nakagami Kenji zenshū*, vol. 1, 584.

53. Nakagami Kenji, "Ore, Jūhassai," 23–24.

54. Nakagami Kenji, *Nakagami Kenji zenshū*, vol. 1, 580; "Ore, Jūhassai," 19.

55. My translation of the soldier's name follows the orthography of Nakagami's story: "Ludolph" rather than "Rudolph."

56. Sugahara Maiko, "Nakagami Kenji 'Jūkyūsai no jeikobo': Jazu hyōshō wo megutte," 1.

57. Nakagami Kenji, "Hakai seyo, to Airā wa itta," 17.

58. Nakagami Kenji, *Nihongo ni tsuite*, 130.

59. Gates, *Signifying Monkey*, 105.

60. Gates, *Signifying Monkey*, 105.

61. See Nina Cornyetz, *Dangerous Women, Deadly Words: Phallic Fantasy and Modernity in Three Japanese Writers*, especially the chapter "Dangerous Men and All That Jazz."

62. Atsuko Ueda, "'Nihongo' de kataru koto, 'Nihongo' wo kataru koto: Nakagami Kenji *Nihongo ni tsuite* wo megutte," 343.

63. Nakagami Kenji, "Hakai seyo, to Airā wa itta," 29. I agree with Eve Zimmerman and Ken Ito that *hō/seido* (law/system) is best translated as "code." In "Hakai seyo," however, Nakagami uses both *hō/seido* and *kōdo*—a fact that substantiates Zimmerman and Ito's reasoning. To avoid confusion, I have translated *hō/seido* as "law/system" and *kōdo* as "code."

64. Nakagami Kenji, "Hakai seyo," 29.

65. Nakagami Kenji, "Hakai seyo," 29, my emphasis.

66. To clarify the timeline a bit, Nakagami's documented interest in *monogatari* can be traced back to the 1970s. Nakagami's interest in jazz and its possible avenue to a "destruction of the fixed form" of identities narrated in Japanese, however, is palpable as early as *On the Japanese Language*, hence my suggestion that one should read the novella vis-à-vis Nakagami's articulation of jazz time and its destructive force.

67. Nakagami Kenji, "Hakai seyo," 36.

68. Nakagami Kenji, "Hakai seyo," 43.

69. McKnight, *Nakagami, Japan*, 129.

70. Nakagami Kenji, "Hakai seyo," 43.

71. Zimmerman, *Out of the Alleyway*, 151. The passage quoted here is from an interview of Nakagami conducted by Zimmerman; the translation of Nakagami is Zimmerman's.

72. Zimmerman, *Out of the Alleyway*, 152.

73. Zimmerman, *Out of the Alleyway*, 152.

74. Nakagami Kenji, "Toshi shōsetsu no minamoto wo tsuku anyu toshite no sogai ya sabetsu: Toni Morison-cho 'Aoi me ga hoshi' shohyō," 472.

75. Nakagami Kenji, "Hakai seyo," 36.

76. Nakagami Kenji, *Nihongo ni tsuite*, 135.

77. Nakagami Kenji, *Nihongo ni tsuite*, 133, 139.

78. Nakagami Kenji, *Nihongo ni tsuite*, 161.

79. Nakagami Kenji, *Nihongo ni tsuite*, 179.

80. Nakagami Kenji, *Nihongo ni tsuite*, 193, emphasis in original.

81. Nakagami Kenji, *Nihongo ni tsuite*, 178.

82. Nakagami Kenji, *Nihongo ni tsuite*, 162.

83. Nakagami Kenji, *Nihongo ni tsuite*, 192.

84. James Baldwin, *Nobody Knows My Name*, 98–99, my emphasis.

85. Nakagami Kenji, *Nihongo ni tsuite*, 194.

86. Atsuko Ueda, "'Nihongo de kataru koto, 'Nihongo' wo kataru koto," 337.

87. Nakagami Kenji, *Jazu to bakudan*, 32.

88. Nakagami Kenji, *Nihongo ni tsuite*, 168.

89. Nakagami Kenji, *Nihongo ni tsuite*, 187.

90. James Baldwin, *Notes of a Native Son*, 15.

91. Baldwin, *Notes of a Native Son*, 13.

92. Nakagami Kenji, *Hakai seyo, to Airā wa itta*, 45.

93. Nakagami Kenji, *Nihongo ni tsuite*, 129. Capitalized "Fujiyama," and "courage" in bold print in the original.

94. Nakagami Kenji, *Nihongo ni tsuite*, 206–7. "Help me!" is in English in the Japanese original.

95. Atsuko Ueda, "'Nihongo de kataru koto, 'Nihongo' wo kataru koto," 345; Nakagami Kenji, "Watashi wa 'Nihon'-jin na no ka," 345.

96. Jacques Derrida, "The Tower of Babel," 226.

97. Nakagami Kenji, *Nihongo ni tsuite*, 129.

98. Nakagami Kenji, *Nihongo ni tsuite*, 203.

99. Nakagami Kenji, *Nihongo ni tsuite*, 207.

100. Nakagami Kenji, *Nihongo ni tsuite*, 206, my emphasis.

101. Ueda, "'Nihongo de kataru koto, 'Nihongo' wo kataru koto," 345.

102. Derrida, "Tower of Babel," 226.

103. Derrida, "Tower of Babel," 226.

104. Butler, *Bodies That Matter*, 219.

105. Butler, *Bodies That Matter*, 221.

106. Butler, *Bodies That Matter*, 221.

107. Butler, *Bodies That Matter*, 221.

108. Nakagami Kenji, "Hakai seyo, to Airā wa itta," 54, 21.

109. Nakagami Kenji, *Baffarō Sorujā*, 251–53.

Chapter 4

1. Jacques Derrida and Avital Ronell, "The Law of Genre," 57.

2. Derrida and Ronell, "Law of Genre," 57.

3. C. Douglas Lummis, *Radical Democracy*, 58.

4. Sawada Miki, heiress of the Mitsubishi fortune, founded the Elizabeth Saunders Home for biracial war orphans. Attuned to what Michael Molasky has called a darker shade of difference, Sawada believed that black war orphans in Japan would face more pernicious discrimination than their white counterparts did. It is for this reason that her social work aimed to, among other objectives, uphold social justice for black Japanese orphans.

5. Yoshida Ruiko, *Hāremu no atsui hibi*, 45.

6. Yoshida Ruiko, *Hāremu no atsui hibi*, 45.

7. Yoshida Ruiko, *Hāremu no atsui hibi*, 43, 44.

8. Yoshida Ruiko, *Hāremu no atsui hibi*, 46.

9. Yoshida Ruiko and Kijima Hajime, *Hāremu: Kuroi tenshitachi*, 108. *Harlem: Black Angels* is a bilingual text. The translation of Kijima's poetry here is not mine; it is quoted from the translation provided in the book.

10. Yoshida Ruiko and Kijima Hajime, *Hāremu*, 108.

11. Yoshida Ruiko, *Hāremu no atsui hibi*, 20.

12. Yoshida Ruiko, *Hāremu no atsui hibi*, 194.

13. Miura Masahiro, "Yoshida Ruiko to kokujin-tachi," 31.

14. Yoshida Ruiko, *Hāremu no atsui hibi*, 183, 184.

15. Yoshida Ruiko, *Hāremu no atsui hibi*, 82.

16. Yoshida Ruiko, *Hāremu no atsui hibi*, 9.

17. Yoshida Ruiko, *Hāremu no atsui hibi*, 9.

18. Yoshida Ruiko, *Hāremu no atsui hibi*, 216.

19. Yoshida Ruiko, *Hāremu no atsui hibi*, 217.

20. Russell, "Race and Reflexivity," 15.

21. W. E. B. Du Bois, "The Criteria of Negro Art," 259.

22. Yoshida Ruiko, *Hāremu no atsui hibi*, 196.

23. Yoshida Ruiko, *Hāremu no atsui hibi*, 87.

24. Honda Katsu'ichi, *Amerika gasshūkoku*, 287.

25. Yoshida Ruiko, *Hāremu no atsui hibi*, 199.

26. Honda Katsu'ichi, *Amerika gasshūkoku*, 58.

27. Honda Katsu'ichi, *Amerika gasshūkoku*, 285.

28. Honda Katsu'ichi, *Reporutāju no hōhō*, 98.

29. Honda Katsu'ichi, *Reporutāju no hōhō*, 98.

30. John Lie, "Introduction: Honda Katsuichi and Political and Intellectual Life in Postwar Japan," 18.

31. Lie, "Introduction," 18.

32. Honda Katsu'ichi, *Amerika gasshūkoku*, 141.

33. Honda Katsu'ichi, *Amerika gasshūkoku*, 105.

34. Honda Katsu'ichi, *Amerika gasshūkoku*, 30, emphasis in original.

35. Honda Katsu'ichi, *Amerika gasshūkoku*, 174.

36. Honda Katsu'ichi, *Amerika gasshūkoku*, 174.

37. Honda Katsu'ichi, *Amerika gasshūkoku*, 102.

38. Honda Katsu'ichi, *Amerika gasshūkoku*, 176.

39. Benedict Anderson, *Imagined Communities: Reflections on the Origin and Spread of Nationalism*, 178, emphasis in original.

40. Honda Katsu'ichi, *Amerika gasshūkoku*, 47.

41. Honda Katsu'ichi, *Amerika gasshūkoku*, 147.

42. Honda Katsu'ichi, *Amerika gasshūkoku*, 46, 138.

43. Honda Katsu'ichi, *Amerika gasshūkoku*, 46, 138.

44. Honda Katsu'ichi, *Amerika gasshūkoku* 154, emphasis in original.

45. Honda Katsu'ichi, *Amerika gasshūkoku*, 138.

46. Honda Katsu'ichi, *Korosareru gawa no ronri*, 52.

47. The pun in Honda's title, which substitutes the homophone 州 (state) for 衆 (people, also a key character in the Japanese word for *democracy*), initiates his gambit: it is the states, rather than the people, that are united. To see the United States calls for a view from the parallax perspectives of its people.

48. Honda Katsu'ichi, *Nihongo no sakubun gijutsu*, 202.

49. Honda Katsu'ichi, *Amerika gasshūkoku*, 283.

50. Ariyoshi Sawako, *Hishoku*, 96.

51. Ariyoshi Sawako, *Hishoku*, 176.

52. Ariyoshi Sawako, *Hishoku*, 14.

53. Molasky, *American Occupation of Japan and Okinawa*, 71.

54. Molasky, *American Occupation of Japan and Okinawa*, 71.

55. Ariyoshi Sawako, *Hishoku*, 16.

56. Ariyoshi Sawako, *Hishoku*, 29.

57. Ariyoshi Sawako, *Hishoku*, 29.

58. Toni Morrison, *Beloved*, 200.

59. Morrison, *Beloved*, 251.

60. Ariyoshi Sawako, *Hishoku*, 73.

61. Trudier Harris, *From Mammies to Militants: Domestics in Black American Literature*, 12.

62. Ariyoshi Sawako, *Hishoku*, 85.

63. Ariyoshi Sawako, *Hishoku*, 112.

64. Ariyoshi Sawako, *Hishoku*, 127.

65. The ship metaphor used to describe life in Harlem also resonances with any number of Japanese literary tropes in which the sea voyage transports characters to a world of racial and cultural difference. In addition to the ships used to transport war brides from Japan to the United States, other examples include ships carrying Japanese soldiers to and from their imperial posts, Japanese laborers sailing to plantations in Hawaii and Latin America, and Endō Shūsaku's fictional journeys to racial awakening in France. I highlight the slave ship here in order to note the link between Ariyoshi's description of Harlem and *Not Because of Color*'s westward journey around Africa.

For more on Endō Shūsaku, see Christopher Hill's "Crossed Geographies: Endō and Fanon in Lyon." My thanks to an anonymous reader for bringing this insight to my attention.

66. Ariyoshi Sawako, *Hishoku*, 137.

67. Ariyoshi Sawako, *Hishoku*, 321.

68. Ariyoshi Sawako, *Hishoku*, 395.

69. Ariyoshi Sawako, *Hishoku*, 322–23.

70. Ariyoshi Sawako, *Hishoku*, 406.

71. Frantz Fanon, "The Fact of Blackness," 17, ellipses in original.

72. See Yoko McClain, "Ariyoshi Sawako: Creative Social Critic," 215. McClain writes that the conclusion of *Not Because of Color* is "disappointingly simplistic and weak," but it represents "Emiko's realization that she is the wife of a black man and the mother of black children, and thus she herself should also live her life as a Negro without shunning the responsibilities assigned to her, no matter how harsh her life becomes."

73. Morimura Seiichi, "Shohan atogaki," 500. This rationale is drawn from the original postscript to *Ningen no shōmei* (Human Proof). In the afterword to the 2004 edition, Morimura would amend this assessment, writing that the text was not a product of chance but "a work that the era demanded" (*jidai ga yōkyū shita sakuhin*). Morimura Seiichi, "Shin-seihan atogaki," 502. Given the content of *Human Proof*, Morimura's updated assessment speaks to the ways in which the long 1970s served as a milieu for the genericity discussed in the final section of this chapter.

74. Morimura Seiichi, "Shin-seihan atogaki," 502.

75. Morimura Seiichi, "Ningen no shōmei."

76. The date of birth noted on Johnny's passport, which is recovered after his death, would make him twenty-four years old at the time of his murder. Toward the end of the novel, however, it is revealed that Johnny was born in Japan in the immediate postwar period and his date of birth, October 1950, was mostly likely fabricated by his father.

77. Morimura Seiichi, *Ningen no shōmei*, 7.

78. In both French and Japanese transliteration, *étranger* also carries the connotation of an alien in the legal sense of the term.

79. Morimura Seiichi, *Ningen no shōmei*, 47.

80. Morimura Seiichi, *Ningen no shōmei*, 7.

81. Morimura Seiichi, *Ningen no shōmei*, 18.

82. The plot of *Human Proof* is composed of three intertwined mysteries: the search for Johnny's killer, the search for a missing person due to an unreported death caused by a hit-and-run, and the search for the identity of American soldiers who assaulted Detective Munesue's father. In each of these mysteries, the human body itself serves as the physical evidence needed to solve the case. This is a second argument for the *Human Proof* translation.

83. See Morimura Seiichi, "Shohan atogaki."

84. Saijō Yaso, "Boku no bōshi," 27. Although the excerpts translated here are from a different volume, this version is an exact reproduction of the poem as it is recorded in *The Complete Anthology of Saijō Yaso*, the collection found by the detectives in *Human Proof*.

85. Saijō Yaso, "Boku no bōshi," 27.

86. Saijō Yaso, "Boku no bōshi," 27.

87. This translation is by Joan Ericson in "Introduction," *A Rainbow in the Desert: An Anthology of Early Twentieth-Century Japanese Children's Literature*, xii.

88. Morimura Seiichi, "Shohan atogaki," 497, 498.

89. "allusion, n," *OED Online*.

90. Morimura Seiichi, *Ningen no shōmei*, 34.

91. The hotel is located in Chiyoda ward, the seat of political power in Japan. The ward houses, among other buildings, the Imperial Palace, the National Diet building, and the Supreme Court.

92. Chris Baldick, *The Oxford Dictionary of Literary Terms*, 9.

93. Morimura Seiichi, *Ningen no shōmei*, 212.

94. Nielsen, *Writing between the Lines*, 22.

95. Ronald Thomas, *Detective Fiction and the Rise of Forensic Science*, 3–4.

96. Christopher Bolton, *Sublime Voices: The Fictional Science and Scientific Fiction of Abe Kōbō*, 133.

97. Ōe Kenzaburō, "Kaisetsu," 348–49.

98. Darko Suvin, "On the Poetics of the Science Fiction Genre," 374.

99. Suvin, "On the Poetics of the Science Fiction Genre," 374, 375.

100. Arthur C. Clarke, "Foreword," ix.

101. Bolton, *Sublime Voices*, 57.

102. Abe Kōbō, *Tanin no kao*, 313.

103. This is the passing reference to racism: "Undoubtedly, it's doubtful whether or not things like the problems of racial discrimination . . . could even exist if humans didn't have faces." Abe Kōbō, "Tanin no kao," 195. The musings of the narrator of *Tanin no kao* are recorded in three notebooks: (in the order they are presented in the novel) a black notebook, a white notebook, and a gray notebook. The final notebook, which concludes *Tanin no kao* and includes the passage on the Harlem Riots, was not published in *Gunzo* magazine.

104. Abe Kōbō, *Tanin no kao*, 313.

105. Richard Calichman, *Beyond Nation: Time, Writing, and Community in the Work of Abe Kobo*, 142.

106. Calichman, *Beyond Nation*, 142.

107. Fanon, "Fact of Blackness," 291.

108. Calichman, *Beyond Nation*, 142.

109. See Calichman, *Beyond Nation*, 142.

110. Ellison, *Invisible Man*, 3, emphasis in original.

111. Derrida and Ronell, "Law of Genre," 57.

112. John Frow, *Genre*, 28.

113. Derrida and Ronell, "Law of Genre," 65, emphasis in original.

114. Frow, *Genre*, 2.

115. Morimura Seiichi, *Ningen no shōmei*, 325.

116. Morimura Seiichi, *Ningen no shōmei*, 330, 331.

117. Yoshida Ruiko, *Hāremu no atsui hibi*, 12.

118. Yoshida Ruiko, *Hāremu no atsui hibi*, 12.

119. Honda Katsu'ichi, *Amerika gasshūkoku*, 141.

120. Ariyoshi Sawako, *Hishoku*, 17.

121. Sheldon Garon, *Molding Japanese Minds: The State in Everyday Life*, 58.

122. Eddie Glaude, *Democracy in Black: How Race Still Enslaves the American Soul*, 9.

123. Matt. 25:40–43: "And the king will answer, 'Truly I tell you: anything you did for one of my brothers here, however insignificant [the brother], you did for me.' Then he will say to those on his left, 'A curse is on you; go from my sight to the eternal fire that is ready for the devil and his angels. For when I was hungry, you gave me nothing to eat; when thirsty, nothing to drink; when I was a stranger, you did not welcome me; when I was naked, you did not clothe me; when I was ill and in prison, you did not come to my help." *The Oxford Study Bible: Revised English Bible with the Apocrypha*, 1298.

124. Abe Kōbō, "Discovering America," 53, 57. The translation of Abe is Calichman's.

125. Sarutya Kaname, *Hāremu no atsui hibi*, 227.

126. Honda Katsu'ichi, *Amerika gasshūkoku*, 48, 47.

127. Ariyoshi Sawako, *Hishoku*, 124.

128. Ariyoshi Sawako, *Hishoku*, 138.

129. Morimura Seiichi, *Ningen no shōmei*, 79, 82.

130. John Russell, *Sambo's Step-Children: Western Hegemony and the Construction of the Black Other in Japan*, 187.

131. Yoshida Ruiko, *Hāremu no atsui hibi*, 16.

132. This compromise, reached during the 1787 US Constitutional Convention, stipulated that three-fifths of the slave population would be "counted" in calculations of the population of slave states, which in turn impacted the number of seats slave states would hold in the US House of Representatives.

133. Takuma Hideo. "Chibikuro sambo de kangaeru koto," 27.

134. Ōe Kenzaburō. "Sengo sedai no imēji," 17. Nina Cornyetz and I have written about the gendered implications of this claim in the introduction to Bridges and Cornyetz, *Traveling Texts and the Work of Afro-Japanese Cultural Production*.

135. Elaine Scarry, *The Body in Pain: The Making and Unmaking of the World*, 125.

136. Honda Katsu'ichi, *Korosareru gawa no ronri*, 87; Ariyoshi Sawako, *Hishoku*, 364; Abe Kōbō, *Tanin no kao*, 313.
137. James Baldwin, *The Fire Next Time*, 4, 21.
138. Yoshida Ruiko, *Hāremu no atsui hibi*, 226.
139. Ariyoshi Sawako, *Hishoku*, 408.
140. Honda Katsu'ichi, *Amerika gasshūkoku*, 169, 170.
141. Abe Kōbō, *Tanin no kao*, 340.
142. Morimura Seiichi, *Ningen no shōmei*, 45.
143. Morimura Seiichi, *Ningen no shōmei*, 493.
144. Morimura Seiichi, *Ningen no shōmei*, 494.
145. Morimura Seiichi, *Ningen no shōmei*, 494–95.
146. Carolyn Miller, "Genre as Social Action," 36.
147. Jonathan Crimmins, "Gender, Genre, and the Near Future in Derrida's 'The Law of Genre,'" 51.
148. Crimmins, "Gender, Genre, and the Near Future in Derrida's 'The Law of Genre,'" 51.
149. Rey Chow, "The Interruption of Referentiality: Poststructuralism and the Conundrum of Critical Multiculturalism," 184.

Chapter 5

1. To provide a historical answer to this question, the 1983 release in Japan of *Wild Style*, a classic of hip hop cinema, catalyzed the creation of Japanese hip hop culture. The film was promoted in Japan by the cast of *Wild Style*, which furthered the popularity of both the film and hip hop. Shortly after the debut of *Wild Style*, Japanese musicians and B-Boys (or break-boys, that is, hip hoppers who dance during the lyricless breaks of songs) took to Yoyogi Park, which quickly became an incubator for Japanese hip hop culture. This was followed by the 1985 release of Itō Seikō's *Gyōkai-kun monogatari*, which was arguably Japan's first rap album. This chapter considers novels, music, and music criticism composed between 1985 and 2004.
2. Imani Perry, "Justin Timberlake, 'The 20/20 Experience': Is There a Visual Preference for Whiteness?"
3. Zora Neale Hurston, "Characteristics of Negro Expression," 1042; Nina Eidsheim, "Race and the Aesthetics of Vocal Timbre," 341.
4. Condry, *Hip-Hop Japan*, 30.
5. David A. Hollinger, "The Concept of Post-racial: How Its Easy Dismissal Obscures Important Questions," 174–75, my emphasis.
6. Touré, "Visible Young Man," *New York Times Book Review*, quoted in Hollinger, "Concept of Post-Racial," 177.
7. President of the Spokane, Washington, chapter of the NAACP from 2014–15,

Rachel Dolezal, who was born to white parents, resigned from her post as president after she was outed for "passing" as African American.

8. Kuchiroro, "Hippu hoppu no shoki shōdō." The Far East Network is now the American Forces Network. I have taken liberties in the translation in order to preserve the rhyme.

9. Noriko Manabe, "Globalization and Japanese Creativity: Adaptations of Japanese Language to Rap," 5.

10. Tricia Rose, *Black Noise: Rap Music and Black Culture in Contemporary America*, 2.

11. This concern has plagued Japanese hip hop since its inception. Japanese hip hop had a bifurcated origin: college-educated rappers such as Itō Seikō and the B-boy crews that took to Yoyogi Park, who tended to be more worldly than their college-educated counterparts (e.g., DJ Krush dropped out of high school and worked for the *yakuza*). This split portended the debates on the authenticity of underground rap compared to that of so-called party rap, a topic of serious conversation in Japanese hip hop circles in the 1990s. For more on this, see Gotō Akio, *J rappu izen: Hippu hoppu karuchā wa kōshite umareta*.

12. Itō Seikō and Saeki Kenzō, "Ai shiteru o kowasanakya Nihongo wa kaerarenai," 83.

13. Noriko Manabe, "Globalization and Japanese Creativity," 1.

14. Itō Seikō and Saeki Kenzō "Ai shiteru o kowasanakya Nihongo wa kaerarenai," 82.

15. Itō Seikō and Saeki Kenzō "Ai shiteru o kowasanakya Nihongo wa kaerarenai," 79.

16. Itō Seikō and Saeki Kenzō "Ai shiteru o kowasanakya Nihongo wa kaerarenai," 79.

17. Itō Seikō and Saeki Kenzō "Ai shiteru o kowasanakya Nihongo wa kaerarenai," 80.

18. Itō Seikō, "Itō Seikō," 257.

19. Itō Seikō, "Itō Seikō," 257.

20. Itō Seikō, "Oretachi datte, damashite yo: J poppu na Nihongo, sono imi wa," 74. This desire to destroy artificial Japanese with rhyme and leave a creative, clever vernacular in its wake was already on display in the *Music* magazine dialogue, hence Seikō's preface to his thoughts on artificial Japanese and clever black vernaculars: "Actually, when you're rapping, there's a way to escape from the Japanese language." For the *Music* rendition, see Itō Seikō and Saeki Kenzō, "Ai shiteru o kowasanakya Nihongo wa kaerarenai," 80.

21. According to Seikō, his pre-1988 hip hop ventures (his work on the 1985 *Gyōkai-kun monogatari* [The Tale of Mr. Business] and his 1986 *Kensetsuteki* [Constructive]) placed less emphasis on rhyme. A listen to either of these albums evinces this claim. For more on this, see Itō Seikō, "Itō Seikō."

22. Itō Seikō, *Mess/Age* liner notes. All quotations from *Mess/Age* are based on the 1995 rerelease.

23. Condry, *Hip Hop Japan*, 135.

24. Itō Seikō, "Mess/Age."

25. Itō Seikō, "Mess/Age."

26. Itō Seikō, "Mess/Age."

27. Definitions here from the *Oxford English Dictionary*.

28. Itō Seikō, "Itō Seikō," 257.

29. One way of reading this understanding of *affinity* is to consider it against the history of Japanese rap. The 1990s would see debates between Japanese exponents of "party" and "underground" rap. Preempting the spirit of those debates, this tension can be read as the before-and-after commentary of Japanese rappers first facing the question of how to determine the authenticity of one's rap. Another way of reading this notion of affinity would be to consider it as a kind of respectful refusal to cross the color line of rap, an admission that Japanese rappers might not have the bona fides required for admission.

30. Condry, *Hip Hop Japan*, 29.

31. Condry, *Hip Hop Japan*, 28.

32. Condry, *Hip Hop Japan*, 29, my emphasis.

33. Condry, *Hip Hop Japan*, 34.

34. Condry, *Hip Hop Japan*, 41, 46, 45, my emphasis.

35. I am reminded here of Stephen Henderson, who begins with the premise that "structurally speaking, Black poetry is most distinctly and effectively *Black* [when] it derives its form from two basic sources, Black speech and Black music," and ends up with the question of whether black poetry can be "Poetry which is somehow *structurally* Black, irrespective of authorship. . . . What distinguishes a Claude McKay sonnet from a sonnet by Longfellow? . . . Is it possible that, given a Black Poetic Structure, a non-Black can create in this form—as whites play jazz for example?" Stephen Henderson, *Understanding the New Black Poetry: Black Speech and Black Music as Poetic References*, 30–31, 8–9.

36. West, "New Cultural Politics of Difference," 109.

37. Itō Seikō and Kenzō Saeki, "Ai shiteru o kowasanakya Nihongo wa kaerarenai," 83.

38. Condry, *Hip-Hop Japan*, 45.

39. Noriko Manabe, "Hip-Hop in Japan: Alternative Stories," 249.

40. Imani Perry, *Prophets of the Hood: Politics and Poetics of Hip Hop*, 63.

41. Justin A. Williams, "Intertextuality, Sampling, and Copyright," 207.

42. Itō Seikō, @seikoito, 6 April 2015.

43. Itō Seikō, "Message."

44. John Szwed, *Space Is the Place: The Lives and Times of Sun Ra*, 134.

45. Itō Seikō, *Sōzō rajio*, 10.

46. Williams, "Intertextuality, Sampling, and Copyright," 209.

47. Noriko Manabe, "Representing Japan: 'National' Style among Japanese Hip-Hop DJs," 44.

48. Nina Cornyetz, "The Theatrics of Japanese Blackface: Body as Mannequin," 49.

49. Cornyetz, "Theatrics of Japanese Blackface," 49.

50. Lawrence Grossberg, "Reflections of a Disappointed Popular Music Scholar," 47.

51. Grossberg, "Reflections of a Disappointed Popular Music Scholar," 47.

52. Grossberg, "Reflections of a Disappointed Popular Music Scholar," 47.

53. In his early days, Itō Seikō positioned himself as a kind of rap pedagogue for a Japanese audience. His teaching tools included the aforementioned "rhyme bible," which lined the cover of *Mess/Age*, and brief lectures on rap delivered to his live audiences at hip hop venues.

54. The Akutagawa Prize committee was split in its assessment of *Kaigo nyūmon*. Some saw Mobu's hip hop narration as a gimmick (Kono Taeko's assessment is particularly scathing). Others saw it as a technique for giving voice to an otherwise voiceless generation.

55. Miyamoto Teru, "Yokei na kyōzatsubutsu," 383.

56. Mobu Norio, *Kaigo nyūmon*, 5.

57. Mobu Norio, *Kaigo nyūmon*, 11.

58. Mobu Norio, *Kaigo nyūmon*, 37.

59. Mobu Norio, *Kaigo nyūmon*, 38.

60. Condry, *Hip-Hop Japan*, 142, 141.

61. Mobu Norio, *Kaigo nyūmon*, 40.

62. Mobu Norio, *Kaigo nyūmon*, 45.

63. Mobu Norio, *Kagio nyūmon*, 88.

64. Jennifer Robertson, "Human Rights vs. Robot Rights: Forecasts from Japan," 578.

65. Mobu Norio, *Kagio nyūmon*, 24–25.

66. Mobu Norio, *Kagio nyūmon*, 28–29.

67. Mobu Norio, *Kagio nyūmon*, 16–17. The narrator's father and grandfather are both deceased, which raises the stakes of the narrator's hip hop redefinition of productive masculinity.

68. Mobu Norio, *Kagio nyūmon*, 42–43.

69. Cornel West, "Black Culture and Postmodernism," 395.

70. Miyamoto Teru, "Yokei na kyōzatsubutsu," 384, 383.

71. Ishihara Shintaro, "Mosho, natsugare," 380.

72. "Cloud, or Silver Linings?"

73. Mobu Norio, *Kaigo nyūmon*, 85.

74. As cited by Kristina Iwata-Weickgenannt, "Kirino Natsuo's *Metabola* or the Okinawan Stage, Fractured Selves, and the Precarity of Contemporary Existence," 27.

75. Mobu Norio, *Kaigo nyūmon*, 97.

76. bell hooks, "Postmodern Blackness," 514.

77. Mobu Norio, *Kaigo nyūmon*, 105.

78. Mobu Norio, "Bungaku kara ataerareta chikara," 238–39.

79. See Sterling, "Searching for Self in the Global South."

80. Mobu Norio, *Kaigo nyūmon*, 52.

81. Yamada Eimi, "Senpyō," 385.

82. Seikō is referring to Yamada's popular Pon-chan series. Pon-chan (Ms. Pon) is an alter ego of Yamada. The series features autobiographical essays and cultural critiques written in the no-holds-barred voice of Pon-chan. One signature of the series is interstitial mock advertisements, which separate the essays in the collection. The advertisements typically include puns on "Pon." One example is an advertisement for a "frying pon." Seikō's comment refers to a similar pun on the Japanese expression for "I love you."

83. Satō Ai, "Kokujin to chokorēto: Yamada Eimi *Beddo taimu aizu* ron," 128. There is a way in which Satō's critique is not characteristic of Japanese scholarship on Yamada. It has more in common with American criticism of Yamada. Compare Satō, for example, to Richard Okada, who writes that "Yamada's discursive appropriations are ultimately self-serving and narcissistic . . . and somehow true to a 'self' whose desire remains unquestioned." There is a skein of Japanese critics who laud Yamada for the "realism" and ethics of her portrayals of blackness. See, for example, Kono Taeko's claim that Yamada is "well beyond the realism of yesteryear," Shibata Shōji's claim that Yamada's black characters (unlike those in "Shiiku" and "American School") are portrayed as everyday people living with Japanese people, or Akasaki Moeko's claim that Yamada takes an ethical stance as she "stares at reality and tries to ascertain it to the fullest." Richard Okada, "Positioning Subjects Globally: A Reading of Yamada Eimi," 122; Kono Taeko, quoted in Hasegawa Kei, "Seiai no gensetsu: Beddo taimu aizu," 67; Shibata Shōji, "Nichijō no seiritsu *Jesshī no seboni* Yamada Eimi"; Akasaki Moeko, "Yamada Eimi: Ningen byōsha ni miru sakka no rinri," 179.

84. Okada, "Positioning Subjects Globally," 123

85. Russell, "Consuming Passions," 128, 129, 130.

86. Yamada Eimi, *Watashi wa henondōbutsu*, 169–70.

87. I use "style lately" not as a synonym for "contemporary" but to differentiate Yamada's 2003 *Payday!!!* from her works from the mid-1980s and early 1990s. I also have in mind the fact that Said's notion of "late style" refers to artistic shifts prompted by grappling with mortality and impending death, and I assume that this phase in Yamada's work is a newfound style rather than a closing chapter. With that said, ele-

ments of what I call Yamada's style lately can be seen in some of her more contemporary works. One example is her 2010 *Tainī sutōrīzu* (Tiny Stories).

88. Yamada Eimi, *Payday!!!*, 14.

89. Yamada Eimi, *Payday!!!*, 208. The parenthetical explanation of "beat" and "flow" is in the Japanese original. I discuss this narratival strategy momentarily.

90. Yamada Eimi, *Payday!!!*, 14.

91. Yamada Eimi, *Payday!!!*, 14.

92. Yamada Eimi, *Payday!!!*, 206.

93. Yamada Eimi, *Payday!!!*, 17.

94. Yamada Eimi, *Payday!!!*, 275.

95. Yamada Eimi, *Payday!!!*, 208.

96. Yamada Eimi, *Payday!!!*, 208.

97. David Morris, "The Sakura of Madness: Japan's Nationalist Hip Hop and the Parallax of Globalized Identity Politics," 476.

98. Yamada Eimi, *Soul Music Lovers Only*, 214–15.

99. Yamada Eimi, *Soul Music Lovers Only*, 214–15.

100. Kubota Toshinobu and Yamada Eimi, "Nihonjin dakara daseru kokujinpoi shinsensa, omoshirosa," 74.

101. The three elements noted here are not exhaustive. We might add, for example, the level of the paratext. All the chapter titles of *Payday!!!*, as well as the title of the novel itself, are written in English and glossed with Japanese translations. This, in conjunction with the techniques discussed in this section, gives the reader the impression that *Payday!!!* is a "black" story presented in Japanese translation. Here black characters "speak for themselves," and Yamada simply serves as our Japanese amanuensis.

102. Yamada Eimi, *Payday!!!*, 15.

103. Yamada Eimi, *Payday!!!*, 16.

104. Roland Barthes, "The Reality Effect," 141, 148.

105. Nina Cornyetz, "Power and Gender in the Narratives of Yamada Eimi," 452–53.

106. That Robin discovers Harmony's black masculinity through Charlie Patton is a testament to the transition from sensual blackness to performed, "postracial" blackness that Yamada attempts to style lately. Indeed, as Stephen Calt and Gayle Wardlow note in *King of the Delta Blues: The Life and Music of Charlie Patton*, there was something racially ambiguous about Patton's face, and he was able to pass for white. His life and race, Calt and Wardlow propose, was thus interpreted through his musical performances rather than the other way around.

107. Yamada Eimi, *Payday!!!*, 65.

108. I should note that this is a technique that Yamada employs in other texts as well. Although the intertextual focus in *Payday!!!* (for reasons discussed in the preceding section) is a mix of hip hop and non-hip-hop texts, Yamada's primary intertextual

link is with James Baldwin. When Spoon is described as reminiscent of "Brother Rufus in the Baldwin novel," or when *Animal Logic* becomes reminiscent of *Giovanni's Room*, Yamada intimates that she is literate in black fiction, thereby bolstering her qualifications to write black fiction in Japanese. Yamada Eimi, *Beddo taimu aizu*, 41.

109. Butler, *Bodies That Matter*, 95, emphasis in original.

110. Butler, *Bodies that Matter*, 95, 118.

111. Yamada Eimi, *Payday!!!*, 221.

112. Yamada Eimi, *Payday!!!*, 221.

113. Yamada Eimi, *Payday!!!*, 26.

114. Yamada Eimi, *Payday!!!*, 89.

115. Yamada Eimi, *Payday!!!*, 90.

116. Yamada Eimi, *Payday!!!*, 94.

117. Yamada Eimi, *Payday!!!*, 274.

118. Yamada Eimi, *Payday!!!*, 273.

119. Yamada Eimi, *Payday!!!*, 274.

120. Yamada Eimi, *Payday!!!*, 108.

121. Eduardo Bonilla-Silva, *Racism without Racists: Color-Blind Racism and the Persistence of Racial Inequality in America*, 8.

122. Bonilla-Silva, *Racism without Racists*, 179.

123. Yamada Eimi, *Payday!!!*, 17.

124. Bonilla-Silva, *Racism without Racists*, 9.

125. Stuart Hall, *Stuart Hall: Race, the Floating Signifier*, 15, 16.

126. See David Goldberg, *Are We All Postracial Yet?*

127. Andre Craddock-Willis, "Rap Music and the Black Musical Tradition," quoted in Rose, *Black Noise*, 23.

128. Rose, *Black Noise*, 25, 34.

129. Azuma Hiroki, *Otaku*, 16.

130. Hikita Kunio, *Kyōki no sakura*, 199. Here I have taken a line from Hikita's 2000 novel and read it against its film adaptation, which was directed by Sonoda Kenji and released in 2002. I have taken this liberty because Hikita was involved in the writing of the screenplay for the film adaptation.

131. Paul Gilroy, *Against Race: Imagining Political Culture beyond the Color Line*, 51.

132. Butler, *Bodies That Matter*, 219.

133. Gilroy, *Against Race*, 324.

134. Giorgio Agamben, *The Coming Community*, 2, emphasis in original.

Conclusion

1. Morris, "Sakura of Madness," 467.

2. Morris, "Sakura of Madness," 467.

3. Morris, "Sakura of Madness," 468.

4. Chandler, "Introduction," 5.

5. Chandler, "Introduction," 27.

6. Russell, "Race and Reflexivity," 4.

7. Rey Chow, "Brushes with the-Other-as-Face: Stereotyping and Cross-Ethnic Representation," 52.

8. Chandler, "Introduction," 5.

9. Gerald Horne, "Tokyo Bound: African Americans and Japan Confront White Supremacy," 16.

10. George Schuyler, *Black No More*, 228.

11. Schuyler, *Black No More*, 221.

12. Richard Wright, *Haiku: Kono bessekai*, 156, 144, 117.

13. Kevin Allen Leonard, "'In the Interest of All Races': African Americans and Interracial Cooperation in Los Angeles during and after World War II," quoted in Keith Wilhite, "Mapping Black and Brown L.A.: Zoot Suit Riots as Spatial Subtext in *If He Hollers Let Him Go*," 131.

14. Chester Himes, *If He Hollers Let Him Go*, 4–5.

15. Arimitsu Michio, "Playing the Dozens on Zen: Amiri Baraka's Journey from a 'Pre-black' Bohemian Outsider to a 'Post-American Low Coup' Poet," 90.

16. Amiri Baraka, *Digging: The Afro-American Soul of American Classical Music*, 403, quoted in Arimitsu, "Playing the Dozens on Zen," 91.

17. Amiri Baraka, *Un Poco Low Coups*, 4.

18. Neal Stephenson, *Snow Crash*, 2.

19. Neal Stephenson, *Snow Crash*, 19–20.

20. Stephenson, *Snow Crash*, 30.

21. Junot Diaz, *The Brief Wondrous Life of Oscar Wao*, 18.

22. Michiko Kakutani, "Travails of an Outcast."

23. Diaz, *The Brief Wondrous Life of Oscar Wao*, 21, 48.

24. Diaz, *The Brief Wondrous Life of Oscar Wao*, 197.

25. Junot Diaz, "The Search for Decolonial Love: An Interview with Junot Diaz."

Bibliography

@seikoito. *Twitter*, 6 April 2015.

Abe, Kōbō. "Discovering America." *The Frontier Within: Essays by Abe Kobo*. Trans. Richard Calichman. Columbia University Press, 2013. 47–60.

Abe, Kōbō. "Tanin no kao." *Gunzō* 19, no. 1 (1964): 118–201.

Abe, Kōbō. *Tanin no kao*. Shinchōsha, 2013.

Abe, Tomoji. *Koi to afurika*. Shinchōsha, 1935.

Abel, Jonathan. *Redacted: The Archives of Censorship in Transwar Japan*. University of California Press, 2012.

Abel, Marco. *Violent Affect: Literature, Cinema, and Critique after Representation*. University of Nebraska Press, 2007.

Affeldt, Steven. "The Force of Freedom: Rousseau on Forcing to Be Free." *Political Theory* 27, no. 3 (1999): 299–333.

Agamben, Giorgio. "Example." *The Coming Community*. Trans. Michael Hardt. University of Minnesota Press, 1993.

Agamben, Giorgio. *The Coming Community*. Trans. Michael Hardt. University of Minnesota Press, 1993.

Akasaki, Moeko. "Yamada Eimi: Ningen byōsha ni miru sakka no rinri." *Fukuoka daigaku Nihongo Nihon bungaku* 16 (2006): 152–81.

Amos, Timothy. *Embodying Difference: The Making of Burakumin in Modern Japan*. University of Hawaii Press, 2011.

Anderson, Benedict. *Imagined Communities: Reflections on the Origin and Spread of Nationalism*. 2nd ed. Verso, 1991.

Andō, Hajime. *Ishikawa Jun ron*. Ōfūsha, 1987.

Arimitsu, Michio. "Playing the Dozens on Zen: Amiri Baraka's Journey from a 'Pre-black' Bohemian Outsider to a 'Post-American Low Coup' Poet." *Traveling Texts and the Work of Afro-Japanese Cultural Production: Two Haiku and a Microphone*. Ed. William H. Bridges and Nina Cornyetz. Lexington Books, 2015. 79–98.

Ariyoshi, Sawako. *Akujo ni tsuite*. Shinchōsha, 1978.

Ariyoshi, Sawako. *Geisha warutsu Itariano.* Chūō Kōronsha, 1959.

Ariyoshi, Sawako. *Hishoku.* Kadokawa, 1999.

Ariyoshi, Sawako. *Onna futari no Nyū Ginia.* Asahi Shimbunsha, 1969.

Ariyoshi, Sawako. *Pueruto Riko nikki.* Bungei Shunjū, 1964.

Atkins, E. Taylor. *Blue Nippon: Authenticating Jazz in Japan.* Duke University Press, 2001.

Azuma, Hiroki. *Otaku: Japan's Database Animals.* Trans. Jonathan Abel and Shion Kono. University of Minnesota Press, 2009.

Baldick, Chris. *The Oxford Dictionary of Literary Terms.* Oxford University Press, 2008.

Baldwin, James. *Another Country.* Dial Press, 1962.

Baldwin, James. "The Black Boy Looks at the White Boy Norman Mailer." *Esquire,* 1 May 1961, 102–6.

Baldwin, James. *The Fire Next Time: Go Tell It On the Mountain, The Fire Next Time, If Beale Street Could Talk.* Black Expressions Book Club, 2004.

Baldwin, James. *Giovanni's Room.* Delta Trade Paperbacks, 2000.

Baldwin, James. "Here Be Dragons." *The Price of the Ticket: Collected Nonfiction, 1948–1985.* St. Martin's, 1985. 677–90.

Baldwin, James. *Nobody Knows My Name* [and] *More Notes of a Native Son.* Dial Press, 1961.

Baldwin, James. *Notes of a Native Son.* Beacon Press, 1955.

Baraka, Amiri. "Black Art." *Selected Poetry of Amiri Baraka/LeRoi Jones.* Morrow, 1979. 106–7.

Baraka, Amiri. *Digging: The Afro-American Soul of American Classical Music.* University of California Press, 2009.

Baraka, Amiri. *Un Poco Low Coups.* Ishmael Reed Publishing, 2004.

Barash, David. "Race (Part 1)." *Chronicle of Higher Education,* 9 April 2012.

Barthes, Roland. "The Reality Effect." *Roland Barthes: The Rustle of Language.* Trans. Richard Howard. Hill and Wang, 1987. 141–48.

"Beigun ga ikan no i wo hyōmei." *Asahi shimbun,* Kitakyushu evening edition, 18 July 1950.

Benjamin, Walter. "The Task of the Translator." *Selected Writings. Vol. 1: 1913–1926.* Ed. Marcus Bullock and Michael Jennings. Harvard University Press, 2004. 253–63.

Bennington, Geoffrey. "A Moment of Madness: Derrida's Kierkegaard." *Oxford Literary Review* 33, no. 1 (2011): 103–27.

Best, Stephen, and Sharon Marcus. "Surface Reading: An Introduction." *Representations* 108, no. 1 (2009): 1–21.

Bolton, Christopher. *Sublime Voices: The Fictional Science and Scientific Fiction of Abe Kōbō.* Harvard University Press, 2009.

Bonilla-Silva, Eduardo. *Racism without Racists: Color-Blind Racism and the Persistence of Racial Inequality in America.* Rowman and Littlefield, 2010.

Bowers, William, William Hammond, and George MacGarrigle. *Black Soldier, White Army: The 24th Infantry Regiment in Korea*. Center of Military History, United States Army, 1996.

Bridges, William H., and Nina Cornyetz, eds. *Traveling Texts and the Work of Afro-Japanese Cultural Production: Two Haiku and a Microphone*. Lexington Books, 2015.

Brooks, Peter. *Reading for the Plot: Design and Intention in Narrative*. Clarendon, 1984.

Buraku kaihō Kyoto-fu rengōkai. "Wareware wa shisei to ika ni tatakau ka: *Ōru romansu* sabetsu kyūdan yōkō." *Kyoto no burakushi*. Vol. 9. Ed. Inoue Kiyoshi. *Kyoto burakushi kenkyūjo*, 1987. 537–58.

Butler, Judith. *Bodies That Matter: On the Discursive Limits of "Sex."* Routledge, 1993.

Calichman, Richard. *Beyond Nation: Time, Writing, and Community in the Work of Abe Kobo*. Stanford University Press, 2016.

Calt, Stephen, and Gayle Wardlow. *King of the Delta Blues: The Life and Music of Charlie Patton*. Rock Chapel Press, 1988.

Carter, Mitzi Uehara. "Nappy Routes and Tangled Tales: Critical Ethnography in a Militarised Okinawa." *Under Occupation: Resistance and Struggle in a Militarised Asia-Pacific*. Ed. Peter Simpson, Daniel Broudy, and Makoto Arakaki. Cambridge Scholars Publishing, 2013. 8–28.

Chance, Linda. *Formless in Form: Kenko, Tsurezuregusa, and the Rhetoric of Japanese Fragmentary Prose*. Stanford University Press, 1997.

Chandler, Nahum. "Introduction: On the Virtues of Seeing—at Least, but Never Only—Double." *CR: The New Centennial Review* 12, no. 1 (2012): 1–39.

Chinen, Seishin. "The Human Pavilion." *Islands of Protest: Japanese Literature from Okinawa*. Ed. Davinder L. Bhowmik and Steve Rabson. Trans. Robert Tierney. University of Hawai'i Press, 2016. 231–91.

Cho, Jung-Min. "Kojima Nobuo 'Amerikan sukūru' ron." *Comparatio* 5 (2001): 156–62.

Chow, Rey. "Brushes with the-Other-as-Face: Stereotyping and Cross-Ethnic Representation." *The Rey Chow Reader*. Ed. Paul Bowman. Columbia University Press, 2010. 48–55.

Chow, Rey. "The Interruption of Referentiality: Poststructuralism and the Conundrum of Critical Multiculturalism." *South Atlantic Quarterly* 101, no. 1 (2002): 171–86.

Chow, Rey. "The Old/New Question of Comparison in Literary Studies: A Post-European Perspective." *ELH* 71, no. 2 (2004): 289–311.

Claremont, Yasuko. *The Novels of Ōe Kenzaburō*. Routledge, 2009.

Clarke, Arthur C. "Foreword." *The Collected Stories of Arthur C. Clarke*. Orb Books, 2000. ix–x.

Clinton, George. "Atomic Dog." *Computer Games*. Capitol Records, 1982.

"Cloud, or Silver Linings?" *The Economist*, 26 July 2007. Accessed 3 October 2015. http://www.economist.com/node/9539825

Condry, Ian. *Hip-Hop Japan: Rap and the Paths of Cultural Globalization*. Duke University Press, 2006.

Cornyetz, Nina. *Dangerous Women, Deadly Words: Phallic Fantasy and Modernity in Three Japanese Writers*. Stanford University Press, 1999.

Cornyetz, Nina. "Murakami Takashi and the Hell of Others: Sexual (In)Difference, the Eye, and the Gaze in ©*Murakami*." *Criticism* 54, no. 2 (2012): 181–95.

Cornyetz, Nina. "Power and Gender in the Narratives of Yamada Eimi." *The Woman's Hand: Gender and Theory in Japanese Women's Writing*. Ed. Paul Schalow and Janet Walker. Stanford University Press, 1996. 425–57.

Cornyetz, Nina. "The Theatrics of Japanese Blackface: Body as Mannequin." *Traveling Texts and the Work of Afro-Japanese: Two Haiku and a Microphone*. Ed. William H. Bridges and Nina Cornyetz. Lexington Books, 2005. 45–56.

Craddock-Willis, Andre. "Rap Music and the Black Musical Tradition: A Critical Assessment." *Radical America* 23, no. 4 (1991): 29–38.

Cramer, Jennifer. "'Do We Really Want to Be Like Them'? Indexing Europeanness through Pronominal Use." *Discourse Society* 21, no. 6 (2010): 619–37.

Crimmins, Jonathan. "Gender, Genre, and the Near Future in Derrida's 'The Law of Genre.'" *Diacritics* 39, no. 1 (2009): 45–51, 53–60.

Damasio, Antonio. *The Self Comes to Mind: Constructing the Conscious Brain*. Pantheon, 2010.

Danow, David. *Models of Narrative: Theory and Practice*. St. Martin's, 1997.

Davis, Colin. "Hauntology, Spectres, and Phantoms." *French Studies* 59, no. 3 (2005): 373–79.

Deleuze, Gilles, and Félix Guattari. *Kafka: Toward a Minor Literature*. Trans. Dana Polan. University of Minnesota Press, 1986.

Derrida, Jacques. "Des Tours de Babel." *Difference in Translation*. Ed. Joseph Graham. Cornell University Press, 1985. 209–48.

Derrida, Jacques. *The Gift of Death*. University of Chicago Press, 1996.

Derrida, Jacques. *Monolingualism of the Other; or, The Prosthesis of Origin*. Trans. Patrick Mensah. Stanford University Press, 1998.

Derrida, Jacques. *Specters of Marx: The State of Debt, the Work of Mourning, and the New International*. Routledge, 1994.

Derrida, Jacques. "Structure, Sign, and Play in the Discourse of the Human Sciences." *A Postmodern Reader*. Ed. Joseph Natoli and Linda Hutcheon. State University of New York Press, 1993. 223–42.

Derrida, Jacques, and Avital Ronell. "The Law of Genre." *Critical Inquiry* 7, no. 1 (1980): 55–81.

Derrida, Jacques, and Bernard Stiegler. "Spectrographies." *Echographies of Television: Filmed Interviews*. Trans. Jennifer Bajorek. Polity, 2002. 113–34.

Deutsch, Nathaniel. "'The Asiatic Black Man': An African American Orientalism?" *Journal of Asian American Studies* 4, no. 3 (2001): 193–208.

Diaz, Junot. *The Brief Wondrous Life of Oscar Wao*. Faber and Faber, 2008.

Diaz, Junot. "The Search for Decolonial Love: An Interview with Junot Diaz." *Boston Review*, 26 June 2012. Accessed 12 May 2017. http://bostonreview.net/books-ideas/paula-ml-moya-decolonial-love-interview-junot-d%C3%ADaz

Dilworth, David, and G. Cameron Hurst, trans. *An Outline of a Theory of Civilization*, by Yukichi Fukuzawa. Columbia University Press, 2009.

Dower, John. "*Black Ships and Samurai: Commodore Perry and the Opening of Japan (1853–1854)*." *MIT Visualizing Cultures*. Accessed 25 June 2019. https://visualiz ingcultures.mit.edu/black_ships_and_samurai/bss_essay01.html

Dower, John. "Black Ships and Samurai." *MIT Visualizing Cultures*. Accessed 2 March 2017. https://ocw.mit.edu/ans7870/21f/21f.027/black_ships_and_samurai/bss_essay05.html

Dower, John. *War without Mercy: Race and Power in the Pacific War*. Pantheon, 1993.

DuBois, W. E. B. "Criteria of Negro Art." *The New Negro: Readings on Race, Representation, and African American Culture, 1892–1938*. Ed. Henry Louis Gates and Gene Andrew Jarret. Princeton University Press, 2007. 257–59.

DuBois, W. E. B. *The Souls of Black Folk*. Signet Classics, 1995.

Dyson, Michael Eric. "Tour(é)ing Blackness." *Who's Afraid of Post-blackness? What It Means to Be Black Now*, by Touré. Free Press, 2011. xi–xviii.

Eidsheim, Nina. "Race and the Aesthetics of Vocal Timbre." *Rethinking Difference in Music Scholarship*. Ed. Olivia Bloechl et al. Cambridge University Press, 2015. 338–65.

Ellison, Ralph. *Invisible Man*. Random House, 1952.

Ellison, Ralph. "What America Would Be Like without Blacks." *Time*, 6 April 1970.

Ema, Shū. "Kokujin no kyōdai." *Nihon puroretaria bungakushū*. Vol. 16. Shin Nihon Shuppansha, 1984. 319–38.

Endō, Shūsaku. *Kuronbō*. Kadokawa Bunko, 1973.

Endoh, Toake. *Exporting Japan: Politics of Emigration to Latin America*. University of Illinois Press, 2009.

Ericson, Joan. "Introduction." *A Rainbow in the Desert: An Anthology of Early Twentieth-Century Japanese Children's Literature*. M. E. Sharpe, 2001. vii–xv.

"Ethiopian Concert." Japan Expedition Press, 1894.

Fabian, Johannes. *Time and the Other: How Anthropology Makes Its Object*. Columbia University Press, 2014.

Fanon, Frantz. "The Fact of Blackness." *Postcolonial Studies: An Anthology*. Ed. Pramod K. Nayar. Wiley, 2015. 15–32.

Feagin, Joe. *Systemic Racism: A Theory of Oppression*. Routledge, 2006.

Felski, Rita. *The Limits of Critique*. University of Chicago Press, 2015.

Field, Norma. "Neitibu to eirian, nanji to ware: Ōe Kenzaburō no shinwa, kindai, kyokō." *Bungakukai* 43 no. 1 (1989): 308–19.

Frow, John. *Genre*. Routledge, 2014.

Fukuoka-ken Keisatsu Honbu. *Fukuoka-ken keisatsushi Showa zenpen*. Fukuoka-ken keisatsu honbu, 1980.

Fukuzawa, Yukichi. *An Outline of a Theory of Civilization*. Trans. David A. Dilworth and G. Cameron Hurst III. Columbia University Press, 2009.

Furukawa, Hiromi, and Furukawa Tetsushi. *Nihonjin to Afurika-kei Amerikajin: Nihchi-Bei kankeishi ni okeru sono shosō*. Akashi Shoten, 2004.

Garon, Sheldon. *Molding Japanese Minds: The State in Everyday Life*. Princeton University Press, 1998.

Gates, Henry Louis. *The Signifying Monkey: A Theory of Afro-American Literary Criticism*. Oxford University Press, 1988.

Gessel, Van C. *The Sting of Life: Four Contemporary Japanese Novelists*. Columbia University Press, 1989.

Gilroy, Paul. *Against Race: Imagining Political Culture beyond the Color Line*. Belknap Press of Harvard University Press, 2000.

Glaude, Eddie. *Democracy in Black: How Race Still Enslaves the American Soul*. Broadway Books, 2016.

Goldberg, David. *Are We All Postracial Yet?* Polity, 2015.

Goosen, Theodore. "Caged Beasts: Black Men in Modern Japanese Literature." *The Walls Within: Images of Westerners in Japan and Images of the Japanese Abroad*. Ed. Tsuruta Kin'ya. Institute of Asian Research, University of British Columbia, 1989. 137–61.

Goosen, Theodore. "'Tasha' no sekai ni hairu toki: Yamada Eimi to Murakami Ryū no gaijin butsugo wo megutte." *Nihon bungaku ni okeru 'tasha.'* Ed. Tsuruta Kin'ya, Shinchōsha, 1994. 398–431.

Gordon, Andrew. *A Modern History of Japan: From Tokugawa Times to Present*. 3rd ed. Oxford University Press, 2013.

Gordon, Brandon. "Physical Sympathy: Hip and Sentimentalism in James Baldwin's *Another Country*." *MFS Modern Fiction Studies* 57, no. 1 (2011): 75–95.

Gotō, Akio. *J rappu izen: Hippu hoppu karuchā wa kōshite*. Tokyo FM Shuppan, 1997.

Green, Michael. *Black Yanks in the Pacific: Race in the Making of American Military Empire after World War II*. Cornell University Press, 2010.

Greenblatt, Stephen. *Learning to Curse: Essays in Early Modern Culture*. Routledge, 1990.

Grossberg, Lawrence. "Reflections of a Disappointed Popular Music Scholar." *Rock Over the Edge: Transformations in Popular Music Culture*. Ed. Roger Beebe et al. Duke University Press, 2002. 25–59.

Hall, Stuart. *Stuart Hall: Race, the Floating Signifier.* Accessed 5 October 2015. https://www.mediaed.org/assets/products/407/transcript_407.pdf

Hamaker, Susan. "Nago Mayor Says US Bases 'A Legacy of Misery' in Okinawa." *Japanculture-NYC.* Accessed 5 May 2017. http://www.japanculture-nyc.com/2014/05/21/nago-mayor-says-us-bases-a-legacy-of-misery-in-okinawa

Hanscom, Christopher, and Dennis Washburn, eds. *The Affect of Difference: Representations of Race in East Asian Empire.* University of Hawai'i Press, 2016.

Haraway, Donna. *Simians, Cyborgs, and Women: The Reinvention of Nature.* Free Association Books, 1991.

Hardimon, Michael. *Rethinking Race: The Case for Deflationary Realism.* Harvard University Press, 2017.

Harris, Trudier. *From Mammies to Militants: Domestics in Black American Literature.* Temple University Press, 1982.

Harris, Trudier. "Passing." *The Oxford Companion to Women's Writing in the United States.* Ed. Cathy Davidson and Linda Wagner-Martin. Oxford University Press, 2005. 653–54.

Hartley, Barbara. "Writing the Body of the Mother: Narrative Moments in Tsushima Yūko, Ariyoshi Sawako and Enchi Fumiko." *Japanese Studies* 23, no. 3 (2003): 293–305.

Hasegawa, Kei. "Seiai no gensetsu: Beddo taimu aizu." *Jenda de yomu ai sei kazoku.* Ed. Iwabuchi Hiroko et al. Tokyodo, 2006. 64–76.

Hashimoto, Fukuo. "Atogaki." *Kokujin bungaku zenshū.* Vol. 1. Hayakawa shobō, 1961. 255–65.

Hayakawa, Junko. "Spatial Complexity: Musically Urbanized Kokura Gion Festival." *Journal of the Human Development Research, Minamikyushu University* 3 (2013): 69–76.

Henderson, Stephen. *Understanding the New Black Poetry: Black Speech and Black Music as Poetic References.* Morrow, 1973.

Hikita, Kunio. *Kyōki no sakura.* Shinchōsha, 2000.

Hill, Christopher. "Crossed Geographies: Endō and Fanon in Lyon." *Representations* 128, no. 1 (2014): 93–123.

Himes, Chester. *If He Hollers Let Him Go.* Doubleday, 1945.

Hirose, Masahiro. "Neitibu supīkā no inai eikaiwa: Senji sengo no renzoku to "Amerikan sukūru." *Kokugo kokubungaku* 88 (2001): 1–14.

Hollinger, David A. "The Concept of Post-racial: How Its Easy Dismissal Obscures Important Questions." *Daedalus* 140, no. 1 (2011): 174–82.

Honda, Katsu'ichi. *Amerika gasshūkoku.* Asahi shimbunsha, 1981.

Honda Katsu'ichi. *Korosareru gawa no ronri.* Asahi shimbunsha, 1982.

Honda Katsu'ichi. *Nihongo no sakubun gijitsu.* Asahi shimbunsha, 1976.

Honda Katsu'ichi. *Reporutāju no hōhō.* Suzusawa shoten, 1980.

hooks, bell. "An Aesthetic of Blackness: Strange and Oppositional." *Lenox Avenue: A Journal of Interarts Inquiry* 1 (1995): 65–72.

hooks, bell. "Postmodern Blackness." *A Postmodern Reader.* Ed. Linda Hutcheon and Joseph Natoli. State University of New York Press, 1993. 510–18.

Horne, Gerald. "Tokyo Bound: African Americans and Japan Confront White Supremacy." *Souls: A Critical Journal of Black Politics, Culture, and Society* 3, no. 3 (2011): 16–28.

Huang, Yunte. *Transpacific Imaginations: History, Literature, Counterpoetics.* Harvard University Press, 2008.

Hurston, Zora Neale. "Characteristics of Negro Expression." *The Norton Anthology of African American Literature.* Ed. Henry Louis Gates Jr. et al. 2nd ed. Norton, 2004. 1041–53.

Hutchinson, Rachael. *Nagai Kafū's Occidentalism: Defining the Japanese Self.* State University of New York Press, 2011.

Hutchinson, Rachael, and Mark Williams. "Introduction." *Representing the Other in Modern Japanese Literature: A Critical Approach.* Routledge, 2007. 1–18.

Hwang, Ik-Koo. "'Senryō' to no sōgū: Ishikawa Jun 'Ōgun Densetsu' ni okeru sengo shuyō." *Bungaku kenkyū ronshū 26.* 2008. 125–42.

Ichijō, Takao. *Ōe Kenzaburō: Sono bungaku sekai to haikei.* Izumishoin, 1997.

Ichijō, Takao. "Ōe Kenzaburō to roku jyū nendai no 'Amerika': Rarufu erison no iwayuru 'tayōsei' wo megutte." *Tezukayama gakuin daigaku kenkyū ronshū: Bungakubu* 43 (2008): 1–14.

Inoue, Kota. "Postwar Japanese Fiction and the Legacy of Unequal Japan-US Relations." *Routledge Handbook of Modern Japanese Literature.* Ed. Rachael Hutchinson and Leith Morton. Routledge, 2016. 154–66.

Ishihara, Shintarō. "Mōsho, natsugare." *Bungei shunjū,* September 2004.

Ishikawa, Jun. "Ōgon densetsu." *Ishikawa Jun zenshū.* Vol. 2. Chikuma shobō, 1989. 323–34.

Itō, Seikō. *Gyōkai-kun monogatari.* Universal Music Japan, 1985.

Itō Seikō. "Itō Seikō." *Rappu no kotoba 2.* Ed. Inomata Takashi. Supēsu shawā nettowāku, 2014.

Itō, Seikō. *Mess/Age.* File Records, 1995.

Itō Seikō, "Mess/Age." *Mess/Age.* File Records, 1995.

Itō Seikō. "Message." *Mess/Age.* File Records, 1995.

Itō, Seikō. "Oretachi datte, damashite yo: J poppu na Nihongo, sono imi wa." *Eurika,* May 2003.

Itō, Seikō. *Sōzō rajio.* Kawade shobo, 2013.

Itō Seikō, and Punx Tinnie. *Kensetsuteki.* Pony Canyon, 1986.

Itō Seikō, and Saeki Kenzō. "Ai shiteru o kowasanakya Nihongo wa kaerarenai." *Music* 20, no. 3 (March 1988): 78–83.

Itsuki, Hiroyuki. "Umi wo mite ita Joni." *Umi wo mite ita Joni*. Kōdansha Bunko, 1967, 7–48.

Iwanami kōza Nihon bungakushi. Edited by Kubota Jun et al. Vol. 12. Iwanami Shoten, 1996.

Iwata-Weickgenannt, Kristina. "Kirino Natsuo's *Metabola* or the Okinawan Stage, Fractured Selves, and the Precarity of Contemporary Existence." *Visions of Precarity in Japanese Popular Culture and Literature*. Ed. Kristina Iwata-Weickgenannt and Roman Rosenbaum. Routledge, 2015.

Jakobsen, Janet. "Queers Are Like Jews, Aren't They? Analogy and Alliance Politics." *Queer Theory and the Jewish Question*. Ed. Daniel Boyarin, Daniel Itzkovitz, and Ann Pellegrini. Columbia University Press, 2003. 64–89.

Jauss, Hans Robert, and Elizabeth Benzinger. "Literary History as a Challenge to Literary Theory." *New Literary History* 2, no. 1 (1970): 7–37.

Johnson, James Weldon. "The Creation." *The Penguin Anthology of Twentieth Century American Poetry*. Penguin, 2011. 7–9.

Judaken, Jonathan. "Sartre on Racism: From Existential Phenomenology to Globalization and 'the New Racism.'" *Race after Sartre*. Ed. Jonathan Judaken. State University of New York Press, 2008. 23–54.

"Kaihō." *Kokujin kenkyū*, no. 20 (1963): 37–39.

Kakutani, Michiko. "Travails of an Outcast." *New York Times*, 4 September 2007. Accessed 12 May 2017. http://www.nytimes.com/2007/09/04/books/04diaz.html

Kanagaki, Robun. *Aguranabe. Kanagaki Robun*. Ed. Tsubouchi Yūzō. Chikuma Shobo, 2002. 267–342.

Kanagaki, Robun. *Seiyō dōchū hizakurige. Kanagaki Robun*. Ed. Tsubouchi Yūzō. Chikuma Shobo, 2002. 3–266.

Karatani, Kōjin. *Origins of Modern Japanese Literature*. Trans. Brett de Bary. Duke University Press, 1993.

Keevar, Michael. *Becoming Yellow: A Short History of Racial Thinking*. Princeton University Press, 2011.

Kitakyushu shiritsu Matsumoto Seichō kinenkan. *Kuroji no eten: Kizamareta kioku*. Matsumoto Seichō kinenkan, 2005.

Kojima, Nobuo. "Amerikan sukūru." *Amerikan sukūru*. Shinchōsha, 2008. 227–83.

Kojima, Nobuo. *Hōyō kazoku*. Kōdansha, 1988.

Kojima, Nobuo. *Long Belts and Thin Men: The Postwar Stories of Kojima Nobuo*. Trans. Lawrence Rogers. Kurodahan, 2016.

Kokujin bungaku zenshū. Ed. Hashimoto Fukuo. Hayakawa Shobo, 1960–63.

Kowner, Rotem. *From White to Yellow: The Japanese in European Racial Thought, 1300–1735*. McGill-Queen's University Press, 2014.

Kristeva, Julia. "Word, Dialog, and Novel." *The Kristeva Reader*. Ed. Toril Moi. Columbia University Press, 1986. 34–61.

Kubota Toshinobu, and Yamada Eimi. "Nihonjin dakara daseru kokujinpoi shinsensa, omoshirosa." *Music* 20, no. 3 (March 1988): 72–77.

Kuchiroro. "Hippu hoppu no shoki shōdō." *Everyday Is a Symphony.* Avex Marketing, 2009.

Kumagai, Nobuko. "Kojima Nobuo 'Amerikan sukūru' imejarī ni miru 'shishōsetsu.'" *Geijutsushijōshugi bungei* 27 (2001): 112–17.

Kyōki no sakura. Directed by Sonoda Kenji. Tōei, 2002.

Latour, Bruno. *An Inquiry into Modes of Existence: An Anthropology of the Moderns.* Harvard University Press, 2013.

Leonard, Kevin Allen. "In the Interest of All Races': African Americans and Interracial Cooperation in Los Angeles during and after World War II." *Seeking El Dorado: African Americans in California.* Ed. Lawrence de Graaf, Kevin Mulroy, and Quintard Taylor. University of Washington Press, 2015. 309–40.

Levinas, Emmanuel. *Totality and Infinity: An Essay on Exteriority.* Duquesne University Press, 1969.

Lie, John. "Introduction: Honda Katsuichi and Political and Intellectual Life in Postwar Japan." *The Impoverished Spirit in Contemporary Japan: Selected Essays of Honda Katsuichi.* Monthly Review Press, 1993. 9–44.

Lippit, Akira Mizuta. "Antigraphy: Notes on Atomic Writing and Postwar Japanese Cinema." *Review of Japanese Culture and Society* 10 (1998): 56–65.

Lummis, C. Douglas. *Radical Democracy.* Cornell University Press, 1997.

Macé, Marielle. "Ways of Being, Modes of Reading." *New Literary History* 44 (2013): 213–29.

Mailer, Norman. *Advertisements for Myself.* Harvard University Press, 1992.

Mailer, Norman. "Norman Mailer vs. Nine Writers." *Esquire,* July 1963.

Majima, Ichirō. "Kūhaku no chi kara: Ōe Kenzaburō to Afurika." *Waseda bungaku,* no. 4 (2011): 330–39.

Makibayashi, Koji. "Kojima Nobuo no hōhō: 'Americkan sukūru' no bunseki wo tooshite." *Saga-Dai Kokubun* 1 (1973): 8–17.

Manabe, Noriko. "Globalization and Japanese Creativity: Adaptations of Japanese Language to Rap." *Ethnomusicology* 50 (2006): 1–36.

Manabe, Noriko. "Hip-Hop in Japan: Alternative Stories." *The Cambridge Companion to Hip-Hop.* Ed. Justin A. Williams. Cambridge University Press, 2015. 243–55.

Manabe, Noriko. "Representing Japan: 'National' Style among Japanese Hip-Hop DJs." *Popular Music* 32, no. 1 (2013): 35–50.

Marcus, Sharon. *Between Women: Friendship, Desire, and Marriage in Victorian England.* Princeton University Press, 2007.

Matsumoto, Seichō. "E no gu." *Hansei no ki, Hansei no ki/Atogaki (Matsumoto Seichō zenshu).* Vol. 34. Bungei shunjū, 1974. 77–81.

Matsumoto, Seichō. "Kuroji no e." *Kuroji no e: Kessaku tanpenshū 2.* Shinchōsha, 1995. 69–129.

Matsumura, Wendy. *The Limits of Okinawa: Japanese Capitalism, Living Labor, and Theorizations of Community.* Duke University Press, 2015.

Mayo, Marlene. "Literary Reorientation in Occupied Japan: Incidents of Civil Censorship." *Legacies and Ambiguities: Postwar Fiction and Culture in West Germany and Japan.* Johns Hopkins University Press, 1991. 135–62.

McClain, Yoko. "Ariyoshi Sawako: Creative Social Critic." *Journal of the Association of Teachers of Japanese* 12, nos. 2–3 (1977): 211–28.

McGovern, Ann. *Black Is Beautiful.* Four Winds Press, 1969.

McKnight, Anne. *Nakagami, Japan: Buraku and the Writing of Ethnicity.* University of Minnesota Press, 2011.

Miller, Carolyn. "Genre as Social Action." *Genre in the New Rhetoric.* Ed. Aviva Freedman and Peter Medway. Taylor & Francis, 2003. 20–36.

Miura, Masahiro. "Yoshida Ruiko to kokujin-tachi." *Ōyō shakaigaku kenkyū*, no. 58 (2016): 29–35.

Miyamoto, Teru. "Yokei na kyōzatsubutsu." *Bungei shunjū* 82, no. 12 (2004): 383–84.

Mobu, Norio. "Bungaku kara ataerareta chikara." *Bungakukai* 58, no. 9 (2004): 222–39.

Mobu, Norio. *Kaigo nyūmon.* Bungei shunju, 2004.

Molasky, Michael. *The American Occupation of Japan and Okinawa: Literature and Memory.* Routledge, 1999.

Morimura, Seiichi. *Ningen no shōmei.* Kadokawa, 2004.

Morimura, Seiichi. "Ningen no shōmei." *Morimurau Seiichi kōshiki saito.* Accessed 26 April 2017. http://morimuraseiichi.com/?p=8716

Morimura, Seiichi. "Shin-seihan atogaki." *Ningen no shōmei.* Kadokawa, 2004. 501–4.

Morimura, Seiichi. "Shohan atogaki." *Ningen no shōmei.* Kadokawa, 2004. 496–500.

Morris, David. "The Sakura of Madness: Japan's Nationalist Hip Hop and the Parallax of Globalized Identity Politics." *Communication, Culture, and Critique* 6, no. 3 (2013): 459–80.

Morrison, Toni. *Beloved.* Plume, 1998.

Morrison, Toni. "On the First Black President." *New Yorker,* 5 October 1998.

Morrison, Toni. *Playing in the Dark: Whiteness and the Literary Imagination.* Harvard University Press, 1992.

Morrison, Toni. "Unspeakable Things Unspoken: The Afro-American Presence in American Literature." *A Turbulent Voyage: Readings in African American Studies.* Rowman and Littlefield, 2000. 246–67.

Morris-Suzuki, Tessa. "Lavish Are the Dead: Re-envisioning Japan's Korean War." *Asia-Pacific Journal* 11, no. 3 (2013). Accessed 4 July 2017. http://apjjf.org/2013/11/52/Tessa-Morris-Suzuki/4054/article.html

Moten, Fred. "Blackness and Nothingness (Mysticism in the Flesh)." *South Atlantic Quarterly* 112, no. 4 (2013): 737–80.

Mullen, Bill. *Afro-Orientalism.* University of Minnesota Press, 2004.

Murakami, Haruki. "Hachimitsu pai." *Kami no kodomotachi wa mina odoru.* Shinchōsha, 2002. 187–237.

Murakami, Ryū, and Nakagami Kenji. *Jyazu to bakudan: Nakagami Kenji vs Murakami Ryū.* Kadokawa Shoten, 1982.

Murphy-Shigematsu, Stephen. "'The Invisible Man' and Other Narratives of Living in the Borderlands of Race and Nation." *Transcultural Japan: At the Borderlands of Race, Gender, and Identity.* Edited by Stephen Murphy-Shigematsu and David Willis. Routledge, 2008. 282–87.

Nagai, Kafū. *Amerika monogatari. Gendai Nihon bungaku zenshū (Nagai Kafū shū).* Vol. 22. Kaizōsha, 1927. 175–280.

Nakagami, Kenji. "Amerika no hontō no koe." *Nakagami Kenji zenshū.* Ed. Karatani Kōjin et al. Vol. 15. Shūeisha, 1996. 552–53.

Nakagami, Kenji. *Baffarō Sorujā.* Fukutake Shoten, 1988.

Nakagami, Kenji. "Hakai seyo, to Airā wa itta." *Nakagami Kenji zenshū.* Ed. Karatani Kōjin et al. Vol. 15. Shūeisha, 1996. 9–54.

Nakagami, Kenji. *Kishū: Ki no kuni ne no kuni monogatari.* Asahi shimbunsha, 1978.

Nakagami, Kenji. *Nakagami Kenji zenshū.* Ed. Karatani Kōjin et al. Shūeisha, 1995.

Nakagami, Kenji. *Nihongo ni tsuite. Nakagami Kenji zenshū.* Ed. Karatani Kōjin et al. Vol. 1. Shūeisha, 1995. 127–208.

Nakagami, Kenji. "Ore, Jūhassai." *Nakagami Kenji zenshū.* Ed. Karatani Kōjin et al. Vol. 1. Shūeisha, 1995. 7–32.

Nakagami, Kenji. "Shoki no Ōe Kenzaburō: 'Shiiku' wo chūshin ni." *Nakagami Kenji hatsugen shūsei.* Vol. 6. Daisan bunmeisha, 1999. 289–306.

Nakagami, Kenji. "Toki wa nagareru." *Nakagami Kenji zenshū.* Ed. Karatani Kōjin et al. Vol. 14. Shūeisha, 1996. 239–41.

Nakagami, Kenji. "Toshi shōsetsu no minamoto wo tsuku anyu toshite no sogai ya sabetsu: Toni Morison-cho 'Aoi me ga hoshi' shohyō." *Nakagami Kenji zenshū.* Ed. Karatani Kōjin et al. Vol. 15. Shūeisha, 1996. 470–71.

Nakagami, Kenji. *Yasei no no kaenju.* Chikuma bunko, 1993.

Nakagami, Kenji. "Watashi wa 'Nihon'-jin na no ka." *Nakagami Kenji hatsugen shūsei.* Vol. 6. Daisan bunmeisha, 1999. 337–45.

Nakagami Kenji, Noma Hiroshi, and Yasuoka Shōtarō. "Shimin ni hisomu sabetsu shinri." *Nakagami Kenji hatsugen shūsei.* Vol. 6. Daisan bunmeisha, 1999. 10–61.

NARA II. RG 3a38, Entry 37042, Box 4469.

NARA II. RG 338, Entry 37042, Box 5550.

NARA II. RG 338, Entry 37042, Box 5551.

National Human Genome Research Institute. Accessed 2 March 2017. www.genome.gov/10001356/june-2000-white-house-event

Natsume, Soseki. *Sanshirō.* Iwanami Shoten, 1938.

Nielsen, Aldon. *Writing between the Lines: Race and Intertextuality.* University of Georgia Press, 1994.

Nishida, Kiriko. "Nakagami Kenji *Yasei no kaenju* ni okeru ekkyō no kanōsei to fukanōsei: 'Kuronbo,' 'dojin,' 'konketsu,' to mizukara wo kataru koto." *Taminzoku kenkyū* 7 (2014): 157–77.

Noguchi, Takehiko. "Ishikawa Jun." *Nihon kindai bungaku daijiten.* Vol. 1. Kōdansha, 1977. 94–97.

Nussbaum, Martha. "Fictions of the Soul." *Love's Knowledge: Essays on Philosophy and Literature.* Oxford University Press, 1990. 245–60.

Ōe, Kenzaburō. "Ajia Afurika ningen no kaigi." *Sekai,* no. 186 (1961): 177–83.

Ōe, Kenzaburō. "Amerika no yume." *Shinchō* 62, no. 8 (1965): 184–85.

Ōe, Kenzaburō. "Amerikaron." *Kakujidai no sōzōryoku.* Shinchō, 2007. 79–102.

Ōe, Kenzaburō. "Dai sanbu no tame no nōto." *Genshuku na tsunawatari.* Bungei shunjū, 1991. 205–7.

Ōe, Kenzaburō. "Dosutoefuskī: Hakuchi to Bōrudouin." *Genshuku na tsunawatari.* Bungei shunjū, 1991. 599–603.

Ōe, Kenzaburō. "Fukashi ningen to tayōsei. *Sekai,* no. 263 (1967): 137–45.

Ōe, Kenzaburō. "Gendai bungaku to sei." *Genshuku na tsunawatari.* Bungei shunjū, 1991. 366–75.

Ōe, Kenzaburō. *Genshuku na tsunawatari.* Kōdansha, 1991.

Ōe, Kenzaburō. *Hiroshima Notes.* Trans. David Swain and Toshi Yonezawa. Grove Press, 1995.

Ōe, Kenzaburō. "Jigoku ni yuku Hakkuruberī Fin." *Sekai,* no. 250 (1966): 229–40.

Ōe, Kenzaburō. "Kaisetsu." *Tanin no kao.* Shinchōsha, 2013. 343–50.

Ōe, Kenzaburō. "Kodoku na seinen no kyūka." *Kodoku na seinen no kyūka.* Shinchōsha, 1969. 5–98.

Ōe, Kenzaburō. *Kojinteki na taiken.* Shinchōsha, 1964.

Ōe, Kenzaburō. "Kokujin no suijaku to katsuryoku: Āto Bureikī to sono gakudan." *Asahi jānaru,* 22 January 1961.

Ōe, Kenzaburō. "Konnan no kankaku ni tsuite: Wa ga sosaku taiken." *Bungaku* 31, no. 11 (1963): 1267–72.

Ōe, Kenzaburō. "Kurai kawa omoi kai." *Ōe Kenzaburō zensakuhin.* Vol. 2. Shinchōsha, 1966. 5–22.

Ōe, Kenzaburō. "Kyōdai na amerika-zō no kuzureta ato ni . . ." *Shūkan Asahi,* 20 April 1968, 89–100.

Ōe, Kenzaburō. "Kyōken ni kakushitsu wo kamosu kokorozashi." *Sekai,* no. 187 (1961): 61–64.

Ōe, Kenzaburō. *Man'en gannen no futtobōru.* Kōdansha, 1988.

Ōe, Kenzaburō. "Modan jazu to boku jishin." *Genshuku na tsunawatari.* Bungei shunjū, 1991. 538–45.

Ōe, Kenzaburō. "Prize Stock." *Teach Us to Outgrow Our Madness: Four Short Novels.* Trans. John Nathan. Grove Press, 1977.

Ōe, Kenzaburō. "Ryūkeisha no dokusho." *Tosho,* no. 143 (1961): 2–3.

Ōe, Kenzaburō. *Sakebigoe.* Kōdansha, 1990.

Ōe, Kenzaburō. "Sengo sedai no imēji." *Ōe Kenzaburō dōjidai ronshū 1.* Iwanami Shoten, 1980. 8–37.

Ōe, Kenzaburō. "Shiiku." *Shisha no ogori, Shiiku.* Shinchōsha, 2013. 89–160.

Ōe, Kenzaburō. "Tatakai no konnichi." *Ōe Kenzaburō zensakuhin.* Vol. 2. Shinchōsha, 1966. 81–126.

Ōe, Kenzaburō. "Toni Morison, Ōe Kenzaburō (erum no kokage yori)." *Asahi shimbun,* 11 March 1997, evening ed., 5.

Okada, Richard. *Figures of Resistance: Language, Poetry, and Narrating in the 'Tale of Genji' and Other Mid-Heian Texts.* Duke University Press, 1991.

Okada, Richard. "Positioning Subjects Globally: A Reading of Yamada Eimi." *U.S.-Japan Women's Journal English Supplement,* no. 9 (1995). 111–26.

Okuno, Takeo. "Ishikawa Jun no shōsetsu no gainen." *Bungakukai,* March–April 1966, 151–59.

Onishi, Yuichiro. *Transpacific Antiracism: Afro-Asian Solidarity in Twentieth-Century Black America, Japan, and Okinawa.* New York University Press, 2013.

Orbaugh, Sharalyn. *Japanese Fiction of the Allied Occupation: Vision, Embodiment, Identity.* Brill, 2007.

The Oxford Study Bible: Revised English Bible with the Apocrypha. Ed. M. Jack Suggs, Katharine Sakenfeld, and James Mueller. Oxford University Press, 1992.

Palumbo-Liu, David. *The Deliverance of Others: Reading Literature in a Global Age.* Duke University Press, 2012.

Perpich, Diane. *The Ethics of Emmanuel Levinas.* Stanford University Press, 2008.

Perry, Imani. "Justin Timberlake, 'The 20/20 Experience': Is There a Visual Preference for Whiteness?" Interview with Marc Lamont Hill. *HuffPost Live,* 27 March 2013. Accessed 8 May 2017. http://www.huffingtonpost.com/2013/03/27/justin-timberlake-the-2020-experience-is-there-a-visual-preference-for-whiteness_n_2965509.html

Perry, Imani. *Prophets of the Hood: Politics and Poetics of Hip Hop.* Duke University Press, 2004.

Perry, Matthew Calbraith. *Narrative of the Expedition of an American Squadron to the China Seas and Japan, Performed in the Years 1852, 1853, and 1854, under the Command of Commodore M. C. Perry, United States Navy.* Congress of the United States, 1856–58.

Pratt, Mary Louise. "Arts of the Contact Zone." *Profession,* 1991. 33–40.

"Race and Human Variation." American Anthropological Association. Accessed 2 March 2017. www.understandingrace.org/humvar/race_humvar

Ricoeur, Paul. *Freud and Philosophy: An Essay on Interpretation.* Trans. Denis Savage. Yale University Press, 1970.

Ricoeur, Paul. *From Text to Action: Essays in Hermeneutics.* Trans. Kathleen Blamey and John B. Thompson. Vol. 2. Northwestern University Press, 2007.

Rizawa, Yukio. "Kojima Nobuo ni okeru fūshi to chūshō." *Kokubungaku: Kaishaku to kanshō* 37, no. 2 (1972): 10–16.

Robertson, Jennifer. "Human Rights vs. Robot Rights: Forecasts from Japan." *Critical Asian Studies* 46, no. 4 (2014): 571–98.

Rose, Tricia. *Black Noise: Rap Music and Black Culture in Contemporary America*. University Press of New England, 1994.

Russell, John. "Consuming Passions: Spectacle, Self-Transformation, and the Commodification of Blackness in Japan." *positions: east asia cultures critique* 6, no. 1 (1998): 113–77.

Russell, John. "Playing with Race/Authenticating Alterity: Authenticity, Mimesis, and Racial Performance in the Transcultural Diaspora." *CR: The New Centennial Review* 12, no. 1 (2012): 41–92.

Russell, John. "Race and Reflexivity: The Black Other in Contemporary Japanese Mass Culture." *Cultural Anthropology* 6, no. 1 (1991): 3–25.

Russell, John. "Sambo's Step-Children: Western Hegemony and the Construction of the Black Other in Japan." Manuscript.

Russell, John. "Taishū bungaku ni miru Nihonjin Kokujinkan." *Nihonjin no kokujin kan: Mondai wa "Chibikuro Sanbo" dake de wa nai*. Shinhyōron, 1991.

Ryang, Sonia. *Writing Selves in Diaspora: Ethnography of Autobiographies of Korean Women in Japan and the United States*. Lexington Books, 2008.

Saijō, Yaso. "Boku no bōshi." *Nihon jidō bungaku taikei*. Vol. 8. Horupu shuppan, 1978. 27.

Sartre, Jean-Paul. *Being and Nothingness: A Phenomenological Essay on Ontology*. Trans. Hazel Barnes. Washington Square Press, 1992.

Sartre, Jean-Paul. "Black Orpheus." *"What Is Literature?" and Other Essays*. Harvard University Press, 1988. 289–332

Sartre, Jean-Paul. *Notebooks for an Ethics*. Trans. David Pellauer. University of Chicago Press, 1992.

Saruya, Kaname. "Kaisetsu: Mizu Yoshida in Hāremu." *Hāremu no atsui hibi Black Is Beautiful*. Kōdansha, 1979. 227–32.

Satō, Ai. "Kokujin to chokorēto: Yamada Eimi *Beddo taimu aizu* ron." *Geijutsu shijoshugi bungei* 27 (2001): 124–30.

Satō, Kōjirō. *Nichi-bei sensō yume monogatari*. Nippon Hyōronsha, 1921.

Sawada, Miki. *Kuroi jūjika no Agasa*. Mainichi Shinbunsha, 1967.

Scarry, Elaine. *The Body in Pain: The Making and Unmaking of the World*. Oxford University Press, 1988.

Schuyler, George. *Black No More. Harlem Renaissance: Four Novels of the 1930s*. Ed. Rafia Zafar. Library of America, 2011. 220–372.

Sexton, Jared. "The Social Life of Social Death: On Afro-Pessimism and Black Optimism." *InTensions Journal*, no. 5 (2011). Accessed 3 March 2017. http://www.yorku.ca/intent/issue5/articles/pdfs/jaredsextonarticle.pdf

Shibata, Shōji. "Nichijō no seiritsu *Jesshi no seboni* Yamada Eimi." *Kokubungaku* 42, no. 12 (1997): 107–11.

Shimazaki, Tōson. *The Broken Commandment.* University of Tokyo Press, 1974.

"Shōgen kokujinhei shūdan dassō." *Asahi shimbun,* Kitakyushū ed., 9 July 1975.

"Shōgen kokujinhei shūdan dassō." *Asahi shimbun,* Kitakyushū ed., 12 July 1975.

"Shōgen kokujinhei shūdan dassō." *Asahi shimbun,* Kitakyushū ed., 16 July 1975.

"Shōgen kokujinhei shūdan dassō." *Asahi shimbun,* Kitakyushū ed., 23 July 1975.

Slaymaker, Douglas. *The Body in Postwar Japanese Fiction.* Routledge, 2004.

Spivak, Gayatri. "Can the Subaltern Speak?" *Colonial Discourse and Post-colonial Theory: A Reader.* Ed. Patrick Williams and Laura Chrisman. Columbia University Press. 66–111.

Stephenson, Neal. *Snow Crash.* Bantam Books, 1992.

Sterling, Marvin. "Searching for Self in the Global South: Japanese Literary Representations of Afro-Jamaican Blackness." *Japanese Studies* 31, no. 1 (2011): 53–71.

Sugahara, Maiko. "Nakagami Kenji 'Jūkyūsai no jeikobo': Jazu hyōshō wo megutte." *Ningen bunka sōsei kagaku ronsō* 11 (2008): 6.1–6.9.

Sugiyama, Seiichi. "Tokushu buraku." *Kyoto no burakushi.* Vol. 9. Ed. Inoue Kiyoshi. *Kyoto burakushi kenkyūjo,* 1987. 559–81.

Suvin, Darko. "On the Poetics of the Science Fiction Genre." *College English* 34, no. 3 (1972): 372–82.

Suzuki, Sadami. "Kaidai." *Ishikawa Jun zenshū.* Vol. 2. Chikuma shobō, 1989. 753–69.

Szwed, John. *Space Is the Place: The Lives and Times of Sun Ra.* Da Capo, 1998.

Tachibana, Reiko. "Structures of Power: Ōe Kenzaburō's 'Shiiku' ('Prize Stock')." *World Literature Today* 76, no. 2 (2002): 37–48.

Takano, Yoshitomo. "Ishikawa Jun sengo no shuppatsu: 'Ōgon densetsu' ni okeru zetsubō ni tsuite." *Geijutsushijōshugi bungei* 14 (1988): 61–72.

Takano, Yoshitomo. "Ōgon densetsu ron: Zetsubō kara no saisei ni tsuite." *Ishikawa Jun kenkyū.* Miyai shoten, 1991. 122–34.

Takemae, Eiji. *Inside GHQ: The Allied Occupation of Japan and Its Legacy.* Continuum International, 2002.

Takeuchi, Nobuo. "Nihon bungaku ni okeru tasha no keifu." *Nihon bungaku ni okeru tasha.* Ed. Tsuruta Kin'ya. Shin'yōsha, 1994. 68–96.

Takuma, Hideo. "Chibikuro Sambo de kangaeru koto." *Gekkan ehon* 2, no. 11 (December 1974): 25–27.

Tanaka, Minoru. "'Genbun' to 'katari' saikō: *Kami no kodomotachi wa mina odoru* no shinsō hihyō." *Kokubungaku: Kaishaku to kanshō* 76, no. 7 (2011): 6–25.

Tanaka, Minoru. "'Jiko-tōkai' to 'shutai' no saikōchiku: 'Bishin,' 'Dai-ichiya,' 'Takasebune' no tajigen sekai to 'Rashōmon' no koto." *Nihon bungaku* 65, no. 8 (2016): 2–15.

Tanaka, Minoru. "'Yomi no hairi' wo toku mittsu no kagi: Tekusuto, 'genbun' no kage, 'jikotōkai,' soshite 'katarite no jikohyōshutsu.'" *Kokubungaku: Kaishaku to kanshō* 73, no. 7 (2008): 6–16.

Tanizaki, Jun'ichirō. *Chijin no ai: Tanizaki Jun'ichirō shū*. Kaizōsha, 1927.

Tanizaki, Jun'ichirō. *Fūten rōjin nikki. Kagi: Fūten rōjin nikki*. Shinchōsha, 1968.

Tanizaki, Jun'ichirō. *In Praise of Shadows*. Trans. Thomas J. Harper and Edward G. Seidensticker. Leet's Island Books, 1977.

Tansman, Alan. "History, Repetition, and Freedom in the Narratives of Nakagami Kenji." *Journal of Japanese Studies* 24, no. 2 (1998): 257–88.

Thomas, Ronald. *Detective Fiction and the Rise of Forensic Science*. Cambridge University Press, 2003.

"Tōbōhei wa hōkoku wo, Kokura kenpeitai kara." *Asahi shimbun*, Kitakyushu evening ed., 15 July 1950.

Toeda, Hirokazu. "Matsumoto Seichō to shimbun shōsetsu." *Matsumoto Seicho kenkyū* 16 (2015): 30–41.

Tompkins, Jane. *Sensational Designs: The Cultural Work of American Fiction, 1790–1860*. Oxford University Press, 1986.

Toombs, Charles. "Black-Gay-Man Chaos in *Another Country*." *Re-viewing James Baldwin: Things Not Seen*. Ed. D. Quentin Miller. Temple University Press, 2000. 105–27.

Touré. "Visible Young Man," *New York Times Book Review*. Accessed 19 July 2019. https://www.nytimes.com/2009/05/03/books/review/Toure-t.html

"translation, n." *OED Online*. Oxford University Press, 2017.

Treat, John. *Writing Ground Zero: Japanese Literature and the Atomic Bomb*. University of Chicago Press, 1996.

Tyler, William, trans. *The Legend of Gold and Other Stories*. University of Hawai'i Press, 1998.

Tyler, William. "On 'The Legend of Gold' and 'The Jesus of the Ruins.'" *The Legend of Gold and Other Stories*. Trans. William Tyler. University of Hawai'i Press, 1998. 201–22.

Ueda, Atsuko. "'Nihongo' de kataru koto, 'Nihongo' wo kataru koto: Nakagami Kenji Nihongo ni tsuite wo megutte." *Bungaku no yami/Kindai no "chinmoku."* Ed. Nakayama Akihiko et al. Seori Shobō, 2003. 329–52.

Watanabe, Naomi. *Nihon kindai bungaku to "sabetsu."* Ota Shuppan, 1994.

West, Cornel. "Black Culture and Postmodernism." *A Postmodern Reader*. Ed. Joseph Natoli and Linda Hutcheon. State University of New York Press, 1993. 390–97.

West, Cornel. "The New Cultural Politics of Difference." *October* 53 (1990): 93–109.

West, Cornel. *Race Matters*. Beacon, 1993.

Wild Style. Directed by Charlie Ahearn. Submarine Entertainment, 1983.

Wilhite, Keith. "Mapping Black and Brown L.A.: Zoot Suit Riots as Spatial Subtext in *If He Hollers Let Him Go*." *Arizona Quarterly: A Journal of American Literature, Culture, and Theory* 66, no. 2 (2010): 121–48.

Williams, Justin A. "Intertextuality, Sampling, and Copyright." *The Cambridge Companion to Hip-Hop*. Ed. Justin A. Williams. Cambridge University Press, 2015. 206–22.

Wilson, Michiko. *The Marginal World of Ōe Kenzaburō: A Study in Themes and Techniques*. M. E. Sharpe, 1986.

Wright, Richard. *Haiku: Kono bessekai*. Sairyūsha, 2007.

Wright, Richard. *Native Son*. Harper Perennial, 2005.

Wright, Richard. *Uncle Tom's Children: Four Novellas*. Harper & Brothers, 1938.

Yamada, Eimi. *Animaru rojikku*. Shinchōsha, 1996.

Yamada, Eimi. *Beddo taimu aizu*. Kawade shobo, 1985.

Yamada, Eimi. *Payday!!!* Shinchōsha, 2003.

Yamada, Eimi. "Senpyō." *Bungei shunjū* 82, no. 12 (2004): 384–85.

Yamada, Eimi. *Soul Music Lovers Only*. Kadokawa shoten, 1987.

Yamada, Eimi. *Tainī sutōrīzu*. Bungei shunjū, 2010.

Yamada, Eimi. *Watashi wa henondōbutsu*. Kōdansha, 1991.

Yamaguchi, Masao. *Dōke no minzokugaku*. Shinchōsha, 1977.

Yamaguchi, Toshio. *Ishikawa Jun sakuhin kenkyū: "Kajin" kara "Yakeato no Iesu" made*. Sōbunsha Shuppan, 2005.

Yamamoto, Yukimasa. "Hisenryōki-ka ni okeru kotoba no fūkei: Kojima Nobuo 'Amerikan sukūru' wo megutte." *Kokubungaku kenkyū* 150 (2006): 125–35.

Yellin, Victor. "Mrs. Belmont, Matthew Perry, and the 'Japanese Minstrels.'" *American Music* 14, no. 3 (1996): 257–75.

Yokote, Kazuhiko. "Ōgon densetsu wa ni do to tsukurareta." *Kindai bungaku ronshū* 23 (1997): 13–25. 1997.

Yomota, Inuhiko. *Kishu to tensei: Nakagami Kenji*. Shinchōsha, 1996.

Yoshida, Ruiko. *Hāremu no atsui hibi Black Is Beautiful*. Kōdansha, 1979.

Yoshida, Ruiko, and Kijima Hajime. *Hāremu: Kuroi tenshitachi*. Kōdansha, 1974.

Zamberlin, Mary. *Rhizosphere: Gilles Deleuze and the "Minor" American Writings of William James, W. E. B. DuBois, Gertrude Stein, Jean Toomer, and William Faulkner*. Routledge, 2006.

Zimmerman, Eve. *Out of the Alleyway: Nakagami Kenji and the Poetics of Outcaste Fiction*. Harvard University Press, 2007.

Index

Abe Kōbō, 22, 25, 140, 164–67, 169, 171, 173, 174–75, 177, 227
Abe Tomoji, 15
Abel, Jonathan, 62
Advertisements for Myself (Mailer), 83–84
affinity: Abe and, 165; black-Japanese affinity, 95; definitions of, 18, 190–91; focus on, 19; Honda and, 149, 154; improvisational affinity, 21; Itō Seikō, 190–91, 217; Nakagami and, 101–2, 109, 126, 226; Ōe's sense of, 66, 67, 71, 86, 88; politics of, 24, 121; postblack two-step and, 183; racial affinity, 23; transracial, 99, 202; understandings of, 258n29; without association, 192, 194
African Americans: African American studies, 13; civil rights era, 19; contributions to war effort, 16; history of, 27; Perry's display of, 1–2; postwar enlistment, 17; post-WWII Japanese authors' cultural exchange with, 2
Afro-Asian solidarity, 18, 71
Afro-Asian Writers Association, 138–39
Afro-Jamaican blackness, 12
Afro-Japanese analogy: overview, 19; creation of, 66; falsity in, 19; historical amnesia and, 87–88; long 1970s literature and, 22; as precedent, 21; racial gaze dialectics and, 71–76; violence of, 21

Afro-Japanese contact zone, 17
Afro-Japanese cultural exchange: during 1960s, 18; overview, 3, 18; American administration of Okinawa and, 20; golden age of, 18; hip-hop and, 22; misrepresentation in modern history of, 5; rate of, 22; richest chapters of, 16; stakes and techniques of, 14
Afro-Japanese literary exchange, 3
Afro-Japanese racial difference, Otherness (term), 6–7
Afro-Japanese solidarity, fiction of postwar, 10
Afro-Japonisme, 224
Afro-Orientalism (Mullen), 229
Against Race (Gilroy), 219
Agamben, Giorgio, 7, 219
Agatha of the Black Cross (*Kuroi jujika no Agasa*) (Sawada Miki), 139
Aguranabe (*The Beefeater*) (Kanagaki), 15
Akasaki Moeko, 260n83
Akujo ni tsuite (*About an Evil Woman*) (Ariyoshi), 154–55
Akutagawa Prize, 21
Ali, Muhammad, 6, 19
Ali, Muhammad (formerly Cassius Clay), 73, 74
Allied Occupation, 17; African American influx of, 16; censorship under, 18; contact zones of, 18; as context, 44; hauntology of blackness and, 29–

Printed and bound by CPI Group (UK) Ltd, Croydon, CR0 4YY

09/06/2025

14686097-0001